# Measuring the User Experience

# The Morgan Kaufmann Series in Interactive Technologies

*Series Editors:* Stuart Card, PARC; Jonathan Grudin, Microsoft; Jakob Nielsen, Nielsen Norman Group

*Moderating Usability Tests: Principles and Practices for Interacting*
Joseph Dumas and Beth Loring

*Keeping Found Things Found: The Study and Practice of Personal Information Management*
William Jones

*GUI Bloopers 2.0: Common User Interface Design Don'ts and Dos*
Jeff Johnson

*Visual Thinking for Design*
Colin Ware

*User-Centered Design Stories: Real-World UCD Case Studies*
Carol Righi and Janice James

*Sketching User Experiences: Getting the Design Right and the Right Design*
Bill Buxton

*Text Entry Systems: Mobility, Accessibility, Universality*
Scott MacKenzie and Kumiko Tanaka-ishi

*Letting Go of the Words: Writing Web Content that Works*
Janice "Ginny" Redish

*Personas and User Archetypes: A Field Guide for Interaction Designers*
Jonathan Pruitt and Tamara Adlin

*Cost-Justifying Usability*
Edited by Randolph Bias and Deborah Mayhew

*User Interface Design and Evaluation*
Debbie Stone, Caroline Jarrett, Mark Woodroffe, and Shailey Minocha

*Rapid Contextual Design*
Karen Holtzblatt, Jessamyn Burns Wendell, and Shelley Wood

*Voice Interaction Design: Crafting the New Conversational Speech Systems*
Randy Allen Harris

*Understanding Users: A Practical Guide to User Requirements: Methods, Tools, and Techniques*
Catherine Courage and Kathy Baxter

*The Web Application Design Handbook: Best Practices for Web-Based Software*
Susan Fowler and Victor Stanwick

*The Mobile Connection: The Cell Phone's Impact on Society*
Richard Ling

*Information Visualization: Perception for Design, 2nd Edition*
Colin Ware

*Interaction Design for Complex Problem Solving: Developing Useful and Usable Software*
Barbara Mirel

*The Craft of Information Visualization: Readings and Reflections*
Written and edited by Ben Bederson and Ben Shneiderman

*HCI Models, Theories, and Frameworks: Towards a Multidisciplinary Science*
Edited by John M. Carroll

*Web Bloopers: 60 Common Web Design Mistakes, and How to Avoid Them*
Jeff Johnson

*Observing the User Experience: A Practitioner's Guide to User Research*
Mike Kuniavsky

*Paper Prototyping: The Fast and Easy Way to Design and Refine User Interfaces*
Carolyn Snyder

# Measuring the User Experience
## Collecting, Analyzing, and Presenting Usability Metrics

**Tom Tullis**

**Bill Albert**

AMSTERDAM • BOSTON • HEIDELBERG • LONDON
NEW YORK • OXFORD • PARIS • SAN DIEGO
SAN FRANCISCO • SINGAPORE • SYDNEY • TOKYO

ELSEVIER    Morgan Kaufmann Publishers is an imprint of Elsevier

MORGAN KAUFMANN PUBLISHERS

Publisher: Denise E. M. Penrose
Publishing Services Manager: George Morrison
Project Manager: Marilyn E. Rash
Assistant Editor: Mary E. James
Copyeditor: Debbie Prato
Proofreader: Dianne Wood
Indexer: Ted Laux
Cover Design: Joanne Blank
Cover Images: © Veer
Typesetting/Illustration Formatting: Integra
Interior Printer: Sheridan Books
Cover Printer: Phoenix Color Corp.

Morgan Kaufmann Publishers is an imprint of Elsevier.
30 Corporate Drive, Suite 400, Burlington, MA 01803

This book is printed on acid-free paper.

**Library of Congress Cataloging-in-Publication Data**
Tullis, Tom (Thomas)
Measuring the user experience : collecting, analyzing, and presenting usability metrics /
    Tom Tullis, Bill Albert.
      p.   cm. — (The Morgan Kaufmann interactive technologies series)
Includes bibliographical references and index.
ISBN-13: 978-0-12-373558-4 (alk. paper)
1. User interfaces (Computer systems)   2. User interfaces (Computer systems)—
Measurement.   3. Measurement.   4. Technology assessment.   I. Albert, Bill (William)
II. Title.
 QA76.9.U83T95 2008
 303.48'34—dc22                                                              2007043050

For information on all Morgan Kaufmann publications, visit our
Web site at *www.mkp.com* or *www.books.elsevier.com.*

Printed in the United States
   10  11  12   10 9 8 7 6 5 4

*To my wife, Susan, and my daughters, Cheryl and Virginia*
                  – Tom

*To my mother, Sara Albert*
              – Bill

# About the Authors

**Thomas S. (Tom) Tullis** is senior vice president of User Insight at Fidelity Investments. He joined Fidelity in 1993 and was instrumental in the development of the company's User Experience department; its facilities include a state-of-the-art Usability Lab. Prior to working at Fidelity, Tom held positions at Canon Information Systems, McDonnell Douglas, Unisys Corporation, and Bell Laboratories. He and Fidelity's usability team have been featured in a number of publications, including *Newsweek*, *Business 2.0*, *Money*, *The Boston Globe*, *The Wall Street Journal*, and *The New York Times*. Tullis received a B.A. from Rice University, an M.A. in experimental psychology from New Mexico State University, and a Ph.D. in engineering psychology from Rice University. During his 30 years of experience in human–computer interface studies, he has published more than 50 papers in numerous technical journals and has been an invited speaker at national and international conferences. Tom also holds eight U.S. patents and is an instructor in the Human Factors in Information Design Program at Bentley College.

**William (Bill) Albert** is the Director of the Design and Usability Center at Bentley University. Previously he was Director of User Experience at Fidelity Investments. Prior to joining Fidelity, he was a Senior User Interface Researcher at Lycos and Post Doctoral Research Scientist at Cambridge Basic Research. Over the past decade, Bill has used nearly every type of usability metric as part of his research. He has published more than 20 papers and has presented his research at many professional and academic conferences. Albert has been awarded prestigious fellowships through the University of California and the Japanese government for his research in human factors and spatial cognition. He received B.A. and M.A. degrees from the University of Washington and a Ph.D. from Boston University.

# Contents

Preface   xv

Acknowledgments   xvii

**CHAPTER 1  Introduction** ............................................................... 1
  **1.1** Organization of This Book.......................................... 2
  **1.2** What Is Usability? ...................................................... 4
  **1.3** Why Does Usability Matter? ..................................... 5
  **1.4** What Are Usability Metrics? ..................................... 7
  **1.5** The Value of Usability Metrics................................. 8
  **1.6** Ten Common Myths about Usability Metrics................. 10

**CHAPTER 2  Background** ............................................................. 15
  **2.1** Designing a Usability Study..................................... 15
      2.1.1 Selecting Participants ...................................... 16
      2.1.2 Sample Size..................................................... 17
      2.1.3 Within-Subjects or Between-Subjects Study............. 18
      2.1.4 Counterbalancing............................................. 19
      2.1.5 Independent and Dependent Variables.................. 20
  **2.2** Types of Data .......................................................... 20
      2.2.1 Nominal Data.................................................. 20
      2.2.2 Ordinal Data................................................... 21
      2.2.3 Interval Data................................................... 22
      2.2.4 Ratio Data ...................................................... 23
  **2.3** Metrics and Data ..................................................... 23
  **2.4** Descriptive Statistics ............................................... 24
      2.4.1 Measures of Central Tendency .......................... 25
      2.4.2 Measures of Variability..................................... 26
      2.4.3 Confidence Intervals ....................................... 27
  **2.5** Comparing Means..................................................... 28
      2.5.1 Independent Samples ...................................... 28
      2.5.2 Paired Samples ............................................... 29
      2.5.3 Comparing More Than Two Samples.................... 30
  **2.6** Relationships between Variables ............................... 31
      2.6.1 Correlations ................................................... 32
  **2.7** Nonparametric Tests ................................................ 33
      2.7.1 The Chi-Square Test ........................................ 33
  **2.8** Presenting Your Data Graphically ............................. 35
      2.8.1 Column or Bar Graphs...................................... 36

**vii**

        2.8.2 Line Graphs .............................................. 38
        2.8.3 Scatterplots............................................. 40
        2.8.4 Pie Charts .............................................. 42
        2.8.5 Stacked Bar Graphs ................................. 42
    **2.9** Summary.................................................... 44

**CHAPTER 3**   **Planning a Usability Study** ............................ 45
    **3.1** Study Goals ................................................ 45
        3.1.1 Formative Usability ................................ 45
        3.1.2 Summative Usability ............................... 46
    **3.2** User Goals ................................................. 47
        3.2.1 Performance............................................ 47
        3.2.2 Satisfaction ............................................ 47
    **3.3** Choosing the Right Metrics: Ten Types of Usability
        Studies....................................................... 48
        3.3.1   Completing a Transaction ......................... 48
        3.3.2   Comparing Products................................. 50
        3.3.3   Evaluating Frequent Use of the Same Product ......... 50
        3.3.4   Evaluating Navigation and/or Information
                Architecture........................................ 51
        3.3.5   Increasing Awareness............................... 52
        3.3.6   Problem Discovery ................................. 52
        3.3.7   Maximizing Usability for a Critical Product............. 53
        3.3.8   Creating an Overall Positive User Experience ......... 54
        3.3.9   Evaluating the Impact of Subtle Changes.............. 54
        3.3.10  Comparing Alternative Designs ..................... 55
    **3.4** Other Study Details ....................................... 55
        3.4.1 Budgets and Timelines................................ 55
        3.4.2 Evaluation Methods................................... 57
        3.4.3 Participants............................................ 58
        3.4.4 Data Collection ...................................... 59
        3.4.5 Data Cleanup ........................................ 60
    **3.5** Summary.................................................... 61

**CHAPTER 4**   **Performance Metrics**.................................. 63
    **4.1** Task Success ............................................... 64
        4.1.1 Collecting Any Type of Success Metric ................. 65
        4.1.2 Binary Success......................................... 66
        4.1.3 Levels of Success ..................................... 69
        4.1.4 Issues in Measuring Success.......................... 73

**4.2** Time-on-Task............................................. 74
    4.2.1 Importance of Measuring Time-on-Task ................ 74
    4.2.2 How to Collect and Measure Time-on-Task ............. 74
    4.2.3 Analyzing and Presenting Time-on-Task Data ........... 77
    4.2.4 Issues to Consider When Using Time Data ............. 79
**4.3** Errors.................................................... 81
    4.3.1 When to Measure Errors ........................... 81
    4.3.2 What Constitutes an Error?......................... 82
    4.3.3 Collecting and Measuring Errors ..................... 83
    4.3.4 Analyzing and Presenting Errors...................... 84
    4.3.5 Issues to Consider When Using Error Metrics .......... 86
**4.4** Efficiency ................................................ 87
    4.4.1 Collecting and Measuring Efficiency.................... 87
    4.4.2 Analyzing and Presenting Efficiency Data............... 88
    4.4.3 Efficiency as a Combination of Task Success and Time .. 90
**4.5** Learnability .............................................. 92
    4.5.1 Collecting and Measuring Learnability Data............. 93
    4.5.2 Analyzing and Presenting Learnability Data............. 94
    4.5.3 Issues to Consider When Measuring Learnability ........ 96
**4.6** Summary.................................................. 97

**CHAPTER 5  Issues-Based Metrics** ................................... 99
**5.1** Identifying Usability Issues ................................. 99
**5.2** What Is a Usability Issue?................................. 100
    5.2.1 Real Issues versus False Issues ...................... 101
**5.3** How to Identify an Issue ................................. 102
    5.3.1 In-Person Studies ................................. 103
    5.3.2 Automated Studies................................. 103
    5.3.3 When Issues Begin and End......................... 103
    5.3.4 Granularity ....................................... 104
    5.3.5 Multiple Observers ................................ 104
**5.4** Severity Ratings .......................................... 105
    5.4.1 Severity Ratings Based on the User Experience ........ 105
    5.4.2 Severity Ratings Based on a Combination of Factors ... 106
    5.4.3 Using a Severity Rating System ..................... 107
    5.4.4 Some Caveats about Severity Ratings ................. 108
**5.5** Analyzing and Reporting Metrics for Usability Issues ........ 108
    5.5.1 Frequency of Unique Issues......................... 109
    5.5.2 Frequency of Issues per Participant .................. 111
    5.5.3 Frequency of Participants ........................... 111
    5.5.4 Issues by Category ................................. 112

5.5.5 Issues by Task . . . . . . . . . . . . . . . . . . . . . . . . . . . . . . . . . . . . 113
5.5.6 Reporting Positive Issues. . . . . . . . . . . . . . . . . . . . . . . . . . . 114
**5.6** Consistency in Identifying Usability Issues . . . . . . . . . . . . . . . . . 114
**5.7** Bias in Identifying Usability Issues . . . . . . . . . . . . . . . . . . . . . . . . 116
**5.8** Number of Participants. . . . . . . . . . . . . . . . . . . . . . . . . . . . . . . . . . 117
5.8.1 Five Participants Is Enough . . . . . . . . . . . . . . . . . . . . . . . . 118
5.8.2 Five Participants Is *Not* Enough . . . . . . . . . . . . . . . . . . . . 119
5.8.3 *Our* Recommendation . . . . . . . . . . . . . . . . . . . . . . . . . . . . . 119
**5.9** Summary. . . . . . . . . . . . . . . . . . . . . . . . . . . . . . . . . . . . . . . . . . . . . 121

**CHAPTER 6  Self-Reported Metrics**. . . . . . . . . . . . . . . . . . . . . . . . . . . **123**
**6.1** Importance of Self-Reported Data . . . . . . . . . . . . . . . . . . . . . . . . 123
**6.2** Collecting Self-Reported Data. . . . . . . . . . . . . . . . . . . . . . . . . . . . 124
6.2.1 Likert Scales . . . . . . . . . . . . . . . . . . . . . . . . . . . . . . . . . . . . 124
6.2.2 Semantic Differential Scales . . . . . . . . . . . . . . . . . . . . . . . . 125
6.2.3 When to Collect Self-Reported Data . . . . . . . . . . . . . . . . . . 125
6.2.4 How to Collect Self-Reported Data . . . . . . . . . . . . . . . . . . . 126
6.2.5 Biases in Collecting Self-Reported Data . . . . . . . . . . . . . . . 126
6.2.6 General Guidelines for Rating Scales . . . . . . . . . . . . . . . . . . 127
6.2.7 Analyzing Self-Reported Data. . . . . . . . . . . . . . . . . . . . . . . 127
**6.3** Post-Task Ratings. . . . . . . . . . . . . . . . . . . . . . . . . . . . . . . . . . . . . . 128
6.3.1 Ease of Use . . . . . . . . . . . . . . . . . . . . . . . . . . . . . . . . . . . . . 128
6.3.2 After-Scenario Questionnaire . . . . . . . . . . . . . . . . . . . . . . . 129
6.3.3 Expectation Measure. . . . . . . . . . . . . . . . . . . . . . . . . . . . . . 129
6.3.4 Usability Magnitude Estimation. . . . . . . . . . . . . . . . . . . . . . 132
6.3.5 Comparison of Post-Task Self-Reported Metrics . . . . . . . . 133
**6.4** Post-Session Ratings . . . . . . . . . . . . . . . . . . . . . . . . . . . . . . . . . . . . 135
6.4.1 Aggregating Individual Task Ratings . . . . . . . . . . . . . . . . . . 137
6.4.2 System Usability Scale. . . . . . . . . . . . . . . . . . . . . . . . . . . . . 138
6.4.3 Computer System Usability Questionnaire . . . . . . . . . . . . . 139
6.4.4 Questionnaire for User Interface Satisfaction . . . . . . . . . . 139
6.4.5 Usefulness, Satisfaction, and Ease of Use
Questionnaire . . . . . . . . . . . . . . . . . . . . . . . . . . . . . . . . . . . . 142
6.4.6 Product Reaction Cards . . . . . . . . . . . . . . . . . . . . . . . . . . . . 142
6.4.7 Comparison of Post-Session Self-Reported Metrics . . . . . 144
**6.5** Using SUS to Compare Designs . . . . . . . . . . . . . . . . . . . . . . . . . . . 147
6.5.1 Comparison of "Senior-Friendly" Websites . . . . . . . . . . . . 147
6.5.2 Comparison of Windows ME and Windows XP . . . . . . . . 147
6.5.3 Comparison of Paper Ballots . . . . . . . . . . . . . . . . . . . . . . . 148
**6.6** Online Services . . . . . . . . . . . . . . . . . . . . . . . . . . . . . . . . . . . . . . . . 150
6.6.1 Website Analysis and Measurement Inventory . . . . . . . . . 150

6.6.2 American Customer Satisfaction Index ............... 151
6.6.3 OpinionLab.............................................. 153
6.6.4 Issues with Live-Site Surveys ......................... 157
**6.7** Other Types of Self-Reported Metrics........................ 158
6.7.1 Assessing Specific Attributes ......................... 158
6.7.2 Assessing Specific Elements........................... 161
6.7.3 Open-Ended Questions ............................... 162
6.7.4 Awareness and Comprehension....................... 163
6.7.5 Awareness and Usefulness Gaps...................... 165
**6.8** Summary.................................................... 166

**CHAPTER 7  Behavioral and Physiological Metrics** ................. 167
**7.1** Observing and Coding Overt Behaviors...................... 167
7.1.1 Verbal Behaviors.................................... 168
7.1.2 Nonverbal Behaviors................................ 169
**7.2** Behaviors Requiring Equipment to Capture.................. 171
7.2.1 Facial Expressions .................................. 171
7.2.2 Eye-Tracking........................................ 175
7.2.3 Pupillary Response ................................. 180
7.2.4 Skin Conductance and Heart Rate.................... 183
7.2.5 Other Measures..................................... 186
**7.3** Summary.................................................... 188

**CHAPTER 8  Combined and Comparative Metrics**................... 191
**8.1** Single Usability Scores...................................... 191
8.1.1 Combining Metrics Based on Target Goals ........... 192
8.1.2 Combining Metrics Based on Percentages ............ 193
8.1.3 Combining Metrics Based on $z$-Scores ............... 198
8.1.4 Using SUM: Single Usability Metric .................. 202
**8.2** Usability Scorecards ........................................ 203
**8.3** Comparison to Goals and Expert Performance.............. 206
8.3.1 Comparison to Goals ............................... 206
8.3.2 Comparison to Expert Performance ................. 208
**8.4** Summary.................................................... 210

**CHAPTER 9  Special Topics** .................................... 211
**9.1** Live Website Data.......................................... 211
9.1.1 Server Logs ........................................ 211
9.1.2 Click-Through Rates ................................ 213
9.1.3 Drop-Off Rates..................................... 215

9.1.4 A/B Studies ........................................... 216
**9.2** Card-Sorting Data ........................................ 217
9.2.1 Analyses of Open Card-Sort Data .................... 218
9.2.2 Analyses of Closed Card-Sort Data.................... 225
**9.3** Accessibility Data ........................................ 227
**9.4** Return-on-Investment Data ................................. 231
**9.5** Six Sigma ................................................ 234
**9.6** Summary.................................................. 236

**CHAPTER 10    Case Studies** ........................................ 237
**10.1** Redesigning a Website Cheaply and Quickly
*Hoa Loranger*............................................. 237
10.1.1 Phase 1: Testing Competitor Websites ............. 237
10.1.2 Phase 2: Testing Three Different Design Concepts .... 239
10.1.3 Phase 3: Testing a Single Design ................... 243
10.1.4 Conclusion ....................................... 244
10.1.5 Biography ........................................ 244
**10.2** Usability Evaluation of a Speech Recognition IVR
*James R. Lewis*........................................... 244
10.2.1    Method ........................................ 244
10.2.2    Results: Task-Level Measurements ................ 245
10.2.3    PSSUQ ........................................ 246
10.2.4    Participant Comments........................... 246
10.2.5    Usability Problems ............................. 247
10.2.6    Adequacy of Sample Size ........................ 247
10.2.7    Recommendations Based on Participant
          Behaviors and Comments ........................ 250
10.2.8    Discussion ...................................... 251
10.2.9    Biography....................................... 251
10.2.10 References ...................................... 252
**10.3** Redesign of the CDC.gov Website    *Robert Bailey,
*Cari Wolfson, and Janice Nall*............................. 252
10.3.1 Usability Testing Levels ........................... 253
10.3.2 Baseline Test ...................................... 253
10.3.3 Task Scenarios..................................... 254
10.3.4 Qualitative Findings .............................. 255
10.3.5 Wireframing and FirstClick Testing ................ 256
10.3.6 Final Prototype Testing (Prelaunch Test)........... 258
10.3.7 Conclusions ...................................... 261
10.3.8 Biographies....................................... 262
10.3.9 References ....................................... 262

**10.4** Usability Benchmarking: Mobile Music and Video
*Scott Weiss and Chris Whitby* ................................. 263

    10.4.1   Project Goals and Methods ........................ 263

    10.4.2   Qualitative and Quantitative Data................. 263

    10.4.3   Research Domain .............................. 263

    10.4.4   Comparative Analysis........................... 264

    10.4.5   Study Operations: Number of Respondents ....... 264

    10.4.6   Respondent Recruiting .......................... 265

    10.4.7   Data Collection................................. 265

    10.4.8   Time to Complete............................... 266

    10.4.9   Success or Failure .............................. 266

    10.4.10 Number of Attempts ........................... 266

    10.4.11 Perception Metrics ............................. 266

    10.4.12 Qualitative Findings ........................... 267

    10.4.13 Quantitative Findings........................... 267

    10.4.14 Summary Findings and SUM Metrics .............. 267

    10.4.15 Data Manipulation and Visualization .............. 267

    10.4.16 Discussion .................................... 269

    10.4.17 Benchmark Changes and Future Work............. 270

    10.4.18 Biographies ................................... 270

    10.4.19 References..................................... 270

**10.5** Measuring the Effects of Drug Label Design and Similarity
on Pharmacists' Performance   *Agnieszka Bojko*............ 271

    10.5.1 Participants........................................ 272

    10.5.2 Apparatus ......................................... 272

    10.5.3 Stimuli ............................................ 272

    10.5.4 Procedure ......................................... 275

    10.5.5 Analysis ........................................... 276

    10.5.6 Results and Discussion.............................. 277

    10.5.7 Biography ......................................... 279

    10.5.8 References ......................................... 279

**10.6** Making Metrics Matter   *Todd Zazelenchuk*................ 280

    10.6.1 OneStart: Indiana University's Enterprise Portal
            Project ............................................ 280

    10.6.2 Designing and Conducting the Study................ 281

    10.6.3 Analyzing and Interpreting the Results.............. 282

    10.6.4 Sharing the Findings and Recommendations ........ 283

    10.6.5 Reflecting on the Impact .......................... 286

    10.6.6 Conclusion ........................................ 287

    10.6.7 Acknowledgment................................... 287

10.6.8 Biography . . . . . . . . . . . . . . . . . . . . . . . . . . . . . . . . . . . . . . 287
10.6.9 References . . . . . . . . . . . . . . . . . . . . . . . . . . . . . . . . . . . . . . 287

**CHAPTER 11   Moving Forward**. . . . . . . . . . . . . . . . . . . . . . . . . . . . . . . . **289**
**11.1**   Sell Usability and the Power of Metrics . . . . . . . . . . . . . . . . . . . 289
**11.2**   Start Small and Work Your Way Up. . . . . . . . . . . . . . . . . . . . . . 290
**11.3**   Make Sure You Have the Time and Money . . . . . . . . . . . . . . 291
**11.4**   Plan Early and Often . . . . . . . . . . . . . . . . . . . . . . . . . . . . . . . . 292
**11.5**   Benchmark Your Products . . . . . . . . . . . . . . . . . . . . . . . . . . . 293
**11.6**   Explore Your Data . . . . . . . . . . . . . . . . . . . . . . . . . . . . . . . . . 294
**11.7**   Speak the Language of Business . . . . . . . . . . . . . . . . . . . . . . 295
**11.8**   Show Your Confidence. . . . . . . . . . . . . . . . . . . . . . . . . . . . . . 295
**11.9**   Don't Misuse Metrics. . . . . . . . . . . . . . . . . . . . . . . . . . . . . . . 296
**11.10** Simplify Your Presentation . . . . . . . . . . . . . . . . . . . . . . . . . . . 297

References   299
Index   307

# Preface

User experience, or UX as it's often abbreviated, refers to all aspects of someone's interaction with a product, application, or system. Many people seem to think of the user experience as some nebulous quality that can't be measured or quantified. We think it can be. And the tools for measuring it are usability metrics such as the following:

- How long does it take users to make a flight reservation using a travel website?
- How many errors do users make in trying to log onto a system?
- How many users are successful when trying to instruct their digital video recorder that they want to record all episodes of their favorite TV show?
- How many users get into a new "destination-based" elevator without first choosing their desired floor, only to discover there are no floor buttons?
- How many users fail to notice the link on a web page that would let them do exactly what they want with only one click?
- How many users get frustrated trying to read the tiny serial number on the back of their new MP3 player when registering it?
- How many users are delighted by how easy it was to assemble their new bookcase that came with wordless instructions?

These are all examples of behaviors and attitudes that can be measured. Some may be easier to measure than others, but they can all be measured. Task success rates, task times, number of mouse clicks or keystrokes, self-reported ratings of frustration or delight, and even the number of visual fixations on a link on a web page are all examples of usability metrics. And these metrics can give you invaluable insight into the user experience.

Why would you want to measure the user experience? The answer is, to help you improve it. With most consumer products and websites these days, if you're not improving, you're falling behind. Usability metrics can help you determine where you stand relative to your competition and help you pinpoint where you should focus your improvement efforts—the areas that users find the most confusing, inefficient, or frustrating.

This book is a how-to guide, not a theoretical treatise. We provide practical advice about what usability metrics to collect in what situations, how to collect them, how to make sense of the data using various analysis techniques, and how to present the results in the clearest and most compelling way. We're sharing practical lessons we've learned from our 40+ combined years of experience in this field.

*Measuring the User Experience* is intended for anyone interested in improving the user experience for any type of product, whether it's a consumer product, computer system, application program, website, or something else altogether. If it's something people use, then you can measure the user experience associated with it. Those who are interested in improving the user experience and who could benefit from this book come from many different perspectives and disciplines, including usability and user experience (UX) professionals, interaction designers, information architects, product designers, web designers and developers, software developers, graphic designers, marketing and market-research professionals, as well as project and product managers.

We hope you find this book helpful in your quest to improve the user experience for your products. We'd like to hear about your successes (and failures!). You can contact us through our website, *www.MeasuringUserExperience.com*. You will also find supplementary material there, such as the actual spreadsheets and graphs for many of the examples in this book, as well as information about tools that can help in measuring the user experience.

\* \* \*

The material, examples, and case studies presented in this book have been included for their instructional value. The publisher and the authors offer NO WARRANTY OF FITNESS OR MERCHANTABILITY FOR ANY PARTICULAR PURPOSE and do not accept any liability with respect to the material, examples, and case studies.

The opinions expressed in this book are those of the authors and do not represent any official position or endorsement by their employer or the publisher.

# Acknowledgments

First of all, we thank Diane Cerra, Denise Penrose, Mary James, and Marilyn Rash from Morgan Kaufmann. You gave us many practical suggestions and pushed us at all the right times. We also thank Jim Lewis and Joyce Oghi for many thorough and timely reviews of the manuscript. We owe a debt of gratitude to all the authors who contributed case studies: Hoa Loranger, Bob Bailey, Cari Wolfson, Janice Nall, Jim Lewis, Scott Weiss, Chris Whitby, Aga Bojko, and Todd Zazelenchuk. The book is far more useful because of your willingness to share your experiences with our readers.

\* \* \*

I would like to thank my wife, Susan, and my daughters, Cheryl and Virginia, for your support and for putting up with my long evenings and weekends at the computer! I'd especially like to thank Susan for your reviews and comments on a number of the chapters in this book. You've helped me become a better writer.

*Tom*

I would like to thank my family. Devika, you helped me write a few sentences. I hope your love of writing continues to grow. Arjun, you gave me some creative ideas for different metrics. I know your curiosity will take you far. To my wife Monika, thank you for all the support, encouragement, and faith you had in me while writing this book and especially for your patience on all those evenings when I was writing while you were helping the kids with their homework.

*Bill*

# Introduction

The goal of this book is to show how usability metrics can be a powerful tool for successfully evaluating the user experience for any product. When some people think about usability metrics, they feel overwhelmed by complicated formulas, contradictory research, and advanced statistical methods. We hope to demystify much of the research and focus on the practical application of usability metrics. We'll walk you through a step-by-step approach to collecting, analyzing, and presenting usability metrics. We'll help you choose the right metrics for each situation or application, and show you how to use them to produce reliable, actionable results without breaking your budget. We'll give you guidelines and tips for analyzing a wide range of usability metrics and provide many different examples of how to present usability metrics to others in simple and effective ways.

Our intention is to make this book a practical, how-to guide about measuring the usability of any product. We aren't going to give you a lot of formulas; in fact, there are very few. The statistics will be fairly limited, and the calculations can be done easily in Excel or some other common software package or web application. Our goal is to give you the tools you need to evaluate the usability of any product, without overwhelming you with unnecessary details.

This book is both product- and technology-neutral. The usability metrics we describe can be used for practically any type of product and any type of technology. This is one of the great features of usability metrics: They aren't just for websites or any single technology. For example, task success and satisfaction are equally valid whether you evaluate a website, a treadmill, or a toaster. More advanced technologies, such as websites, mobile phones, software, and consumer electronics, are of special concern because they're generally more complicated, but the basic premise remains the same.

The "half-life" of usability metrics is much greater than any specific design or technology. Despite all the changes in technology, the metrics essentially stay the same. Some metrics may change with the development of new technologies to measure usability, but the underlying phenomena being measured don't change. Eye-tracking is a great example. Many researchers wanted a method for determining where exactly a user is looking on the screen. Now, with the latest advances in eye-tracking technology, measurement has become much easier and far more accurate.

So why did we write this book? There's certainly no shortage of books on human factors, statistics, experimental design, and usability methods. Some of those books even cover the more common usability metrics. Does a book that focuses entirely on usability metrics even make sense? Obviously, we think so. In our (humble) opinion, this book makes five unique contributions to the realm of usability publications:

- We take a *comprehensive* look at usability metrics. No other books review so many different usability metrics. We provide details on collecting, analyzing, and presenting nearly every type of usability metric you could possibly use.

- This book takes a *practical approach*. We assume you're interested in applying usability metrics as part of your job. We don't waste your time with unnecessary details. We want you to be able to use these metrics easily every day. If you're interested in the theoretical side, we point you to additional resources.

- We provide help in making the *right decisions* about usability metrics. One of the most difficult aspects of a usability professional's job is deciding whether to collect metrics and, if so, which ones to use. We guide you through the decision process so that you find the right metrics for *your* situation.

- We provide many *examples* of how usability metrics have been applied within different organizations and how they have been used to address specific usability questions. We also provide in-depth case studies to help you determine how best to use the information revealed by the usability metrics.

- We present usability metrics that can be used with *any product or technology*. We take a broad view so that these usability metrics can be helpful throughout your career even as technology and products change.

## 1.1 ORGANIZATION OF THIS BOOK

This book is organized into three main parts. The first one (Chapters 1–3) provides background information needed to get up to speed on usability metrics. This part is intended for those who are less familiar with usability, data analysis, or statistics.

- Chapter 1 provides an *overview* of usability and usability metrics. We define user experience, usability, and different types of usability metrics; discuss the value of measuring the user experience; and dispel some of the common myths about usability metrics.

- Chapter 2 includes *background* information on usability data and some basic statistical concepts. We walk you through a step-by-step process to set up a usability study using different metrics and provide a guide for performing common statistical procedures related to different usability methods.

- Chapter 3 focuses on *planning a usability study,* including defining participant goals and study goals and choosing the right metrics for a wide variety of situations.

The second part (Chapters 4–9) reviews five general types of usability metrics, as well as some special topics that don't fall neatly into any single type. For each metric, we explain what it is, when to use it, and when not to use it. We show you how to collect the data and different ways to analyze and present it. We provide examples of how it has been used in real-world usability studies.

- Chapter 4 covers various *types of performance metrics,* including task success, time on task, errors, efficiency, and ease of learning. These metrics are grouped under an "umbrella" of performance because they measure different aspects of the user's behavior.

- Chapter 5 looks at *measuring usability issues*. Usability issues can easily be quantified by measuring the frequency, severity, and type of issue. We also discuss some of the debates about appropriate sample sizes and how to capture usability issues reliably.

- Chapter 6 focuses on *self-reported metrics,* such as satisfaction, expectations, ease-of-use ratings, usefulness, and awareness. Self-reported metrics are based on what users share about their experiences, not what the usability specialist measures about their actual behaviors.

- Chapter 7 is devoted to *behavioral and physiological metrics*. These metrics include eye-tracking, facial expressions, and various measures of stress. All of these metrics capture something about how the body behaves as a result of the experience of working with a user interface.

- Chapter 8 discusses *how to combine different types of metrics and derive new metrics.* Sometimes it's helpful to get an overall assessment of the usability of any product. This global assessment is achieved by combining different types of metrics into a single usability score, summarizing them in a usability scorecard, or comparing them to expert performance.

- Chapter 9 presents *special topics* that we believe are important but that don't fit squarely into one of the five general categories. These include A/B testing on a live website, card-sorting data, Six Sigma, accessibility data, and return on investment (ROI).

The third part (Chapters 10–11) shows how usability metrics are put into practice. In this part, we highlight how usability metrics are actually used within different types of organizations and how to promote the use of metrics within an organization.

- Chapter 10 presents six *case studies*. Each case study reviews how different types of usability metrics were used, how the data were collected and analyzed, and the results. These case studies were drawn from usability practitioners in various types of organizations, including consulting, government, industry, and not-for-profit/education.

- Chapter 11 provides ten *steps to help you move forward in using metrics* within your organization. We discuss how usability metrics can fit within different types of organizations, practical tips for making metrics work within your organization, and recipes for success.

## 1.2 WHAT IS USABILITY?

Before we try to measure usability, we should know what it is and what it isn't. There are many definitions of usability—maybe even one for every person involved in the field! We're going to focus on three definitions.

The International Standards Organization (ISO 9241-11) identifies three aspects of usability, defining it as "the extent to which a product can be used by specified users to achieve specified goals with *effectiveness*, *efficiency*, and *satisfaction* in a specified context of use."

The Usability Professionals Association (UPA) definition focuses more on the product development process: "Usability is an approach to product development that incorporates direct user feedback throughout the development cycle in order to reduce costs and create products and tools that meet user needs."

In his popular book *Don't Make Me Think*, Steve Krug (2000) provides a simple perspective: "Usability really just means making sure that something works well: that a person of average (or even below average) ability and experience can use the thing—whether it's a website, a fighter jet, or a revolving door—for its intended purpose without getting hopelessly frustrated."

All three of these definitions, as well as other definitions of usability, share some common themes:

- A *user* is involved.
- That user is *doing* something.
- That user is doing something with a *product, system, or other thing*.

Some people distinguish between the terms *usability* and *user experience*. *Usability* is usually considered the ability of the user to use the thing to carry out a task successfully, whereas *user experience* takes a broader view, looking at the individual's entire interaction with the thing, as well as the thoughts, feelings, and perceptions that result from that interaction. We take a very broad view of usability and examine the entire user experience. Therefore, when we talk about "measuring usability," we're really looking at the entire user experience.

## 1.3 WHY DOES USABILITY MATTER?

In any casual conversation about usability, most people would agree that it's good to have something that works well and isn't confusing to use. In our years of evaluating products with thousands of test participants, no one has ever complained that something was too easy to use! Everyone has some favorite stories about how something works remarkably well or really terribly. Even as we write this book, we're challenged in formatting the manuscript to give it to the publisher in an acceptable format. Many other stories demonstrate that the usability of something can actually save lives, bankrupt businesses, and have a tremendous impact on society at large.

Usability can sometimes mean the difference between life and death. For example, the health industry is not immune to poor usability. Usability issues abound in medical devices, procedures, and even diagnostic tools. Jakob Nielsen (2005) cites one study that found 22 separate usability issues that contributed to patients receiving the wrong medicine. Similar situations can arise on a regular basis in the workplace or in the home. Just think of the written instructions for such actions as lighting the pilot light on a furnace or installing a new lighting fixture. An instruction that's misunderstood or misread can easily result in property damage, personal injury, or even death. Similar situations arise outside the home: confusing street signs, complicated or poorly designed automobile dashboards, or distracting devices such as vehicle navigation systems or even cell phones.

Sadly, one of the factors involved in a fatal accident on March 2, 2007, in Atlanta, Georgia, may have been poor usability of the high-occupancy vehicle (HOV) lane and its associated signage (see Figure 1.1). A charter bus was carrying the Bluffton University baseball team to their first playoff game in Sarasota, Florida. The bus was driving south in the predawn hours (when it was still dark) on I-75 in the HOV lane, when the driver, who was not from the area, was faced with the signs in Figure 1.1.

Knowing that he wanted to continue in the HOV lane, the driver had to make a split-second decision about which way to go. At least in the United States, the diamond symbol is a standard symbol for an HOV lane, and it can even be seen marking the HOV lane pavement in the figure. Unfortunately, the driver decided to follow the sign that marked the path that branched to the left. The intent of the sign designer was to mark an *exit* from the HOV lane, not the continuation of the HOV lane itself. The bus reached the end of the ramp, continuing at normal speed, when the driver suddenly saw a stop sign and an abrupt end of the road at an overpass. The driver was unable to stop the bus, and it careened off the other side of the overpass and crashed back onto I-75. Seven people died, including the bus driver. If you had been assigned the task of evaluating possible signage for this exit, how might you have done that? What usability metrics could you have used?

Saving lives is, of course, not the only motivation for good usability. Championing usability in a business setting is often geared toward increasing revenues and/ or decreasing costs. Stories abound of companies that lost money because of the poor usability of a new product. Other companies have made ease of use a key

**FIGURE 1.1**

Signs at the time of the March 2, 2007, bus accident in Atlanta, GA. The "Northside Drive" sign, which marks an exit, may have been interpreted as a continuation of the HOV lane.

selling point and have profited by this approach. Staples, the office supply store, is an excellent example of a company that has embraced the concept of ease of use, even in their advertising. Other companies are also beginning to promote ease of use in their product or brand.

Usability can have a tremendous impact on our society. Consider the infamous "butterfly ballot" used in Florida during the 2000 U.S. presidential election. As a result of the usability problems encountered in that ballot, the Usability Professionals Association started a "design for democracy" group that looks at such things as ballot design, voting machines, and the usability of absentee ballots. Outside the political arena, usability can have a huge impact on providing access to goods and services for different user populations, such as older adults, people with disabilities, or people with language or literacy challenges.

Usability plays a much wider role in our lives than most people realize. It's not just about using a website, a piece of software, or the latest technology. Usability is about setting up a tent, relighting a furnace to heat a home, trying to figure out a tax form, or driving an unfamiliar rental car. Usability impacts everyone, every day. It cuts across cultures, age, gender, and economic class.

Usability takes on an ever-increasing role in our lives as products become more complex. As technologies evolve and mature, they tend to be used by an increasingly diverse set of users. For example, consider the evolution of the written word.

In the earliest days, books were extremely rare (and beautiful) things that were written and illustrated by monks over many years. Precious few people had access to these books or could read them. The invention of the printing press by Johann Gutenberg in 1450 changed that. Books became more widely available, and over many generations more people learned to read. The introduction of electronic books, audio books, and the web brought even more impressive changes. Now even someone who is blind can "read" a book using modern technology.

But this kind of increasing complexity and evolution of technology doesn't necessarily mean that the technologies are becoming easier to use. In fact, just the opposite is likely to happen unless we pay close attention to the user experience. Anyone who's tried to set the time on any of a variety of household devices flashing "12:00" after a power failure can attest to that! As the complexity of technology grows, we believe that usability must be given more attention and importance, and usability metrics will become a critical part of the development process to provide complex technology that's easy to use. We believe that the design process will become more and more user centered.

## 1.4  WHAT ARE USABILITY METRICS?

A *metric* is a way of measuring or evaluating a particular phenomenon or thing. We can say something is longer, taller, or faster because we are able to measure or quantify some attribute of it, such as distance, height, or speed. The process requires agreement on how to measure these things, as well as a consistent and reliable way of doing it. An inch is the same length regardless of who is measuring it, and a second lasts for the same amount of time no matter what the time-keeping device is. Standards for such measures are defined by a society as a whole and are based on standard definitions of each measure.

Metrics exist in many areas of our lives. We're familiar with many metrics, such as time, distance, weight, height, speed, temperature, volume, and so on. Every industry, activity, and culture has its own set of metrics. For example, the auto industry is interested in the horsepower of a car, its gas mileage, and the cost of materials. The computer industry is concerned with processor speed, memory size, and power requirements. At home, we're interested in similar measurements: the bathroom scale (losing or gaining weight), the curfew for our children, and the size of the turkey required to feed everyone on Thanksgiving.

The usability field is no different. We have a set of metrics specific to our profession: task success, user satisfaction, and errors, among others. This book gathers all the usability metrics in one place and explains how to use these metrics to provide maximum benefit to you and your organization.

So what is a usability metric and how does it compare to other types of metrics? Like all other metrics, usability metrics are based on a reliable system of measurement: Using the same set of measurements each time something is measured should result in comparable outcomes. All usability metrics must be *observable* in some way, either directly or indirectly. This observation might be simply noting that a task was completed successfully or noting the time required to complete the task. All usability metrics must be *quantifiable*—they have to be turned into a number or counted in some way. All usability metrics also require that the thing being measured represent some aspect of the user experience, presented in a numeric format. For example, a usability metric might reveal that 65 percent of the users are satisfied with using a product, or that 90 percent of the users are able to complete a set of tasks in less than one minute.

What makes a usability metric different from other metrics? Usability metrics reveal something about the user experience—about the personal experience of the human being using the thing. A usability metric reveals something about the interaction between the user and the thing: some aspect of *effectiveness* (being able to complete a task), *efficiency* (the amount of effort required to complete the task), or *satisfaction* (the degree to which the user was happy with his or her experience while performing the task).

Another difference between usability metrics and other metrics is that they measure something about *people* and their behavior or attitudes. Because people are amazingly diverse and adaptable, we sometimes encounter challenges in our usability metrics. For this reason, we will discuss *confidence intervals* with most of the usability metrics we discuss in order to reflect the variability in the data.

Certain things are not considered usability metrics, such as overall preferences and attitudes not tied to an actual experience of using something. Think of some standard metrics such as the Presidential Approval Ratings, the Consumer Price Index, or the frequency of purchasing specific products. Although these metrics are all quantifiable and may reflect some type of behavior, they are not based on actually using something in order to reflect the variability in the data.

Usability metrics are not an end unto themselves; rather, they are a means to help you reach an informed decision. Usability metrics provide answers to questions that are critical to your organization and that can't be answered by other means. For example, usability metrics can answer these critical questions:

- Will the users like the product?
- Is this new product more efficient to use than the current product?
- How does the usability of this product compare to the competition?
- What are the most significant usability problems with this product?
- Are improvements being made from one design iteration to the next?

## 1.5 THE VALUE OF USABILITY METRICS

We think usability metrics are pretty amazing. Measuring the user experience offers so much more than just simple observation. Metrics add structure to the design and evaluation process, give insight into the findings, and provide information to the decision makers. Without the information provided by usability metrics, important business decisions are made based on incorrect assumptions, "gut feelings," or hunches. As a result, some of these decisions are not the best ones.

During a typical usability evaluation, it's fairly easy to spot some of the more obvious usability issues. But it's much harder to estimate the size or magnitude of the issues. For example, if all eight participants in a study have the same exact problem, you can be quite certain it is a common problem. But what if only two or three of the eight participants encounter the problem? What does that mean for the larger population of users? Usability metrics offer a way to estimate the number of users likely to experience this problem. Knowing the magnitude of the problem could mean the difference between delaying a major product launch and simply adding an additional item to the bug list with a low priority. Without usability metrics, the magnitude of the problem is just a guess.

Usability metrics show whether you're actually improving the user experience from one product to the next. An astute manager will want to know as close to certain as possible that the new product will actually be better than the current product. Usability metrics are the only way to really know if the desired improvements have been realized. By measuring and comparing the current with new, "improved" product and evaluating the potential improvement, you create a win-win situation. There are three possible outcomes:

- The new version tests better than the current product: Everyone can sleep well at night knowing that improvements were made.

- The new version tests worse than the current version: Steps can be taken to address the problem or put remediation plans into place.

- No difference between the current product and the new product is apparent: The impact on the user experience does not affect the success or failure of the new product. However, improvements in other aspects of the product could make up for the lack of improvement in the user experience.

Usability metrics are a key ingredient in calculating a ROI. As part of a business plan, you may be asked to determine how much money is saved or how revenue increases as a result of a new product design. Without usability metrics, this task is impossible. With usability metrics, you might determine that a simple change in a data input field on an internal website could reduce data entry errors by 75 percent, reduce the time required to complete the customer service task, increase the number of transactions processed each day, reduce the backlog in customer orders, cut the delay in customer shipments, and increase both customer satisfaction and customer orders, resulting in an overall rise in revenue for the company.

Usability metrics can help reveal patterns that are hard or even impossible to see. Evaluating a product with a very small sample size (without collecting any metrics) usually reveals the most obvious usability problems. However, there are many more subtle problems that require the power of metrics. For example, sometimes it's difficult to see small inefficiencies, such as the need to reenter user data whenever a transaction displays a new screen. Users may be able to complete their tasks—and maybe even say they like it—but a bunch of small inefficiencies can eventually build up to impact the user experience and slow down the process. Usability metrics help you gain new insights and lead toward a better understanding of user behavior.

## 1.6 TEN COMMON MYTHS ABOUT USABILITY METRICS

There are many common myths about usability metrics. Some of these myths may come from of a lack of experience with using metrics. Perhaps these myths arose from a negative experience (such as someone from marketing screaming about your sample size) or even other usability professionals complaining about the hassles and costs associated with using metrics. Ultimately the source of these myths doesn't matter. What matters is to separate fact from fiction. We've listed ten of the most common myths surrounding usability metrics and a few examples that dispel these myths.

### Myth 1: Metrics take too much time to collect

At best, usability metrics can speed up the design process and, at worst, should not impact the overall timeline. Metrics are quickly and easily collected as part of normal iterative usability evaluation. Project team members may incorrectly assume that full-blown surveys need to be launched or that you have to be testing in the lab for two straight weeks to collect even basic usability metrics. In fact, there are some fairly simple usability metrics you can collect as part of your everyday testing. Adding a few extra questions at the beginning or end of each usability session will not impact the length of the session. Participants can quickly answer a few key questions as part of either a typical background questionnaire or follow-up activities.

Participants can also rate tasks for ease of use or satisfaction after each task or at the end of all tasks. If you have easy access to a large group of target users or a user panel, you can send out an e-mail blast with a few key questions, perhaps with some screenshots. It's possible to collect data from hundreds of users in just one day. Some data can also be quickly collected without even involving the user. For example, you can quickly and easily report the frequency and severity of specific issues with each new design iteration. The time it takes to collect metrics doesn't have to be weeks or even days. Sometimes it's just a few extra hours or even minutes.

### Myth 2: Usability metrics cost too much money

Some people believe that the only way to get reliable usability data is to outsource the study to a market research firm or usability consultancy. Although this may be helpful in some situations, it can also be quite costly. Many reliable metrics don't cost an arm and a leg. Even as part of your everyday testing, you can collect incredibly valuable data on the frequency and severity of different usability issues. You can also collect huge amounts of quantitative data by sending out short e-mail surveys to fellow employees or a panel of targeted users. Also, some of the best analysis tools are actually free on the web. Although money does help in certain situations, it is by no means necessary to get some great metrics.

## Myth 3: Usability metrics are not useful when focusing on small improvements

Some project team members may question the usefulness of metrics when they are interested in only some fairly small improvements. They may say it's best to focus on a narrow set of improvements and not worry about metrics. They may not have any extra time or budget to collect any usability metrics. They may say that metrics have no place in a rapid-pace iterative design process. Analyzing usability issues is an obvious and incredibly valuable solution. For example, looking at the severity and frequency of usability issues and why they occur is an excellent way to focus resources during the design process. This approach saves the project both money and time. You can easily derive usability metrics based on previous studies that might help you answer key usability questions. Usability metrics are useful for large and small projects alike.

## Myth 4: Usability metrics don't help us understand causes

Some people argue that metrics don't help us understand the root cause of usability problems. They assume (incorrectly) that metrics serve only to highlight the magnitude of the problem. But if they concentrate on only success rates or completion time data, it's easy to see why some might have this perception. Metrics, however, can tell you much more about the root cause of usability issues than you might initially think. You can analyze verbatim comments to reveal the source of the problem and how many users experience it. You can identify where in the system users experience a problem and use metrics to tell where and even why some problems occur. Depending on how the data are coded and the methods used, there is a wealth of usability data that can help reveal the root cause of many usability issues.

## Myth 5: Usability data are too noisy

One big criticism of usability metrics is that the data are too "noisy": Too many variables prevent getting a clear picture of what's going on. The classic example of "noisy" data is measuring task completion time in an automated usability study when the participant goes out for a cup of coffee or, worse, home for the weekend. Although this may happen on occasion, it should not deter you from collecting task time data or any other type of usability data. There are some simple things that can be done to minimize or even remove noise in the data. Usability data can be cleaned up so that extreme values are not used in the analysis. Also, specific metrics can be carefully chosen to mitigate noisy data. Well-defined procedures can be used to ensure that appropriate levels of consistency are achieved in evaluating tasks or usability issues. Many standard usability questionnaires have already been widely validated by many researchers. The bottom line is that with some careful thought and a few simple techniques, a lot of the noise in usability data can be significantly reduced to show a clear picture of user behavior and attitudes.

## Myth 6: You can just trust your gut

A lot of usability decisions are made on a "gut level." There's always someone on the project team who proclaims, "This decision just feels right!" One of the beauties of metrics is that having the data takes a lot of the guesswork out of usability decisions. Some design options are truly borderline cases, but they might actually have an impact on a large population. Sometimes the right design solutions are counterintuitive. For example, a design team may ensure that all the information on a web page is above the fold, thereby eliminating the need to scroll. However, usability data (perhaps in the form of task completion times) may reveal longer task completion times because there's not enough white space between the various visual elements. Intuition is certainly important, but data are better.

## Myth 7: Metrics don't apply to new products

Some people shy away from metrics when evaluating a new product. They may argue that since there is no point of comparison, metrics don't make sense. We would argue just the opposite. When evaluating a new product, it's critical to establish a set of baseline metrics against which future design iterations can be compared. It's the only way to really know if the design is improving or not. In addition, it's helpful to establish target metrics for new products. Before a product is released, it should meet basic usability metrics around task success, satisfaction, and efficiency.

## Myth 8: No metrics exist for the type of issues we are dealing with

Some people believe that there aren't any metrics related to the particular product or project they are working on. Whatever the goal of the project, at least a couple of metrics should tie directly to the business goals of the project. For example, some people say they are only interested in the emotional response of users and not in actual task performance. In this case, several well-established ways of measuring emotional responses are available. In other situations, someone might be concerned only with awareness. Very simple ways to measure awareness also exist, even without investing in eye-tracking equipment. Some people say that they are only interested in more subtle reactions of users, such as their level of frustration. There are ways to measure stress levels without actually asking the user. In our years of usability research, we have yet to come across a business or user goal that was not measurable in some way. You may have to be creative in how you collect the data, but it's always possible.

## Myth 9: Metrics are not understood or appreciated by management

Although some managers view usability as providing only qualitative feedback about a design or product, most managers see the value of measurement. It has been our experience that usability metrics are not only understood but very much appreciated by upper-level management. They can relate to metrics. Metrics provide credibility to the team, the product, and the design process. Metrics can be used to calculate ROI (return on investment). Most managers love metrics, and usability metrics are one type of metric they will quickly embrace. Usability metrics can also be real attention-grabbers with management. It's one thing to say there's a problem with the online checkout process, but it's an entirely different thing to say that 52 percent of users are unable to successfully purchase a product online once they've found it.

## Myth 10: It's difficult to collect reliable data with a small sample size

A widely held belief is that a large sample size is required to collect any reliable usability metrics. Many people assume that you need at least 30 participants to even start looking at usability data. Although having a larger sample size certainly helps increase the confidence level, smaller sample sizes of eight or ten participants can still be meaningful. We will show you how to calculate a confidence interval that takes into account the sample size when making any conclusion. Also, we will show you how to determine the sample size you need to identify usability issues. Most of the examples in this book are based on fairly small sample sizes (fewer than 20 participants). So not only are metrics possible to analyze with fairly small sample sizes, doing so is quite common!

# Background

In this chapter we review some basic statistical concepts, walk you through a few common statistical procedures, and discuss how to design a well-thought-out usability study. We won't burden you with too many formulas or complicated statistics. Instead, we focus on the practical side to give you a step-by-step guide to analyzing your usability data in the simplest possible way. We want to get you comfortable with these methods as easily and quickly as possible before you continue with the material in the rest of the book.

The first part of this chapter covers basic information about understanding data and designing a usability study. The second part includes a step-by-step guide to analyzing different types of usability data. We show you how to calculate and interpret descriptive statistics, how to compare means, how to examine relationships between variables, and how to use some nonparametric statistics. We address the techniques you will use most often as part of everyday usability testing. In our examples, we use Microsoft Excel for our calculations because it is so widely available. Many similar statistical software packages provide the same calculations with only minor variations in presentation and use.

## 2.1 DESIGNING A USABILITY STUDY

Many factors must be considered when you design a usability study. A well-thought-out study can save you time and effort and answer your research questions clearly. A poorly designed study can be just the opposite: a waste of time, money, and effort, without giving you the answers you need. To design a well-thought-out usability study, you need to answer these questions:

- What type of participants do I need?
- How many participants do I need?
- Am I going to compare the data from a single group of participants or from several different groups?
- Do I need to counterbalance (adjust for) the order of tasks?

We examine each of these questions and try to help you find the answers.          **15**

### 2.1.1 Selecting Participants

Selecting participants for a usability study should be a set of deliberate decisions based on factors such as cost, availability, appropriateness, and study goals. One of the most common criticisms of some usability studies is that the participants are not representative of the larger population or don't match the target audience. You should consider carefully how you select participants for your study and try to get all the interested parties to agree on the sampling strategy *before* you begin.

The first question you must answer is how well your participants should reflect your target audience. We recommend you try to recruit truly representative participants whenever you can. For example, if you're designing a new medical application for doctors to use in their practices, try to get practicing physicians as your participants. In some situations, however, you may have to settle for participants who are only close approximations of the target users. In those cases, be aware of the limitations of the data you collect. Many of the statistics you will calculate assume that the sample data reflects the larger population.

The second important question when selecting participants is whether you're going to divide your data by different types of participants. If you plan to separate your participants into distinct groups, think about what those groups are and about how many participants you want in each group. In usability, there are a few common types of groups or segments:

- Self-reported expertise in some domain (novice, intermediate, expert)
- Frequency of use (e.g., number of web visits or interactions per month)
- Amount of experience with something relevant (days, months, years)
- Demographics (gender, age, location, etc.)
- Activities (use of particular functionality or features)

The third question involves sampling strategy. The goal of larger (or quantitative) usability studies is to be able to generalize the findings to the larger population. To attain that goal, you need to develop a sampling strategy that allows you to say something about the overall user population. Here are some different sampling techniques:

*Random sampling:* Everyone in the population has a roughly equal probability of being selected to participate in the study. Random sampling involves numbering everyone on a list of all potential recruits and using a random number generator to select participants according to the desired sample size.

*Systematic sampling:* You select each participant based on predefined criteria. For example, you might select every tenth person from a list of users or every one hundredth person who passes through a turnstile at a sporting event.

*Stratified sampling:* You create subsamples of the entire population and ensure that certain sample sizes are achieved for each subgroup. The goal is to ensure that the sample reflects the larger population. For example, you might recruit 50 percent males and 50 percent females, or recruit a group of participants in which 20 percent are older than 65.

*Samples of convenience:* This approach, which is very common is usability studies, includes anyone willing to participate in a study. Locating participants for these samples might be done through an advertisement or by using a list of people who came to the lab for past testing. It's important to know how well a sample of convenience reflects the general population and to be aware of any special biases that may be reflected in their feedback or data.

### 2.1.2 Sample Size

One of the most commonly asked questions in the usability field concerns the sample size for a usability study. Everyone involved—usability professionals, project managers, market researchers, developers, designers—wants to know how many participants are enough in a usability study. There's no rule that says if you don't have at least *x* number of participants in a study, the data won't be valid. The sample size you choose should be based on two factors: the goals of your study and your tolerance for a margin of error.

If you are interested only in identifying major usability issues as part of an iterative design process, you can get useful feedback from three or four representative participants. This small sample means that you will not identify all or even most of the usability issues, but you can identify some of the more significant ones. If you have lots of tasks or several different parts of the product to evaluate, then you will certainly need more than four participants. As a general rule of thumb, during the early stages of design, you need fewer participants to identify the major usability issues. As the design gets closer to completion, you need more participants to identify the remaining issues. (Chapter 5 provides more discussion of this issue, as well as some simple statistics for determining sample sizes.)

The other issue to consider is how much error you're willing to accept. Table 2.1 shows how the degree of confidence (or confidence interval) changes based on an average 80 percent success rate for different sample sizes. We'll talk more about confidence intervals later, but the basic idea is that they show what projections you can make about the true value of a statistic for the whole population based on what you observed in your sample. For example, if eight out of ten participants in a usability test successfully completed a task, can you say that 80 percent of users in the larger population will be able to complete it? No, you can't.

As Table 2.1 shows, you can say (with 95 percent confidence) that somewhere between 48 and 95 percent of the people in the larger population will be able to successfully complete the task. But you can see that as the sample size increases, the lower and upper bounds of the 95 percent confidence interval move closer together. So if you ran 100 participants, and 80 of them completed the task successfully, you can say that 71 to 86 percent of the larger population will be able to complete the task (with 95 percent confidence). We'll talk more later about how you calculate confidence intervals.

**Table 2.1** Example of How Confidence Intervals Change as a Function of Sample Size

| Number Successful | Number of Participants | Lower 95% Confidence | Upper 95% Confidence |
|---|---|---|---|
| 4 | 5 | 36% | 98% |
| 8 | 10 | 48% | 95% |
| 16 | 20 | 58% | 95% |
| 24 | 30 | 62% | 91% |
| 40 | 50 | 67% | 89% |
| 80 | 100 | 71% | 86% |

Note: These numbers indicate how many participants in a usability test successfully completed a given task and the confidence interval for that mean completion rate in the larger population.

### 2.1.3 Within-Subjects or Between-Subjects Study

Another important decision to make is whether you are going to be comparing different data for each participant (such as success rates for different designs of the product) or data from each participant to the other participants (such as success rates for different age groups). The first approach is commonly referred to as a within-subjects design, and the second is known as a between-subjects design. Both approaches have their strengths and weaknesses.

A within-subjects, or repeated-measures, design is most commonly used in studies when you want to evaluate how easily a participant can learn to use a particular product. By comparing metrics such as task completion times or errors across several trials with the same set of participants, you can determine how quickly and easily the participant becomes familiar with the product. A within-subjects study does not require as large a sample size, and you don't have to worry about differences across groups. Because each participant is being compared to himself, the differences you observe in the data cannot be attributed to differences between participants. The downside of a within-subjects design is that you may need to worry about "carryover effects," where performance in one condition impacts performance in another condition. A carryover effect might be the result of practice (improving performance) or fatigue (decreasing performance). If there is a possible carryover effect, you can counterbalance for this effect as you design the study and analyze the data.

A between-subjects study is used to compare results for different participants, such as differences in satisfaction between novices and experts or in task completion times for younger versus older participants. In another type of between-subjects design, participants are randomly assigned to groups and then receive different treatments, such as different prototype designs for the same product. Because there is generally more variance across a group of  participants than within a single participant, a between-subjects design requires a larger sample size. One advantage of a between-subjects design is the elimination of carryover effects, because any potential carryover effects would impact both groups equally.

If neither a between-subjects nor a within-subjects design meets your needs, consider a mixed design. A mixed design contains a between-subjects factor, such as gender, *and* a within-subjects factor, such as three trials distributed over time. For example, you could use a mixed-design study to find out if there is a difference in the way men and women perform some task across several trials. Mixed designs can be a very powerful technique in a usability study, and because they may eliminate the need for separate studies for each question that arises, they can also save time and money.

## 2.1.4 Counterbalancing

Sometimes the order in which participants perform their tasks has a significant impact on the results. Participants usually learn the product as their experience with it grows. As a result, you must consider the order in which the data are collected, which is usually the order of tasks. It's possible that you may see improvement in performance or satisfaction as the usability session continues. Can you determine if the improvement occurs because the fifth task is easier than the first task or if some learning takes place between the first and fifth tasks that makes the fifth task easier to perform? The only way to address this question is to control for order effects through a technique called counterbalancing.

Counterbalancing involves simply changing the order in which different tasks are performed. There are a few ways to do this. You can randomize the order of tasks by "shuffling" the task order prior to each participant, or you can create various orders ahead of time so that each participant performs each task in a different order. Table 2.2 shows one example of how to counterbalance task order. Notice how each task appears in each position only once. Task 2 (T2) is performed as the second task only once by participant 1. Participant 2 performs task 2 as the last task.

**Table 2.2** Example of How to Counterbalance Task Order for Four Participants and Four Tasks

| Participant | First Task | Second Task | Third Task | Fourth Task |
| --- | --- | --- | --- | --- |
| P1 | T1 | T2 | T3 | T4 |
| P2 | T3 | T1 | T4 | T2 |
| P3 | T2 | T4 | T1 | T3 |
| P4 | T4 | T3 | T2 | T1 |

If you suspect that there might be an order effect, we recommend you counter-balance task order. However, there are a few situations when it is not necessary or may even be detrimental to your findings. First, if the tasks are totally unrelated to each other, learning between tasks is unlikely. Performing one task successfully will not help in any other task. Second, counterbalancing is not appropriate when a natural order of tasks is present. Sometimes the order cannot be juggled because the test session would not make sense. In this situation, acknowledge order effects as part of the general learning process rather than as a symptom of a poorly designed usability study.

### 2.1.5 Independent and Dependent Variables

In any usability study you must identify both independent and dependent variables. An independent variable of a study is an aspect that you manipulate. Choose the independent variables based on your research questions. For example, you may be concerned with differences in performance between males and females, or between novices and experts, or between two different designs. All of these are independent variables that can be manipulated to answer specific research questions.

Dependent variables (also called outcome or response variables) describe what happened as the result of the study. A dependent variable is something you measure as the result of, or as dependent on, how you manipulate the independent variables. Dependent variables include metrics or measurements such as success rates, number of errors, user satisfaction, completion times, and many more. Most of the metrics we discuss in this book are dependent variables.

When you design a usability study, you must have a clear idea of what you plan to manipulate (independent variables) and what you plan to measure (dependent variables). If you don't have a clear idea of those, go back to the research goals. If you can draw a logical connection between the research goals and your independent and dependent variables, you and your study should be successful.

## 2.2 TYPES OF DATA

Data, the cornerstone of usability metrics, exist in many forms. In the world of usability, types of data include task completion rates, web traffic, responses to a satisfaction survey, or the number of problems a participant encounters in a lab test. To analyze usability data, you need to understand the four general types of data: nominal, ordinal, interval, and ratio. Each type of data has its own strengths and limitations. When collecting and analyzing usability data, you should know what type of data you're dealing with and what you can and can't do with each type.

### 2.2.1 Nominal Data

Nominal data are simply unordered groups or categories. Without order between the categories, you can say only that they are different, not that one is any better than the other. For example, consider apples, oranges, and bananas. They are just different; no one fruit is inherently better than any other.

In usability, nominal data might be characteristics of different types of users, such as Windows versus Mac users, users in different geographic locations, or males as opposed to females. These are typically independent variables that allow you to segment the data by these different groups. Nominal data also include some commonly used dependent variables, such as task success. Nominal data could also be the number of participants who clicked on link A instead of link B, or participants who chose to use a remote control instead of the controls on a DVD player itself.

Among the statistics you can use with nominal data are simple descriptive statistics such as counts and frequencies. For example, you could say that 45 percent of the participants are female, or 200 participants have blue eyes, or 95 percent were successful on a particular task.

One important thing to remember when you work with nominal data is how you code the data. In statistical analysis programs such as Excel, it's common to represent the membership in each group using numbers. For example, you might code males as group "1" and females as group "2." Remember that those figures are not data to be analyzed as numbers: An average of these values would be meaningless. (You could just as easily code them as "F" and "M.") The software can't distinguish between numbers used strictly for coding purposes, like these, and numbers whose values have true meaning. One useful exception to this is task success. If you code task success as a "1" and task failure as "0," the average will be the same as the proportion of users who were successful.

## 2.2.2 Ordinal Data

Ordinal data are ordered groups or categories. As the name implies, the data are organized in a certain way. However, the intervals between the measurements are not meaningful. Some people think of ordinal data as ranked data. The list of the top 100 movies, as rated by the American Film Institute (AFI), shows that the tenth best movie of all time, *Singing in the Rain,* is better than the twentieth best movie of all time, *One Flew Over the Cuckoo's Nest.* But these ratings don't say that *Singing in the Rain* is *twice* as good as *One Flew Over the Cuckoo's Nest.* One film is just *better* than the other, at least according to the AFI. Because the distance between the ranks is not meaningful, you cannot say one is twice as good as the other. Ordinal data might be ordered as better or worse, more satisfied or less satisfied, or more severe or less severe. The relative ranking (the order of the rankings) is the only thing that matters.

In usability, the most common occurrence of ordinal data comes from self-reported data on questionnaires. For example, a participant might rate a website as excellent, good, fair, or poor. These are relative rankings: The distance between excellent and good is not necessarily the same distance between good and fair. Severity ratings are another example of ordinal data. A usability specialist might assign a severity rating of high, medium, or low for each problem that the participant encountered. The distance between high and medium is not necessarily the same as that between medium and low.

The most common way to analyze ordinal data is by looking at frequencies. For example, you might report that 40 percent of the participants rated the site as excellent, 30 percent as good, 20 percent as fair, and 10 percent as poor. Calculating an average ranking may be tempting, but it's statistically meaningless.

### 2.2.3 Interval Data

Interval data are continuous data where the differences between the measurements are meaningful but there is no natural zero point. An example of interval data familiar to most of us is temperature, either Celsius or Fahrenheit. Defining zero as the freezing point (in the case of Celsius) or as the point at which pipes begin to burst (in the case of Fahrenheit) is completely arbitrary. Zero degrees does not mean the absence of heat; it only identifies a meaningful point on the scale of temperatures.

In usability, the System Usability Scale (SUS) is one example of interval data. SUS (described in detail in Chapter 6) is based on self-reported data from a series of questions about the overall usability of any system. Scores range from 0 to 100, with a higher SUS score indicating better usability. The distance between each point along the scale is meaningful in the sense that it represents an incremental increase or decrease in perceived usability.

Interval data allow you to calculate a wide range of descriptive statistics (including averages, standard deviation, etc.). There are also many inferential statistics that can be used to generalize about a larger population. Interval data provide many more possibilities for analysis than either nominal or ordinal data. Much of this chapter will review statistics that can be used with interval data.

One of the debates you can get into with people who collect and analyze subjective ratings is whether you must treat the data as purely ordinal or you can treat it as being interval. Consider these two rating scales:

○ Poor ○ Fair ○ Good ○ Excellent
Poor ○ ○ ○ ○ ○ Excellent

At first glance, you might say the two scales are the same, but the difference in presentation makes them different. Putting explicit labels on the items in the first scale makes the data ordinal. Leaving the intervening labels off in the second scale and only labeling the end points make the data more "interval-like." That's the reason that most subjective rating scales only label the ends, or "anchors," and not every data point.

Consider a slightly different version of the second scale:

Poor ○ ○ ○ ○ ○ ○ ○ ○ ○ ○ Excellent

Presenting it this way, with 10 points along the scale, makes it even more obvious that the data can be treated as if they were interval data. The reasonable interpretation of this scale by a user is that the distances between all the data points along the scale are equal. A question to ask yourself when deciding whether you can treat some data like these as interval or not is whether a point halfway between any two of the defined data points makes sense. If it does, then it makes sense to analyze the data as interval data.

## 2.2.4 **Ratio Data**

Ratio data are the same as interval data, with the addition of an absolute zero. These data mean that the zero value is not arbitrary, as with interval data, but has some inherent meaning. With ratio data, the differences between the measurements are interpreted as a ratio. Examples of ratio data are age, height, and weight. In each example, zero indicates the absence of age, height, or weight.

In usability, the most obvious example of ratio data is time to completion. Zero seconds left would mean no time or duration remaining. Ratio data let you say something is twice as fast or half as slow as something else. For example, you could say that one participant is twice as fast as another user in completing a task.

There aren't many additional analyses you can do with ratio data compared to interval data in usability. One exception is calculating a geometric mean, which might be useful in measuring differences in time (Nielsen, 2001a). Aside from that calculation, there really aren't many differences between interval and ratio data in terms of the available statistics.

## 2.3 **METRICS AND DATA**

Choosing the right statistics is critical. Choosing the wrong statistical test and ending up with an incorrect conclusion could invalidate your results and negate your entire usability test. Table 2.3 shows some of the common statistical tests

**Table 2.3** Choosing the Right Statistics for Different Data Types and Usability Metrics

| Data Type | Common Metrics | Statistical Procedures |
|---|---|---|
| Nominal (categories) | Task success (binary), errors (binary), top-2-box scores | Frequencies, crosstabs, Chi-square |
| Ordinal (ranks) | Severity ratings, rankings (designs) | Frequencies, crosstabs, chi-square, Wilcoxon rank sum tests, Spearman rank correlation |
| Interval | Likert scale data, SUS scores | All descriptive statistics, $t$-tests, ANOVAs, correlation, regression analysis |
| Ratio | Completion time, time (visual attention), average task success (aggregated) | All descriptive statistics (including geometric means), $t$-tests, ANOVAs, correlation, regression analysis |

described in the rest of this chapter. The type of data you are examining will dictate different tests. In Chapter 3 we discuss the reasons you should choose one metric over another.

## 2.4 DESCRIPTIVE STATISTICS

Descriptive statistics are essential for any interval or ratio-level data. Descriptive statistics, as the name implies, describe the data without saying anything about the larger population. Inferential statistics let you draw some conclusions or infer something about a larger population above and beyond your sample. Descriptive statistics are very easy to calculate using most statistical software packages. Let's assume we have the time data shown in Figure 2.1.

For our examples, we use Excel to analyze the data. First click on "Tools," then on "Data Analysis." (*Note:* If you do not see a "Data Analysis" option on the "Tools" menu, you must first install it by choosing "Tools" > "Add-ins" and then checking "Analysis Toolpak.") In the "Data Analysis" window, choose "Descriptive Statistics" from the list of analysis options. Next, define the range of data on which you want to run the descriptive statistics. In our example, we identify as the input range of data column B from row 1 through row 13. (Notice that the first row in the spreadsheet data is the label, so we check the box indicating "labels in first row." Including the label is optional, but it helps you keep your data more organized.) Next, select the output range (the top, left corner of the area where you want the results to be placed). Finally, we indicate that we want to see the summary statistics and the 95 percent confidence interval. (The 95 percent confidence interval is the default selection in Excel.)

The results of the descriptive statistics are shown in Figure 2.2. Our hypothetical raw task time data for 12 participants are shown on the left side (columns A and B). The descriptive statistics are shown on the right side (columns D and E). We will review this output in the next several sections.

**FIGURE 2.1**

Time to complete a task, in seconds, for 12 participants in a usability study.

|   | A | B |
|---|---|---|
| 1 | Participant | Task Time |
| 2 | P1 | 34 |
| 3 | P2 | 33 |
| 4 | P3 | 28 |
| 5 | P4 | 44 |
| 6 | P5 | 46 |
| 7 | P6 | 21 |
| 8 | P7 | 22 |
| 9 | P8 | 53 |
| 10 | P9 | 22 |
| 11 | P10 | 29 |
| 12 | P11 | 39 |
| 13 | P12 | 50 |
| 14 | | |

| | A | B | C | D | E |
|---|---|---|---|---|---|
| 1 | Participant | Task Time | | Task Time | |
| 2 | P1 | 34 | | | |
| 3 | P2 | 33 | | Mean | 35.08333333 |
| 4 | P3 | 28 | | Standard Error | 3.246112671 |
| 5 | P4 | 44 | | Median | 33.5 |
| 6 | P5 | 46 | | Mode | 22 |
| 7 | P6 | 21 | | Standard Deviation | 11.24486415 |
| 8 | P7 | 22 | | Sample Variance | 126.4469697 |
| 9 | P8 | 53 | | Kurtosis | -1.321525965 |
| 10 | P9 | 22 | | Skewness | 0.251441718 |
| 11 | P10 | 29 | | Range | 32 |
| 12 | P11 | 39 | | Minimum | 21 |
| 13 | P12 | 50 | | Maximum | 53 |
| 14 | | | | Sum | 421 |
| 15 | | | | Count | 12 |
| 16 | | | | Confidence Level(95.0%) | 7.144645813 |
| 17 | | | | | |

**FIGURE 2.2**

Example data showing the output of the descriptive statistics option in Excel.

## 2.4.1 Measures of Central Tendency

Measures of central tendency are the first thing you should look at when you run descriptive statistics. Central tendency is simply the middle, or central, part of any distribution. The three most common measures of central tendency are mean, median, and mode. In Figure 2.2, the mean, or average, is 35.1, so the average time to complete this task was just over 35 seconds. The mean of most usability metrics is extremely useful and is probably the most common statistic cited in a usability report.

The median is the midway point in the distribution: Half the participants are below the median and half are above the median. In Figure 2.2, the median is equal to 33.5 seconds: Half of the participants were faster than 33.5 seconds, and half of the participants were slower than 33.5 seconds. In some cases, the median can be more revealing than the mean. In an example of salaries, median salaries for a company are more commonly reported because the higher executive salaries will skew the mean value so much that the average salary appears much higher than the majority really are. In such cases involving possible extreme values (as is sometimes the case with time data), consider using the median.

The mode is the most commonly occurring value. In Figure 2.2, the mode is 22 seconds: Two participants completed the task in 22 seconds. It's not common to report the mode in usability test results, but it may be useful to know it. When the data are continuous over a broad range, such as the completion times shown in Figure 2.2, the mode is generally less useful. When data have a more limited set of values (such as subjective rating scales), the mode is more useful.

---

**HOW MANY DECIMAL PLACES TO USE WHEN REPORTING DATA**

One of the most common mistakes usability specialists make is reporting the data from a usability test (mean times, task completion rates, etc.) with more precision than they really deserve. For example, Figure 2.2 shows that the mean time was 35.08333333 seconds. Is that the way you should report the mean? Of course not. That many decimal places may be mathematically correct, but it's ridiculous from a practical standpoint. Who cares whether the mean was 35.083 or 35.085 seconds? When you're dealing with tasks that took *about* 35 seconds to complete, a few milliseconds or a few hundredths of a second make no difference whatsoever. So how many decimal places should you use?

There's no universal answer, but some of the factors to consider are the accuracy of the original data, their magnitude, and its variability. The original data in Figure 2.2 appear to be accurate to the nearest second. One rule of thumb is that the number of significant digits you should use when reporting a statistic, such as the mean, is no more than one additional significant digit in comparison to the original data. So in this example, you could report that the mean was 35.1 seconds.

---

### 2.4.2 Measures of Variability

Measures of variability show how the data are spread or dispersed across the range of all the data. These measures help answer the question "Do most users have similar completion times, or is there a wide range of times?" Determining the variability is critical if you want to know how confident you can be of the data. The greater the variability or spread in the data, the less dependable the data are relative to understanding the general population. The less the variability or spread, the more confidence you can have in relating the findings to a larger population. There are three common measures of variability: the range, the variance, and the standard deviation.

The range is the distance between the minimum and maximum data points. In Figure 2.2, the range is 32, with a minimum time of 21 seconds and a maximum time of 53 seconds. The range can vary wildly depending on the metric. For example, in many kinds of rating scales, the range is usually limited to five or seven, depending on the number of values used in the scales. When you study completion times, the range is very important because it will identify "outliers" (data points that are at the extreme top and bottom of the range). Looking at the range is also a good check to make sure that the data are coded properly. If the range is supposed to be from one to five, and the data include a seven, you know there is a problem.

Variance, another common and important measure of variability, tells you how spread out the data are relative to the average or mean. The formula for calculating variance measures the difference between each individual data point and the mean, squares that value, sums all of those squares, and then divides the result by the sample size minus 1. In Figure 2.2, the variance is 126.4.

Once you know the variance, you can easily calculate the standard deviation, the most commonly used measure of variability. The standard deviation is simply the square root of the variance. The standard deviation in the example shown in Figure 2.2 is 11 seconds. Interpreting this measure of variability is a little easier than interpreting the variance, since the unit of the standard deviation is the same as the original data (seconds in this example).

### 2.4.3 **Confidence Intervals**

Confidence intervals are extremely valuable for any usability professional. A confidence interval is a range that estimates the true population value for a statistic. For example, assume that you need to estimate the mean for the entire population and you want to be 95 percent certain about what that mean is. In Figure 2.2 the 95 percent confidence interval is just over 7 seconds. This means that you can have a 95 percent confidence that the population mean is 35 seconds plus or minus 7 seconds, or between 28 seconds and 42 seconds.

Alternatively, you can quickly calculate the confidence interval using the CONFIDENCE function in Excel. The formula is very easy to construct:

$$= \text{confidence (alpha, standard deviation, sample size)}$$

The alpha is your significance level, which is typically 5 percent, or 0.05. The standard deviation is easily calculated using the Excel "stdev" function. The sample size is simply the number of cases or data points you are examining, which is easily calculated using the "Count" function. Figure 2.3 shows an example.

The CONFIDENCE function in Excel works a little differently from the confidence level calculated as part of the descriptive statistics function shown in Figure 2.2. Remember, however, that this function is based on the standard deviation of the population, which in many cases is unknown. As a result, the

**FIGURE 2.3**

Example of how to calculate a 95 percent confidence interval using the CONFIDENCE function in Excel.

| | B17 | | $f_x$ =CONFIDENCE(0.05,B16,B15) | | |
|---|---|---|---|---|---|
| | A | | B | C | D |
| 1 | Participant | | Task Time | | |
| 2 | P1 | | 34 | | |
| 3 | P2 | | 33 | | |
| 4 | P3 | | 28 | | |
| 5 | P4 | | 44 | | |
| 6 | P5 | | 46 | | |
| 7 | P6 | | 21 | | |
| 8 | P7 | | 22 | | |
| 9 | P8 | | 53 | | |
| 10 | P9 | | 22 | | |
| 11 | P10 | | 29 | | |
| 12 | P11 | | 39 | | |
| 13 | P12 | | 50 | | |
| 14 | Mean | | 35.08333 | | |
| 15 | Count | | 12 | | |
| 16 | Standard Deviation | | 11.24486 | | |
| 17 | 95% Confidence Level | | 6.362264 | | |
| 18 | | | | | |

confidence intervals don't quite match up between Figures 2.2 and 2.3. We recommend that you take a more conservative perspective and use the confidence level as part of the descriptive statistics (Figure 2.2), since this does not make any assumptions about the standard deviation of the population.

Ultimately, which calculation method you choose does not matter a great deal. As your sample size increases, the difference between the two calculations gets smaller. What really matters is that you use one of them. We cannot emphasize enough the importance of calculating and presenting confidence levels with your metrics.

## 2.5 COMPARING MEANS

One of the most useful things you can do with interval or ratio data is to compare different means. If you want to know whether one design has higher satisfaction rates than another, or if error rates are higher for one group of participants compared to another, your best approach is through statistics. This is quite easy using Excel or many other analysis packages. Therefore, instead of providing all the formulas for the various ways of comparing means, we will explain when to use each, how to use each, and how to interpret the results.

There are several ways to compare means, but before you jump into the statistics, you should know the answers to a few questions:

1. Is the comparison *within* the same set of participants or *across* different participants? For example, if you are comparing some data for men and women, it is highly likely that these are different participants. Comparing different samples like this is called independent samples. But if you're comparing the same group of participants on two different products or designs (a within-subjects design), you will use something called repeated measures analysis or paired samples.

2. What is the sample size? If the sample size is less than 30, use a *t*-test. If the sample is 30 or more, use a *z*-test.

3. How many samples are you comparing? If you are comparing two samples, use a *t*-test. If you are comparing three or more samples, use an analysis of variance (also called ANOVA).

### 2.5.1 Independent Samples

Frequently in usability studies you're comparing means based on independent samples. This only means that the groups are different. For example, you might be interested in comparing satisfaction rates between expert and novice participants. The most common question is whether the two groups are different. Doing this is easy in Excel. First, go to "Data" > "Tools" and choose the option of "*t*-test: Two Samples

| | A | B | C | D | E | F |
|---|---|---|---|---|---|---|
| 1 | Expert_time | Novice_time | | t-Test: Two Samples Assuming Equal Variance | | |
| 2 | 34 | 45 | | | | |
| 3 | 33 | 48 | | | Expert_time | Novice_time |
| 4 | 28 | 53 | | Mean | 35.08333333 | 49.33333333 |
| 5 | 44 | 66 | | Variance | 126.4469697 | 229.6969697 |
| 6 | 46 | 67 | | Observations | 12 | 12 |
| 7 | 21 | 35 | | Pooled Variance | 178.0719697 | |
| 8 | 22 | 39 | | Hypothesized Mean Difference | 0 | |
| 9 | 53 | 21 | | df | 22 | |
| 10 | 22 | 34 | | t Stat | -2.61572876 | |
| 11 | 29 | 55 | | P(T<=t) one-tail | 0.007892632 | |
| 12 | 39 | 59 | | t Critical one-tail | 1.717144335 | |
| 13 | 50 | 70 | | P(T<=t) two-tail | 0.015785265 | |
| 14 | | | | t Critical two-tail | 2.073873058 | |

**FIGURE 2.4**

Output from an independent samples $t$-test in Excel.

Assuming Equal Variances" (of course, assuming that the two variances are roughly equal). Next, input the data for both variables. In this example, the data are coming from columns A and B in our Excel spreadsheet (Figure 2.4). We decided to include the labels in each row, so we check the label option. Because we hypothesize that there is no difference in means, we enter 0. (You might hear this called the "null hypothesis.") This means we are testing whether there is a difference between the two variables. We select an alpha level equal to 0.05. This means we want to be 95 percent confident of our results. Another way to think of this is that we are willing to be wrong 5 percent of the time by concluding there is a difference when there really is not one.

The output from this analysis is shown in Figure 2.4. The first thing you might notice is the difference in means between the novices and the experts. Experts are faster (35 seconds) compared to novices (49 seconds). The other very important piece of data here is the $p$-value. Because we aren't making any assumptions ahead of time about who might be faster (experts or novices), we look at the $p$-value for the two-tailed distribution. The $p$-value is about 0.016, which is well below our 0.05 threshold. Therefore, we can say there is a statistically significant difference in completion times between novices and experts, at the 0.05 level. It's important to remember to state the alpha level because it shows how much error you are willing to accept.

## 2.5.2 Paired Samples

A paired samples $t$-test is used when you're comparing means within the same set of participants. For example, you may be interested in knowing whether there is a difference between two prototype designs. If you have the same set of participants perform tasks using prototype A and then prototype B, and you are measuring variables such as self-reported ease of use and time, you will use a paired samples $t$-test.

Running this test is simple in Excel. On the main menu, go to "Tools" > "Data Analysis." Choose the option "$t$-Test: Paired Two Samples for Means." Next, select

| | A | B | C | D | E | F | G |
|---|---|---|---|---|---|---|---|
| 1 | Participant | Design A_SUS | Design B_SUS | | t-Test: Two Samples for Means | | |
| 2 | P1 | 80 | 48 | | | | |
| 3 | P2 | 88 | 55 | | | Design A_SUS | Design B_SUS |
| 4 | P3 | 76 | 53 | | Mean | 77.7500000 | 57.0833333 |
| 5 | P4 | 90 | 80 | | Variance | 125.4772727 | 153.7196970 |
| 6 | P5 | 93 | 81 | | Observations | 12.0000000 | 12.0000000 |
| 7 | P6 | 67 | 51 | | Pearson Correlation | 0.6521213 | |
| 8 | P7 | 68 | 61 | | Hypothesized Mean Difference | 0.0000000 | |
| 9 | P8 | 55 | 41 | | df | 11.0000000 | |
| 10 | P9 | 77 | 55 | | t Stat | 7.2295917 | |
| 11 | P10 | 71 | 57 | | P(T<=t) one-tail | 0.0000084 | |
| 12 | P11 | 88 | 59 | | t Critical one-tail | 1.7958848 | |
| 13 | P12 | 80 | 44 | | P(T<=t) two-tail | 0.0000169 | |
| 14 | | | | | t Critical two-tail | 2.2009852 | |

**FIGURE 2.5**

Output from a paired samples t-test in Excel.

the two columns that will be compared. In this example, columns B and C are being compared, from row 2 through row 13 (Figure 2.5). Next, indicate the "Hypothesized Mean Difference." In this example, we chose 0 because we are hypothesizing that there is no difference between the means of columns B and C. Next, we set an alpha value to 0.05, saying that we want to be 95 percent confident in our findings. The output options are where you want to see the results. This dialog box is set up exactly like the independent samples t-test. The main difference, of course, is that the comparisons are within the same participant as opposed to across different participants.

The outcome is shown in Figure 2.5. The raw data are on the left side, and the results are on the right side. As with the independent samples output, it's important to look at the mean and the variance. The p-value of 0.0000169 indicates that there is a significant difference between the two designs, since this number is considerably smaller than 0.05.

Notice that in a paired samples test, you should have an equal number of values in each of the two distributions you're comparing (although it is possible to have missing data). In the case of independent samples, the number of values does not need to be equal. You might happen to have more participants in one group than the other.

## 2.5.3 Comparing More Than Two Samples

We don't always compare only two samples. Sometimes we want to compare three, four, or even six different samples. Fortunately, there is a way to do this without a lot of pain. An analysis of variance (commonly referred to as an ANOVA) lets you determine whether there is a significant difference across more than two groups.

Excel lets you perform three types of ANOVA. We will give an example for just one type of ANOVA, called a single-factor ANOVA. A single-factor ANOVA is used

| | A | B | C | D | E | F | G | H | I | J | K |
|---|---|---|---|---|---|---|---|---|---|---|---|
| 1 | Design 1_time | Design 2_time | Design 3_time | | Anova: Single Factor | | | | | | |
| 2 | 34 | 45 | 66 | | | | | | | | |
| 3 | 33 | 48 | 45 | | SUMMARY | | | | | | |
| 4 | 28 | 53 | 89 | | Groups | Count | Sum | Average | Variance | | |
| 5 | 44 | 66 | 49 | | Design 1_time | 12 | 421 | 35.08333 | 126.447 | | |
| 6 | 46 | 67 | 55 | | Design 2_time | 12 | 592 | 49.33333 | 229.697 | | |
| 7 | 21 | 35 | 77 | | Design 3_time | 12 | 802 | 66.83333 | 333.4242 | | |
| 8 | 22 | 39 | 90 | | | | | | | | |
| 9 | 53 | 21 | 43 | | | | | | | | |
| 10 | 22 | 34 | 56 | | ANOVA | | | | | | |
| 11 | 29 | 55 | 66 | | Source of Variation | SS | df | MS | F | P-value | F crit |
| 12 | 39 | 59 | 69 | | Between Groups | 6069.5 | 2 | 3034.75 | 13.20283 | 0.00006 | 3.284918 |
| 13 | 50 | 70 | 97 | | Within Groups | 7585.25 | 33 | 229.8561 | | | |
| 14 | | | | | | | | | | | |
| 15 | | | | | Total | 13654.75 | 35 | | | | |

**FIGURE 2.6**

Output from a single-factor ANOVA in Excel.

when you have just one variable you want to examine. For example, you might be interested in comparing task completion times across three different prototypes.

To run an ANOVA in Excel, first select "ANOVA: Single Factor" from "Tools" > "Data Analysis." This just means that you are looking at one variable (factor). Next, define the range of data. In our example (Figure 2.6), the data are in columns A, B, and C. We have set an alpha level to 0.05 and have included our labels in the first row.

The results are shown in two parts (see Figure 2.6). The top part is a summary of the data. As you can see, the average time for Design 3 is quite a bit slower, and Design 1 completion times are faster. Also, the variance is greater for Design 3 and less for Design 1. The second part of the output lets us know whether this difference is significant. The $F$-value is equal to 13.20. The critical value that we need to achieve significance is 3.28. The $p$-value of 0.00006 reflects the statistical significance of this result. Understanding exactly what this means is important: It means that there is a significant effect due to the "designs" variable. It does not necessarily mean that each of the design means is significantly different from each of the others—only that there *is* an effect overall. To see if any two means are significantly different from each other, you could do a two samples $t$-test on just those two sets of values.

## 2.6 RELATIONSHIPS BETWEEN VARIABLES

Sometimes it's important to know about the relationship between different variables. We've seen many cases where someone observing a usability test for the first time remarks that what participants say and what they do don't always correspond with each other. Many participants will struggle to complete just a few tasks with a prototype, but when asked to rate how easy or difficult it was, they often give it good ratings. In this section we provide examples of how to perform analyses that investigate these kinds of relationships (or the lack thereof).

### 2.6.1 Correlations

When you first begin examining the relationship between two variables, it's important to visualize what the data look like. In Excel, it's easy to create a scatterplot of the two variables. Figure 2.7 is an example of a scatterplot that shows the relationship between months of experience (*x*-axis) and average errors per day (*y*-axis). Notice that as the months of experience increase, the average number of errors drops. This is called a negative relationship because as one variable increases (months of experience), the other variable decreases (errors per day). The line that runs through the data is called a trend line and is easily added to the chart in Excel by right-clicking on any one of the data points and selecting "Add Trend Line." The trend line helps you to better visualize the relationship between the two variables. You can also have Excel display the $R^2$ value (a measure of the strength of the relationship) by clicking on the "Options" tab and checking the box next to "Display *R*-squared value on chart."

Plotting your data in a scatterplot is just the first step. You also want to understand the degree of association between the two variables. This can be done by choosing the CORRELATION function in the "Data Analysis" tool.

Next, specify the range of data. In Figure 2.8, the data are in columns B and C. We have also included the first row, which is the label for the row. The only decision here is to choose the output range (where you see the results). The output from the correlation is something called a correlation coefficient, or *r* value. A correlation coefficient is a measure of the strength of the relationship between the two variables and has a range from −1 to +1. The stronger the relationship, the closer the value is to −1 or +1, and the weaker the relationship, the closer the correlation coefficient is to 0.

Figure 2.8 shows a correlation coefficient of −0.76. The negative correlation coefficient means that it is a negative relationship (as experience increases, errors decrease). This correlation also tells us that there is a pretty strong relationship

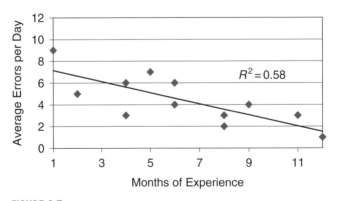

**FIGURE 2.7**

An example of a scatterplot (with trend line) in Excel.

| | A | B | C | D | E | F | G |
|---|---|---|---|---|---|---|---|
| 1 | **Participant** | **Months of Experience** | **Errors** | | | *Months of Experience* | *Errors* |
| 2 | P1 | 6 | 4 | | Months of Exp | 1 | |
| 3 | P2 | 6 | 6 | | Errors | –0.76160463 | 1 |
| 4 | P3 | 8 | 3 | | | | |
| 5 | P4 | 5 | 7 | | | | |
| 6 | P5 | 4 | 3 | | | | |
| 7 | P6 | 12 | 1 | | | | |
| 8 | P7 | 11 | 3 | | | | |
| 9 | P8 | 1 | 9 | | | | |
| 10 | P9 | 9 | 4 | | | | |
| 11 | P10 | 8 | 2 | | | | |
| 12 | P11 | 4 | 6 | | | | |
| 13 | P12 | 2 | 5 | | | | |

**FIGURE 2.8**

Output data from a correlation in Excel.

between experience and errors. Another way of thinking about it is that if you knew one of the two values, you could predict the other one reasonably well.

## 2.7 NONPARAMETRIC TESTS

Nonparametric tests are used for analyzing nominal and ordinal data. For example, you might want to know if there is a significant difference between men and women for success and failure on a particular task. Or perhaps you're interested in determining whether there is a difference between experts, intermediates, and novices on how they ranked different websites. To answer questions that involve nominal and ordinal data, you will need to use some type of nonparametric test.

Nonparametric statistics make different assumptions about the data than the statistics we've reviewed for comparing means and describing relationships between variables. For instance, when we run *t*-tests and correlation analysis, we assume that data are normally distributed and variances are approximately equal. The distribution is not normal for nominal or ordinal data. Therefore, we don't make the same assumptions about the data in nonparametric tests. For example, in the case of (binary) success, when there are only two possibilities, the data are based on the binomial distribution. Some people like to refer to nonparametric tests as "distribution-free" tests. There are a few different types of nonparametric tests, but we will just cover the chi-square test because it is probably the most commonly used.

### 2.7.1 The Chi-Square Test

The chi-square test is used when you want to compare categorical (or nominal) data. Let's consider an example. Assume you're interested in knowing whether there is a significant difference in task success between three different groups: novices, intermediates, and experts. You run a total of 60 participants in your study, 20 in each group. You measure task success or failure on a single task. You count the number of participants who were successful in each group. For the novices, only 6 out of 20 were successful, 12 out of 20 intermediates were successful, and 18 out of 20 experts were successful. You want to know if there is a statistically significant difference between the groups.

To perform a chi-square test in Excel, you use the `CHITEST` function. This function calculates whether the differences between the observed and expected values are simply due to chance. The function is relatively easy to use: `=CHITEST(actual_range, expected_range)`. The actual range is the number of people who were successful on the task for each group. The expected range is the total number of participants successful (33) divided by the number of groups (3), or equivalent to 11 in this example. The expected value is what you would expect if there were no differences between any of the three groups.

Figure 2.9 shows what the data look like and the output from the `CHITEST` function. In this example, the likelihood that this distribution is due to chance is about 2.9 percent (0.028856). Because this number is less than 0.05 (95 percent confidence), we can reasonably say that there is a difference in success rates between the three groups.

In this example we were just examining the distribution of success rates across a single variable (experience group). There are some situations in which you might want to examine more than one variable, such as experience group and design prototype. Performing this type of evaluation works the same way. Figure 2.10

C7 =CHITEST(B2:B4,C2:C4)

| | A | B | C | D |
|---|---|---|---|---|
| 1 | **Group** | **Observed** | **Expected** | |
| 2 | Novice | 6 | 11 | |
| 3 | Intermediate | 9 | 11 | |
| 4 | Experts | 18 | 11 | |
| 5 | **Total** | **33** | **33** | |
| 6 | | | | |
| 7 | | Chi-test | 0.028856 | |

**FIGURE 2.9**

Output from a chi-square test in Excel.

C13 =CHITEST(B3:C5,B9:C11)

| | A | B | C | D |
|---|---|---|---|---|
| 1 | | ***Observed*** | ***Observed*** | |
| 2 | **Group** | **Design A** | **Design B** | |
| 3 | Novice | 4 | 2 | |
| 4 | Intermediate | 6 | 3 | |
| 5 | Experts | 12 | 6 | |
| 6 | | | | |
| 7 | | ***Expected*** | ***Expected*** | |
| 8 | **Group** | **Design A** | **Design B** | |
| 9 | Novice | 5.5 | 5.5 | |
| 10 | Intermediate | 5.5 | 5.5 | |
| 11 | Experts | 5.5 | 5.5 | |
| 12 | | | | |
| 13 | | Chi-test | 0.003111 | |

**FIGURE 2.10**

Output from a chi-square test with two variables.

shows data based on two different variables: group and design. For a more detailed example of using the chi-square to test for differences in live website data for two alternative pages (so-called A/B tests), see section 9.1.4.

## 2.8 PRESENTING YOUR DATA GRAPHICALLY

You might have collected and analyzed the best set of usability data ever, but it's of little value if you can't communicate it effectively to others. Data tables are certainly useful in some situations, but in most cases you'll want to present your data graphically. A number of excellent books on the design of effective data

---

**GENERAL TIPS FOR DATA GRAPHS**

*Label the axes and units.* It might be obvious to you that a scale of 0 to 100 percent represents the task completion rate, but it may not be obvious to your audience. Or you might know that the times being plotted on a graph are minutes, but your audience may be left pondering whether they could be seconds or even hours. Sometimes the labels on an axis make it clear what the scale is (e.g., "Task 1," "Task 2," etc.), in which case adding a label for the axis itself (e.g., "Tasks") would be redundant.

*Don't imply more precision in your data than they deserve.* Labeling your time data with "0.00" seconds to "30.00" seconds is almost never appropriate, nor is labeling your task completion data with "0.0%" to "100.0%." Whole numbers work best in most cases. Exceptions include some metrics with a very limited range and some statistics that are almost always fractional (e.g., correlation coefficients).

*Don't use color alone to convey information.* Of course, this is a good general principle for the design of any information display, but it's worth repeating. Color is commonly used in data graphs, but make sure it's supplemented by positional information, labels, or other cues that help someone who can't clearly distinguish colors to interpret the graph.

*Display labels horizontally whenever possible.* When you try to squeeze too many items onto the horizontal axis, you may be tempted to display the labels vertically. But you don't want to give your audience a sore neck from constantly tilting their heads to read the axis! An exception is that the main title for the vertical axis is normally shown vertically.

*Show confidence intervals whenever possible.* This mainly applies to bar graphs and line graphs that are presenting means of individual participant data (times, ratings, etc.). Showing the 95 or 90 percent confidence intervals for the means via error bars is a good way to visually represent the variability in the data.

*Don't overload your graphs.* Just because you *can* create a single graph that shows the task completion rate, error rate, task times, and subjective ratings for each of 20 tasks, broken down by novice versus experienced participants, doesn't mean you *should*.

*Be careful with 3D graphs.* If you're tempted to use a 3D graph, ask yourself whether it really helps. In some cases, the use of 3D makes it harder to see the values being plotted.

graphs are available, including those written by Edward Tufte (1990, 1997, 2001, 2006), Stephen Few (2004, 2006), and Robert Harris (1999). Our intent in this section is simply to introduce some of the most important principles in the design of data graphs, particularly as they relate to usability data.

We've organized this section around tips and techniques for five basic types of data graphs:

- Column or bar graphs
- Line graphs
- Scatterplots
- Pie charts
- Stacked bar graphs

We will begin each of the following sections with one good example and one bad example of that particular type of data graph.

## 2.8.1 Column or Bar Graphs

Column graphs and bar graphs (Figure 2.11) are the same thing; the only difference is their orientation. Technically, column graphs are vertical and bar graphs are horizontal. In practice, most people refer to both types simply as bar graphs, which is what we will do.

Bar graphs are probably the most common way of displaying usability data. Almost every presentation of data from a usability test that we've seen has included at least one bar graph, whether it was for task completion rates, task times, self-reported data, or something else. The following are some of the principles for using bar graphs:

- Bar graphs are appropriate when you want to present the values of continuous data (e.g., times, percentages, etc.) for discrete items or categories (e.g., tasks, participants, designs, etc.). If both variables are continuous, a line graph is appropriate.

- The axis for the continuous variable (the vertical axis in Figure 2.11) should normally start at 0. The whole idea behind bar graphs is that the lengths of the bars represent the values being plotted. By not starting the axis at 0, you're artificially manipulating their lengths. The bad example in Figure 2.11 gives the impression that there's a larger difference between the tasks than there really is. A possible exception is when you include error bars, making it clear which differences are real and which are not.

- Don't let the axis for the continuous variable go any higher than the maximum value that's theoretically possible. For example, if you're plotting percentages of users who successfully completed each task, the theoretical maximum is 100 percent. If some values are close to that maximum, Excel and other packages will tend to automatically increase the scale beyond the maximum, especially if error bars are shown.

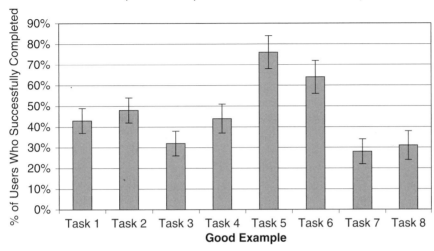

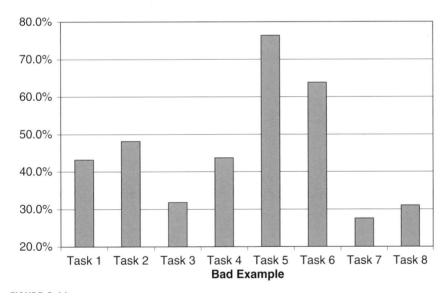

**FIGURE 2.11**

Good and bad examples of bar graphs for the same data. The mistakes in the bad version (*bottom*) include failing to label the data, not starting the vertical axis at 0, not showing confidence intervals when you can, and showing too much precision in the vertical axis labels.

**LINE GRAPHS VERSUS BAR GRAPHS**

Some people have a hard time deciding whether it's appropriate to use a line graph or a bar graph to display a set of data. Perhaps the most common data-graph mistake we see is using a line graph when a bar graph is more appropriate. If you're considering presenting some data with a line graph, ask yourself a simple question: Do the places along the line *between* the data points make sense? In other words, even though you don't have data for those locations, would they make sense if you did? If they don't make sense, a bar graph is more appropriate.

For example, it's technically possible to show the data in Figure 2.11 as a line graph, as follows.

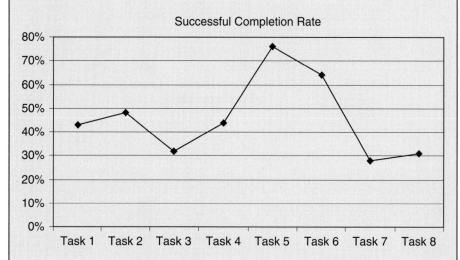

Successful Completion Rate

However, you should ask yourself whether things like "Task 1½" or "Task 6¾" make any sense, because the lines imply that they should. Obviously, they don't, so a bar graph is the correct representation. The line graph might make an interesting picture, but it's a misleading picture.

## 2.8.2 Line Graphs

Line graphs (Figure 2.12) are most commonly used to show trends in continuous variables, often over time. Although not as common as bar graphs in presenting usability data, they certainly have their place. The following are some of the key principles for using line graphs:

- Line graphs are appropriate when you want to present the values of one continuous variable (e.g., percent correct, number of errors, etc.) as a function of another

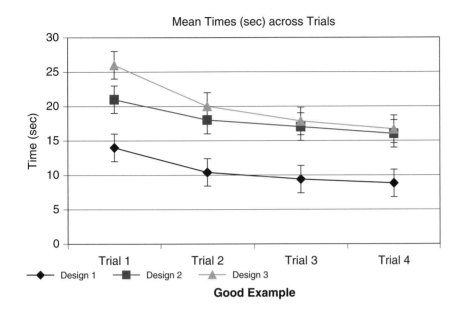

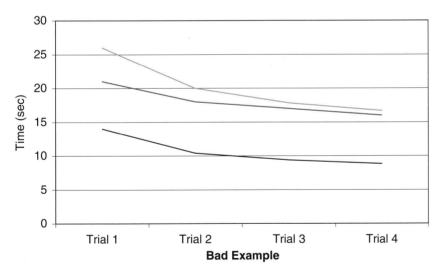

**FIGURE 2.12**

Good and bad examples of line graphs for the same data. The mistakes in the bad version (*bottom*) include failing to label the vertical axis, not showing the data points, not including a legend, not showing confidence intervals, and using lines that are too lightweight.

continuous variable (e.g., age, trial, etc.). If one of the variables is discrete (e.g., gender, participant, task, etc.), then a bar graph is more appropriate.

■ Show your data points. Your actual data points are the things that really matter, not the lines. The lines are just there to connect the data points and to make the trends more obvious. You may need to increase the default size of the data points in Excel.

■ Use lines that have sufficient weight to be clear. Very thin lines are not only hard to see, but it's harder to detect their color and they may imply a greater precision in the data than is appropriate. You may need to increase the default weight of lines in Excel.

■ Include a legend if you have more than one line. In some cases, it may be clearer to manually move the labels from the legend into the body of the graph and put each label beside its appropriate line. It may be necessary to do this in Power-Point or some other drawing program.

■ As with bar graphs, the vertical axis normally starts at 0, but it's not as important with a line graph to always do that. There are no bars whose length is important, so sometimes it may be appropriate to start the vertical axis at a higher value. In that case, you should mark the vertical axis appropriately. The traditional way of doing this is with a "discontinuity" marker on that axis: ⸜. Again, it may be necessary to do that in a drawing program.

### 2.8.3 Scatterplots

Scatterplots (Figure 2.13), or X/Y plots, show pairs of values. Although they're not very common in usability reports, they can be very useful in certain situations. Here are some of the key principles for using scatterplots:

■ You must have paired values that you want to plot. A classic example is heights and weights of a group of people. Each person would appear as a data point, and the two axes would be height and weight.

■ Normally, both of the variables would be continuous. In Figure 2.13, the vertical axis shows mean values for a visual appeal rating of 42 web pages (from Tullis & Tullis, 2007). Although that scale originally had only four values, the means come close to being continuous. The horizontal axis shows the size, in $k$ pixels, of the largest nontext image on the page, which truly is continuous.

■ You should use appropriate scales. In Figure 2.13, the values on the vertical axis can't be any lower than 1.0, so it's appropriate to start the scale at that point rather than 0.

■ Your purpose in showing a scatterplot is usually to illustrate a relationship between the two variables. Consequently, it's usually helpful to add a trend line to the scatterplot, as in the good example in Figure 2.13. You may want to include the $R^2$ value to indicate the goodness of fit.

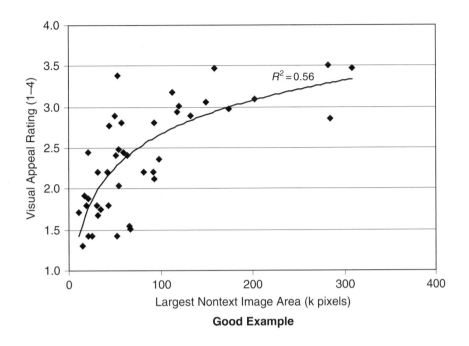

**Good Example**

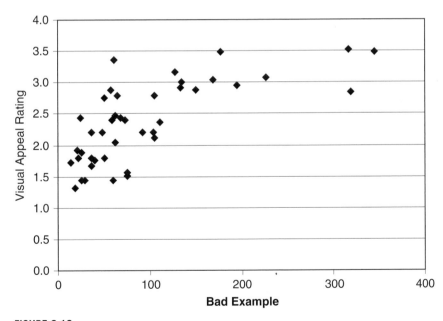

**Bad Example**

**FIGURE 2.13**

Good and bad examples of scatterplots for the same data. The mistakes in the bad version include an inappropriate scale for the vertical axis, not showing the scale for the visual appeal ratings (1–4), not showing a trend line, and not showing the goodness of fit ($R^2$).

### 2.8.4 Pie Charts

Pie charts (Figure 2.14) illustrate the parts or percentages of a whole. They can be useful any time you want to illustrate the relative proportions of the parts of a whole to each other (e.g., how many participants in a usability test succeeded, failed, or gave up on a task). Here are some key principles for their use:

- Pie charts are appropriate only when the parts add up to 100 percent. You have to account for all cases. In some situations, this might mean creating an "other" category.

- Minimize the number of segments in the pie chart. Even though the bad example in Figure 2.14 is technically correct, it's almost impossible to make any sense of it because it has so many segments. Try to use no more than six segments. Logically combine segments, as in the good example, to make the results clearer.

- In almost all cases, you should include the percentage and label for each segment. Normally these should be next to each segment, connected by leader lines if necessary. Sometimes you have to manually move the labels to prevent them from overlapping.

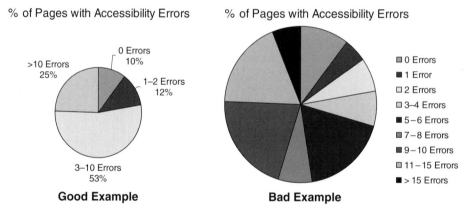

**FIGURE 2.14**

Good and bad examples of pie charts for the same data. The mistakes in the bad version (*right*) include too many segments, poor placement of the legend, and not showing percentages for each segment.

### 2.8.5 Stacked Bar Graphs

Stacked bar graphs (Figure 2.15) are basically multiple pie charts shown in bar form. They're appropriate whenever you have a series of datasets, each of which represents parts of the whole. Their most common use in usability data is to show different task completion states for each task. Here are some key principles for their use:

- Like pie charts, stacked bar graphs are only appropriate when the parts for each item in the series add up to 100 percent.

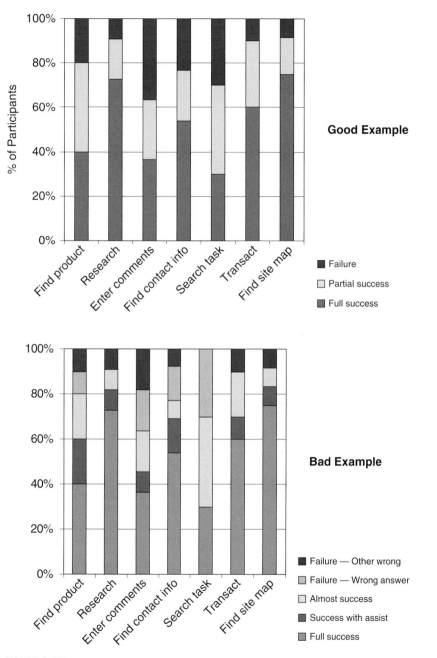

**FIGURE 2.15**

Good and bad examples of stacked bar graphs for the same data. The mistakes in the bad version (*bottom*) include too many segments, poor color coding, and failing to label the vertical axis.

- The items in the series are normally categorical (e.g., tasks, participants, etc.).

- Minimize the number of segments in each bar. More than three segments per bar can make it difficult to interpret. Combine segments as appropriate.

- When possible, make use of color coding conventions that your audience is likely to be familiar with. For many U.S. audiences, green is good, yellow is marginal, and red is bad. Playing off these conventions can be helpful but don't rely solely on them.

## 2.9 SUMMARY

In a nutshell, this chapter is about knowing your data. The better you know your data, the more likely you are to clearly answer your research questions. The following are some of the key takeaways from this chapter.

1. It's important to consider questions about how to select participants for your study, how to order tasks, what participants perform what tasks, and how many participants you need to get reasonably reliable feedback.

2. Knowing your data is critical when analyzing your results. The specific type of data you have will dictate what statistics you can (and can't) perform.

3. Nominal data are categorical, such as binary task success or males and females. Nominal data are usually expressed as frequencies or percentages. Chi-square tests can be used when you want to learn whether the frequency distribution is random or there is some underlying significance to the distribution pattern.

4. Ordinal data are rank orders, such as a severity ranking of usability issues. Ordinal data are also analyzed using frequencies, and the distribution patterns can be analyzed with a chi-square test.

5. Interval data are continuous data where the intervals between each point are meaningful but without a natural zero. The SUS score is one example. Interval data can be described by means, standard deviations, and confidence intervals. Means can be compared to each other for the same set of users (paired samples *t*-test) or across different users (independent samples *t*-test). ANOVA can be used to compare more than two sets of data. Relationships between variables can be examined through correlations.

6. Ratio data are the same as interval data but with a natural zero. One example is completion times. Essentially, the same statistics that apply to interval data also apply to ratio data.

7. When presenting your data graphically, use the appropriate types of graphs. Use bar graphs for categorical data and line graphs for continuous data. Use pie charts or stacked bar graphs when the data sum to 100 percent.

# Planning a Usability Study

3

The Boy Scouts' motto is "Be Prepared." This is true not only when you head off into the wilderness but also when you collect usability data. Preparation is the key to any successful usability study. If nothing else, we hope this chapter convinces you to plan ahead when running a usability study, particularly where data collection is involved.

A few high-level questions must be answered when planning any usability study. First, you need to understand the goals of the study. For example, are you trying to ensure optimal usability for a new piece of functionality, or are you benchmarking the user experience for an existing product? Next, you need to understand the goals of the users. Are users looking to simply complete a task and then stop using the product, or will they use the product many times on a daily basis? Knowing both the study goals and the user goals will lead toward choosing the right metrics.

Many practical details come into play as well. For example, you must decide on the most appropriate evaluation method, how many participants are enough to get reliable feedback, how collecting metrics will impact the timeline and budget, and how the data will be collected and analyzed. By answering these questions, you will be well prepared to carry out any usability study involving metrics. In the end, you will likely save time and money and have a greater impact on the product.

## 3.1 STUDY GOALS

The first decision to make when planning a usability study is how the data will ultimately be used within the product development life cycle. There are essentially two general ways to use data: formative and summative.

### 3.1.1 Formative Usability

When running a formative study, a usability specialist is much like a chef who periodically checks a dish while it's being prepared and makes adjustments to positively impact the end result. The chef might add a little salt, then a few more **45**

*Generate*
*Nielsen —*
*present*
*usability*

spices, and finally a dash of chili pepper right before serving. The chef is periodically evaluating, adjusting, and reevaluating. The same is true in formative usability. A usability specialist, like a chef, periodically evaluates a product or design, identifies shortcomings, makes recommendations, and then repeats the process, until, ideally, the product comes out as close to perfect as possible.

What distinguishes formative usability is the iterative nature of the testing. The goal is to make improvements in the design. This means identifying or diagnosing the problems, making recommendations, and then evaluating again. Formative usability is always done before the design has been finalized. In fact, the earlier the formative evaluation, the more impact the usability evaluations will have on the design.

Here are a few key questions you will be able answer with a formative approach:

- What are the most significant usability issues that are preventing users from completing their goals or that are resulting in inefficiencies?
- What aspects of the product work well for the users? What do they find frustrating?
- What are the most common errors or mistakes users are making?
- Are improvements being made from one design iteration to the next?
- What usability issues can you expect to remain after the product is launched?

The most appropriate situation to run a formative usability study is when an obvious opportunity to improve the design presents itself. Ideally, the design process allows for multiple usability evaluations. If there's no opportunity to impact the design, then running a formative test is probably a waste of time. Generally, though, selling the value of formative usability shouldn't be a problem. Most people will see the importance of it. The biggest obstacles tend to be a limited budget or time rather than a failure to see the value.

### 3.1.2 Summative Usability

Continuing with our cooking metaphor, summative usability is about evaluating the dish after it comes out of the oven. The usability specialist running a summative test is like a food critic who evaluates a few sample dishes at a restaurant or perhaps compares the same meal in multiple restaurants. The goal of summative usability is to evaluate how well a product or piece of functionality meets its objectives. Summative testing can also be about comparing several products to each other. Although formative testing focuses on identifying ways of making improvements, summative testing focuses on evaluating against a certain set of criteria. Summative usability evaluations answer these questions:

- Did we meet the usability goals of the project?
- How does our product compare against the competition?
- Have we made improvements from one product release to the next?

Running a successful summative usability test should always involve some follow-up activities. Just knowing is usually not enough for most organizations. Potential outcomes of a summative usability test might be securing funding to enhance functionality on your product, or launching a new project to address some outstanding usability issues, or even benchmarking changes to the user experience against which senior managers will be evaluated. We recommend that follow-up actions be planned along with any summative usability study.

## 3.2 USER GOALS

When planning a usability study, you need to know something about the users and what they are trying to accomplish. For example, are users forced to use the product every day as part of their job? Are they likely to use the product only once or just a few times? Are they using it frequently as a source of entertainment? It's critical to understand what matters to the user. Does the user simply want to complete a task, or is their efficiency the primary driver? Do users care at all about the design aesthetics of the product? All these questions boil down to measuring two main aspects of the user experience: performance and satisfaction.

### 3.2.1 Performance

Performance is all about what the user actually *does* in interacting with the product. It includes measuring the degree to which users can successfully accomplish a task or set of tasks. Many measures related to the performance of these tasks are also important, including the time it takes to perform each task, the amount of effort to perform each (such as number of mouse clicks or amount of cognitive effort), the number of errors committed, and the amount of time it takes to become proficient in performing the tasks (learnability). Performance measures are critical for many different types of products and applications, especially those where the user doesn't really have much choice in how they are used (such as a company's internal applications). If users can't successfully perform key tasks when using a product, it's likely to fail. Chapter 4 reviews different types of performance measures.

### 3.2.2 Satisfaction

Satisfaction is all about what the user *says* or *thinks* about his interaction with the product. The user might report that it was easy to use, that it was confusing, or that it exceeded his expectations. The user might have opinions about the product being visually appealing or untrustworthy. User satisfaction has many different aspects. Satisfaction, and many other self-reported metrics, is important for products where the user has some choice in their usage. This would certainly be true for most websites, software applications, and consumer products. Satisfaction metrics are reviewed in Chapter 6.

---

**DO PERFORMANCE AND SATISFACTION ALWAYS CORRELATE?**

Perhaps surprisingly, performance and satisfaction don't always go hand-in-hand. We've seen many instances of a user struggling to perform key tasks with an application and then giving it glowing satisfaction ratings. Conversely, we've seen users give poor satisfaction ratings to an application that worked perfectly. So it is important that you look at both performance and satisfaction metrics to get an accurate overall picture of the user experience.

---

## 3.3 CHOOSING THE RIGHT METRICS: TEN TYPES OF USABILITY STUDIES

You should consider many issues when choosing metrics for a usability study, including the goals of the study and the user, the technology that's available to collect and analyze the data, and the budget and time you have to turn around your findings. Because every usability study has unique qualities, we can't prescribe the exact metrics to use for every type of study. Instead, we've identified ten proto-typical categories of usability studies and developed recommendations about metrics for each. The recommendations we offer are simply suggestions that you should consider when running a usability study with a similar set of characteristics. Conversely, metrics that may be essential to your study may not be on the list. Also, we strongly recommend that you explore your raw data and develop new metrics that are meaningful to your project goals.

Ten common usability study scenarios are listed in Table 3.1. (Many of the usability metrics in Table 3.1 are discussed in detail later in the book.) The metrics that are commonly used or are appropriate for each of the usability study scenarios are indicated. The sections that follow discuss each of the ten scenarios.

### 3.3.1 Completing a Transaction

Many usability studies are aimed at making transactions run as smoothly as possible. These might take the form of a user completing a purchase, registering a new piece of software, or selling a stock. A transaction usually has a well-defined beginning and end. For example, on an e-commerce website, a transaction may start when a user places something in his shopping cart and ends when he has completed the purchase on the confirmation screen.

Perhaps the first metric that you will want to examine is *task success.* Each task is scored as a success or failure. Obviously the tasks need to have a clear end-state, such as reaching a confirmation that the transaction was successful.

**Table 3.1** Ten Common Usability Study Scenarios and Their Most Appropriate Metrics

| Usability Study Scenario | Task Success | Task Time | Errors | Efficiency | Learn-ability | Issues-Based Metrics | Self-Reported Metrics | Behavioral and Physiological Metrics | Combined and Comparative Metrics | Live Website Metrics | Card-Sorting Data |
|---|---|---|---|---|---|---|---|---|---|---|---|
| 1. Completing a transaction | X | | | X | | X | X | | | X | |
| 2. Comparing products | X | | | X | | | X | | X | | |
| 3. Evaluating frequent use of the same product | X | X | | X | X | | X | | | | |
| 4. Evaluating navigation and/or information architecture | X | | X | X | | | | | | | X |
| 5. Increasing awareness | | | | | | | X | X | | X | |
| 6. Problem discovery | | | | | | X | X | | | | |
| 7. Maximizing usability for a critical product | X | | X | X | | | | | | | |
| 8. Creating an overall positive user experience | | | | | | | X | X | | | |
| 9. Evaluating the impact of subtle changes | | | | | | | X | | | X | |
| 10. Comparing alternative designs | X | X | | | | X | X | | X | | |

Reporting the percentage of participants who were successful is an excellent measure of the overall effectiveness of the transaction. If the transaction involves a website, some *live website metrics,* such drop-off rate from the transaction, can be very useful. By knowing where users are dropping off, you will be able to focus your attention on the most problematic steps in the transaction.

Calculating *issue severity* can help narrow down the cause of specific usability problems with a transaction. By assigning a severity to each usability issue, you will be able to focus on the high-priority problems with any transaction. Two types of *self-reported metrics* are also very useful: likelihood to return and user expectations. In cases where users have a choice of where to perform their transactions, it's important to know what they thought of their experience. One of the best ways to learn this is by asking participants whether they would use the same product again and whether the product met or exceeded their expectations. *Efficiency* is an appropriate metric when a user has to complete the same transaction many times. Efficiency is often measured as task completion per unit of time.

### 3.3.2 Comparing Products

It's always useful to know how your product compares to the competition or to previous releases. By making comparisons, you can determine your product's strengths and weaknesses and whether improvements have been made from one release to another. The best way to compare different products or releases is through the use of various metrics. The type of metrics you choose should be based on the product itself. Some products aim to maximize efficiency, whereas others try to create an exceptional user experience.

For most types of products, we recommend three general classes of metrics to get an overall sense of usability. First, we recommend looking at some task success measures. Being able to complete a task correctly is essential for most products. It's also important to pay attention to efficiency. Efficiency might be task completion time, number of page views (in the case of some websites), or number of action steps taken. By looking at efficiency, you will get a good sense of how much effort is required to use the product. Some self-reported metrics of satisfaction provide a good summary of the user's overall experience. Satisfaction measures make the most sense with products where people have choices. Finally, one of the best ways to compare usability across products is by *combined and comparative metrics*. This will give an excellent big picture of how the products compare from a usability perspective.

### 3.3.3 Evaluating Frequent Use of the Same Product

Many products are intended to be used on a frequent or semifrequent basis. Examples might include microwave ovens, DVD players, web applications used as part of your job, and even the software program we used to write this book. These products need to be both easy to use and highly efficient. The amount of effort required to burn a DVD or *not* burn popcorn in a microwave needs to be kept to a minimum. Most of us have very little time or patience for products that are difficult to use.

The first metric we would recommend is task time. Measuring the amount of time required to complete a set of core tasks will reveal the effort involved. For most products, the faster the completion time, the better. Because some tasks are naturally more complicated than others, it may be helpful to compare task completion times to expert performance. Other efficiency metrics such as the number of steps or page views (in the case of some websites) can also be helpful. The time for each step may be short, but the separate decisions that must be made to accomplish a task can be numerous.

*Learnability* metrics assess how much time or effort is required to achieve maximum efficiency. Learnability can take the form of any of the previous efficiency metrics examined over time. In some situations, consider self-reported metrics, such as awareness and usefulness. By examining the difference between users' awareness and perceived usefulness, you will be able to identify aspects of the product that should be promoted or highlighted. For example, users may have low awareness for some parts of the product, but once they use it, they find out it is extremely useful.

### 3.3.4 Evaluating Navigation and/or Information Architecture

Many usability studies focus on improving the navigation and/or information architecture. This is probably most common for websites, software programs, or consumer electronics. It may involve making sure that users can quickly and easily find what they are looking for, easily navigate around the product, know where they are within the overall structure, and know what options are available to them. Typically, these studies involve the use of wire-frames or partially functional prototypes because the navigation and information mechanisms and information architecture are so fundamental to the design that they have to be figured out before almost anything else.

One of the best metrics to evaluate navigation is task success. By giving participants tasks to find key pieces of information (a "scavenger hunt"), you can tell how well the navigation and information architecture works for them. Tasks should touch on all the different areas of the product. An efficiency metric that's useful for evaluating navigation and information architecture is *lostness,* which looks at the number of steps the participant took to complete a task (e.g., web page visits) relative to the minimum number to complete the task.

*Card sorting* is a particularly useful method to understand how participants organize information. One type of card-sorting study is called a closed sort, which has participants put items into predefined categories. A useful metric to come from a closed card sort study is the percentage of items placed into the correct category. This metric indicates the intuitiveness of the information architecture.

### 3.3.5 **Increasing Awareness**

Not every design that goes through a usability evaluation is about making something easier or more efficient to use. Some design changes are aimed at increasing awareness of a specific piece of content or functionality. This is certainly true for online advertisements, but it's also true for products that have important but underutilized functionality. There can be many reasons why something is not noticed or used, including some aspect of the visual design, labeling, or placement.

First, we recommend monitoring the number of interactions with the element in question. This is not foolproof, since a participant might notice something but not click on it or interact with it in some way. The opposite would not be very likely: interaction without noticing. Because of this, the data can help confirm awareness but not demonstrate lack of awareness. Sometimes it's useful to ask for self-reported metrics about whether the participants noticed or were aware of a specific design element. Measuring noticeability involves pointing out specific elements to the participants and then asking whether they had noticed those elements during the task. Measuring awareness involves asking the participants if they were aware of the feature before the study began. However, it's unclear how reliable these data are. Not everyone has a good memory, and some people try to save face and say they saw something when they didn't. Therefore, we don't recommend that this be your sole measure; you should complement it with other data sources.

Memory is another useful self-reported metric. For example, you can show participants several different elements, only one of which they had actually seen previously, and ask them to choose which one they saw during the task. If they noticed the element, their memory should be better than chance. But perhaps the best way to assess awareness, if you have the technology available, is through the use of *behavioral and physiological metrics* such as eye-tracking data. Using eye-tracking technology, you can determine the average time spent looking at a certain element, the percentage of participants who looked at it, and even the average time it took to first notice it. Another metric to consider, in the case of websites, is a change in live website data. Looking at how traffic patterns change between different designs will help you determine relative awareness. Simultaneous testing of alternative designs (A/B testing) on live sites is an increasingly common way to measure how small design changes impact user behavior.

### 3.3.6 **Problem Discovery**

The goal of problem discovery is to identify major usability issues. In some situations you may not have any preconceived ideas about what the significant usability issues are with a product, but you want to know what annoys users. This is often done for a product that is already built but has not gone through usability evaluation before. A problem discovery study also works well as a periodic checkup to get back in touch with how users are interacting with your product. A discovery study is a little different from other types of usability studies because it is generally open-ended. Participants in a problem discovery study may be generating their own tasks, as opposed to being given a list of specific tasks. It's important to strive for realism as much as possible. This might involve using the live product and their own accounts and performing tasks that are relevant only to them. It might also include evaluating the product in the participants' environments, such as homes or workplaces.

Because they may be performing different tasks and their contexts of use may be different, comparing across participants may be a challenge. *Issues-based metrics* may be the most appropriate for problem discovery. Assuming you capture all the usability issues, it's fairly easy to convert those data into frequency and type. For example, you might discover that 40 percent of the usability issues pertain to high-level navigation and 20 percent of the issues to confusing terminology. Even though the exact problems encountered by each participant might be different, you are still able to generalize into a higher-level category of issue. Examining the frequency and severity of specific issues will reveal how many repeat issues are being observed. Is it a one-time occurrence or part of a recurring problem? By cataloging all the issues and assigning severity ratings, you may come away with a quick-hit list of design improvements.

### 3.3.7 Maximizing Usability for a Critical Product

Although some products *strive* to be easy to use and efficient, such as a cell phone or washing machine, other products *have* to be easy to use and efficient, such as a defibrillator machine, voting machine, or emergency exit instructions on an airplane. What differentiates a critical product from a noncritical product is that the entire reason for the critical product's existence is for the user to complete a very important task. Not completing that task will have a significant negative outcome.

Measuring usability for any critical product is essential. Just running a few participants through the lab is rarely good enough. It's important that user performance be measured against a target goal. Any critical product that doesn't meet its target usability goal should undergo a redesign. Because of the degree of certainty you want from your data, you may have to run relatively large numbers of participants in the study. One very important metric is user *errors*. This might include the number of errors or mistakes made while performing a specific task. Errors are not always easy to tabulate, so special attention must be given to how you define an error. It's always best to be very explicit about what constitutes an error and what doesn't.

Task success is also important to measure. We recommend using a binary approach to success in this situation. For example, the true test of a portable defibrillator machine is that someone can use it successfully by themselves. In some cases, you may wish to tie task success to more than one metric, such as completing the task successfully within a specific amount of time and with no errors. Other efficiency metrics are also useful. In the example of the defibrillator machine, simply using it correctly is one thing but doing so in a timely manner is altogether different. Self-reported metrics are relatively less important with critical products. What users think about their use of the product is much less important than their actual success.

### 3.3.8 Creating an Overall Positive User Experience

Some products strive to create an exceptional user experience. It's simply not enough to be usable. These products need to be engaging, thought-provoking, entertaining, and maybe even slightly addictive. The iPod and TiVo are two such products that come to mind. These are products that you tell a friend about and are not embarrassed to mention at a party. Their popularity usually grows at phenomenal rates. Even though the characteristics of what constitutes a great user experience are subjective, they are still measurable.

Although some performance metrics may be useful, what really matters is what the user thinks, feels, and says with respect to his or her experience. In some ways, this is the opposite perspective of measuring usability of a critical product. If the user struggles a little at first, it may not be the end of the world. What matters is how the user feels at the end of the day. Many self-reported metrics must be considered when measuring the overall user experience.

Satisfaction is perhaps the most common self-reported metric, but it may not always be the best one. Being "satisfied" is usually not enough. One of the most valuable self-reported metrics we've used relates to the participant's expectation. The best experiences are those that *exceed* a participant's expectations. When the participant says something is much easier, more efficient, or more entertaining than expected, you know you are onto something.

Another set of self-reported metrics relates to future use. For example, you might ask questions related to likelihood to purchase, recommend to a friend, or use in the future. Another interesting set of metrics relates to subconscious reactions that users may be having. For example, if you want to make sure your product is engaging, you can look at *physiological metrics*. Changes in pupil diameter can be used to gauge the level of arousal, or if you're trying to eliminate stress as much as possible, you can measure heart rate or skin conductance.

### 3.3.9 Evaluating the Impact of Subtle Changes

Not all design changes have an obvious impact on user behavior. Some design changes are much more subtle, and their impact on user behavior is less clear. Small trends, given enough users, can have huge implications for a large population of users. The subtle changes may involve different aspects of the visual design, such as font choice and size, placement, visual contrast, color, and image choice. Nonvisual design elements, such as subtle changes to content or terminology, can also have an impact on the user experience.

Perhaps the best way to measure the impact of subtle design changes is through *live-site metrics* from A/B tests. A/B testing involves comparing a control design against an alternative design. For websites, this usually involves diverting a portion of web traffic to an alternative design and comparing metrics such as traffic or purchases to a control design. An online usability study with a large population can also be very useful. If you don't have access to the technology to run A/B tests or online studies, we recommend using e-mail and online surveys to get feedback from as many representative participants as you can.

### 3.3.10 Comparing Alternative Designs

One of the most common types of usability studies involves comparing more than one design alternative. Typically, these types of studies take place early in the design process, before any one design has been fully developed. (We often refer to these as "design bakeoffs.") Different design teams put together semifunctional prototypes, and we evaluate each design using a predefined set of metrics. Setting up these studies can be a little tricky. Because the designs are often similar, there is a high likelihood of a learning effect from one design to another. Asking the same participant to perform the same task with all designs usually does not yield valuable information, even when counterbalancing design and task order.

There are two solutions to this problem. You can set up the study as purely between-subjects whereby each participant only uses one design, which provides a clean set of data but requires significantly more participants. Alternatively, you can ask participants to perform the tasks using one primary design (counterbalancing the designs) and then show the other design alternatives and ask for their preference. This way you can get feedback about all the designs from each participant.

The most appropriate metrics to use when comparing multiple designs may be issues-based metrics. Comparing the frequency of high-, medium-, and low-severity issues across different designs will help shed light on which design or designs are more usable. Ideally, one design ends up with fewer issues overall and fewer high-severity issues. Performance metrics such as task success and task times can be useful, but because sample sizes are typically small, these data tend to be of limited value. A couple of self-reported metrics are particularly relevant. One is asking each participant to choose which prototype they would most like to use in the future (as a forced choice comparison). Also, asking each participant to rate each prototype along dimensions such as ease of use and visual appeal can be insightful.

## 3.4 OTHER STUDY DETAILS

Many other details must be considered when planning a usability study. Several important issues to consider are budget/timelines, evaluation methods, participants, and data cleanup.

### 3.4.1 Budgets and Timelines

The time and cost of running a usability study with metrics depends on the evaluation method, metrics, participants, and available tools. It's impossible for us to give even approximate costs or time estimates for any particular type of usability study. The best we can do is provide a few general rules of thumb for estimating time and costs for some common types of studies. When making these estimates, we recommend that you carefully consider all the variables that go into any usability study and communicate those estimates to business sponsors (or whoever is funding the study) as early as possible. Also, it's wise to add at least a 10 percent buffer for both time and costs, knowing that there may be some unforeseen costs and delays.

If you are running a formative study with a small number of participants (ten or fewer), collecting metrics should have little, if any, impact on the overall timeline or budget. Collecting and analyzing basic metrics on issue frequency and severity should at most add a few hours to any study. Just allow yourself a little time to analyze the data once the study is complete. If you're not yet very familiar with collecting these metrics, give yourself some extra time to set up tasks and agree on severity ratings prior to starting the test. Because it is a formative study, you should make every attempt to get the findings back to the stakeholders as quickly as possible to influence the next design iteration and not slow down the project.

In the case of running a lab test with a larger number of participants (usually more than a dozen), including metrics may have more of an impact on the budget and timeline. The most significant cost impact may be any additional costs for recruiting and compensating the participants. These costs depend on who they are (e.g., internal to your company versus external) and how participants are recruited. The most significant impact on the timeline is likely to be the additional time required to run the larger number of participants. Depending on your billing or cost-recovery model, there may also be additional costs because of the increased time for the usability specialists. Keep in mind that you will also need extra time to clean up and analyze the data.

Running an online study is quite different in terms of costs and time. Typically, about half of the time is usually spent setting up the study, from identifying and validating tasks, creating questions and scales, evaluating the prototypes or designs, identifying and/or recruiting participants, and developing the online script. Unlike traditional lab tests where a lot of time is spent collecting the data, running an online study requires little, if any, time on the part of the usability specialist for data collection. With most online usability testing technologies you simply flip the switch and then monitor the data as they pour in.

The other half of the time is spent cleaning up and analyzing the data. It's very common to underestimate the time required for this. Data are often not in a format that readily allows analysis. For example, you will need to filter out extreme values (particularly when collecting time data), check for data inconsistencies, and code new variables based on the raw data (such as creating top-2-box variables for self-reported data). We have found that we can run an online study in about 100 to 200 person-hours. This includes everything from the planning phase through data collection, analysis, and presentation. The estimate can vary by up to 50 percent in either direction based on the scope of the study.

### 3.4.2 Evaluation Methods

One of the great features of collecting usability metrics is that you're not restricted to a certain type of evaluation method (e.g., lab test, online test). Metrics can be collected using almost any kind of evaluation method. This may be surprising because there is a common misperception that metrics can only be collected through large-scale online studies. As you will see, this is simply not the case.

Choosing an evaluation method to collect metrics boils down to how many participants are needed and what metrics you're going to use. The most common usability method is a lab test that requires a relatively small number of participants (typically four to ten). The lab test involves a one-on-one session between a moderator (usability specialist) and a test participant. The moderator asks questions of the participants and gives them a set of tasks to perform on the product in question. The test participant is likely to be thinking aloud as she performs the various tasks. The moderator notes the participant's behavior and responses to questions. Lab tests are best used in formative studies where the goal is to make iterative design improvements. The most important metrics to collect are about issues, including issue frequency, type, and severity. Also, collecting performance data such as task success, errors, and efficiency may also be helpful.

Self-reported metrics can also be collected by having participants answer questions regarding each task or at the conclusion of the study. However, we recommend that you approach performance data and self-reported data very carefully because it's easy to overgeneralize the results to a larger population without an adequate sample size. In fact, we typically only report the frequency of successful tasks or errors. We hesitate even to state the data as a percentage for fear that someone (who is less familiar with usability data or methods) will overgeneralize the data.

Usability tests are not always run with a small number of participants. In some situations you might want to spend some extra time and money by running a larger group of participants (perhaps 10–50 users). The main advantage of running a test with more participants is that as your sample size increases, so does your confidence in the data. This will afford you the ability to collect a wider range of data. In fact, all performance, self-reported, and physiological metrics are fair game. But there are a few metrics that you should be cautious about. For example, inferring website traffic patterns from usability-lab data is probably not very reliable, nor is looking at how subtle design changes might impact the user experience. In these cases, it is better to test with hundreds or even thousands of participants in an online study.

Online studies involve testing with many participants at the same time. They are an excellent way to collect a lot of data in a relatively short amount of time. Online studies are usually set up similarly to a lab test in that there are some background questions, tasks, and follow-up questions. Participants go through a well-defined script of questions and tasks, and all their data are collected automatically using the particular tool. You can collect a wide range of data, including many performance metrics and self-reported metrics. It may be difficult to collect issues-based data because you're not directly observing participants. But the performance and self-reported data can point to issues, and verbatim comments can help infer their causes.

Online surveys are also appropriate for capturing data on more subtle designs. For example, you can gauge emotional responses to specific visual design elements. The main drawback of online usability studies is that the data you get from each participant is less rich than what you can get in a lab, but that may be offset by the larger number of participants. Another limitation is that online studies only work well with websites or software. Products such as consumer electronics can't easily be tested using an online study.

Focus groups are a great way to get at people's perceptions and attitudes about any particular product or concept. In most cases, there is no direct interaction with the product. All the data from a focus group are in the form of self-reported metrics. Some usability specialists prefer to administer short questionnaires before the focus group begins or at its conclusion. Some of the more useful questions revolve around the likelihood to use the new functionality or to recommend the product to friends. Typical focus groups include about eight to ten participants. We recommend that you conduct at least three groups whenever possible. Data from only one focus group of eight or ten participants may not be very reliable, partly because of the possibility of only one particularly vocal participant swaying the group's opinions.

---

**FOCUS GROUPS VERSUS USABILITY TESTS**

When some people first hear about usability testing, they believe it is the same as a focus group. But in our experience, the similarity between the two methods begins and ends with the fact that they both involve representative participants. In a focus group, the participants commonly watch someone demonstrate or describe a potential product, and then react to it. In a usability test, the participants actually try to use some version of the product themselves. We've seen many cases where a prototype got rave reviews from focus groups and then failed miserably in a usability test.

---

### 3.4.3 Participants

The participants in any usability study have a major impact on its findings. It's critical that you carefully plan how to include the most representative participants as possible in your study. The steps you will go through in recruiting participants are essentially the same whether you're collecting metrics or not.

The first step is to identify the recruiting criteria that will be used to determine whether a specific person is eligible to participate in the study. Criteria should be as specific as possible to reduce the possibility of recruiting someone who does not fit the profile(s). We often recruit participants based on many characteristics, including their experience with the web, years away from retirement, or experience with various financial transactions. As part of identifying the criteria, you may segment participant types. For example, you may recruit a certain number of new participants as well as ones who have experience with the existing product.

After deciding on the types of participants you want, you need to figure out how many you need. As you saw in section 2.1.2, the number of participants needed for a usability test is one of the most hotly debated issues in the field. Many factors enter into the decision, including the diversity of the user population, the complexity of the product, and the specific goals of the study. But as a general rule of thumb, testing with about six to eight participants for each iteration in a formative study works well. The most significant usability findings will be observed with the first six or so participants. If there are distinct groups of users, it's helpful to have at least four from each group.

For summative usability studies, we recommend having data from 50 to 100 representative users. If you're in a crunch, you can go as low as 20 participants, but the variance in the data will be quite high, making it difficult to generalize the findings to a broader population. In the case of studies where you are testing the impact of potentially subtle design changes, having at least 100 participants is advisable.

After determining the sample size, you will need to plan the recruiting strategy. This is essentially how you are actually going to get people to participate in the study. You might generate a list of possible participants from customer data and then write a screener that a recruiter uses when contacting potential participants. You might send out requests to participate via e-mail distribution lists. You can screen or segment participants through a series of background questions. Or you might decide to use a third party to handle all of the recruiting. Some of these companies have quite extensive user panels to draw on. Other options exist, such as posting an announcement on the web or e-mailing a specific group of potential participants. Different strategies work for different organizations.

### 3.4.4 Data Collection

It's important to think about how the data are going to be collected. You should plan out well in advance how you are going to capture all the data that you need for your study. The decisions you make may have a significant impact on how much work you have to do further down the road when you begin analysis.

In the case of a lab test with a fairly small number of participants, Excel probably works as well as anything for collecting data. Make sure you have a template in place for quickly capturing the data during the test. Ideally, this is not done by the moderator but by a note taker or someone behind the scenes who can quickly and easily enter the data. We recommend that data be entered in numeric format as much as possible. For example, if you are coding task success, it is best to code it as a "1" (success) and "0" (failure). Data entered in a text format will eventually have to be converted, with the exception of verbatim comments.

The most important thing when capturing data is for everyone on the usability team to know the coding scheme extremely well. If anyone starts flipping scales (confusing the high and low values) or does not understand what to enter for certain variables, you will have to either recode or throw the data out. We strongly recommend that you offer training to others who will be helping you collect data. Just think of it as cheap insurance to make sure you end up with clean data.

For studies involving larger numbers of participants, consider using a data-capture tool. If you are running an online study, data are typically collected automatically. You should also have the option of downloading the raw data into Excel.

### 3.4.5 Data Cleanup

Data rarely come out in a format that is instantly ready to analyze. Some sort of cleanup is usually needed to get your data in a format that allows for quick and easy analysis. Data cleanup might include the following:

*Filtering data.* You should check for extreme values in the data set. The most likely culprit will be task completion times (in the case of online studies). Some participants may have gone out to lunch in the middle of the study, and their task times will be unusually large. Also, some participants may have taken an impossibly short amount of time to complete the task. This is likely an indicator that they were not truly engaged in the study. Some general rules for how to filter time data are included in section 4.2. You should also consider filtering out data for participants who do not reflect your target audience or where outside factors impacted the results. We've had more than a few usability testing sessions interrupted by a fire drill!

*Creating new variables.* Building on the raw data set is very useful. For example, you might want to create a top-2-box variable for self-reported rating scales by counting the number of participants who gave one of the two highest ratings. Perhaps you want to aggregate all the success data into one overall success average representing all tasks. Or you might want to combine several metrics using a *z*-score transformation (described in section 8.1.3) to create an overall usability score.

*Verifying responses.* In some situations, particularly for online studies, participant responses may need to be verified. For example, if you notice that a large percentage of participants are all giving the same wrong answer, this should be investigated.

*Checking consistency.* It is important to make sure that data are captured properly. A consistency check might include comparing task completion times and successes to self-reported metrics. If many participants completed a task in a relatively short period of time and were successful but gave the task a very low rating, there may be a problem with either how the data were captured or participants confusing the scales of the question. This is quite common with scales involving self-reported ease of use.

*Transferring data.* It's common to capture and clean up the data using Excel, then use another program such as SPSS to run some statistics (although all the basic statistics can be done with Excel), and then move back to Excel to create the charts and graphs.

Data cleanup can take anywhere from one hour to a couple of weeks. For pretty simple usability studies, with just a couple of metrics, cleanup should be very quick. Obviously, the more metrics you are dealing with, the more time it will take. Also, online studies can take longer because more checks are being done. You want to make sure that the technology is correctly coding all the data.

## 3.5 SUMMARY

Running a usability study including metrics requires some planning. The following are some of the key points to remember.

1. The first decision you must make is whether you are going to take a formative or summative approach. A formative approach involves collecting data to help improve the design before it is launched or released. It is most appropriate when you have an opportunity to positively impact the design of the product. A summative approach is taken when you want to measure the extent to which certain target goals were achieved. Summative testing is also sometimes used in competitive usability studies.

2. When deciding on the most appropriate metrics, two main aspects of the user experience to consider are performance and satisfaction. Performance metrics characterize what the user *does* and include measures such as task success, task time, and the amount of effort required to achieve a desired outcome. Satisfaction metrics relate to what users *think* or *feel* about their experience.

3. Budgets and timelines need to be planned out well in advance when running any usability studies involving metrics. If you are running a formative study with a relatively small number of participants, collecting metrics should have little, if any, impact on the overall timeline or budget. Otherwise, special attention must be paid to estimating and communicating costs and time for larger-scale studies.

4. Three general types of evaluation methods are used in collecting usability data. Lab tests with small numbers of participants are best in formative testing. These studies typically focus on issues-based metrics. Lab tests with large numbers of participants (more than a dozen) are best to capture a combination of qualitative and quantitative data. These studies usually measure different aspects of performance such as success, completion time, and errors. Online studies with very large numbers of participants (more than one hundred) are best to examine subtle design changes and preferences.

5. Clearly identify the criteria for recruiting participants for the usability test, making sure they are truly representative of the target users. In a formative usability study, testing with about six to eight participants for each iteration is usually enough. If there are distinct groups of users, it's helpful to have at least four from each group. For summative usability studies, we recommend collecting data from 50 to 100 representative users, if possible.

6. Plan well in advance how you are going to capture all the data you need for your study. Make sure you have a template in place for quickly capturing the data during the test and that everyone who will be assisting with the data collection is familiar with any coding conventions. Consider using data-logging tools for larger-scale studies.

7. Data cleanup involves manipulating the data in a way to make them usable and reliable. For example, filtering data means removing extreme values or removing records that are problematic. Consistency checks and verifying responses are important steps in making sure that participants' intentions map to their responses.

# Performance Metrics

4

Anyone who uses technology has to interact with some type of interface to accomplish his or her goals. For example, a user of a website clicks on different links, a user of a word-processing application enters information via a keyboard, and a user of a DVD player pushes buttons on a remote control. No matter the technology, users are behaving or interacting with a product in some way. These behaviors form the cornerstone of performance metrics.

Every type of user behavior is measurable in some way. For example, you can measure whether users clicking through a website found what they were looking for. You can measure how long it took users to enter and properly format a page of text in a word-processing application or how many incorrect buttons users pressed in trying to play a DVD. All performance metrics are calculated based on specific user behaviors.

Performance metrics rely not only on user behaviors but also on the use of scenarios or tasks. For example, if you want to measure success, the user needs to have specific tasks or goals in mind. The task may be to find the price of a CD or submit an expense report. Without tasks, performance metrics aren't possible. You can't measure success if the user is only aimlessly browsing a website or playing with a piece of software. How do you know if he or she was successful?

Performance metrics are among the most valuable tools for any usability professional. They're the best way to evaluate the effectiveness and efficiency of many different products. If users are making many errors, you know there are opportunities for improvement. If users are taking four times longer to complete a task than what was expected, efficiency can be greatly improved. Performance metrics are the best way of knowing how well users are actually using a product.

Performance metrics are also useful to estimate the *magnitude* of a specific usability issue. Many times it is not enough to know that a particular issue exists. You probably want to know *how many* people are likely to encounter the same issue after the product is released. For example, by calculating a success rate that includes a confidence interval, you can derive a reasonable estimate of how big a usability issue really is. By measuring task completion times, you can determine what percentage of your target audience will be able to complete a task within a specified amount of time. If only 20 percent of the target users are successful at a particular task, it should be fairly obvious that the task has a usability problem.

Senior managers and other key stakeholders on a project usually sit up and pay attention to performance metrics, especially when they are presented effectively. Managers will want to know how many users are able to successfully complete a core set of tasks using a product. They see these performance metrics as a strong indicator of overall usability and a potential predictor of cost savings or increases in revenue.

Performance metrics are not the magical elixir for every situation. Similar to other metrics, an adequate sample size is required. Although the statistics will work whether you have 2 or 100 participants, your confidence level will change dramatically depending on the sample size. If you're only concerned about identifying the lowest of the low-hanging fruit, performance metrics are probably not a good use of time or money. But if you have the time to collect data from at least eight participants, and ideally more, you should be able to derive meaningful performance metrics with reasonable confidence levels.

Overrelying on performance metrics may be a danger for some. When reporting task success or completion time, it may be easy to lose sight of the underlying issues behind the data. Performance metrics tell the *what* very effectively but not the *why*. Performance data can point to tasks or parts of an interface that were particularly problematic for participants, but you will usually want to supplement with other data, such as observational or self-reported data, to better understand why they were problems and how they might be fixed.

Five basic types of performance metrics are covered in this chapter.

1. *Task success* is perhaps the most widely used performance metric. It measures how effectively users are able to complete a given set of tasks. Two different types of task success will be reviewed: binary success and levels of success.

2. *Time-on-task* is a common performance metric that measures how much time is required to complete a task.

3. *Errors* reflect the mistakes made during a task. Errors can be useful in pointing out particularly confusing or misleading parts of an interface.

4. *Efficiency* can be assessed by examining the amount of effort a user expends to complete a task, such as the number of clicks in a website or the number of button presses on a cell phone.

5. *Learnability* is a way to measure how performance changes over time.

## 4.1 TASK SUCCESS

The most common usability metric is task success, which can be calculated for practically any usability study that includes tasks. It's almost a universal metric because it can be calculated for such a wide variety of *things* being tested—from websites to kitchen appliances. As long as the user has a well-defined task, you can measure success.

Task success is something that almost anyone can relate to. It doesn't require elaborate explanations of measurement techniques or statistics to get the point across. If your participants can't complete their tasks, then you know something is wrong. Seeing participants fail to complete a simple task can be pretty compelling evidence that something needs to be fixed.

### 4.1.1 Collecting Any Type of Success Metric

To measure task success, each task that participants are asked to perform must have a clear end-state, such as purchasing a product, finding the answer to a specific question, or completing an online application form. To measure success, you need to know what constitutes success, so you should define the success criteria for each task prior to the data collection. If you don't predefine the criteria, you run the risk of constructing a poorly worded task and not collecting clean success data. Here are examples of two tasks with clear and not-so-clear end-states:

- Find the current price for a share of Google stock (clear end-state)
- Research ways to save for your retirement (not a clear end-state)

Although the second task may be perfectly appropriate in certain types of usability studies, it's not appropriate for measuring task success.

The most common way of measuring success in a lab-based usability test is to have the participant verbally articulate the answer after completing the task. This is natural for the participant, but sometimes it results in answers that are difficult to interpret. Participants might give extra or arbitrary information that makes it difficult to interpret the answer. In these situations, you may need to probe the participants to make sure they actually completed the task successfully.

Another way to collect success data is by having participants provide their answers in a more structured way, such as using an online tool or paper form. Each task might have a set of multiple-choice responses. Participants might choose the correct answer from a list of four to five distracters. It's important to make the distracters as realistic as possible. Try to avoid write-in answers if possible. It's much more time consuming to analyze each write-in answer, and it may involve judgment calls, thereby adding more noise to the data.

In some cases the correct solution to a task may not be verifiable because it depends on the user's specific situation, and testing is not being performed in person. For example, if you ask participants to find the balance in their savings account, there's no way to know what that amount really is unless you're sitting next to them while they do it. So in this case, you might use a proxy measure of success. For example, you could ask the participant to identify the title of the page that shows the balance. This works well as long as the title of the page is unique and obvious and you're confident that they are able to actually see the balance if they reach this page.

### 4.1.2 Binary Success

Binary success is the simplest and most common way of measuring task success. Either participants complete a task successfully or they don't. It's kind of like a "pass/fail" course in college. Binary success is appropriate to use when the success of the product depends on users completing a task or a set of tasks. Getting close doesn't count. The only thing that matters is that they accomplish their tasks. For example, when evaluating the usability of a defibrillator device (to resuscitate people during a heart attack), the only thing that matters is being able to use it correctly without making any mistakes. Anything less would be a major problem, especially for the recipient! A less dramatic example might be a task that involves purchasing a book on a website. Although it may be helpful to know where in the process someone failed, if your company's revenue depends on selling those books, that's what really matters.

#### *How to Collect and Measure Binary Success*

Each time users perform a task, they should be given a "success" or "failure" score. Typically, these scores are in the form of 1's (for success) and 0's (for failure). (The analysis is easier if you assign a numeric score rather than a text value of "success" or "failure.") By having a numeric score, you can easily calculate the average as well as perform any other statistics you might need. Simply calculate the average of the 1's and 0's to determine the binary success rate. In addition to showing the average, it's best to also include the confidence interval as part of the binary success data. Figure 4.1 shows how to organize binary success data. Assuming the answers are predefined, it should be very easy to assign a success or failure

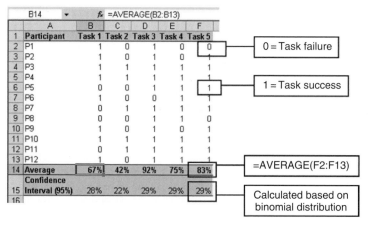

**FIGURE 4.1**

An example of how binary success data should be organized. Confidence intervals were calculated based on a binomial distribution.

score for each user on each task. If you are unsure whether to count an answer as a task success or failure, it's critical to look at the degree to which the task was accomplished by obtaining that answer.

### How to Analyze and Present Binary Success

The most common way to analyze and present binary success rates is by individual task. This involves simply presenting the percentage of participants who successfully completed each task (Figure 4.2). This approach is most useful when you want to compare success rates for tasks. You can then do a more detailed analysis of each task by looking at specific problems to determine what changes may be needed to address them. If you're interested in knowing whether there is a statistically significant difference between the various tasks, you will need to perform a *t*-test or ANOVA (see Chapter 2). In the figure, the average binary success rate for task 1 is 67 percent, but there is a 95 percent chance that the true mean is between 39 and 95 percent (as shown by the confidence interval).

Another common way of looking at binary success is by user or type of user. As always in reporting usability data, you should be careful to maintain the anonymity of the participants in the study by using numbers or other nonidentifiable descriptors. The main value of looking at binary success data from a user perspective is that you can identify different groups of participants who perform differently or encounter different sets of problems. Here are some of the common ways to segment different participants:

- Frequency of use (infrequent users versus frequent users)
- Previous experience using the product
- Domain expertise (low-domain knowledge versus high-domain knowledge)
- Age group

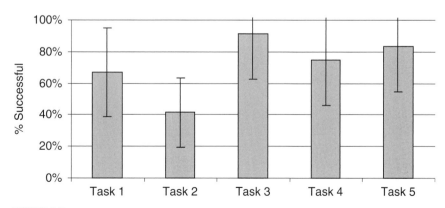

**FIGURE 4.2**

An example of how to present binary success data for individual tasks. The error bars represent the 95 percent confidence interval based on a binomial distribution.

One of the advantages of looking at success data by participant is that you can then calculate a percentage of tasks that each successfully completed, assuming everyone was given more than one task. In this way, the data is no longer binary, and it becomes continuous. For example, if you are testing an application for use by both managers and non-managers, and you find that six out of six managers failed to complete a given task, but none of the six non-managers failed the task, you should investigate why that happened. There may be something in the product for that particular task that works well for the non-managers but is confusing for the managers. Of course, you must be careful drawing conclusions about different groups of participants based on small sample sizes.

If you have a fairly large number of participants in a usability study (at least 12, ideally more than 20), it may be helpful to present binary success data as a frequency distribution (Figure 4.3). This is a convenient way to visually represent the variability in binary task success data. For example, in Figure 4.3, six participants in the evaluation of the original website completed 61 to 70 percent of the tasks successfully, one completed fewer than 50 percent, and two completed as many as 81 to 90 percent. In a revised design, six participants had a success rate of 91 percent or greater, and no participant had a success rate below 61 percent. Illustrating that the two distributions of task success barely overlap is a much more dramatic way of showing the improvement across the iterations than simply reporting the two means.

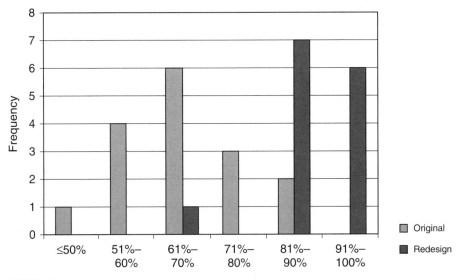

**FIGURE 4.3**

Frequency distributions of binary success rates from usability tests of the original version of a website and the redesigned version. *Source:* Adapted from LeDoux, Connor, and Tullis (2005); used with permission.

### Calculating Confidence Intervals for Binary Success

One of the most important aspects of analyzing and presenting binary success is including confidence intervals. Confidence intervals are essential because they reflect your trust or confidence in the data. In most usability studies, binary success data are based on relatively small samples (e.g., 5–20 participants). Consequently, the binary success metric may not be as reliable as we would like it to be. For example, if 4 out of 5 participants successfully completed a task, how confident can we be that 80 percent of the larger population of participants will be able to successfully complete that task? Obviously, we would be more confident if 16 out of 20 participants successfully completed the task and even more confident if 80 out of 100 did.

Fortunately, there is a way to take this into account. Binary success rates are essentially proportions: the proportion of the participants who successfully completed a given task. The appropriate way to calculate a confidence interval for a proportion like this is to use is a binomial confidence interval. Several methods are available for calculating binomial confidence intervals, such as the Wald Method and the Exact Method. But as Sauro and Lewis (2005) have shown, many of those methods are too conservative or too liberal in their calculation of the confidence interval when you're dealing with the small sample sizes we commonly have in usability tests. They found that a modified version of the Wald Method, called the Adjusted Wald, yielded the best results when calculating a confidence interval for task success data.

Jeff Sauro has provided a very useful calculator for determining confidence intervals for binary success on his website: *http://www.measuringusability.com/ wald.htm*. By entering the total number of participants who attempted a given task and how many of them successfully completed it, this tool will automatically perform the Wald, Adjusted Wald, Exact, and Score calculations of the confidence interval for the mean task completion rate. You can choose to calculate a 99, 95, or 90 percent confidence interval. If you really want to calculate confidence intervals for binary success data yourself, the details are included on our website: *www.MeasuringUserExperience.com*.

If 4 out of 5 participants successfully completed a given task, the Adjusted Wald Method yields a 95 percent confidence interval for that task completion rate ranging from 36 to 98 percent—a rather large range! On the other hand, if 16 out of 20 participants completed the task successfully (the same proportion), the Adjusted Wald Method yields a 95 percent confidence interval of 58 to 93 percent. If you got *really* carried away and ran a usability test with 100 participants, of whom 80 completed the task successfully, the 95 percent confidence interval would be 71 to 87 percent. As is always the case with confidence intervals, larger sample sizes yield smaller (or more accurate) intervals.

## 4.1.3 Levels of Success

Identifying levels of success is useful when there are reasonable shades of gray associated with task success. The participant receives some value from partially completing a task. Think of it as partial credit on a homework assignment if you showed your work, even though you got the wrong answer. For example, assume that a participant's task is to find the cheapest digital camera with at least 5 megapixel resolution, at least 6X optical zoom, and weighing no more than 3 pounds. What if the participant found a camera that met most of those criteria but had a 5X optical zoom instead of a 6X?

According to a strict binary success approach, that would be a failure. But you're losing some important information by doing that. The participant actually came very close to successfully completing the task. In some cases this might be acceptable. For some types of products, coming close to fully completing a task may provide value to the participant. Also, it may be helpful for you to know why some participants failed to complete a task or with which particular tasks they needed help.

### How to Collect and Measure Levels of Success

Collecting and measuring levels of success data are very similar to collecting and measuring binary success data, except that you must define the various levels. There are three perspectives on levels of success:

- Levels of success might be based on the extent or degree to which a participant completed the task. This could be defined by whether he received any assistance or got only part of an answer.

- Levels of success might be based on the experience in completing a task. Some participants might struggle, whereas others can complete their tasks without any difficulty.

- Levels of success might be based on the participant accomplishing the task in different ways. Some participants might accomplish the task in an optimal way, whereas others might accomplish it in ways that are less than optimal.

Between three and six levels of success based on the degree to which participants complete a task are typical. A common approach is to use three levels: complete success, partial success, and complete failure.

Levels of success data are almost as easy to collect and measure as binary success data. It just means defining what you mean by "complete success" and by "complete failure." Anything in between is considered a partial success. A more granular approach is to break out each level according to whether assistance was given or not. The following are examples of six different levels of completion:

- Complete success
  - With assistance
  - Without assistance
- Partial success
  - With assistance
  - Without assistance

- Failure
  - Participant thought it was complete, but it wasn't
  - Participant gave up

If you do decide to use levels of success, it's important to clearly define the levels beforehand. Also, consider having multiple observers independently assess the levels for each task and then reach a consensus.

A common issue when measuring levels of success is deciding what constitutes "giving assistance" to the participant. Here are some examples of situations we define as giving assistance:

- Moderator takes the participant back to a homepage or resets to an initial (pretask) state. This form of assistance may reorient the participant and help avoid certain behaviors that initially resulted in confusion.

- Moderator asks probing questions or restates the task. This may cause the participant to think about her behavior or choices in a different way.

- Moderator answers a question or provides information that helps the participant complete the task.

- Participant seeks help from an outside source. For example, the participant calls a phone representative, uses some other website, consults a user manual, or accesses an online help system.

Levels of success based on completion can be organized in many different ways. One of the most straightforward methods is to assign a numeric value for each level. Here is one way of assigning weights for various levels of success:

- Complete success (without assistance) = 1.0
- Partial success = 0.5
- Gives up or wrong answer = 0.0

This method allows you to derive a usability "success score," and you can easily calculate an average. This is not a traditional success rate but a success score. One obvious limitation is that it does not differentiate between different types of failure (giving up versus wrong answers). So if it's important to know the difference between participants who gave the wrong answer and those who just gave up, numeric scoring may not be the best solution.

Level of success can also be examined in terms of the user experience. We commonly find that some tasks are completed without any difficulty and others are completed with minor or major problems along the way. It's important to distinguish between these different experiences. A 4-point scoring method can be used for each task:

**1** = *No problem.* The participant successfully completed the task without any difficulty or inefficiency.

**2** = *Minor problem*. The participant successfully completed the task but took a slight detour. He made one or two small mistakes but quickly recovered and was successful.

**3** = *Major problem.* The participant successfully completed the task but had major problems. She struggled and took a major detour in her eventual successful completion of the task.

**4** = *Failure/gave up.* The participant provided the wrong answer or gave up before completing the task, or the moderator moved on to the next task before successful completion.

When using this scoring system, it's important to remember that these data are ordinal (section 2.2.2). Therefore, you should not report an average score. Rather, present the data as frequencies for each level of completion. This scoring system is relatively easy to use, and we usually see agreement on the various levels by different usability specialists observing the same interactions. Also, you can aggregate the data into a binary success rate if you need to. Finally, this scoring system is usually easy to explain to your audience.

Another way of organizing levels of success data is according to different answers given by participants. For example, you could assign a score of 1.0 for an optimal answer(s) and a score or 0.75 or 0.5 for acceptable (but suboptimal) answers, depending on the quality of the answer. You don't have to assign a numeric score, but it's convenient if you want to do any in-depth analysis. The same can also be done for different navigation strategies used to reach a particular answer. If you are evaluating a website, sometimes the participant clicks on the best link and completes the task without any issues. Other times a participant might click on a suboptimal link but eventually be successful.

### How to Analyze and Present Levels of Success

In analyzing levels of success, the first thing you should do is create a stacked bar chart. This will show the percentage of participants who fall into each category or level, including failures. Make sure that the bars add up to 100 percent. Figure 4.4 is an example of a common way to present levels of success.

Another approach to analyzing and presenting levels of success based on task completion is to report a "usability score." As mentioned in the previous section, you can assign a numeric score to each level of success ranging from 0 (failure) to 1.0 (full success without assistance). Obviously there are many different ways to do this. These data would look very much like binary success (Figure 4.2), except instead of the *y*-axis showing "% successful," it would be "average success score."

Keep in mind that it's important to communicate the scoring system used to the audience, because it's easy to misinterpret these charts as common success rates.

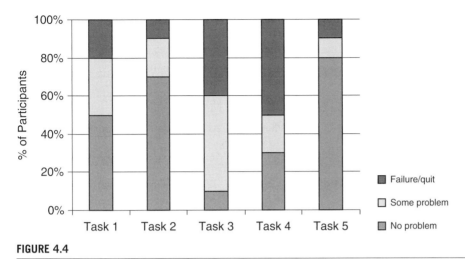

**FIGURE 4.4**

Stacked bar chart showing different levels of success based on task completion.

### 4.1.4 Issues in Measuring Success

Obviously, an important issue in measuring task success is simply how you define whether a task was successful. The key is to clearly define beforehand what the criteria are for *successfully* completing each task. Try to think through the various situations that might arise for each task and decide whether they constitute success. For example, is a task successful if the participant finds the right answer but reports it in the wrong format? Also, what happens if he reports the right answer but then restates his answer incorrectly? When unexpected situations arise during the test, make note of them and afterward try to reach a consensus among the observers about those cases.

One issue that commonly arises during a usability evaluation is how or when to end a task if the participant is not successful. In essence, this is the "stopping rule" for unsuccessful tasks. Here are some of the common approaches to ending an unsuccessful task:

1. Tell the participants at the beginning of the session that they should continue to work on each task until they either complete it or reach the point at which, in the real world, they would give up or seek assistance (from technical support, a colleague, etc.).

2. Apply a "three strikes and you're out" rule. This means that the participants make three attempts to complete a task before you stop them. The main difficulty with this approach is defining what is meant by an "attempt." It could be three different strategies, three wrong answers, or three different "detours" in finding specific information. However you define it, there will be a considerable amount of discretion on behalf of the moderator or scorer.

**3.** "Call" the task after a prespecified amount of time has passed. Set a time limit, such as five minutes. After the time has expired, move on to the next task. In most cases, it is better not to tell the participant that you are timing him. By doing so, you create a more stressful, "testlike" environment.

Of course, you always have to be sensitive to the participant's state in any usability session and potentially end a task (or even the session) if you see that the participant is becoming particularly frustrated or agitated.

## 4.2  TIME-ON-TASK

Time-on-task (sometimes referred to as task completion time or simply task time) is an excellent way to measure the efficiency of any product. The time it takes a participant to perform a task says a lot about the usability of the product. In almost every situation, the faster a participant can complete a task, the better the experience. In fact, it would be pretty unusual for a user to complain that a task took less time than expected.

There are a couple of exceptions to the assumption that faster is better. One is a game where you may not want the participant to finish it too quickly. The main purpose of most games is the experience itself rather than the quick completion of a task. Another exception may be learning. For example, if you're putting together an online training course, slower may be better. It may be better that participants not rush through the course but spend more time completing their tasks.

### 4.2.1  Importance of Measuring Time-on-Task

Time-on-task is particularly important for products where tasks are performed repeatedly by the user. For example, if you're designing an application for use by customer service representatives of an airline, the time it takes to complete a phone reservation would be an important measure of efficiency. The faster the airline agent can complete a reservation, presumably the more calls can be handled and, ultimately, the more money can be saved. The more often a task is performed by the same participant, the more important efficiency becomes. One of the side benefits of measuring time-on-task is that it can be relatively straightforward to calculate cost savings due to an increase in efficiency and then derive an actual ROI (return on investment). Calculating ROI is discussed in more detail in section 9.4.

### 4.2.2  How to Collect and Measure Time-on-Task

Time-on-task is simply the time elapsed between the start of a task and the end of a task, usually expressed in minutes and seconds. Logistically, time-on-task can be measured in many different ways. The moderator or note taker can use a stopwatch or any other time-keeping device that can measure at the minute and second levels. Using a digital watch, you could simply record the start and end times. When videotaping a usability session, we find it's helpful to use the time-stamp feature of most recorders to display the time and then to mark those times as the task start and stop times. If you choose to record time-on-task manually, it's important to be very diligent about when to start and stop the clock and/or record the start and stop times. It may also be helpful to have two people record the times.

### Automated Tools for Measuring Time-on-Task

A much easier and less error-prone way of recording task times is using an automated tool. Usability testing products such as Ergo Browser, Data Logger, or Bailey's Usability Testing Environment (UTE) all capture task time automatically. In fact, tools such as UTE will calculate average task completion times for you. The automated method has several advantages. Not only is it less error-prone but it's also much less obtrusive. The last thing you want is a participant in a usability session to feel nervous from watching you press the start and stop button on your stopwatch.

---

**WORKING WITH TIME DATA IN EXCEL**

If you use Excel to log data during a usability test, it's often convenient to use times that are formatted as hours, minutes, and (sometimes) seconds (hh:mm:ss). Excel provides a variety of formats for time data. This makes it easy to enter the times, but it slightly complicates matters when you need to calculate an elapsed time. For example, assume that a task started at 12:46 PM and ended at 1:04 PM. Although you can look at those times and determine that the elapsed time was 18 minutes, how to get Excel to calculate that isn't so obvious. Internally, Excel stores all times as a number reflecting the number of seconds elapsed since midnight. So to convert an Excel time to minutes, multiply it by 60 (the number of minutes in an hour) and then by 24 (the number of hours in a day). To convert to seconds, multiply by another 60 (the number of seconds in a minute).

---

### Turning on and off the Clock

Not only do you need a way to measure time, but you also need some rules about *how* to measure time. Perhaps the most important rule is when to turn the clock on and off. Turning on the clock is fairly straightforward: If you have the participants read the task aloud, you start the clock as soon as they finish reading the task.

Turning off the clock is a more complicated issue. Automated time-keeping tools typically have an "answer" button. Participants are required to hit the "answer" button, at which point the timing ends, and they are asked to provide an answer and perhaps answer a few questions. If you are not using an automated method, you can have participants verbally report the answer or perhaps even write it down. However, there are many situations in which you may not be sure if they have found the answer. In these situations, it's important for participants to indicate their answer as quickly as possible. In any case, you want to stop timing when the participant has stopped interacting with the product. Because this is largely a matter of interpretation, the data might contain a fair bit of noise.

### Tabulating Time Data

The first thing you need to do is arrange the data in a table, as shown in Table 4.1. Typically, you will want a list of all the participants in the first column, followed by the time data for each task in the remaining columns (expressed in seconds, or in minutes if the tasks are long). Table 4.1 also shows summary data, including the average, median, geometric mean, and confidence intervals for each task.

**Table 4.1** Time-on-Task Data for 20 Participants and 5 Tasks

| Participant | Task 1 | Task 2 | Task 3 | Task 4 | Task 5 |
| --- | --- | --- | --- | --- | --- |
| P1 | 259 | 112 | 135 | 58 | 8 |
| P2 | 253 | 64 | 278 | 160 | 22 |
| P3 | 42 | 51 | 60 | 57 | 26 |
| P4 | 38 | 108 | 115 | 146 | 26 |
| P5 | 33 | 142 | 66 | 47 | 38 |
| P6 | 33 | 54 | 261 | 26 | 42 |
| P7 | 36 | 152 | 53 | 22 | 44 |
| P8 | 112 | 65 | 171 | 133 | 46 |
| P9 | 29 | 92 | 147 | 56 | 56 |
| P10 | 158 | 113 | 136 | 83 | 64 |
| P11 | 24 | 69 | 119 | 25 | 68 |
| P12 | 108 | 50 | 145 | 15 | 75 |
| P13 | 110 | 128 | 97 | 97 | 78 |
| P14 | 37 | 66 | 105 | 83 | 80 |
| P15 | 116 | 78 | 40 | 163 | 100 |
| P16 | 129 | 152 | 67 | 168 | 109 |
| P17 | 31 | 51 | 51 | 119 | 116 |
| P18 | 33 | 97 | 44 | 81 | 127 |
| P19 | 75 | 124 | 286 | 103 | 236 |
| P20 | 76 | 62 | 108 | 185 | 245 |
| **Average** | **86.6** | **91.5** | **124.2** | **91.35** | **80.3** |
| **Median** | **58.5** | **85** | **111.5** | **83** | **66** |

| Table 4.1 cont. | | | | | |
| --- | --- | --- | --- | --- | --- |
| Participant | Task 1 | Task 2 | Task 3 | Task 4 | Task 5 |
| Geometric mean | 65.216 | 85.225 | 104.971 | 73.196 | 60.323 |
| Upper bound | 119.8 | 108.0 | 159.5 | 116.6 | 110.2 |
| Lower bound | 53.4 | 75.0 | 119.9 | 66.1 | 50.4 |
| Confidence interval | 33.2 | 16.5 | 19.8 | 25.2 | 29.9 |

Note: Data are all expressed in seconds.

### 4.2.3 Analyzing and Presenting Time-on-Task Data

You can analyze and present time-on-task data in many different ways. Perhaps the most common way is to look at the average amount of time spent on any particular task or set of tasks by averaging all the times for each participant by task (Figure 4.5). This is a straightforward and intuitive way to report time-on-task data. One downside is the potential variability across participants. For example, if you have several participants who took an exceedingly long time to complete a task, it may increase the average considerably. Therefore, you should always report a confidence interval to show the variability in the time data. This will not only show the

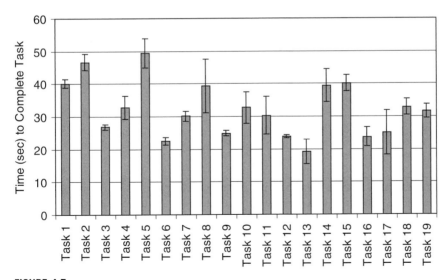

**FIGURE 4.5**

Mean time-on-task for 19 tasks. Error bars represent a 95 percent confidence interval. These data are from an online study of a prototype website.

variability within the same task but also help visualize the difference across tasks to determine whether there is a statistically significant difference between tasks.

Some usability specialists prefer to summarize time-on-task data using the median rather than the mean. The median is the middle point in an ordered list of all the times: Half of the times are below the median and half are above the median. Similarly, some usability specialists suggest that the geometric mean is potentially less biased. Time data is typically skewed, in which case geometric means may be more appropriate. These alternatives can be calculated in Excel using the =MEDIAN or =GEOMEAN functions. In practice, we find that using these other methods of summarizing the time data may change the overall level of the times, but the kinds of patterns you're interested in (e.g., comparisons across tasks) usually stay the same; the same tasks still took the longest or shortest times overall.

### Ranges

A variation on calculating average completion time by task is to create ranges, or discrete time intervals, and report the frequency of participants who fall into each time interval. This is a useful way to visualize the spread of completion times by all participants. In addition, this might be a helpful approach to look for any patterns in the type of participants who fall within certain segments. For example, you may want to focus on those who had particularly long completion times to see if they share any common characteristics.

### Thresholds

Another useful way to analyze task time data is by using a threshold. In many situations, the only thing that matters is whether users can complete certain tasks within an acceptable amount of time. In many ways, the average is unimportant. The main goal is to minimize the number of users who need an excessive amount of time to complete a task. The main issue is determining what the threshold should be for any given task. One way is to perform the task yourself, keep track of the time, and then double that number. Alternatively, you could work with the product team to come up with a threshold for each task based on competitive data or even a best guess. Once you have set your threshold, simply calculate the percentage of users above or below the threshold and plot as illustrated in Figure 4.6.

### Distributions and Outliers

When analyzing time data, it's critical to look at the distribution. This is particularly true for time-on-task data collected via automated tools (when the moderator is not present). Participants might take a phone call or even go out to lunch in the middle of a task. The last thing you want is to include a task time of two hours among other times of only 15 to 20 seconds when calculating an average! It's perfectly acceptable to exclude outliers from your analysis, and many statistical techniques for identifying them are available. Sometimes we exclude any times that are more than three standard deviations above the mean. Alternatively, we sometimes set up

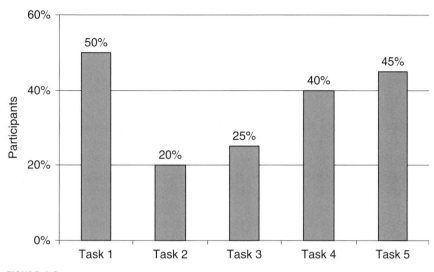

**FIGURE 4.6**

An example showing the percentage of participants who completed each task in less than one minute.

thresholds, knowing that it should never take a user more than $x$ seconds to complete a task. There is a real art to this last approach. Therefore, you should have some rationale for using an arbitrary threshold for excluding outliers.

The opposite problem—participants apparently completing a task in unusually short amounts of time—is actually more common in online studies. Some participants may be in such a hurry, or only care about the compensation, that they simply fly through the study as fast as they can. In most cases, it's very easy to identify these individuals through their time data. For each task, determine the fastest possible time. This would be the time it would take someone with perfect knowledge and optimal efficiency to complete the task. For example, if there is no way you, as an expert user of the product, can finish the task in less than eight seconds, then it is highly unlikely than a typical participant could complete the task any faster. Once you have established this minimum acceptable time, simply filter out those times that fall below the minimum. You can expect anywhere from 5 to 10 percent of all participants in an online study to be in it only for the compensation!

### 4.2.4 Issues to Consider When Using Time Data

Some of the issues to think about when analyzing time data is whether to look at all tasks or just the successful tasks, what the impact of using a think-aloud protocol might be, and whether to tell test participants that time is being measured.

### Only Successful Tasks or All Tasks?

Perhaps the first issue to consider is whether you should include only successful tasks or all tasks in the analysis. The main advantage of only including successful tasks is that it is a cleaner measure of efficiency. For example, time data for unsuccessful tasks are often very difficult to estimate. Some participants will keep on trying until you practically unplug the computer. Any task that ends with the participant giving up or the moderator "pulling the plug" is going to result in highly variable time data.

The main advantage of analyzing time data for *all* tasks, successful or not, is that it is a more accurate reflection of the overall user experience. For example, if only a small percentage of participants were successful, but that particular group was very efficient, the overall time-on-task is going to be low. Therefore, it is easy to misinterpret time-on-task data when only analyzing successful tasks. Another advantage of analyzing time data for all tasks is that it is an independent measure in relation to the task success data. If you only analyze the time data for successful tasks, you're introducing a dependency between the two sets of data.

A good rule is that if the participant always determined when to give up on unsuccessful tasks, you should include all times in the analyses. If the moderator sometimes decided when to end an unsuccessful task, then use only the times for the successful tasks.

### Using a Think-Aloud Protocol

Another important issue to consider is whether to use a think-aloud protocol when collecting time data. Most usability specialists rely heavily on a think-aloud protocol to gain important insight into the user experience. A think-aloud protocol is almost certainly going to have an impact on the time-on-task data. The last thing you want to do is measure time-on-task as a participant is giving a ten-minute diatribe on the importance of fast-loading web pages. A good solution, when you want to capture time-on-task, is to ask participants to "hold" most of their comments for the time between tasks. Then you can have a dialog with the participant about the just-completed task after the "clock is stopped." This is sometimes called a retrospective probing technique (e.g., Birns, Joffre, Leclerc, & Paulsen, 2002).

> **THINK-ALOUD PROTOCOL AND TASK TIMES**
>
> Does using a think-aloud protocol always increase task times? Maybe not. Sometimes it actually might decrease task times. It can be argued that the process of thinking aloud sometimes helps the participant to focus more on the task and the interface, perhaps more readily identifying ways of accomplishing the task.

### Should You Tell the Participants about the Time Measurement?

An important question to consider is whether to tell the participants you are recording their time. It's possible that if you don't, participants won't behave in an efficient manner. It's not uncommon for participants to explore different parts of a website when they are in the middle of a task. On the flip side, if you tell them they are being timed, they may become nervous and feel they are the ones being tested and not the product. A good compromise is to ask participants to perform the tasks as quickly and accurately as possible without volunteering that they are being explicitly timed. If the participants happen to ask (which they rarely do), then simply state that you are noting the start and finish times for each task.

## 4.3 ERRORS

Some usability professionals believe errors and usability issues are essentially the same thing. Although they are certainly related, they are actually quite different. A usability issue is the underlying *cause* of a problem, whereas one or more errors are a possible *outcome*. For example, if users are experiencing a problem in completing a purchase on an e-commerce website, the issue (or cause) may be confusing labeling of the products. The error, or the result of the issue, may be the act of choosing the wrong options for the product they want to buy. Essentially, errors are incorrect actions that may lead to task failure.

### 4.3.1 When to Measure Errors

In some situations it's very helpful to identify and classify errors rather than just document usability issues. Measuring errors is useful when you want to understand the specific action or set of actions that may result in task failure. For example, a user may make the wrong selection on a web page and sell a stock instead of buying more. A user may push the wrong button on a medical device and deliver the wrong medication to a patient. In both cases, it's important to know what errors were made and how different design elements may increase or decrease the frequency of errors.

Errors are a useful way of evaluating user performance. While being able to complete a task successfully within a reasonable amount of time is important, the number of errors made during the interaction is also very revealing. Errors can tell you how many mistakes were made, where they were made within the product, how various designs produce different frequencies and types of errors, and generally how usable something really is.

Measuring errors is not right for every situation. We've found that there are three general situations where measuring errors might be useful:

1. When an error will result in a significant loss in efficiency—for example, when an error results in a loss of data, requires the user to reenter information, or significantly slows the user in completing a task.

2. When an error will result in significant costs—for example, if an error will result in increased call volumes to customer support or in increased product returns.

3. When an error will result in task failure—for example, if an error will cause a patient to receive the wrong medication, a voter to accidentally vote for the wrong candidate, or a web user to buy the wrong product.

## 4.3.2 What Constitutes an Error?

Surprisingly, there is no widely accepted definition of what constitutes an error. Obviously, it's some type of incorrect action on the part of the user. Generally an error is any action that prevents the user from completing a task in the most efficient manner. Errors can be based on many different types of actions by the user, such as the following:

■ Entering incorrect data into a form field (such as typing the wrong password during a login attempt)

■ Making the wrong choice in a menu or drop-down list (such as selecting "Delete" when they should have selected "Modify")

■ Taking an incorrect sequence of actions (such as reformatting their DVD drive when all they were trying to do was play a taped TV show)

■ Failing to take a key action (such as clicking on a key link on a web page)

Obviously, the range of possible actions will depend on the product you are studying (website, cell phone, DVD player, etc.). When you're trying to determine what constitutes an error, first make a list of all the possible actions a user can take on your product. Once you have the universe of possible actions, you can then start to define many of the different types of errors that can be made using the product.

### A Real-World Example: Errors in Election Ballots

One of the most publicized examples of possible user errors occurred in the 2000 U.S. presidential election in Palm Beach County, Florida. They used the now-infamous "butterfly ballot" shown in Figure 4.7. With this ballot, you record your vote by punching one of the holes in the center strip. The crux of the usability problem is that although Al Gore was the *second* candidate listed on the left, a vote for him was indicated using the *third* hole. The second hole corresponded to Pat Buchanan on the right (no pun intended). How many voters might have accidentally voted for Buchanan when they intended to vote for Gore is not known. Whatever your political leanings, this is a situation where measuring errors in a usability study of the election ballot prior to the actual election would have been very helpful!

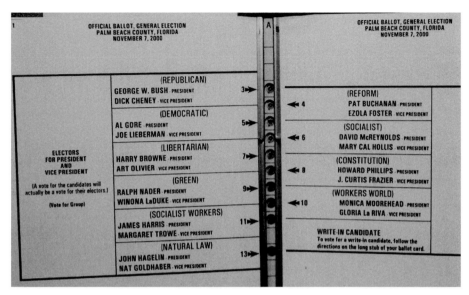

**FIGURE 4.7**

The ballot used in the 2000 presidential election in Palm Beach County.

### 4.3.3 Collecting and Measuring Errors

Measuring errors is not always easy. As with other performance metrics, you need to know what the correct action should be or, in some cases, the correct set of actions. For example, if you're studying a password reset form, you need to know what is considered the correct set of actions to successfully reset the password and what is not. The better you can define the universe of correct and incorrect actions, the easier it will be to measure errors.

An important consideration is whether a given task presents only a single error opportunity or multiple error opportunities. An error opportunity is basically a chance to make a mistake. For example, if you're measuring the usability of a login screen, two error opportunities are possible: making an error when entering the username and making an error when entering the password. If you're measuring the usability of an online form, there could be as many error opportunities as there are fields on the form.

In some cases there might be multiple error opportunities for a task but you only care about one of them. For example, you might be interested only in whether users click on a specific link that you know will be critical to completing their task. Even though errors could be made in other places on the page, you're narrowing your scope of interest to that single link. If users don't click on the link, it is considered an error.

The most common way of organizing error data is by task. Simply record the number of errors for each task and each user. If there is only a single opportunity for error, the numbers will be 1's and 0's:

$$0 = \text{No error} \quad 1 = \text{One error}$$

If multiple error opportunities are possible, the numbers will vary between 0 and the maximum number of error opportunities. The more error opportunities, the harder and more time consuming it will be to tabulate the data. You can count errors while observing participants during a lab study, by reviewing videos after the sessions are over, or by collecting the data using an automated or online tool.

### 4.3.4 Analyzing and Presenting Errors

The analysis and presentation of error data differ slightly depending on whether a task has only one error opportunity or multiple error opportunities.

#### Tasks with a Single Error Opportunity

The most common way to analyze errors for tasks with single error opportunities is to look at the frequency of the error for each task. This will indicate which tasks are associated with the most errors and thus have the most significant usability issues. This can be done in either of two ways, with slightly different forms of interpretation:

- Run a frequency of errors by task and plot out the number of errors. This would show the number of errors made on each task. Note that you do not need to use confidence intervals in this type of analysis because you are not trying to extrapolate to a more general population; you are only interested in seeing which tasks have the most errors.

- Divide the number of errors by the total number of participants for each task. This will tell you the percentage of participants who made an error for each task. This is especially useful if different numbers of participants performed each task. Figure 4.8 is an example of presenting errors based on a single opportunity. In this example, they were interested in the percentage of participants who experienced an error when using different types of on-screen keyboards (Tullis, Mangan, & Rosenbaum, 2007). The control condition is the current QWERTY keyboard layout.

Another way to analyze and present error metrics for tasks with single error opportunities is from an aggregate perspective. You may not always be concerned about a specific task but about how participants performed overall. Here are some options:

- You could average the error rates for each task into a single error rate. This would tell you the overall error rate for the study. For example, you might be able to say that the tasks had an average error rate of 25 percent. This is a useful bottom-line metric for reporting errors.

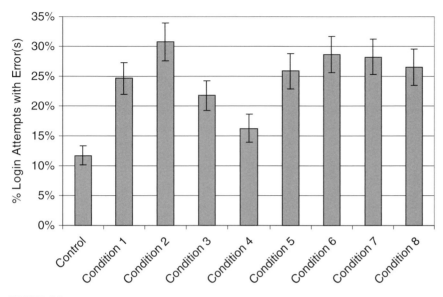

**FIGURE 4.8**

An example showing how to present data for single error opportunities. In this study, only one error opportunity per task (entering a password incorrectly) was possible, and the graph shows the percentage of participants who made an error for each condition.

- You could take an average of all the tasks that had a certain number of errors. For example, if you are looking at a large number of tasks, you could report that 50 percent of all the tasks had an error rate of 10 percent or greater. Or you might state that at least one participant made an error on 80 percent of the tasks.

- You could establish maximum acceptable error rates for each task. For example, you might only be interested in identifying the tasks that have an error rate above a particular threshold, such as 10 percent. You could then calculate the percentage of tasks above and below this threshold. For example, you might simply state that 25 percent of the tasks exceeded an acceptable error rate.

### Tasks with Multiple Error Opportunities

Here are some of the more common ways to analyze the data from tasks that provide multiple error opportunities:

- A good place to start is to look at the frequency of errors for each task. You will be able to see which tasks are resulting in the most errors. But this may be misleading if each task has a different number of error opportunities. In that case, it might be better to divide the total number of errors for the task by the total number of error opportunities. This creates an error rate that takes into account the number of opportunities.

■ You could calculate the average number of errors made by each participant for each task. This will also tell you which tasks are producing the most errors. However, it may be more meaningful because it suggests that a typical user might experience $x$ number of errors on a particular task when using the product. Another advantage is that it takes into account the extremes. If you are simply looking at the frequency of errors for each task, some participants may be the source of most of the errors, whereas many others are performing the task error-free. By taking an average number of errors by each participant, this bias is reduced.

■ In some situations it might be interesting to know which tasks fall above or below a threshold. For example, for some tasks an error rate above 20 percent is unacceptable, whereas for others an error rate above 5 percent is unacceptable. The most straightforward analysis is to first establish an acceptable threshold for each task or each participant. Next, calculate whether that specific task's error rate or participant error count was above or below the threshold.

■ In some situations you want to take into account that not all errors are created equal. Some errors are much more serious than others. It is possible to weight each type of error with a different value and then calculate an "error score"—for example, trivial, moderate, and serious. You could then weight each of those errors with a value of 1 (trivial), 2 (moderate), or 3 (serious). Then, simply add up the score for each participant using these weights. Divide all the scores by the number of participants for each task. This will produce an average "error score" for each task. The interpretation is a little different from an error rate. Essentially, you will be able to report that certain tasks have more frequent and/ or serious errors than other tasks.

### 4.3.5 Issues to Consider When Using Error Metrics

Several important issues must be considered when looking at errors. First, make sure you are not double-counting errors. Double-counting happens when you assign more than one error to the same event. For example, assume you are counting errors in a password field. If a user typed an extra character in the password, you could count that as an "extra character" error, but you shouldn't also count it as an "incorrect character" error.

Sometimes you need to know more than just an error rate; you need to know *why* different errors are occurring. The best way to do this is by looking at each type of error. Basically, you want to try to code each error by type of error. Coding should be based on the various types of errors that occurred. Continuing with the password example, the types of errors might include "missing character," "transposed characters," "extra character," and so on. Or at a higher level, you might have "navigation error," "selection error," "interpretation error," and so on. Once you have coded each error, you can run frequencies on the error type for each task to better understand exactly where the problems lie. This will also help improve the efficiency with which you collect the error data.

In some cases, an error is the same as failing to complete a task—for example, on a login page. If no errors occur while logging in, it is the same as task success. If an error occurs, it is the same as task failure. In this case, it might be easier to report errors as task failure. It's not so much a data issue as it is a presentation issue. It's important to make sure your audience clearly understands your metrics.

## 4.4 EFFICIENCY

Time-on-task is often used as a measure of efficiency, but another way to measure efficiency is to look at the amount of effort required to complete a task. This is typically done by measuring the number of actions or steps that participants took in performing each task. An action can take many forms, such as clicking a link on a web page, pressing a button on a microwave oven or a mobile phone, or flipping a switch on an aircraft. Each action a participant performs represents a certain amount of effort. The more actions taken by a participant, the more effort involved. In most products, the goal is to minimize the number of discrete actions required to complete a task, thereby minimizing the amount of effort.

What do we mean by effort? There are at least two types of effort: cognitive and physical. Cognitive effort involves finding the right place to perform an action (e.g., finding a link on a web page), deciding what action is necessary (should I click this link?), and interpreting the results of the action. Physical effort involves the physical activity required to take action, such as moving your mouse, inputting text on a keyboard, turning on a switch, and many others.

Efficiency metrics work well if you are concerned with not only the time it takes to complete a task but also the amount of cognitive and physical effort involved. For example, if you are designing an automobile navigation system, you need to make sure that it does not take much effort to interpret its navigation directions, since the driver's attention must be focused on the road. It would be important to minimize both the physical and cognitive effort to use the navigation system.

### 4.4.1 Collecting and Measuring Efficiency

There are five important points to keep in mind when collecting and measuring efficiency.

*Identify the action(s) to be measured:* For websites, mouse clicks or page views are common actions. For software, it might be mouse clicks or keystrokes. For appliances or consumer electronics, it could be button presses. Regardless of the product being evaluated, you should have a clear idea of all the possible actions.

*Define the start and end of an action:* You need to know when an action begins and ends. Sometimes the action is very quick, such as a press of a button, but other actions can take much longer. An action may be more passive in nature, such as looking at a web page. Some actions have a very clear start and end, whereas other actions are less defined.

*Count the actions:* You must be able to count the actions. Actions must happen at a pace that can be identified visually or, if they are too fast, by an automated system. Try to avoid having to review hours of videotape to collect efficiency metrics.

*Actions must be meaningful:* Each action should represent an incremental increase in cognitive and/or physical effort. The more actions, the more effort. For example, each click of a mouse on a link is almost always an incremental increase in effort.

*Look only at successful tasks:* When measuring efficiency using the number of actions, you should only calculate it for successful tasks. It does not make sense to include task failures. For example, a participant may quit a task after only a few steps when he becomes hopelessly lost. If you used this data, it may look like he performed at the same level of efficiency as another participant who completed the task successfully with the minimum number of steps required.

Once you have identified the actions you want to capture, counting those actions is relatively simple. You can do it manually, such as by counting page views or presses of a button. This will work for fairly simple products, but in most cases it is not practical. Many times a participant is performing these actions at amazing speeds. There may be more than one action every second, so using automated data-collection tools is far preferable.

## 4.4.2 Analyzing and Presenting Efficiency Data

The most common way to analyze and present efficiency metrics is by looking at the number of actions each participant takes to complete a task. Simply calculate an average for each task (by participant) to see how many actions are taken. This analysis is helpful in identifying which tasks required the most amount of effort, and it works well when each task requires about the same number of actions. However, if some tasks are more complicated than others, it may be misleading. It's also important to represent the 95 percent confidence intervals (based on a continuous distribution) for this type of chart.

Shaikh, Baker, and Russell (2004) used an efficiency metric based on number of clicks to accomplish the same task on three different weight-loss sites: Atkins, Jenny Craig, and Weight Watchers. They found that users were significantly more efficient (needed fewer clicks) with the Atkins site than with the Jenny Craig or Weight Watchers site.

### Lostness

Another measure of efficiency sometimes used in studying behavior on the web is called "lostness" (Smith, 1996). Lostness is calculated using three values:

$N$: The number of *different* web pages visited while performing the task

$S$: The *total* number of pages visited while performing the task, counting revisits to the same page

$R$: The *minimum* (optimum) number of pages that must be visited to accomplish the task

Lostness, $L$, is then calculated using the following formula:

$$L = \mathrm{sqrt}[(N/S - 1)^2 + (R/N - 1)^2]$$

Consider the example shown in Figure 4.9. In this case, the participant's task is to find something on Product Page C1. Starting on the homepage, the minimum number of page visits ($R$) to accomplish this task is three. On the other hand, Figure 4.10 illustrates the path a particular participant took in getting to that target item. This participant started down some incorrect paths before finally getting to the right place, visiting a total of six different pages ($N$), or a total of eight page visits ($S$). So for this example:

$$N = 6$$
$$S = 8$$
$$R = 3$$

$$L = \mathrm{sqrt}[(6/8 - 1)^2 + (3/6 - 1)^2] = 0.56$$

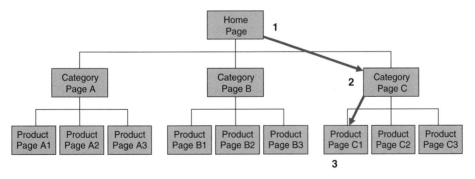

**FIGURE 4.9**

Optimum number of steps (three) to accomplish a task that involves finding a target item on Product Page C1 starting from the homepage.

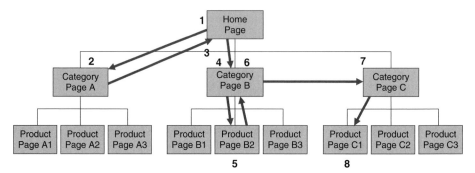

**FIGURE 4.10**

Actual number of steps a participant took in getting to the target item on Product Page C1. Note that each revisit to the same page is counted, giving a total of eight steps.

A perfect lostness score would be 0. Smith (1996) found that participants with a lostness score less than 0.4 did not exhibit any observable characteristics of being lost. On the other hand, participants with a lostness score greater than 0.5 definitely did appear to be lost.

Once you calculate a lostness value, you can easily calculate the average lostness value for each task. The number or percent of participants who exceed the ideal number of actions can also be indicative of the efficiency of the design. For example, you could show that 25 percent of the participants exceeded the ideal or minimum number of steps, and you could break it down even further by saying that 50 percent of the participants completed a task with the minimum number of actions.

### 4.4.3 Efficiency as a Combination of Task Success and Time

Another view of efficiency is that it's a combination of two of the metrics discussed in this chapter: task success and time-on-task. The Common Industry Format (CIF) for Usability Test Reports (NIST, 2001) specifies that the "core measure of efficiency" is the ratio of the task completion rate to the mean time per task. Basically, it expresses task success per unit time. Most commonly, time per task is expressed in minutes, but seconds could be appropriate if the tasks are very short, or even hours if they are unusually long. The unit of time used determines the scale of the results. Your goal is to choose a unit that yields a "reasonable" scale (i.e., one where most of the values fall between 1 and 100 percent).

Table 4.2 shows an example of calculating an efficiency metric, which is simply the ratio of the task completion to the task time in minutes. Of course, higher values of efficiency are better. In the example in the table, participants appear to have been more efficient when performing Tasks 5 and 6 than the other tasks. Figure 4.11 shows how this efficiency metric looks in a chart.

**Table 4.2** Calculating an Efficiency Metric

| Task | Completion Rate Percentage | Task Time (mins) | Percent Efficiency |
|------|----------------------------|------------------|--------------------|
| 1 | 65 | 1.5 | 43 |
| 2 | 67 | 1.4 | 48 |
| 3 | 40 | 2.1 | 19 |
| 4 | 74 | 1.7 | 44 |
| 5 | 85 | 1.2 | 71 |
| 6 | 90 | 1.4 | 64 |
| 7 | 49 | 2.1 | 23 |
| 8 | 33 | 1.3 | 25 |

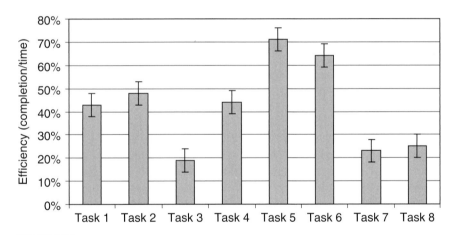

**FIGURE 4.11**

An example showing efficiency as a function of completion rate/time.

A slight variation on this approach to calculating efficiency is to count the number of tasks successfully completed by each participant and divide that by the total time spent by the participant on all the tasks (successful and unsuccessful). This gives you a very straightforward efficiency score for each participant: number of tasks successfully completed per minute (or whatever unit of time you used). If a participant completed ten tasks successfully in a total time of ten minutes, then that participant was successfully completing one task per minute overall. This works best when all participants attempted the same number of tasks and the tasks are relatively comparable in terms of their level of difficulty.

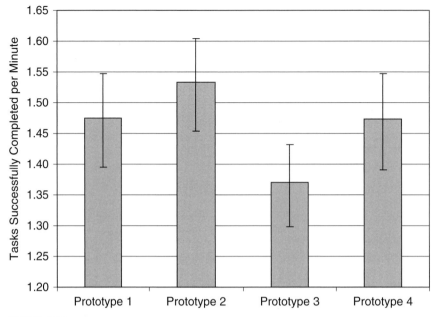

**FIGURE 4.12**

Average number of tasks successfully completed per minute in an online study of four different prototypes of navigation for a website. More than 200 participants attempted 20 tasks for each prototype. Participants using Prototype 2 were significantly more efficient (i.e., completed more tasks per minute) than those using Prototype 3.

Figure 4.12 shows the data from an online study comparing four different navigation prototypes for a website. This was a between-subjects study, in which each participant used only one of the prototypes, but all participants were asked to perform the same 20 tasks. More than 200 participants used each prototype. We were able to count the number of tasks successfully completed by each participant and divide that by the total time that participant spent. The averages of these (and the 95 percent confidence intervals) are shown in Figure 4.12.

## 4.5 LEARNABILITY

Most products, especially new ones, require some amount of learning. Usually learning does not happen in an instant but occurs over time as experience increases. Experience is based on the amount of time spent using a product and the variety of tasks performed. Learning is sometimes quick and painless, but it is at other times quite arduous and time consuming. Learnability is the extent to which something can be learned. It can be measured by looking at how much time and effort are required to become proficient with something. We believe that learnability is an important usability metric that does not receive as much attention as it should. It's an essential metric if you need to know how someone develops proficiency with a product over time.

Consider the following example. Assume you're a usability specialist who has been asked to evaluate a time-keeping application for employees within the organization. You could go into the lab and test with ten participants, giving each one a set of core tasks. You might measure task success, time-on-task, errors, and even overall satisfaction. Using these metrics will allow you to get some sense of the usability of the application.

Although these metrics are useful, they can also be misleading. Because the use of a time-keeping application is not a one-time event, but happens with some degree of frequency, learnability is very important. What really matters is how much time and effort are required to become *proficient* using the time-keeping application. Yes, there may be some initial obstacles when first using the application, but what really matters is "getting up to speed." It's quite common in usability studies to only look at a participant's initial exposure to something, but sometimes it's more important to look at the amount of effort needed to become proficient.

Learning can happen over a short period of time or over longer periods of time. When learning happens over a short period of time, the participant tries out different strategies to complete the tasks. A short period of time might be several minutes, hours, or days. For example, if participants have to submit their time-sheets every day using a time-keeping application, they try to quickly develop some type of mental model about how the application works. Memory is not a big factor in learnability; it is more about adapting strategies to maximize efficiency. Within a few hours or days, maximum efficiency is hopefully achieved.

Learning can also happen over a longer time period, such as weeks, months, or years. This is the case where there are significant gaps in time between each use. For example, if you only fill out an expense report every few months, learnability can be a significant challenge because you may have to relearn the application each time you use it. In this situation, memory is very important. The more time there is between experiences with the product, the greater the reliance on memory.

## 4.5.1  Collecting and Measuring Learnability Data

Collecting and measuring learnability data are basically the same as they are for the other performance metrics, but you're collecting the data at multiple times. Each instance of collecting the data is considered a trial. A trial might be every five minutes, every day, or once a month. The time between trials, or when you collect the data, is based on expected frequency of use.

The first decision is which types of metric you want to use. Learnability can be measured using almost any performance metric over time, but the most common are those that focus on efficiency, such as time-on-task, errors, number of steps, or task success per minute. As learning occurs, you expect to see efficiency improve.

After you decide which metrics to use, you need to decide how much time to allow between trials. What do you do when learning occurs over a very long time? What if users interact with a product once every week, month, or even year? The ideal situation would be to bring the same participants into the lab every week, month, or even year. In many cases, this is not very practical. The developers and the business sponsors might not be very pleased if you told them the study will take three years to complete. A more realistic approach is to bring in the same participants over a much shorter time span and acknowledge the limitation in the data. Here are a few alternatives:

*Trials within the same session.* The participant performs the task, or set of tasks, one right after the other, with no breaks in between. This is very easy to administer, but it does not take into account significant memory loss.

*Trials within the same session but with breaks between tasks.* The break might be a distracter task or anything that might promote forgetting. This is fairly easy to administer, but it tends to make each session relatively long.

*Trials between sessions.* The participant performs the same tasks over multiple sessions, with at least one day in between. This may be the least practical, but most realistic, if the product is used sporadically over an extended period of time.

### 4.5.2 Analyzing and Presenting Learnability Data

The most common way to analyze and present learnability data is by examining a specific performance metric (such as time-on-task, number of steps, or number of errors) by trial for each task or aggregated across all tasks. This will show you how that performance metric changes as a function of experience, as illustrated in Figure 4.13. You could aggregate all the tasks together and represent them as a single line of data, or you could look at each task as separate lines of data. This can help to determine how the learnability of different tasks compares, but it can also make the chart harder to interpret.

The first aspect of the chart you should notice is the slope of the line(s). Ideally, the slope (sometimes called the learning curve) is fairly flat and low on the *y*-axis (in the case of errors, time-on-task, number of steps, or any other metric where a smaller number is better). If you want to determine whether a statistically significant difference between the learning curves (or slopes) exists, you need to perform an analysis of variance and see if there is a main effect of trial.

You should also notice the point of *asymptote*, or essentially where the line starts to flatten out. This is the point at which a participant has learned as much as she can and there is very little room for improvement. Project team members are

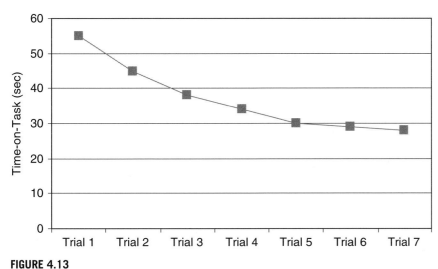

**FIGURE 4.13**

An example of how to present learnability data based on time-on-task.

always interested in how long it will take someone to reach maximum performance.

Finally, you should look at the difference between the highest and lowest values on the *y*-axis. This will tell you how much learning must occur to reach maximum performance. If the gap is small, users will be able to quickly learn the product. If the gap is large, users may take quite some time to become proficient with the product. One easy way to analyze the gap between the highest and lowest scores is by looking at the ratio of the two. Here is an example:

- If the average time on the first trial is 80 seconds and on the last trial is 60 seconds, the ratio shows that participants are initially taking 1.3 times longer.

- If the average number of errors on the first trial is 2.1 and on the last trial is 0.3, the ratio shows a 7 times improvement from the first trial to the last trial.

It may be helpful to look at how many trials are needed to reach maximum performance. This is a good way to characterize the amount of learning required to become proficient in using the product.

In some cases you might want to compare learnability across different conditions, as shown in Figure 4.14. In this study (Tullis, Mangan, & Rosenbaum, 2007), they were interested in how speed (efficiency) of entering a password changed over time using different types of on-screen keyboards. As you can see from the data, there is an improvement from the first trial to the second trial, but then the times flatten out pretty quickly. Also, all the on-screen keyboards were significantly slower than the control condition, which was a real keyboard.

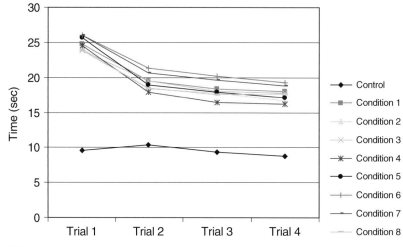

**FIGURE 4.14**

Looking at the learnability of different types of on-screen keyboards.

### 4.5.3 Issues to Consider When Measuring Learnability

Two of the key issues to address when measuring learnability are (1) what should be considered a trial and (2) how many trials to include.

#### *What Is a Trial?*

In some situations learning is continuous. This means that the user is interacting with the product fairly continuously without any significant breaks in time. Memory is much less a factor in this situation. Learning is more about developing and modifying different strategies to complete a set of tasks. The whole concept of trials does not make much sense for continuous learning. What do you do in this situation? One approach is to take measurements at specified time intervals. For example, you may need to take measurements every 5 minutes, every 15 minutes, or every hour.

In one usability study we conducted, we wanted to evaluate the learnability of a new suite of applications that would be used many times every day. We started by bringing the participants into the lab for their first exposure to the applications and their initial tasks. They then went back to their regular jobs and began using the applications to do their normal work. We brought them back into the lab one month later and had them perform basically the same tasks again (with minor changes in details) while we took the same performance measures. Finally, we brought them back one more time after another month and repeated the procedure. In this way, we were able to look at learnability over a two-month period.

#### *Number of Trials*

How many trials do you need? Obviously there must be at least two, but in most cases there should be at least three or four. Sometimes it's difficult to predict where in the sequence of trials the most learning will take place, or even *if* it will take place. In this situation, you should err on the side of more trials than you think you might need to reach stable performance.

## 4.6  SUMMARY

Performance metrics are powerful tools to evaluate the usability of any product. They are the cornerstone of usability and can inform key decisions, such as whether a new product is ready to launch. Performance metrics are always based on participants' behavior rather than what they say. There are five general types of performance metrics.

1. *Task success* metrics are used when you are interested in whether participants are able to complete tasks using the product. Sometimes you might only be interested in whether a user is successful or not based on a strict set of criteria (binary success). Other times you might be interested in defining different levels of success based on the degree of completion, the experience in finding an answer, or the quality of the answer given.

2. *Time-on-task* is helpful when you are concerned about how quickly users can perform tasks with the product. You might look at the time it takes all participants to complete a task, a subset of participants, or the proportion of participants who can complete a task within a desired time limit.

3. *Errors* are a useful measure based on the number of mistakes made while attempting to complete a task. A task might have a single error opportunity or multiple error opportunities, and some types of errors may be more important than others.

4. *Efficiency* is a way of evaluating the amount of effort (cognitive and physical) required to complete a task. Efficiency is often measured by the number of steps or actions required to complete a task or by the ratio of the task success rate to the average time per task.

5. *Learnability* involves looking at how any efficiency metric changes over time. Learnability is useful if you want to examine how and when participants reach proficiency in using a product.

# Issues-Based Metrics

Most usability professionals probably consider identifying usability issues and providing design recommendations the most important part of their job. A usability issue might involve confusion around a particular term or piece of content, method of navigation, or just not noticing something that should be noticed. These types of issues, and many others, are typically identified as part of an iterative process in which designs are being evaluated and improved. This process provides tremendous value to product design and is the cornerstone of the usability profession.

Usability issues are generally thought of as purely qualitative. They typically include a description of a problem one or more participants experienced and, in many cases, an assessment of the underlying cause of the problem. Most usability professionals also include specific recommendations for remedying the problem, and some usability professionals report positive findings (i.e., something that worked particularly well).

Most usability professionals don't strongly associate metrics with usability issues. This may be because of the gray areas in identifying issues or because identifying issues is part of an iterative design process, and metrics are perceived as adding no value. However, not only is it possible to measure usability issues, but doing so also adds value in product design while not slowing down the iterative process.

In this chapter we review some simple metrics around usability issues. We will also discuss different ways of identifying usability issues, prioritizing the importance of different types of issues, and factors you need to think about when measuring usability issues.

## 5.1 IDENTIFYING USABILITY ISSUES

Identifying usability issues can be easy or difficult and everything in between. Sometimes the problems that participants encounter are so obvious that the issues practically punch you in the face. Other times usability issues are much more **99** subtle and require careful observation. At the highest level, three things help to identify usability issues:

*Understanding what is (and isn't) an issue.* The more issues you've observed over the course of your professional career, the easier it is to know which issues are real and which are not. This is the value of being a usability expert.

*Knowing both the product and the usability questions that arise.* The better you know the product, the easier it is to know when someone has trouble with it. When you know what to look for, spotting an issue is much easier.

*Being very observant of participant behavior.* Listen carefully with an open mind and observe different types of behavior, such as facial expressions and body language. The more you pay attention, the easier it is to spot a usability issue.

## 5.2  WHAT IS A USABILITY ISSUE?

What do we mean by usability issues? There's no simple definition, so perhaps the best way to characterize them is to give some examples:

- Anything that prevents task completion
- Anything that takes someone "off-course"
- Anything that creates some level of confusion
- Anything that produces an error
- Not seeing something that should be noticed
- Assuming something is correct when it is not
- Assuming a task is complete when it is not
- Performing the wrong action
- Misinterpreting some piece of content
- Not understanding the navigation

A key point to consider in defining usability issues is how they will be used. The most common use is in an iterative design process focused on improving the product. In that context, the most useful issues are those that point to possible improvements in the product. In other words, it helps if issues are reasonably actionable. If they don't directly point to a part of the interface that was causing a problem, they should at least give you some hint of where to begin looking. For example, we once saw an issue in a usability test report that said, "The mental model of the application does not match the user's mental model." And that was it. Although this may be an interesting observation in some theoretical sense, it does very little to guide designers and developers in addressing the issue.

On the other hand, consider an issue like this: "Many participants were confused by the top-level navigation menu, often jumping around from one section to another, trying to find what they were looking for." Particularly if this issue is followed by a variety of detailed examples describing what happened, it could be very helpful. It tells you where to start looking (the top-level navigation), and the more detailed examples may help focus on some possible solutions. Molich, Jeffries, and Dumas (2007) conducted an interesting study of usability recommendations and ways to make them more useful and usable.

Of course, not all usability issues should be avoided. Some usability issues are positive, such as aspects of a product that exceed a user's expectation for ease of use, efficiency, or satisfaction. These are sometimes called usability "findings," since the term *issues* often has negative connotations. Here are some examples of positive findings:

- Supporting the user in completing a complex transaction without any confusion and in the most efficient way possible
- Anticipating a user's needs at every step of a process
- Educating a user without any effort involved
- Displaying complex information in a clear, simple format that users can easily understand

The main reason for reporting positive findings, in addition to providing some positive reinforcement for the project team, is to make sure that these aspects of the interface don't get "broken" in future design iterations.

## 5.2.1 Real Issues versus False Issues

One of the most difficult parts of any usability professional's job is determining which usability issues are real and which are merely an aberration. Obvious issues are those that most, if not at all, participants encounter. For example, it may be obvious when participants select the wrong option from a poorly worded menu, get taken down the wrong path, and then spend a significant amount of time looking for their target in the wrong part of the application. These are the "no-brainer" issues that are easy for almost anyone to identify.

Some usability issues are much less obvious, or it's not completely clear whether something is a real issue. For example, what if only 1 out of 10 participants expresses some confusion around a specific piece of content or terminology on a website? Or if only 1 out of 12 participants doesn't notice something she should have? At some point the usability specialist must decide whether what he observed is likely to be repeatable with a larger population. In these situations, ask whether the participant's behavior, thought process, perception, or decisions during the task were *logical*. In other words, is there a consistent story or reasoning behind her actions or thoughts? If so, then it may be an issue even if only one participant encountered it. On the other hand, no apparent rhyme or reason behind the behavior may be evident. If the participant can't explain why he did what he did, and it only happened once, then it's likely to be idiosyncratic and should probably be ignored.

For example, assume that you observed one participant click on a link on a web page that started him down the wrong path for accomplishing the task. At the end of the task, you might ask him why he clicked on that link. If he says that he clicked on it simply because it was there in front of him, you might discount this as a false issue. On the other hand, if he says that the wording of the link made it seem like a reasonable place to begin the task, it may be a genuine issue.

## 5.3  HOW TO IDENTIFY AN ISSUE

The most common way to identify usability issues is during a study in which you are directly interacting with a participant. This might be in person or over the phone using remote testing technology. A less common way to identify usability issues is through some automated techniques such as an online study. This is where you don't have an opportunity to directly observe participants but only have access to their behavioral and self-reported data. Identifying issues through this type of data is more challenging but still quite possible.

Possible usability issues might be predicted beforehand and tracked during test sessions. But be careful that you're really *seeing* the issues and not just finding them because you expected to. Your job is certainly easier when you know what to look for, but you might also miss other issues that you never considered. In our testing, we typically have an idea of what to look for, but we also try to keep an open mind to spot the surprise issues. There's no "right" approach; it all depends on the goals of the evaluation. When evaluating products that are in an early conceptual stage, it's more likely that you don't have preset ideas about what the usability issues are. As the product is further refined, you may have a clearer idea of what specific issues you're looking for.

---

**THE ISSUES YOU EXPECT MAY NOT BE THE ONES YOU FIND**

One of the earliest sets of guidelines for designing software interfaces was published by Apple (1982). It was called the *Apple IIe Design Guidelines,* and it contained a fascinating story of an early series of usability tests Apple conducted. They were working on the design of a program called *Apple Presents Apple,* which was a demonstration program for customers to use in computer stores. One part of the interface to which the designers paid little attention was asking users whether their monitor was monochrome or color. The initial design of the question was "Are you using a black-and-white monitor?" (They had predicted that users might have trouble with the word *monochrome.*) In the first usability test, they found that a majority of the participants who used a monochrome monitor answered this question incorrectly because their monitor actually displayed text in green, not white!

What followed was a series of hilarious iterations involving questions such as "Does your monitor display multiple colors?" or "Do you see more than one color on the screen?"—all of which kept failing for some participants. In desperation, they were considering including a developer with every computer just to answer this question, but then they finally hit on a question that worked: "Do the words above appear in several different colors?" In short, the issues you expect may not be the issues you find.

### 5.3.1 **In-Person Studies**

The best way to facilitate identifying usability issues during an in-person study is using a think-aloud protocol. This involves having participants verbalize their thoughts as they are working through the tasks. Typically, the participants are reporting what they are doing, what they are trying to accomplish, how confident they are about their decisions, their expectations, and why they performed certain actions. Essentially, it's a stream of consciousness focusing on their interaction with the product. During a think-aloud protocol, you might observe the following:

- Verbal expressions of confusion, frustration, dissatisfaction, pleasure, or surprise
- Verbal expressions of confidence or indecision about a particular action that may be right or wrong
- Participants *not* saying or doing something that they should have done or said
- Nonverbal behaviors such as facial expressions and/or eye movements

Any of these might point to usability issues.

### 5.3.2 **Automated Studies**

Identifying usability issues through automated studies requires careful data collection. The key is to allow participants to enter verbatim comments at a page or task level. In most automated studies, several data points are collected for each task: success, time, ease-of-use rating, and verbatim comments. The verbatim comments are the best way to understand any possible issues.

One way to collect verbatim comments is to require the participant to provide a comment at the conclusion of each task. This might yield some interesting results, but it doesn't always yield the best results. An alternative that seems to work better is to make the verbatim comment conditional. If the participant provides a low ease-of-use score (e.g., not one of the two highest ratings), then she is asked to provide feedback about why she rated the task that way. Having a more pointed question usually yields more specific, actionable comments. For example, participants might say that they were confused about a particular term or that they couldn't find the link they wanted on a certain page. This type of task-level feedback is usually more valuable than one question after they complete all the tasks (post-study).

### 5.3.3 **When Issues Begin and End**

When does a usability issue begin? It might start with some initial confusion or deviation away from ideal behavior. For example, a participant may express some question about a link on a website, click on it, and then get taken down a black hole. In this case, the issue really started when the question or doubt first arose within the participant's mind. In another situation, a participant may voice some confusion about what button to press on a remote control. In many cases the participant is not even aware that he is experiencing an issue until the very end, when he discovers that he didn't get the answer or result he was looking for. For example, a user might be going along a series of steps to install some software, only to realize at the end of the process that she made a mistake. In this case, the issue began at the point of departure from the ideal process.

The next obvious question is, when does an issue end? There are a few situations that typically indicate the end of an issue. In one common situation, an issue ends with task failure. The participant either realizes that she got the wrong answer or gives up. This is when the participant throws up her hands and the facilitator says, "Okay, let's move on to the next task." Other usability issues end when another one begins—in other words, a different problem arises and takes the place of the original issue. The new problem is sufficiently different from the original problem, and it has become the driving force behind her current behavior. Finally, in some situations, the participant recovers from the issue. This is when a participant says, "Oh, *now* I get it!" They identified the source of the confusion and might even go back several steps and show you where they were confused and why. This is always enlightening, since it gives you direct access to their thoughts about what originally precipitated the issue. An issue might also end when it's no longer relevant. The participant either recovered in some way or it just became insignificant.

### 5.3.4 Granularity

One of the most important decisions when identifying usability issues is how detailed or granular they should be. High granularity is useful for identifying very specific problems but makes it easy to miss the big picture. This level of detail usually focuses on one particular behavior at a specific point in time. For example, a user might fail to notice a particular link on a web page or might misinterpret a specific field label on a form. In either case, the issue is described in a fairly detailed way.

When you're looking for usability issues with less granularity, it's easier to see the big picture. For example, you might state that a user often jumped around from one section of the site to another in search of information and was obviously confused about the overall organization of the site. Or maybe the information density was so high on many of the pages that the user missed many of the links.

Identifying issues at a granular level or at a high level can both be appropriate and useful. Just keep in mind the audience and the goals of the study. If the product is at an early stage of design, capturing the big issues is probably more important. If the design is fairly well developed, then a more detailed examination of the issues may be more helpful.

### 5.3.5 Multiple Observers

There is power in numbers. Whenever possible, try to have multiple observers on hand to identify usability issues—ideally at least two or three observers. This is particularly true when you are the one moderating the sessions. Things happen quickly in a usability session, and the moderator must be focused on the partici-pant rather than on taking notes. Some studies have shown that more observers identify more usability issues than fewer observers (Hertzum, Jacobsen, & Molich, 2002; Molich et al., 1998). Of course, there are some situations where it's not practical to have more than one observer. In this case, it's helpful to review videos of the sessions to capture any issues that you might have originally missed. This is particularly important when you're a one-person team. If you're evaluating a product alone and you don't have access to audio or video recordings, make sure you take good notes!

## 5.4 SEVERITY RATINGS

Not all usability issues are the same: Some are more serious than others. Some usability issues annoy or frustrate users, whereas others cause them to make the wrong decisions or lose data. Obviously, these two different types of usability issues have a very different impact on the user experience, and severity ratings are a useful way to deal with them.

Severity ratings help focus attention on the issues that really matter. There's nothing more frustrating for a developer or business analyst than being handed a list of 82 usability issues that all need to be fixed immediately. By prioritizing usability issues, you're much more likely to have a positive impact on the design, not to mention lessening the likelihood of making enemies with the rest of the design and development team.

The severity of usability issues can be classified in many ways, but most severity rating systems can be boiled down to two different types. In one type of rating system, severity is based purely on the impact on the user experience: The worse the user experience, the higher the severity rating. A second type of severity rating system tries to bring in multiple dimensions or factors. These dimensions usually include impact on the user experience, predicted frequency of use, and impact on the business goals. In this case, the highest severity rating would mean that the participant failed a task that is frequently done and is critical to the business. Think of someone who wants to buy something on a website, finds the product, and then fails at the actual purchase!

### 5.4.1 Severity Ratings Based on the User Experience

Many severity ratings are based solely on the impact on the user experience. These rating systems are easy to implement and provide very useful information. They usually have between three and five levels—often something like low, medium, and high severity. In some rating systems there is a "catastrophe" level, which is essentially a showstopper (delaying product launch or release—Nielsen, 1993). This, of course, is above and beyond a "high," which is normally reserved for the biggest usability issues but might not necessarily delay the launch of the product. Other severity rating systems have a "cosmetic" rating (Nielsen, 1993; Rubin, 1994). These are superficial usability issues that can be addressed if time and budget allow. For example, some participants might comment on the colors or other aspects of the visual design.

Wilson (1999) proposes a five-level rating system: level 5 (minimal error), level 4 (minor but irritating), level 3 (moderate: waste of time but no loss of data), level 2 (severe problem causing loss of data), and level 1 (catastrophic error, causing loss of data or damage to hardware/software). He also suggests that your severity rating system should be consistent with the bug-tracking system used in your organization. This will help with adoption of the system, as well as with tracking and fixing each of the issues.

When choosing a severity rating system, it's important to look at your organization and the product you are evaluating. Often, a three-level system works well in many situations:

*Low:* Any issue that annoys or frustrates participants but does not play a role in task failure. These are the types of issues that may lead someone off course, but he still recovers and completes the task. This issue may only reduce efficiency and/or satisfaction a small amount, if any.

*Medium:* Any issue that contributes to but does not directly prevent task failure. Participants often develop workarounds to get to what they need. These issues have an impact on effectiveness and most likely efficiency and satisfaction.

*High:* Any issue that directly leads to task failure. Basically, there is no way to encounter this issue and still complete the task. This type of issue has a significant impact on effectiveness, efficiency, and satisfaction.

## 5.4.2 Severity Ratings Based on a Combination of Factors

Severity rating systems that use a combination of factors usually are based on the impact on the user experience coupled with frequency of use and/or impact on the business goals. Nielsen (1993) provides an easy way to combine the impact on the user experience and frequency of use on severity ratings (Figure 5.1). This severity rating system is intuitive and easy to explain.

Rubin (1994) offers a different way of looking at the combination of severity and the frequency of occurrence of issues. First, he assigns a *severity rating* on a 4-point scale (1 = irritant, 2 = moderate, 3 = severe, 4 = unusable). Next, he assigns a *frequency of occurrence,* also on a 4-point scale (1 = occurs < 10 percent of the time; 2 = occurs 11 to 50 percent of the time; 3 = occurs 51 to 89 percent of the time; 4 = occurs more than 90 percent of the time). He then simply adds the two scores to arrive at a criticality score between 2 and 8. This approach gives a numeric severity score that may be helpful when combined with other types of data.

| | Few users experiencing a problem | Many users experiencing a problem |
|---|---|---|
| Small impact on the user experience | Low severity | Medium severity |
| Large impact on the user experience | Medium severity | High severity |

**FIGURE 5.1**

Severity rating scale taking into account problem frequency and impact on the user experience. *Source*: Adapted from Nielsen (1993).

Building on Rubin's method for combining different types of scores, it's possible to add a third dimension based on *importance to the business goals*. For example, you might combine three different 3-point scales:

- Impact on the user experience (1 = low, 2 = medium, 3 = high)
- Predicted frequency of occurrence (1 = low, 2 = medium, 3 = high)
- Impact on the business goals (1 = low, 2 = medium, 3 = high)

By adding up the three scores, you now have an overall severity rating ranging from 3 to 9. Of course, a certain amount of guesswork is involved in coming up with the levels, but at least all three factors are being taken into consideration.

## 5.4.3 Using a Severity Rating System

Once you have settled upon a severity rating system, you still need to consider a few more things. First, be consistent: Decide on one severity rating system, and use it for all your studies. By using the same severity rating system, you will be able to make meaningful comparisons across studies, as well as help train your audience on the differences between the severity levels. The more your audience internalizes the system, the more persuasive you will be in promoting design solutions.

Second, clearly communicate what each level means. Provide examples of each level as much as possible. This is particularly important for other usability specialists on your team who might also be assigning ratings. It's important that developers, designers, and business analysts understand each severity level. The more the "nonusability" audience understands each level, the easier it will be to influence design solutions for the highest-priority issues.

Third, try to have more than one usability specialist assign severity ratings to each issue. One approach that works well is to have the usability specialists independently assign severity ratings to each of the issues, then discuss any of the issues where they gave different ratings and try to agree on the appropriate level.

Finally, there's some debate about whether usability issues should be tracked as part of a larger bug-tracking system (Wilson & Coyne, 2001). Wilson argues that it is essential to track usability issues as part of a bug-tracking system because it makes the usability issues more visible, lends more credibility to the usability team, and makes it more likely that the issues will be remedied. Coyne suggests that usability issues, and the methods to fix them, are much more complex than typical bugs. Therefore, it makes more sense to track usability issues in a separate database. Either way, it's important to track the usability issues and make sure they are addressed.

### 5.4.4 Some Caveats about Severity Ratings

Not everyone believes in severity ratings. Kuniavsky (2003) suggests letting your audience provide their own severity ratings. He argues that only those who are deeply familiar with the business model will be able to determine the relative priority of each usability issue.

Bailey (2005) strongly argues against severity rating systems altogether. He cites several studies that show there is very little agreement between usability specialists on the severity rating for any given usability issue (Catani & Biers, 1998; Cockton & Woolrych, 2001; Jacobsen, Hertzum, & John, 1998). All of these studies generally show that there is very little overlap in what different usability specialists identify as a high-severity issue. Obviously, this is troubling given that many important decisions may be based on severity ratings.

Hertzum et al. (2002) highlight a potentially different problem in assigning severity ratings. In their research they found that when multiple usability specialists are working as part of the same team, each usability specialist rates the issues she personally identifies as more severe than issues identified by the other usability specialists on their own team. This is known as an evaluator effect, and it poses a significant problem in relying on severity ratings by a single usability professional.

So where does this leave us? We believe that severity ratings are not perfect, but they still serve a useful purpose. They help direct attention to at least some of the most pressing needs. Without severity ratings, the designers or developers will simply make their own priority list, perhaps based on what's easiest to implement. Even though there is some subjectivity involved in assigning severity ratings, they're better than nothing. Most key stakeholders understand that there is more art than science involved, and they interpret the severity ratings within this broader context.

## 5.5 ANALYZING AND REPORTING METRICS FOR USABILITY ISSUES

Once you've identified and prioritized the usability issues, it's helpful to do some analyses of the issues themselves. This lets you derive some metrics related to the usability issues. Exactly how you do this will largely depend on the type of usability questions you have in mind. Three general questions can be answered by looking at metrics related to usability issues:

- How is the overall usability of the product? This is helpful if you simply want to get an overall sense of how the product did.

- Is the usability improving with each design iteration? Focus on this question when you need to know how the usability is changing with each new design iteration.

- Where should I focus my efforts to improve the design? The answer to this question is useful when you need to decide where to focus your resources.

All of the analyses we will examine can be done with or without severity ratings. Severity ratings simply add a way to filter the issues. Sometimes it's helpful to focus on the high-severity issues. Other times it might make more sense to treat all the usability issues equally.

### 5.5.1 Frequency of Unique Issues

The most common way to measure usability issues is to simply count the unique issues. Analyzing the frequency of unique issues is most useful in an iterative design process when you want some basic data about how the usability is changing with each iteration. For example, you might observe that the number of issues decreased from 24 to 12 to 4 through the first three design iterations. These data are obviously trending in the right direction, but they're not necessarily iron-clad evidence that the design is significantly better. Perhaps the four remaining issues are so much bigger than all the rest that without addressing them, everything else is unimportant. Therefore, we suggest a thorough analysis and explanation of the issues when presenting this type of data.

Keep in mind that this frequency represents the number of *unique issues*, not the *total number of issues* encountered by all participants. For example, assume Participant A encountered ten issues, whereas Participant B encountered 14 issues, but 6 of those issues were the same as those from Participant A. If A and B were the only participants, the total number of unique issues would be 18 (10 + 14 − 6). Figure 5.2 shows an example of how to present the frequency of usability issues when comparing more than one design.

The same type of analysis can be performed using usability issues that have been assigned a severity rating. For example, if you have classified your usability issues into three levels (low, medium, and high severity), you can easily look at the number of issues by each type of severity rating. Certainly the most telling data item would be the change in the number of high-priority issues with each design iteration. Looking at the frequency of usability issues by severity rating, as illustrated in Figure 5.3, can be very informative since it is an indicator of whether the design effort between each iteration is addressing the most important usability issues.

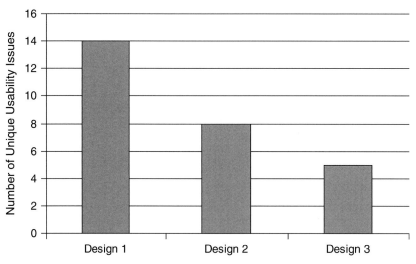

**FIGURE 5.2**

Example data showing the number of unique usability issues by design iteration. Ideally, the number of issues decreases with each new design iteration.

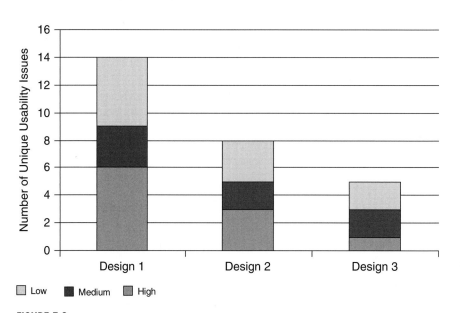

**FIGURE 5.3**

Example data showing the number of unique usability issues by design iteration, categorized by severity rating. The change in the number of high-severity issues is probably of key interest.

### 5.5.2 **Frequency of Issues per Participant**

It can also be informative to look at the number of issues each participant encountered. Over a series of design iterations, you would expect to see this number decreasing along with the total number of unique issues. For example, Figure 5.4 shows the average number of issues encountered by each participant for three design iterations.

Of course, this analysis could also include the average number of issues per participant broken down by severity level. If the average number of issues per participant is not declining over a series of iterations, but the total number of unique issues is declining, then you know there is more consistency in the issues that the participants are encountering. This would indicate that the issues encountered by fewer participants are being fixed whereas those encountered by more participants are not.

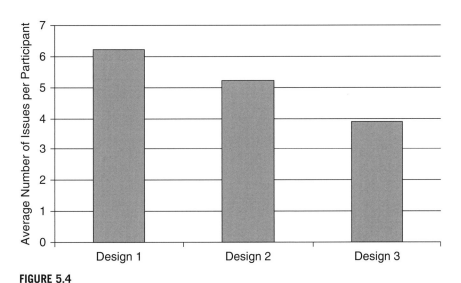

**FIGURE 5.4**

Example data showing the average number of usability issues encountered by participants in each of three usability tests.

### 5.5.3 **Frequency of Participants**

Another useful way to analyze usability issues is to observe the frequency or percentage of participants who encountered a specific issue. For example, you might be interested in whether participants correctly used some new type of navigation element on your website. You report that half of the participants encountered a specific issue in the first design iteration, and only one out of ten encountered the same issue in the second design iteration. This is a useful metric

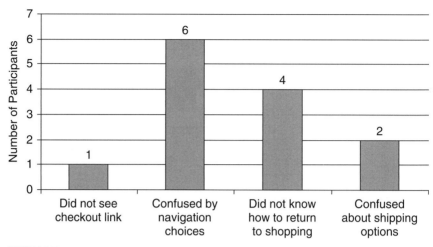

**FIGURE 5.5**

Example data showing the frequency of participants who experienced specific usability issues.

when you need to focus on whether you are improving the usability of specific design elements as opposed to making overall usability improvements.

With this type of analysis, it's important that your criteria for identifying specific issues are consistent between participants and designs. If a description of a specific issue is a bit fuzzy, your data won't mean very much. It's a good idea to explicitly document the issue's exact nature, thereby reducing any interpretation errors across participants or designs. Figure 5.5 shows an example of this type of analysis.

The use of severity ratings with this type of analysis is useful in a couple of ways. First, you could use the severity ratings to focus your analysis only on the high-priority issues. For example, you could report that there are five outstanding high-priority usability issues. Furthermore, the percentage of participants who are experiencing these issues is decreasing with each design iteration. Another form of analysis is to aggregate all the high-priority issues to report the percentage of participants who experienced any high-priority issue. This helps you to see how overall usability is changing with each design iteration, but it is less helpful in determining whether to address a specific usability problem.

### 5.5.4 Issues by Category

Sometimes it's helpful to know where to focus design improvements from a tactical perspective. Perhaps you feel that only certain areas of the product are causing the most usability issues, such as navigation, content, terminology, and so forth. In this situation, it can be useful to aggregate usability issues into broad categories. Simply examine each issue and then categorize it into a type of issue. Then look at the frequencies of issues that fall into each category. Issues can be

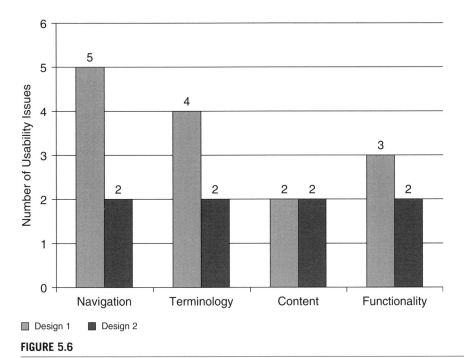

**FIGURE 5.6**

Example data showing the frequency of usability issues categorized by type. Notice that both navigation and terminology issues were improved from the first to the second design iteration.

categorized in many different ways. Just make sure the categorization makes sense to you and your audience, and use a limited number of categories, typically three to eight. If there are too many categories, it won't provide much direction. Figure 5.6 provides an example of usability issues analyzed by category.

## 5.5.5 Issues by Task

Issues can also be analyzed at a task level. You might be interested in which tasks lead to the most issues, and you can report the number of unique issues that occur for each. This will identify the tasks you should focus on for the next design iteration. Alternatively, you could report the frequency of participants who encounter any issue for each task. This will tell you the pervasiveness of a particular issue. The greater the number of issues for each task, the greater the concern should be.

If you have assigned a severity rating to each issue, it might be useful to analyze the frequency of high-priority issues by task. This is particularly effective if you want to focus on a few of the biggest problems and your design efforts are oriented toward specific tasks. This is also helpful if you are comparing different design iterations using the same tasks.

### 5.5.6 Reporting Positive Issues

It's important to report positive issues (e.g., Dumas et al., 2004) for the following reasons:

- Designers and developers should be able to consider you an ally. If you go to them only with problems, it's hard to build any goodwill. In fact, it's better to begin every usability report with at least one positive issue. Starting with a negative issue often sets a somber tone for the rest of the report or presentation.

- You should document positive issues so they can be propagated to other areas of the product as appropriate. It's helpful to know what's working well in the design and to identify other areas that could benefit from a similar solution. It's also important not to mess up the positive aspects across design iterations!

- Reporting positive issues enhances your credibility. It's critical that you are, and appear to be, neutral. If you only report problems, some may question your neutrality.

The analysis and presentation of positive issues are essentially the same as for any other issue. The only unique form of analysis involving positive issues is to calculate a ratio of positive to negative issues. It's questionable whether this is really useful, but some audiences may be interested in it.

## 5.6 CONSISTENCY IN IDENTIFYING USABILITY ISSUES

Much has been written about consistency and bias in identifying and prioritizing usability issues. Unfortunately, the news is not so good. Much of the research shows that there is very little agreement on what a usability issue is or how important it is.

Perhaps the most exhaustive set of studies, called CUE (Comparative Usability Evaluation) was coordinated by Rolf Molich. To date, six separate CUE studies have been conducted, dating back to 1998. Each study was set up in a similar manner. Different teams of usability experts all evaluated the same design. Each team reported their findings, including the identification of the usability issues along with their design recommendations. The first study, CUE-1 (Molich et al., 1998), showed very little overlap in the issues identified. In fact, only 1 out of the 141 issues was identified by all four teams participating in the study, and 128 out of the 141 issues were identified by single teams. Several years later, in CUE-2, the results were no more encouraging: 75 percent of all the issues were reported by only 1 of 9 usability teams (Molich & Dumas, 2006). CUE-4 (Molich & Dumas, 2006) showed similar results: 60 percent of all the issues were identified by only 1 of the 17 different teams participating in the study.

These data certainly do not bode well for the usability profession, but could there be alternative explanations? Some usability professionals have criticized the format of the CUE studies. For example, some have suggested that the teams differed dramatically in terms of professional experience. Others have claimed that the analysis of whether two issues from separate reports were really the same basic issue was too strict: that the criterion for calling two issues the same was set too high.

Tullis (2005) formed two different usability teams from a group of usability professionals who all work together and presumably have relatively consistent usability testing methods. Both teams independently evaluated the same website using a traditional lab test with real end-users (as opposed to an expert evaluation). He found that 38 percent of the usability issues were reported by both teams, 32 percent by one team, and 30 percent by the other team (Figure 5.7). Each team also prioritized the issues (low, medium, and high).

When looking only at the high-severity issues, 88 percent were shared among both teams (Figure 5.8). This is much more encouraging, since it suggests that perhaps many of the issues uniquely identified by each of the teams were the less important ones. Perhaps the bigger the issue, the more likely that it will be observed by different teams.

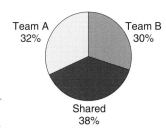

**FIGURE 5.7**

Data showing that 38 percent of the unique usability issues were identified by both teams.

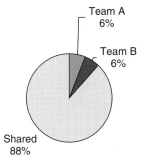

**FIGURE 5.8**

Data showing that 88 percent of the high-priority usability issues were identified by both teams.

## 5.7 BIAS IN IDENTIFYING USABILITY ISSUES

Many different factors can influence how usability issues are identified. Carolyn Snyder (2006) provides a review of many of the ways usability findings might be biased. She concludes that bias cannot be eliminated, but it must be understood. In other words, even though our methods have flaws, they are still useful.

We've distilled the different sources of bias in a usability study into six general categories:

*Participants:* Your participants are critical. Every participant brings a certain level of technical expertise, domain knowledge, and motivation. Some participants may be well targeted, and others may not. Some participants are comfortable in a lab setting, whereas others are not. All of these factors make a big difference in what usability issues you end up discovering.

*Tasks:* The tasks you choose have a tremendous impact on what issues are identified. Some tasks might be well defined with a clear end-state, whereas others might be open-ended, and yet others might be self-generated by each participant. The tasks basically determine what areas of the product are exercised and the ways in which they are exercised. Particularly with a complex product, this can have a major impact on what issues are uncovered.

*Method:* The method of evaluation is critical. Methods might include traditional lab testing or some type of expert review. Other decisions you make are also important, such as how long each session lasts, whether the participant thinks aloud, or how and when you probe.

*Artifact:* The nature of the prototype or product you are evaluating has a huge impact on your findings. The type of interaction will vary tremendously whether it is a paper prototype, functional or semifunctional prototype, or production system.

*Environment:* The physical environment also plays a role. The environment might involve direct interaction with the participant, indirect interaction via a conference call or behind a one-way mirror, or even at someone's home. Other characteristics of the physical environment, such as lighting, seating, observers behind a one-way mirror, and videotaping, can all have an impact on the findings.

*Moderators:* Different moderators will also influence the issues that are observed. A usability professional's experience, domain knowledge, and motivation all play a key role.

An interesting study that sheds some light on these sources of bias was conducted by Lindgaard and Chattratichart (2007). They analyzed the reports from the nine teams in CUE-4 who conducted actual usability tests with real users. They looked at the number of participants in each test, the number of tasks used, and the number of usability issues reported. The number of participants ranged from 5 to 15, the

**AN UNEXPECTED WAY OF BIASING PARTICIPANTS' BEHAVIOR**

One of our funniest experiences in learning how subtle aspects of the environment can impact the identification of usability issues involved a test of a prototype web application. Due to the availability of representative users, we had to set up a makeshift usability lab in a conference room at the participant's location. The participant sat at the conference table along with the moderator. Several of the project team members wanted to observe the sessions, so we agreed to let them sit along the wall as long as they promised not to say anything.

Everything was going fine, but after a while we noticed that some of the participants were showing a similar pattern of behavior: They would reach a page of the prototype that they somehow decided was the right page for their task, but then they couldn't figure out how to complete the task. In fact, it was the right page. Then we figured out what was happening: As the participant was navigating around the prototype trying to find the right page for a task, some of the observers would lean forward, very intently observing. When the participant reached the right page, the observers would lean back in relief, assuming he was almost done. Some of the participants picked up on this, using it as a cue that they had reached the right page! Once we glued the observers to their chairs (not really), this stopped, and we learned that the overriding issue was finding the right page!

number of tasks from 5 to 14, and the number of issues from 20 to 50. Looking across all the reports, a total of 106 unique usability problems categorized as serious or critical were identified. They found no significant correlation between the number of *participants* in the test and the percentage of usability problems found.

On the other hand, they did find a significant correlation between the number of *tasks* used and the percentage of usability problems found ($r = 0.82, p < 0.01$). When looking at the percentage of *new* problems uncovered, the correlation with the number of tasks was even higher ($r = 0.89, p < 0.005$). As Lindgaard and Chattrati-chart concluded, these results suggest "that with careful participant recruitment, investing in wide task coverage is more fruitful than increasing the number of users."

One technique that works well to increase the task coverage in a usability test is to define a core set of tasks that all participants must complete and another set that is derived for each participant. These additional tasks might be selected based on characteristics of the participant (e.g., an existing customer or a prospect), or they might be selected at random. Care must be exercised when making comparisons across participants, since not all participants had the same tasks. In this situation, you may want to limit certain analyses to the core tasks.

## 5.8 NUMBER OF PARTICIPANTS

There has been much debate about how many participants are needed in a usability test to reliably identify usability issues. (See Barnum et al., 2003, for a summary of the debate.) Nearly every usability professional seems to have an opinion. Not only are many different opinions floating around out there, but quite a few compelling studies have been conducted on this very topic. From this research, two different camps have emerged: those who believe that five participants is enough to identify most of the usability issues and those who believe that five is nowhere near enough.

### 5.8.1 Five Participants Is Enough

One camp believes that a majority, or about 80 percent, of usability issues will be observed with the first five participants (Lewis, 1994; Nielsen & Landauer, 1993; Virzi, 1992). This is known as the "magic number 5." One of the most important ways to figure out how many participants are needed in a usability test is to measure $p$, or the probability of a usability issue being detected by a single test participant. It's important to note that this $p$ is different from the $p$-value that is used in tests of significance. The probabilities vary from study to study, but they tend to average around 0.3, or 30 percent. (See Turner, Nielsen, and Lewis, 2002, for a review of different studies.) In the seminal paper, Nielsen and Landauer (1993) found an average probability of 31 percent based on 11 different studies. This basically means that with each participant, about 31 percent of the usability problems are being observed.

Figure 5.9 shows how many issues are observed as a function of the number of participants when the probability of detection is 30 percent. (Notice that this assumes all issues have an equal probability of detection, which may be a big

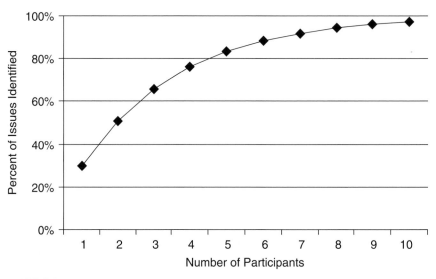

**FIGURE 5.9**

Example showing how many users are required to observe the total number of issues in a usability study, given a probability of detection equal to 30 percent with each participant.

assumption.) As you can see, after the first participant, 30 percent of the problems are detected; after the third participant, about 66 percent of the problems are observed; and after the fifth participant, about 83 percent of the problems have been identified. This claim is backed up not only by this mathematical formula but by anecdotal evidence as well. Many usability professionals only test with five or six participants during an iterative design process. In this situation, it is relatively uncommon to test with more than a dozen, with a few exceptions. If the scope of the product is particularly large or if there are distinctly different audiences, then a strong case can be made for testing with more than five participants.

### 5.8.2  **Five Participants Is *Not* Enough**

More recently, some researchers have challenged this idea of the magic number 5 (Molich et al., 1998; Spool & Schroeder, 2001; Woolrych & Cockton, 2001). Spool and Schroeder (2001) asked participants to purchase various types of products, such as CDs and DVDs, at three different electronics websites. They discovered only 35 percent of the usability issues after the first five participants—far lower than the 80 percent predicted by Nielsen (2000). However, in this study the scope of the websites being evaluated was very large, even though the task of buying something was very well defined. Woolrych and Cockton (2001) discount the assertion that five participants is enough, primarily because it does not take into account individual differences among them.

   The analyses by Lindgaard and Chattratichart (2007) of the nine usability tests from CUE-4 also raise doubts about the magic number 5. They compared the results of two teams, A and H, that both did very well, uncovering 42 and 43 percent, respectively, of the full set of usability problems. Team A used only 6 participants, whereas Team H used 12. At first glance, this might be seen as evidence for the magic number 5, since a team that tested only 6 participants uncovered as many problems as a team that tested 12. But a more detailed analysis reveals a different conclusion. In looking specifically at the overlap of usability issues between just these two reports, they found only 28 percent in common. More than 70 percent of the problems were uncovered by only one of the two teams, ruling out the possibility of the 5-participant rule applying in this case.

### 5.8.3  *Our* **Recommendation**

In our experience, five participants *per significantly different class of user* is usually enough to uncover the most important usability issues. In most of the usability tests we're conducted over the years, regardless of the total number of test participants, we're seen most of the significant issues after the first four or five participants. In fact, it is a rare occurrence when we see a new and significant issue during the fifth or sixth usability session. When we do test more than five participants for a single test, we usually see a major dropoff in attendance from the observers after about the fifth participant. Seeing the same issues over

---

## CALCULATING $p$, OR PROBABILITY OF DETECTION

Calculating the probability of detection is fairly straightforward. Simply line up all the usability issues discovered during the test. Then, for each participant, mark how many of the issues were observed with that participant. Add the total number of issues identified with each participant, and then divide by the total number of issues. Each test participant will have encountered anywhere from 0 to 100 percent of the issues. Then, take the average for all the test participants. This is the overall probability rate for the test. Consider the example shown in this table.

| Participant | Issue 1 | Issue 2 | Issue 3 | Issue 4 | Issue 5 | Issue 6 | Issue 7 | Issue 8 | Issue 9 | Issue 10 | Proportion |
|---|---|---|---|---|---|---|---|---|---|---|---|
| P1 | x |  | x |  | x |  | x | x | x |  | 0.6 |
| P2 | x | x |  | x |  | x |  |  |  |  | 0.4 |
| P3 |  |  | x |  |  | x |  | x | x | x | 0.5 |
| P4 | x | x |  |  | x |  |  | x | x | x | 0.6 |
| P5 |  |  | x | x | x |  |  |  |  |  | 0.3 |
| P6 | x |  |  |  |  | x |  | x | x |  | 0.4 |
| P7 |  | x | x |  | x |  | x | x |  | x | 0.6 |
| P8 | x |  |  | x | x | x | x | x |  |  | 0.7 |
| P9 |  | x | x | x |  | x | x |  | x |  | 0.6 |
| P10 |  | x |  |  | x |  |  |  |  |  | 0.2 |
| Proportion | 0.5 | 0.5 | 0.5 | 0.4 | 0.6 | 0.4 | 0.4 | 0.6 | 0.6 | 0.4 | 0.49 |

Once the average proportion has been determined (0.49 in this case), the next step is to calculate how many users are needed to identify a certain percentage of issues. Use the following formula:

$$1 - (1 - p)^n$$

where $n$ is the number of users.

So if you want to know the proportion of issues that would be identified by a sample of three users:

- $1 - (1 - 0.49)^3$
- $1 - (0.51)^3$
- $1 - 0.133$
- 0.867, or about 87 percent, of the issues would be identified with a sample of three users from this study

---

and over isn't much fun for anyone. From our very unscientific sample, we do seem to find support for the magic number 5.

The magic number 5 has worked well for us but only under the following conditions:

*The scope of the evaluation is fairly limited.* This means we are not doing a product-wide assessment, but rather looking only at a limited set of functions—usually about 5 to 10 tasks and about 20 to 30 web pages.

*The user audience is well defined and represented.* If we pretty much know who we want to test with, and they are well represented in testing, then five is adequate. If we identify more than one unique audience, then we will strive to have about five participants from each user group. Of course, the challenge is knowing when you really do have different user groups. For example, does it matter whether the user is retired? In our experience with websites, sometimes it does and sometimes it doesn't.

## 5.9 SUMMARY

Many usability professionals make their living by identifying usability issues and by providing actionable recommendations for improvement. Providing metrics around usability issues is not commonly done, but it can easily be incorporated into anyone's routine. Measuring usability issues helps you answer some fundamental questions about how good (or bad) the design is, how it is changing with each design iteration, and where to focus resources to remedy the outstanding problems.

You should keep the following points in mind when identifying, measuring, and presenting usability issues.

1. The easiest way to identify usability issues is during an in-person lab study, but it can also be done using verbatim comments in an automated study. The more you understand the domain, the easier it will be to spot the issues. Having multiple observers is very helpful in identifying issues.

2. When trying to figure out whether an issue is real, ask yourself whether there is a consistent story behind the user's thought process and behavior. If the story is reasonable, then the issue is likely to be real.

3. The severity of an issue can be determined in several ways. Severity always should take into account the impact on the user experience. Additional factors, such as frequency of use, impact on the business, and persistence, may also be considered. Some severity ratings are based on a simple high/medium/low rating system. Other systems are number based.

4. Some common ways to measure usability issues are measuring the frequency of unique issues, the percentage of participants who experience a specific issue, and the frequency of issues for different tasks or categories of issue. Additional analysis can be performed on high-severity issues or on how issues change from one design iteration to another.

5. When identifying usability issues, questions about consistency and bias may arise. Bias can come from many sources, and there can be a general lack of agreement on what constitutes an issue. Therefore, it's important to work collaboratively as a team, focusing on high-priority issues, and to understand how different sources of bias impact conclusions. Maximizing task coverage may be key.

# Self-Reported Metrics

6

Perhaps the most obvious way to learn about the usability of something is to ask users to tell you about their experience with it. But exactly how to ask them so that you get good data is not so obvious. The questions you might ask could take on many forms, including various kinds of rating scales, lists of attributes that the participants could choose from, and open-ended questions like "List the top three things you liked the most about this application." Some of the attributes you might ask about include overall satisfaction, ease of use, effectiveness of navigation, awareness of certain features, clarity of terminology, visual appeal, and many others. But the common feature of all of these is that you're asking the participant for information, which is why we think *self-reported metrics* is the best term to use.

Two other terms sometimes used to describe this kind of data include *subjective data* and *preference data*. *Subjective* is used as a counterpart to *objective*, which is often used to describe the performance data from a usability study. But this implies that there's a lack of objectivity to the data you're collecting. Yes, it may be subjective to each participant who's providing the input, but from the perspective of the usability specialist, it is completely objective. Similarly, *preference* is often used as a counterpart to *performance*. Although there's nothing obviously wrong with that, we believe that preference implies a choice of one option over another, which is often not the case in usability studies.

## 6.1 IMPORTANCE OF SELF-REPORTED DATA

Self-reported data give you the most important information about users' *perception* of the system and their interaction with it. At an emotional level, the data may even tell you something about how the users *feel* about the system. In many situations, these kinds of reactions are the main thing that you care about. Even if it takes users forever to perform something with a system, if the experience makes them happy, that may be the only thing that matters.

**123**

Your goal is to make the users think of your product first. For example, when deciding what travel-planning website to use for an upcoming vacation, users are more likely to think of the site that they liked the last time they used it. They're much less likely to remember how long the process was or that it took more mouse clicks than it should have. That's why users' subjective reactions to a website, product, or store may be the best predictor of their likelihood to return or make a purchase in the future.

## 6.2 COLLECTING SELF-REPORTED DATA

The most efficient way to capture self-reported data in a usability test is with some type of rating scale. Open-ended questions can also be very useful, but they are harder to analyze. Two of the classic rating scales are a Likert scale and a semantic differential scale.

### 6.2.1 Likert Scales

A typical item in a Likert scale is a statement to which the respondents rate their level of agreement. The statement may be positive (e.g., "The terminology used in this interface is clear") or negative (e.g., "I found the navigation options confusing"). Usually a 5-point scale of agreement like the following is used:

1. Strongly disagree
2. Disagree
3. Neither agree nor disagree
4. Agree
5. Strongly agree

In the original version of the scale, Likert (1932) provided "anchor terms" for each point on the scale. Some people prefer to use a 7-point scale, but it gets a bit more difficult to come up with descriptive terms for each point as you get to higher numbers. This is one reason many researchers have dropped the intervening labels and just label the two ends (or anchor points). Many variations on Likert scales are still used today, but most Likert-scale purists would say that the two main characteristics of a Likert scale are (1) it expresses degree of agreement with a statement, and (2) it uses an odd number of response options, thus allowing a neutral response.

In designing the statements for Likert scales, you need to be careful how you word them. In general, you should avoid adverbs like *very, extremely,* or *absolutely* in the statements and use unmodified versions of adjectives. For example, the statement "This website is beautiful" may yield results that are quite different from "This website is absolutely beautiful," which may decrease the likelihood of strong agreement.

---

**WHO WAS LIKERT?**

Many people have heard of Likert scales when it comes to subjective rating scales, but not many know where the name came from or even how to pronounce it! It's pronounced "LICK-ert," not "LIKE-ert." This type of scale is named for Rensis Likert, who created it in 1932.

---

## 6.2.2 **Semantic Differential Scales**

The semantic differential technique involves presenting pairs of bipolar, or opposite, adjectives at either end of a series of scales, such as the following:

| | | | | | | | | |
|---|---|---|---|---|---|---|---|---|
| Weak | ○ | ○ | ○ | ○ | ○ | ○ | ○ | Strong |
| Beautiful | ○ | ○ | ○ | ○ | ○ | ○ | ○ | Ugly |
| Hot | ○ | ○ | ○ | ○ | ○ | ○ | ○ | Cold |
| Light | ○ | ○ | ○ | ○ | ○ | ○ | ○ | Dark |

Like the Likert scale, a 5-point or 7-point scale is used. The difficult part about the semantic differential technique is coming up with words that are truly opposites. Sometimes a thesaurus can be helpful since it includes antonyms. But you need to be aware of the connotations of different pairings of words. For example, a pairing of "Friendly/Unfriendly" may have a somewhat different connotation and yield different results from "Friendly/Not Friendly" or "Friendly/Hostile."

---

**OSGOOD'S SEMANTIC DIFFERENTIAL**

The semantic differential technique was developed by Charles E. Osgood (Osgood et al., 1957), who designed it to measure the connotations of words or concepts. Using factor analysis of large sets of semantic differential data, he found three recurring attitudes that people used in assessing words and phrases: evaluation (e.g., "good/bad"), potency (e.g., "strong/weak"), and activity (e.g., "passive/active").

---

## 6.2.3 **When to Collect Self-Reported Data**

The two best times to collect self-reported data are at the end of each task (post-task ratings) and at the end of the entire session (post-study ratings). Post-study ratings tend to be the more common, but both have advantages. Quick ratings immediately after each task can help pinpoint tasks and parts of the interface that are particularly problematic. More in-depth ratings and open-ended questions at the end of the session can provide an effective overall evaluation after the participant has had a chance to interact with the product more fully.

### 6.2.4 How to Collect Self-Reported Data

Logistically, three techniques can be used to collect self-reported data in a usability test: answer questions or provide ratings orally, record responses on a paper form, or provide responses using some type of online tool. Each technique has its advantages and disadvantages. Having the participant provide responses orally is the easiest method from the participant's perspective, but, of course, it means that an observer needs to record the responses. This works best for a single, quick rating after each task.

Paper forms and online forms are suitable for both quick ratings and for longer surveys. Paper forms are generally easier to create than online forms, but they involve manual entry of the data, including the potential for errors in interpreting handwriting. Online forms are getting easier to create, as evidenced by the number of web-based questionnaire tools available, and participants are getting more accustomed to using them. One technique that works well is to have a laptop computer with the online questionnaire next to the participant's computer in the usability lab. The participant can then easily refer to the application or website while completing the online survey.

---

**ONLINE SURVEY TOOLS**

Many tools are available for creating and administering surveys via the web. Doing a search on "online survey tools" turns up a pretty extensive list. Some of them are SnapSurveys.com, SurveyGizmo.com, SurveyMonkey.com, SurveyShare.com, and Zoomerang.com.

Most of these tools support a variety of question types, including rating scales, check boxes, drop-down lists, grids, and open-ended questions. These tools generally have some type of free trial or other limited-functionality subscription that lets you try out the service for free. They provide mechanisms for authoring the surveys online, administering them, and analyzing the results. Most of the tools allow you do some analyses of the data online, and some also provide the option of downloading data to Excel, although that may only be available with paid subscriptions.

---

### 6.2.5 Biases in Collecting Self-Reported Data

Some studies have shown that people who are asked directly for self-reported data, either in person or over the phone, provide more positive feedback than when asked through an anonymous web survey (e.g., Dillman et al., 2001). This is called the social desirability bias (Nancarrow & Brace, 2000), in which respondents tend to give answers they believe will make them look better in the eyes of others or not disappoint the evaluator. For example, people who are called on the phone and asked to evaluate their satisfaction with a product typically report much higher satisfaction than if they reported their satisfaction levels in a more anonymous way. Telephone respondents or participants in a usability lab essentially want to tell us what they think we want to hear, and that is usually positive feedback about our product.

Therefore, we suggest collecting post-test data in such a way that the moderator or facilitator does not see the responses until after the participant has left. This might mean either turning away or leaving the room when the participant fills out the automated or paper survey. Making the survey itself anonymous may also elicit more honest reactions. Some usability researchers have suggested asking participants in a usability test to complete a post-test survey after they get back to their office or home and have received their incentive. This can be done by giving them a paper survey and a postage-paid envelope to mail it back or by e-mailing a pointer to an online survey. The main drawback of this approach is that you will typically have some dropoff in terms of who completes the survey.

### 6.2.6 General Guidelines for Rating Scales

When crafting your own rating scales to assess a specific attribute such as visual appeal, credibility, or responsiveness, the main thing to remember is that you will probably get more reliable data if you can think of a few different ways to ask participants to assess the attribute. In analyzing the results, you would average those responses together to arrive at the participant's overall reaction for that attribute. Likewise, the success of questionnaires that include both positive and negative statements to which participants respond would suggest the value of including both types of statements.

Finally, there's the issue of the number of scale values to use in any rating scales. This topic can be a source of heated debate among usability professionals. Most of the arguments center on the use of an even or odd number of points on the scale. An odd number of points has a center, or neutral, point, whereas an even number does not, thus forcing the user slightly toward one end or the other on the scale. This question is mainly an issue when you have a relatively small number of scale values, such as five or six. We believe that in most real-world situations a neutral reaction to something is perfectly valid and should be allowed on a rating scale. So in most cases we use rating scales with an odd number of points—usually five or seven.

### 6.2.7 Analyzing Self-Reported Data

One common technique for analyzing data from rating scales is to assign a numeric value to each of the scale positions and then compute the averages. For example, in the case of a 5-point Likert scale, you might assign a value of 1 to the "Strongly Disagree" end of the scale and a value of 5 to the "Strongly Agree" end. These averages can then be compared across different tasks, studies, user groups, and so on. This is common practice among most usability professionals as well as market researchers. Even though rating-scale data is not technically interval data, many professionals treat it as such. For example, we assume that the distance between a 1 and a 2 on a Likert scale is the same as the distance between a 2 and a 3 on the same scale. This assumption is called *degrees of intervalness*. We also assume that a value *between* any two of the scale positions has meaning. The bottom line is that it is close enough to interval data that we can treat it as such.

Another common way to analyze rating-scale data is by looking at top-2- and bottom-2-boxes. A top-2-box score refers to someone choosing a 4 or 5 (on a 5-point scale), or a 6 or 7 (on a 7-point scale). The top-2 are those who agree with the statement (somewhat or strongly agree), and the bottom-2 are those who disagree with the statement (somewhat or strongly disagree). Keep in mind that when you convert to a top-2- or bottom-2-box, the data can no longer be considered interval. Therefore, you should just report the data as frequencies (i.e., the percentage of participants who are top-2-box). Sometimes it's helpful to focus just on top-2-box—for example, when you are only interested in those who really like something. However, sometimes it is useful to also look at participants who strongly disagree with something. Depending on your situation, you might want to present just top-2-box or both top-2- and bottom-2-box scores.

Summarizing responses from open-ended questions is always a challenge. We've never been able to come up with a magic solution to doing this quickly and easily. Part of the solution is to be relatively specific in your open-ended questions. For example, a question that asks participants to describe anything they found confusing about the interface is going to be easier to analyze than a general "comments" field. One technique that's sometimes helpful is to bring all the responses to an open-ended question into Word or Excel and then sort them in alphabetical order (having removed articles like *the, a,* and so on, from the beginning of each). This groups together some of the similar comments, but someone still needs to examine those comments and do a logical grouping that takes into account the various ways participants might have expressed similar reactions. Also, having more than one rater perform the groupings helps increase reliability.

## 6.3 POST-TASK RATINGS

The main goal of ratings associated with each task is to give you some insight into which tasks the participants thought were the most difficult. This can then point you toward parts of the system or aspects of the product that need improvement. One way to capture this information is to ask the participant to rate each task on one or more scales. The next few sections examine some of the specific techniques that have been used.

### 6.3.1 Ease of Use

Probably the most common self-reported metric is to ask users to rate how easy or how difficult each task was. This typically involves asking them to rate the task using a 5-point or 7-point scale. Some usability professionals prefer to use a traditional

Likert scale, such as "This task was easy to complete" (1 = Strongly Disagree, 3 = Neither Agree nor Disagree, 5 = Strongly Agree). Others prefer to use a semantic differential technique with anchor terms like "Easy/Difficult." Either technique will provide you with a crude measure of perceived usability on a task level.

### 6.3.2 After-Scenario Questionnaire

Jim Lewis (1991) developed a set of three rating scales—the After-Scenario Questionnaire (ASQ)—designed to be used after the user completes a set of related tasks or a scenario:

1. "I am satisfied with the ease of completing the tasks in this scenario."

2. "I am satisfied with the amount of time it took to complete the tasks in this scenario."

3. "I am satisfied with the support information (online help, messages, documentation) when completing the tasks."

Each of these statements is accompanied by a 7-point rating scale of "strongly disagree" to "strongly agree," as shown in Figure 6.1. You can report the averages or top-2-/bottom-2- box score for each question or aggregated for each task. Note that each of these questions in the ASQ touches on three fundamental areas of usability: effectiveness (question 1), efficiency (question 2), and satisfaction (all three questions).

### 6.3.3 Expectation Measure

Albert and Dixon (2003) proposed a different approach to assessing subjective reactions after each task. Specifically, they argued that the most important thing about each task is how easy or difficult it was *in comparison to* how easy or difficult the participant *thought* it was going to be. So before participants actually did any of the tasks, Albert and Dixon asked them to rate how easy/difficult they *expected* each of the tasks to be, based simply on their understanding of the tasks and the product.

Participants expect some tasks to be easier than others. For example, getting a current quote on a stock should be easier than rebalancing an entire portfolio. Then, after performing each task, participants were asked to rate how easy/difficult the task *actually was*. The "before" rating is called the *expectation* rating, and the "after" rating is called the *experience* rating. They used the same 7-point rating scales (1 = Very Difficult, 7 = Very Easy) for both ratings. For each task you can then calculate an average *expectation rating* and an average *experience rating*. You can then display these two scores for each task as a scatterplot, as shown in Figure 6.2.

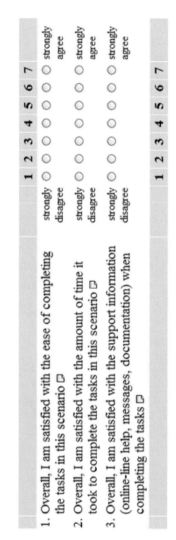

| | 1 | 2 | 3 | 4 | 5 | 6 | 7 | |
|---|---|---|---|---|---|---|---|---|
| 1. Overall, I am satisfied with the ease of completing the tasks in this scenario ▢ | strongly disagree | ○ | ○ | ○ | ○ | ○ | ○ | ○ strongly agree |
| 2. Overall, I am satisfied with the amount of time it took to complete the tasks in this scenario ▢ | strongly disagree | ○ | ○ | ○ | ○ | ○ | ○ | ○ strongly agree |
| 3. Overall, I am satisfied with the support information (online-line help, messages, documentation) when completing the tasks ▢ | strongly disagree | ○ | ○ | ○ | ○ | ○ | ○ | ○ strongly agree |
| | 1 | 2 | 3 | 4 | 5 | 6 | 7 | |

**FIGURE 6.1**

The ASQ developed by Lewis (1991). This implementation is Gary Perlman's web interface, which can be found at *http://www.acm.org/perlman/question.cgi?form=ASQ.*

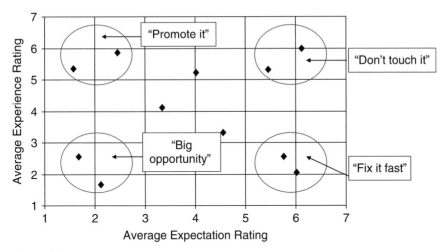

**FIGURE 6.2**

Comparison of the average expectation ratings and average experience ratings for a set of tasks in a usability test. Which quadrants the tasks fall into can help you prioritize which tasks to focus on improving. *Source:* Adapted from Albert and Dixon (2003); used with permission.

The four quadrants of the scatterplot provide some interesting insight into the tasks and where you should focus your attention when making improvements:

1. In the lower right are the tasks that the participants thought would be *easy* but actually turned out to be *difficult*. These probably represent the tasks that are the biggest dissatisfiers for the users—those that were the biggest disappointment. These are the tasks you should focus on first, which is why this is called the "Fix it fast" quadrant.

2. In the upper right are the tasks that the participants thought would be *easy* and actually *were* easy. These are working just fine. You don't want to "break" them by making changes that would have a negative impact. That's why this is called the "Don't touch it" quadrant.

3. In the upper left are the tasks that the participants thought would be *difficult* and actually were *easy*. These are pleasant surprises, both for the users and the designers of the system! These could represent features of your site or system that may help distinguish you from the competition, which is why this is called the "Promote it" quadrant.

4. In the lower left are the tasks that the participants thought would be *difficult* and actually *were* difficult. There are no big surprises here, but there might be some important opportunities to make improvements. That's why this is called the "Big opportunity" quadrant.

### 6.3.4 Usability Magnitude Estimation

A very different approach to task-based metrics has been proposed by Mick McGee (2004), who argued for a departure from the traditional rating-scale approach to self-reported measures. His method goes back to the magnitude estimation technique from classical psychophysics (Stevens, 1957). In traditional psychophysical studies, the experimenter would present a reference stimulus, such as a light source, and ask the subject to assign a value to some attribute of it, such as its brightness. Then, for example, a new light source would be shown, and the subject would be asked to assign a value to its brightness in comparison to the value from the reference light source. One of the keys to this method is that subjects are instructed to maintain a correspondence between the *ratios* of the numbers they assign and their perception of the magnitude. So, for example, a light that the subject perceives as being twice as bright as the reference light should get a value that's twice the reference value.

In adapting this method to usability studies, you may start by giving participants a reference "good design" and "bad design" for the same task. McGee (2004) used two examples illustrating good and bad versions of an interface for logging onto a website. In the good version, there were obvious fields for entering an ID and password and an explanation of what the site is about. This design was not presented as a *perfect* design, just a reasonably good one. The bad version had a long list of problems associated with it: poor contrast, confusing instructions, unlabeled input fields, confusing buttons, and the actual login on a separate page.

Next, you ask the participant to assign "usability values" to the reference good and bad designs. They can be any positive numbers. As illustrated in Figure 6.3, let's assume the participant gave a value of 20 to the reference bad design and a value of 200 to the reference good design. The participant is then asked to make judgments about the tasks she performs and the application's support for those tasks in comparison to these reference values. So, for example, if Task 1 was about three times better than the reference bad design, it would get a rating of 60. If Task 2 was half as good as

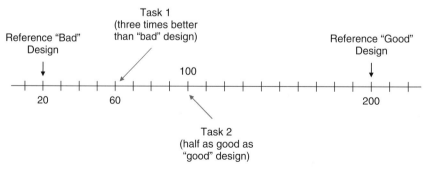

**FIGURE 6.3**

Example of a participant's "usability ruler" and how it might be used for assessing the usability of the system for various tasks.

the reference good design, it would get a rating of 100. In this way, each participant establishes his own "usability ruler" and uses it to express his perceptions.

Usability Magnitude Estimation can also be done without giving the participants reference good and bad designs. In this approach, participants simply start giving usability values for the tasks as they encounter them; in essence, they gradually build their own ruler as they encounter the tasks. In either approach, each participant's data is transformed using geometric averaging (log transformations) to a consistent scale for comparison purposes (McGee, 2003).

### 6.3.5  Comparison of Post-Task Self-Reported Metrics

Tedesco and Tullis (2006) compared a variety of task-based self-reported metrics in an online usability study. Specifically, they tested the following five different methods for eliciting self-reported ratings after each task.

*Condition 1:* "Overall, this task was: Very Difficult ○ ○ ○ ○ ○ Very Easy"
This was a very simple post-task rating scale that some usability teams commonly use.

*Condition 2:* "Please rate the usability of the site for this task: Very Difficult to Use ○ ○ ○ ○ ○ Very Easy to Use"
Obviously, this is very similar to Condition 1 but with an emphasis on the usability of *the site* for the task. Perhaps only usability geeks detect the difference, but they wanted to find out!

*Condition 3:* "Overall, I am satisfied with the ease of completing this task: Strongly Disagree ○ ○ ○ ○ ○ Strongly Agree"
"Overall, I'm satisfied with the amount of time it took to complete this task: Strongly Disagree ○ ○ ○ ○ ○ Strongly Agree"
These are two of the three questions used in Lewis's ASQ (1991). The third question in the ASQ asks about the support information such as online help, which was not relevant in this study, so it was not used.

*Condition 4* (before doing all tasks): "How difficult or easy do you expect this task to be? Very Difficult ○ ○ ○ ○ ○ Very Easy"
(after doing each task): "How difficult or easy did you find this task to be? Very Difficult ○ ○ ○ ○ ○ Very Easy"
This is the expectation measure described by Albert and Dixon (2003).

*Condition 5:* "Please assign a number between 1 and 100 to represent how well the website supported you for this task. Remember: 1 would mean that the site was not at all supportive and completely unusable. A score of 100 would mean that the site was perfect and would require absolutely no improvement."
This condition was originally based on Usability Magnitude Estimation but was significantly modified through iterations in the study planning. In pilot testing using a more traditional version of Usability Magnitude Estimation, they found that

participants had a very difficult time understanding the concepts and using the technique appropriately. As a result, they modified it to this simpler technique. This may mean that Usability Magnitude Estimation is better suited to use in a lab setting, or at least a moderated usability study, than in an online, unmoderated usability study.

The techniques were compared in an online study. The participants performed six tasks on a live application used to look up information about employees (phone number, location, manager, etc.). Each participant used only one of the five self-report techniques. A total of 1,131 employees participated in the online study, with at least 210 of them using each self-report technique.

The main goal of this study was to see whether these rating techniques are sensitive to differences in perceived difficulty of the tasks. But they also wanted to see how perceived difficulty corresponded to the task performance data. They collected task time and binary success data (i.e., whether the participants found the correct answer for each task and how long that took). As shown in Figure 6.4, there were significant differences in the performance data across the tasks. Task 2 appears to have been the most challenging, whereas Task 4 was the easiest.

As shown in Figure 6.5, a somewhat similar pattern of the tasks was reflected by the task ratings (averaged across all five techniques). In comparing task performance with the task ratings, correlations were significant for all five conditions ($p < 0.01$). Overall, Spearman rank correlation comparing the performance data and task ratings for the six tasks was significant: $Rs = 0.83$.

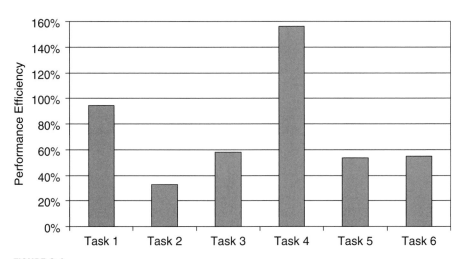

**FIGURE 6.4**

Performance data showing that participants had the most difficulty with Task 2 and the least difficulty with Task 4. *Source:* Adapted from Tedesco and Tullis (2006).

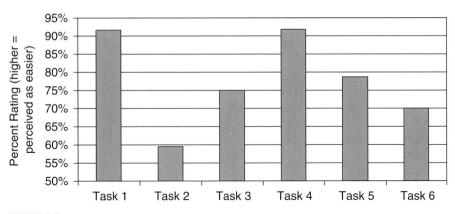

**FIGURE 6.5**

Average subjective ratings across all techniques. Ratings are expressed as a percentage of the maximum possible rating. Similar to the performance data, Task 2 yielded the worst ratings, while Task 4 yielded among the best. *Source:* Adapted from Tedesco and Tullis (2006).

Figure 6.6 shows the averages of the task ratings for each of the tasks, split out by condition. The key finding is that the pattern of the results was very similar regardless of which technique was used. This is not surprising, given the very large sample (total $n = 1,131$). In other words, at large sample sizes, all five of the techniques can effectively distinguish between the tasks.

But what about at the smaller sample sizes more typical of usability tests? To answer that question, they did a subsampling analysis looking at large numbers of random samples of different sizes taken from the full dataset. The results of this are shown in Figure 6.7, where the correlation between the data from the subsamples and the full dataset is shown for each subsample size.

The key finding was that one of the five conditions, Condition 1, resulted in better correlations starting at the smallest sample sizes and continuing. Even at a sample size of only seven, which is typical of many usability tests, its correlation with the full dataset averaged 0.91, which was significantly higher than any of the other conditions. So Condition 1, which was the simplest rating scale ("Overall, this task was Very Difficult ○ ○ ○ ○ ○ Very Easy"), was also the most reliable at smaller sample sizes.

## 6.4 POST-SESSION RATINGS

One of the most common uses of self-reported metrics is as an overall measure of perceived usability that participants are asked to give after having completed their interactions with the product. This can be used as an overall "barometer" of the usability of the product, particularly if you establish a track record with the same

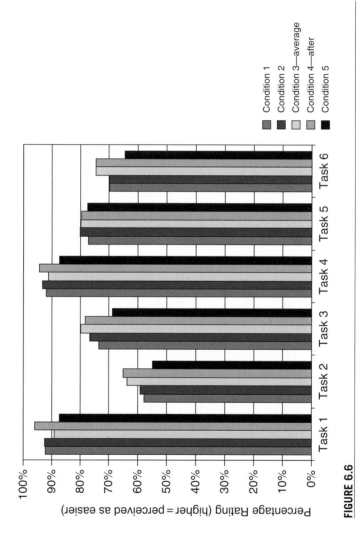

**FIGURE 6.6**

Average subjective ratings split by task and condition. All five conditions (self-report techniques) yielded essentially the same pattern of results for the six tasks. *Source:* Adapted from Tedesco and Tullis (2006).

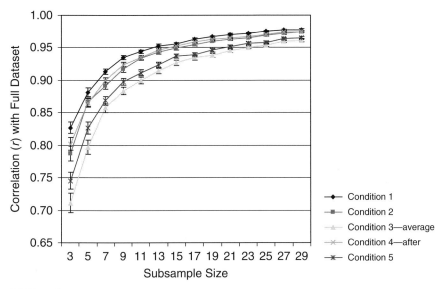

**FIGURE 6.7**

Results of a subsampling analysis showing average correlations between ratings for the six tasks from subsamples of various sizes and the full dataset for each condition. Error bars represent the 95 percent confidence interval for the mean. *Source:* Adapted from Tedesco and Tullis (2006).

measurement technique over time. Similarly, these kinds of ratings can be used to compare multiple design alternatives in a single usability study or to compare your product, application, or website to the competition. Let's look at some of the post-session rating techniques that have been used.

## 6.4.1 Aggregating Individual Task Ratings

Perhaps the simplest way to look at post-session usability is to take an average of the self-reported data across all tasks. Of course, this assumes that you did in fact collect self-reported data after each task. If you did, then simply take an average of them. Keep in mind that these data are a little different from one snapshot at the end of the session. By looking at self-reported data across all tasks, you're really taking an average perception as it changes over time. Alternatively, when you collect the self-reported data just once at the end of the session, you are really measuring the participant's last impression of the experience.

This is the perception participants will leave with, which will likely influence any future decisions they make about your product. So if you want to measure perceived ease of use for the product based on individual task performance, then aggregate self-reported data from multiple tasks. However, if you're interested in knowing the lasting usability perception, then we recommend using one of the following techniques that takes a single snapshot at the end of the session.

## 6.4.2 System Usability Scale

The System Usability Scale (SUS) was originally developed by John Brooke in 1986 while he was working at Digital Equipment Corporation (Brooke, 1996). As shown in Figure 6.8, it consists of ten statements to which participants rate their level of agreement. Half the statements are positively worded and half negatively worded. A 5-point scale of agreement is used for each. A technique for combining the ten ratings into an overall score (on a scale of 0 to 100) is also given. No attempt is made to assess different attributes of the system (e.g., usability, usefulness, etc.). In fact, the intent is that you should not look at the ratings for the ten statements individually but only look at the combined rating.

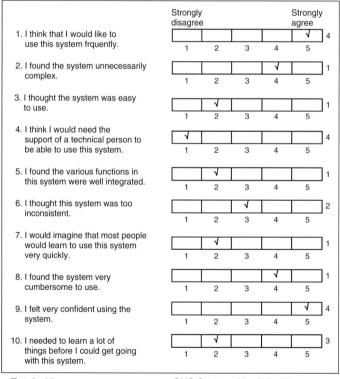

Total = 22                SUS Score = 22 × 2.5 = 55

**FIGURE 6.8**

SUS, developed by John Brooke at Digital Equipment Corporation, and an example of scoring it. *Source:* From Brooke (1996).

It's convenient to think of SUS scores as percentages, since they are on a scale of 0 to 100, with 100 representing a perfect score.

---

**CALCULATING A SUS SCORE**

To calculate a SUS score, first sum the score contributions from each item. Each item's score contribution will range from 0 to 4. For items 1, 3, 5, 7, and 9, the score contribution is the scale position minus 1. For items 2, 4, 6, 8, and 10, the contribution is 5 minus the scale position. Multiply the sum of the scores by 2.5 to obtain the overall SUS score. Consider the sample data in Figure 6.8. The sum of the values, using these rules, is 22. Multiply that by 2.5 to get the overall SUS score of 55 percent. SUS has been made freely available for use in usability studies, for both research purposes and industry use. The only prerequisite for its use is that any published report acknowledge the source of the measure.

---

### 6.4.3 Computer System Usability Questionnaire

Jim Lewis (1995), who developed the ASQ technique for post-task ratings, also developed the Computer System Usability Questionnaire (CSUQ) to do an overall assessment of a system at the end of a usability study. The CSUQ is very similar to Lewis's Post-Study System Usability Questionnaire (PSSUQ), with only minor changes in wording. PSSUQ was originally designed to be administered in person, whereas CSUQ was designed to be administered by mail or online. As shown in Figure 6.9, CSUQ consists of 19 statements to which the user rates agreement on a 7-point scale of "Strongly Disagree" to "Strongly Agree," plus N/A. Unlike SUS, all of the statements in CSUQ are worded positively. Factor analyses of a large number of CSUQ and PSSUQ responses have shown that the results may be viewed in four main categories: System Usefulness, Information Quality, Interface Quality, and Overall Satisfaction.

### 6.4.4 Questionnaire for User Interface Satisfaction

The Questionnaire for User Interface Satisfaction (QUIS) was developed by a team in the Human–Computer Interaction Laboratory (HCIL) at the University of Maryland (Chin, Diehl, & Norman, 1988). As shown in Figure 6.10, QUIS consists of 27 rating scales divided into five categories: Overall Reaction, Screen, Terminology/System Information, Learning, and System Capabilities. The ratings are on 10-point scales whose anchors change depending on the statement. The first six scales (assessing Overall Reaction) are polar opposites with no statements (e.g., Terrible/Wonderful, Difficult/Easy, Frustrating/Satisfying). QUIS can be licensed from the University of Maryland's Office of Technology Commercialization (*http://www.lap. umd.edu/ QUIS/index.html*); it is also available in printed and web versions in multiple languages.

The questionnaire items, each with response options labeled 1–7 (strongly disagree to strongly agree) and NA:

|  | 1 | 2 | 3 | 4 | 5 | 6 | 7 | | NA |
|---|---|---|---|---|---|---|---|---|---|

1. Overall, I am satisfied with how easy it is to use this system ▱
   strongly disagree ○ ○ ○ ○ ○ ○ ○ strongly agree ○

2. It was simple to use this system ▱
   strongly disagree ○ ○ ○ ○ ○ ○ ○ strongly agree ○

3. I can effectively complete my work using this system ▱
   strongly disagree ○ ○ ○ ○ ○ ○ ○ strongly agree ○

4. I am able to complete my work quickly using this system ▱
   strongly disagree ○ ○ ○ ○ ○ ○ ○ strongly agree ○

5. I am able to efficiently complete my work using this system ▱
   strongly disagree ○ ○ ○ ○ ○ ○ ○ strongly agree ○

6. I feel comfortable using this system ▱
   strongly disagree ○ ○ ○ ○ ○ ○ ○ strongly agree ○

7. It was easy to learn to use this system ▱
   strongly disagree ○ ○ ○ ○ ○ ○ ○ strongly agree ○

8. I believe I became productive quickly using this system ▱
   strongly disagree ○ ○ ○ ○ ○ ○ ○ strongly agree ○

9. The system gives error messages that clearly tell me how to fix problems ▱
   strongly disagree ○ ○ ○ ○ ○ ○ ○ strongly agree ○

10. Whenever I make a mistake using the system, I recover easily and quickly ▱
    strongly disagree ○ ○ ○ ○ ○ ○ ○ strongly agree ○

11. The information (such as online help, on-screen messages, and other documentation) provided with this system is clear ▱
    strongly disagree ○ ○ ○ ○ ○ ○ ○ strongly agree ○

12. It is easy to find the information I needed ▱
    strongly disagree ○ ○ ○ ○ ○ ○ ○ strongly agree ○

13. The information provided for the system is easy to understand ▱
    strongly disagree ○ ○ ○ ○ ○ ○ ○ strongly agree ○

14. The information is effective in helping me complete the tasks and scenarios ▱
    strongly disagree ○ ○ ○ ○ ○ ○ ○ strongly agree ○

15. The organization of information on the system screens is clear ▱
    strongly disagree ○ ○ ○ ○ ○ ○ ○ strongly agree ○

16. The interface of this system is pleasant ▱
    strongly disagree ○ ○ ○ ○ ○ ○ ○ strongly agree ○

17. I like using the interface of this system ▱
    strongly disagree ○ ○ ○ ○ ○ ○ ○ strongly agree ○

18. This system has all the functions and capabilities I expect it to have ▱
    strongly disagree ○ ○ ○ ○ ○ ○ ○ strongly agree ○

19. Overall, I am satisfied with this system ▱
    strongly disagree ○ ○ ○ ○ ○ ○ ○ strongly agree ○

|  | 1 | 2 | 3 | 4 | 5 | 6 | 7 | | NA |
|---|---|---|---|---|---|---|---|---|---|

**FIGURE 6.9**

The CSUQ. *Source:* Adapted from the work of Lewis (1995); used with permission.

**OVERALL REACTION TO THE SOFTWARE**

| | 0 | 1 | 2 | 3 | 4 | 5 | 6 | 7 | 8 | 9 | | NA |
|---|---|---|---|---|---|---|---|---|---|---|---|---|
| 1. | terrible | ○ | ○ | ○ | ○ | ○ | ○ | ○ | ○ | ○ | wonderful | ○ |
| 2. | difficult | ○ | ○ | ○ | ○ | ○ | ○ | ○ | ○ | ○ | easy | ○ |
| 3. | frustrating | ○ | ○ | ○ | ○ | ○ | ○ | ○ | ○ | ○ | satisfying | ○ |
| 4. | inadequate power | ○ | ○ | ○ | ○ | ○ | ○ | ○ | ○ | ○ | adequate power | ○ |
| 5. | dull | ○ | ○ | ○ | ○ | ○ | ○ | ○ | ○ | ○ | stimulating | ○ |
| 6. | rigid | ○ | ○ | ○ | ○ | ○ | ○ | ○ | ○ | ○ | flexible | ○ |

**SCREEN**

| | 0 | 1 | 2 | 3 | 4 | 5 | 6 | 7 | 8 | 9 | | NA |
|---|---|---|---|---|---|---|---|---|---|---|---|---|
| 7. Reading characters on the screen 🗅 | hard | ○ | ○ | ○ | ○ | ○ | ○ | ○ | ○ | ○ | easy | ○ |
| 8. Highlighting simplifies task 🗅 | not at all | ○ | ○ | ○ | ○ | ○ | ○ | ○ | ○ | ○ | very much | ○ |
| 9. Organization of information 🗅 | confusing | ○ | ○ | ○ | ○ | ○ | ○ | ○ | ○ | ○ | very clear | ○ |
| 10. Sequence of screens 🗅 | confusing | ○ | ○ | ○ | ○ | ○ | ○ | ○ | ○ | ○ | very clear | ○ |

**TERMINOLOGY AND SYSTEM INFORMATION**

| | 0 | 1 | 2 | 3 | 4 | 5 | 6 | 7 | 8 | 9 | | NA |
|---|---|---|---|---|---|---|---|---|---|---|---|---|
| 11. Use of terms throughout system 🗅 | inconsistent | ○ | ○ | ○ | ○ | ○ | ○ | ○ | ○ | ○ | consistent | ○ |
| 12. Terminology related to task 🗅 | never | ○ | ○ | ○ | ○ | ○ | ○ | ○ | ○ | ○ | always | ○ |
| 13. Position of messages on screen 🗅 | inconsistent | ○ | ○ | ○ | ○ | ○ | ○ | ○ | ○ | ○ | consistent | ○ |
| 14. Prompts for input 🗅 | confusing | ○ | ○ | ○ | ○ | ○ | ○ | ○ | ○ | ○ | clear | ○ |
| 15. Computer informs about its progress 🗅 | never | ○ | ○ | ○ | ○ | ○ | ○ | ○ | ○ | ○ | always | ○ |
| 16. Error messages 🗅 | unhelpful | ○ | ○ | ○ | ○ | ○ | ○ | ○ | ○ | ○ | helpful | ○ |

**LEARNING**

| | 0 | 1 | 2 | 3 | 4 | 5 | 6 | 7 | 8 | 9 | | NA |
|---|---|---|---|---|---|---|---|---|---|---|---|---|
| 17. Learning to operate the system 🗅 | difficult | ○ | ○ | ○ | ○ | ○ | ○ | ○ | ○ | ○ | easy | ○ |
| 18. Exploring new features by trial and error 🗅 | difficult | ○ | ○ | ○ | ○ | ○ | ○ | ○ | ○ | ○ | easy | ○ |
| 19. Remembering names and use of commands 🗅 | difficult | ○ | ○ | ○ | ○ | ○ | ○ | ○ | ○ | ○ | easy | ○ |
| 20. Performing tasks is straightforward 🗅 | never | ○ | ○ | ○ | ○ | ○ | ○ | ○ | ○ | ○ | always | ○ |
| 21. Help messages on the screen 🗅 | unhelpful | ○ | ○ | ○ | ○ | ○ | ○ | ○ | ○ | ○ | helpful | ○ |
| 22. Supplemental reference materials 🗅 | confusing | ○ | ○ | ○ | ○ | ○ | ○ | ○ | ○ | ○ | clear | ○ |

**SYSTEM CAPABILITIES**

| | 0 | 1 | 2 | 3 | 4 | 5 | 6 | 7 | 8 | 9 | | NA |
|---|---|---|---|---|---|---|---|---|---|---|---|---|
| 23. System speed 🗅 | too slow | ○ | ○ | ○ | ○ | ○ | ○ | ○ | ○ | ○ | fast enough | ○ |
| 24. System reliability 🗅 | unreliable | ○ | ○ | ○ | ○ | ○ | ○ | ○ | ○ | ○ | reliable | ○ |
| 25. System tends to be 🗅 | noisy | ○ | ○ | ○ | ○ | ○ | ○ | ○ | ○ | ○ | quiet | ○ |
| 26. Correcting your mistakes 🗅 | difficult | ○ | ○ | ○ | ○ | ○ | ○ | ○ | ○ | ○ | easy | ○ |
| 27. Designed for all levels of users 🗅 | never | ○ | ○ | ○ | ○ | ○ | ○ | ○ | ○ | ○ | always | ○ |

**FIGURE 6.10**

Questionnaire for User Interface Satisfaction. *Source:* Developed by the HCIL at the University of Maryland. Commercial use requires a license from the Office of Technology Commercialization at the University of Maryland. Used with permission.

**GARY PERLMAN'S ONLINE QUESTIONNAIRES**

Several of the questionnaires shown in this chapter, as well as a few others, are available for use online through a web interface created by Gary Perlman (*http://www.acm.org/perlman/ question.html*). The questionnaires include QUIS, ASQ, and CSUQ. Options are provided for specifying which questionnaire to use, an e-mail address to submit results, and the name of the system being evaluated. These can be specified as parameters associated with the URL for the online questionnaire. So, for example, to specify the following:

- Name of System: MyPage
- Questionnaire: CSUQ
- Send Results to: me@gmail.com

the URL would be *http://www.acm.org/perlman/question.cgi?system=MyPage&form= CSUQ&email=me@gmail.com*.

By default, all rating scales also provide a mechanism for the user to enter comments. Once the user clicks on the Submit button, the data is e-mailed to the address specified, formatted in a name=value format with one name and value per line.

## 6.4.5 Usefulness, Satisfaction, and Ease of Use Questionnaire

Arnie Lund (2001) proposed the Usefulness, Satisfaction, and Ease of Use (USE) questionnaire, shown in Figure 6.11, which consists of 30 rating scales divided into four categories: Usefulness, Satisfaction, Ease of Use, and Ease of Learning. Each is a positive statement (e.g., "I would recommend it to a friend"), to which the user rates level of agreement on a 7-point Likert scale. In analyzing a large number of responses using this questionnaire, he found that 21 of the 30 scales (identified in Figure 6.11, on page 144) yielded the highest weights for each of the categories, indicating that they contributed most to the results.

## 6.4.6 Product Reaction Cards

A very different approach to capturing post-session subjective reactions to a product was presented by Joey Benedek and Trish Miner (2002) from Microsoft. As illustrated in Figure 6.12 (on page 145), they presented a set of 118 cards containing adjectives (e.g., Fresh, Slow, Sophisticated, Inviting, Entertaining, Incomprehensible). Some of the words are positive and some are negative. The participants would then simply choose the cards they felt described the system. After selecting the cards, participants were asked to pick the top five cards and explain why they chose each. This technique is intended to be more qualitative in that its main purpose is to elicit commentary. But it can also be used in a somewhat quantitative way by counting the number of positive and negative terms chosen by each participant.

## VISUALIZING DATA USING RADAR CHARTS

Some of the techniques for capturing self-reported data yield values on several dimensions. For example, the USE questionnaire can yield values for Usefulness, Satisfaction, Ease of Use, and Ease of Learning. Similarly, CSUQ can yield values for System Usefulness, Information Quality, Interface Quality, and Overall Satisfaction. One technique that can be useful for visualizing the results in a situation like this is a radar chart. Assume you have the following summary values from a study with the USE questionnaire:

- Usefulness = 90%
- Satisfaction = 50%
- Ease of Use = 45%
- Ease of Learning = 40%

Plotting these values as a radar chart would give you the chart shown here.

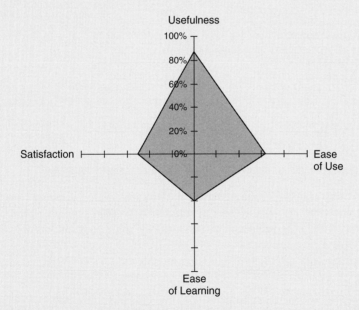

To create these charts, choose "Radar" as the "Chart Type" in Excel. "Filled" radar charts, like the example here, usually work best. The advantage these charts provide is that they help the viewer easily detect patterns as represented by different shapes. For example, a tall, skinny radar chart like the one shown here reflects the fact that users thought the product being evaluated was useful but not particularly easy to use, easy to learn, or satisfying.

**Usefulness**
- It helps me be more effective.
- It helps me be more productive.
- It is useful.
- It gives me more control over the activities in my life.
- It makes the things I want to accomplish easier to get done.
- It saves me time when I use it.
- *It meets my needs.*
- It does everything I would expect it to do.

**Ease of Use**
- It is easy to use.
- It is simple to use.
- It is user friendly.
- It requires the fewest steps possible to accomplish what I want to do with it.
- *It is flexible.*
- *Using it is effortless.*
- *I can use it without written instructions.*
- *I don't notice any inconsistencies as I use it.*
- *Both occasional and regular users would like it.*
- *I can recover from mistakes quickly and easily.*
- *I can use it successfully every time.*

**Ease of Learning**
- I learned to use it quickly.
- I easily remember how to use it.
- It is easy to learn to use it.
- *I quickly became skillful with it.*

**Satisfaction**
- I am satisfied with it.
- I would recommend it to a friend.
- It is fun to use.
- It works the way I want it to work.
- It is wonderful.
- I feel I need to have it.
- It is pleasant to use.

> Users rate agreement with these statements on a 7-point Likert scale, ranging from strongly disagree to strongly agree. Statements in *italics* were found to weight less heavily than the others.

**FIGURE 6.11**

The USE questionnaire. *Source:* From the work of Lund (2001); used with permission.

## 6.4.7 Comparison of Post-Session Self-Reported Metrics

Tullis and Stetson (2004) reported a study that compared a variety of post-session questionnaires for measuring user reactions to websites in an online usability study. They studied the following questionnaires, adapted in the manner indicated for the evaluation of sites.

*SUS:* The word *system* in every question was replaced with *website.*

*QUIS:* Three of the original rating scales that did not seem to be appropriate to websites were dropped (e.g., "Remembering names and use of commands"). The term *system* was replaced with *website,* and the term *screen* was generally replaced by *web page.*

*CSUQ:* The term *system* or *computer system* was replaced by *website.*

*Microsoft's Product Reaction Cards:* Each word was presented with a check box, and participants were asked to choose the words that best describe their interaction with the website. They were free to choose as many or as few words as they wished.

| The Complete Set of 118 Product Reaction Cards | | | | |
|---|---|---|---|---|
| Accessible | Creative | Fast | Meaningful | Slow |
| Advanced | Customizable | Flexible | Motivating | Sophisticated |
| Annoying | Cutting edge | Fragile | Not secure | Stable |
| Appealing | Dated | Fresh | Not valuable | Sterile |
| Approachable | Desirable | Friendly | Novel | Stimulating |
| Attractive | Difficult | Frustrating | Old | Straightforward |
| Boring | Disconnected | Fun | Optimistic | Stressful |
| Business-like | Disruptive | Gets in the way | Ordinary | Time-consuming |
| Busy | Distracting | Hard to use | Organized | Time-saving |
| Calm | Dull | Helpful | Overbearing | Too technical |
| Clean | Easy to use | High quality | Overwhelming | Trustworthy |
| Clear | Effective | Impersonal | Patronizing | Unapproachable |
| Collaborative | Efficient | Impressive | Personal | Unattractive |
| Comfortable | Effortless | Incomprehensible | Poor quality | Uncontrollable |
| Compatible | Empowering | Inconsistent | Powerful | Unconventional |
| Compelling | Energetic | Ineffective | Predictable | Understandable |
| Complex | Engaging | Innovative | Professional | Undesirable |
| Comprehensive | Entertaining | Inspiring | Relevant | Unpredictable |
| Confident | Enthusiastic | Integrated | Reliable | Unrefined |
| Confusing | Essential | Intimidating | Responsive | Usable |
| Connected | Exceptional | Intuitive | Rigid | Useful |
| Consistent | Exciting | Inviting | Satisfying | Valuable |
| Controllable | Expected | Irrelevant | Secure | |
| Convenient | Familiar | Low maintenance | Simplistic | |

**FIGURE 6.12**

The complete set of reaction cards developed by Joey Benedek and Trish Miner at Microsoft. *Source:* From Microsoft—"Permission is granted to use this Tool for personal, academic and commercial purposes. If you wish to use this Tool, or the results obtained from the use of this Tool for personal or academic purposes or in your commercial application, you are required to include the following attribution: Developed by and © 2002 Microsoft Corporation. All rights reserved."

*Their Questionnaire:* They had been using this questionnaire for several years in usability tests of websites. It was composed of nine positive statements (e.g., "This website is visually appealing"), to which the site's user responds on a 7-point Likert scale from "Strongly Disagree" to "Strongly Agree."

They used these questionnaires to evaluate two web portals in an online usability study. There were a total of 123 participants in the study, with each participant using one of the questionnaires to evaluate both websites.

Participants performed two tasks on each website before completing the questionnaire for that site. When the study authors analyzed the data from all the participants, they found that all five of the questionnaires revealed that Site 1 got significantly better ratings than Site 2. The data were then analyzed to determine what the results would have been at different sample sizes from 6 to 14, as shown in Figure 6.13. At a sample size of 6, only 30 to 40 percent of the samples would have identified that Site 1 was significantly preferred. But at a sample size of 8, which is relatively common in many lab-based usability tests, they found that SUS would have identified Site 1 as the preferred site 75 percent of the time—a significantly higher percentage than any of the other questionnaires.

It's interesting to speculate why SUS appears to yield more consistent ratings at relatively small sample sizes. One reason may be its use of both positive and negative statements with which participants must rate their level of agreement. This seems to keep participants more alert. Another reason may be that it doesn't try to break down the assessment into more detailed components (e.g., ease of learning, ease of navigation, etc.). All ten of the rating scales in SUS are simply asking for an assessment of the site as a whole, just in slightly different ways.

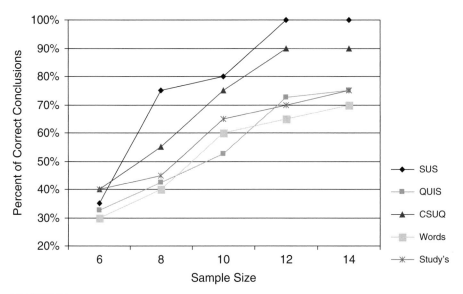

**FIGURE 6.13**

Data illustrating the accuracy of the results from random subsamples ranging from size 6 to size 14. This graph shows what percentage of the random samples yielded the same answer as the full dataset at the different sample sizes. *Source:* Adapted from Tullis and Stetson (2004).

## 6.5 USING SUS TO COMPARE DESIGNS

A number of usability studies that involved comparing different designs for accomplishing similar tasks have used the SUS questionnaire as one of the techniques for making the comparison (typically in addition to performance data).

### 6.5.1 Comparison of "Senior-Friendly" Websites

Traci Hart (2004) of the Software Usability Research Laboratory at Wichita State University conducted a usability study comparing three different websites designed for older adults: SeniorNet, SeniorResource, and Seniors-Place. After attempting tasks on each website, the participants rated each of them using the SUS questionnaire. The results are shown in Figure 6.14. The average SUS score for the SeniorResource site was 80 percent, which was significantly better than the average scores for SeniorNet and Seniors-Place, both of which averaged 63 percent.

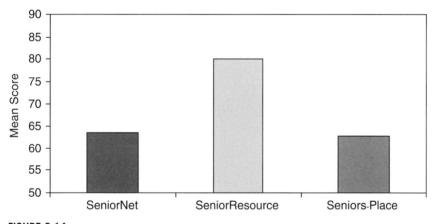

**FIGURE 6.14**

Data showing the average SUS scores from a study of three websites designed for older adults. The average SUS rating for SeniorResource was significantly higher than the average rating for either of the other sites. Participants were 21 adults over the age of 50, who performed tasks on all three sites and then rated all three. *Source:* Adapted from Hart (2004).

### 6.5.2 Comparison of Windows ME and Windows XP

The American Institutes for Research (2001) conducted a usability study comparing Microsoft's Windows ME and Windows XP. They recruited 36 participants whose expertise with Windows ranged from novice to intermediate. They attempted tasks using both versions of Windows and then completed the SUS questionnaire for both. They found that the average SUS score for Windows XP (74 percent) was significantly higher than the average for Windows ME (56 percent) ($p < 0.0001$).

### 6.5.3 Comparison of Paper Ballots

Sarah Everett, Michael Byrne, and Kristen Greene (2006), from Rice University, conducted a usability study comparing three different types of paper ballots: bubble, arrow, and open response. These ballots, which are illustrated in Figure 6.15,

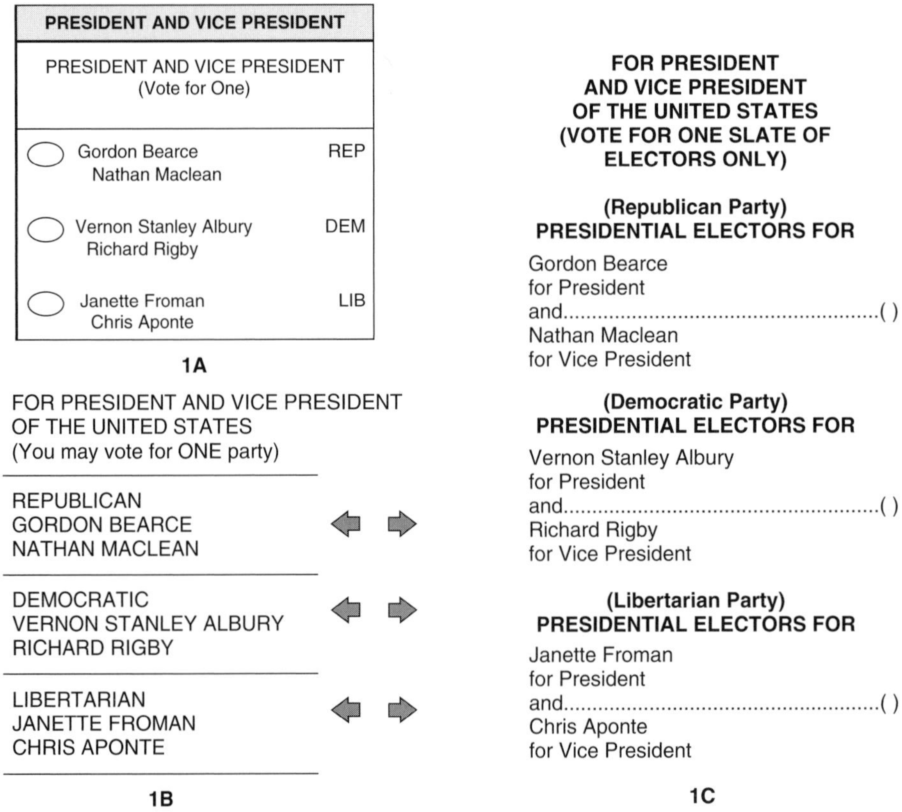

| PRESIDENT AND VICE PRESIDENT |
|---|
| PRESIDENT AND VICE PRESIDENT (Vote for One) |
| ◯ Gordon Bearce  REP<br>Nathan Maclean |
| ◯ Vernon Stanley Albury  DEM<br>Richard Rigby |
| ◯ Janette Froman  LIB<br>Chris Aponte |

**1A**

FOR PRESIDENT AND VICE PRESIDENT
OF THE UNITED STATES
(You may vote for ONE party)

REPUBLICAN
GORDON BEARCE    ⬅ ➡
NATHAN MACLEAN

DEMOCRATIC
VERNON STANLEY ALBURY    ⬅ ➡
RICHARD RIGBY

LIBERTARIAN
JANETTE FROMAN    ⬅ ➡
CHRIS APONTE

**1B**

**FOR PRESIDENT
AND VICE PRESIDENT
OF THE UNITED STATES
(VOTE FOR ONE SLATE OF
ELECTORS ONLY)**

**(Republican Party)
PRESIDENTIAL ELECTORS FOR**

Gordon Bearce
for President
and.....................................................( )
Nathan Maclean
for Vice President

**(Democratic Party)
PRESIDENTIAL ELECTORS FOR**

Vernon Stanley Albury
for President
and.....................................................( )
Richard Rigby
for Vice President

**(Libertarian Party)
PRESIDENTIAL ELECTORS FOR**

Janette Froman
for President
and.....................................................( )
Chris Aponte
for Vice President

**1C**

**FIGURE 6.15**

Three sample ballots. 1A: Bubble ballot; 1B: Arrow ballot; and 1C: Open-response ballot. *Source:* From Everett et al. (2006); reprinted with permission from *Human Factors* 45(4). Copyright © 2003 by the Human Factors and Ergonomics Society. All rights reserved.

were based on actual ballots used in the 2004 U.S. elections. After using each of the ballots in a simulated election, the 42 participants used the SUS questionnaire to rate each one. The results are shown in Figure 6.16. They found that the bubble ballot (1A) received significantly higher SUS ratings than either of the other two ($p < 0.001$).

---

**WHAT IS A GOOD (OR BAD) SUS SCORE?**

After reporting an average of the post-session ratings from a particular study, usability professionals very often hear the question "So, is that good or bad?" It's hard to answer that without having some points for comparison. So we did a review of a large number of published usability studies (using the ACM Digital Library and web search tools) and found 50 studies that reported average SUS scores across a total of 129 different conditions. The studies covered a wide range of subjects, including websites, applications, computer hardware, mobile devices, and voice systems. They were conducted in various parts of the world, including the United States, Germany, Switzerland, the United Kingdom, and New Zealand. The distribution of the average SUS scores from these 129 conditions is shown here.

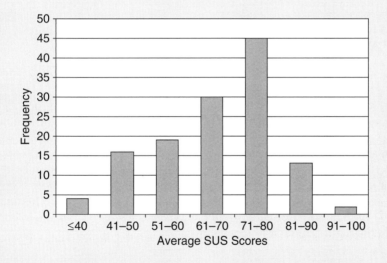

Each of these studies had at least five participants; the maximum number was 81. The average SUS score from the 129 conditions was 66 percent and the median was 69 percent. The 25th percentile was 57 percent and the 75th percentile was 77 percent. (More details can be found on our website at *www.MeasuringUserExperience.com*.) These numbers would tend to suggest that you can think of an average SUS score under about 60 percent as relatively poor, while one over about 80 percent could be considered pretty good. But don't forget to consider the confidence interval for any average SUS score that you calculate.

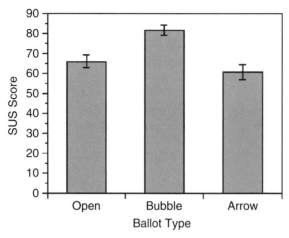

**FIGURE 6.16**

Average SUS ratings for three sample ballots. Error bars represent one standard error of the mean. *Source:* From Everett et al. (2006); reprinted with permission from *Human Factors* 45(4). Copyright © 2003 by the Human Factors and Ergonomics Society. All rights reserved.

## 6.6 ONLINE SERVICES

More and more companies are appreciating the value of getting feedback from the users of their websites. The currently in-vogue term for this process is listening to the *"Voice of the Customer,"* or VoC. This is essentially the same process as in post-session self-reported metrics. The main difference is that VoC studies are typically done on live websites. The common approach is that a randomly selected percentage of live-site users are offered a pop-up survey asking for their feedback at a specific point in their interaction with the site—usually on logout, exiting the site, or completing a transaction. Another approach is to provide a standard mechanism for getting this feedback at various places in the site. The following sections present some of these online services. This list is not intended to be exhaustive, but it is at least representative.

### 6.6.1 Website Analysis and Measurement Inventory

The Website Analysis and Measurement Inventory (WAMMI—*www.wammi.com*) is an online service that grew out of an earlier tool called Software Usability Measurement Inventory (SUMI), both of which were developed by the Human Factors Research Group (HFRG) of University College Cork in Ireland. Although SUMI is designed for evaluation of software applications, WAMMI is designed for evaluation of websites. Note that this same team is now developing a question-naire called Measuring the Usability of Multi-Media Systems (MUMMS).

As shown in Figure 6.17, WAMMI is composed of 20 statements with associated 5-point Likert scales of agreement. Like SUS, some of the statements are positive and some are negative. WAMMI is available in most European languages. The primary advantage that a service like WAMMI has over creating your own questionnaire and associated rating scales is that WAMMI has already been used in the evaluation of hundreds of websites worldwide. When used on your site, the results are delivered in the form of a comparison against their reference database built from tests of these hundreds of sites.

Results from a WAMMI analysis, as illustrated in Figure 6.18, are divided into five areas: Attractiveness, Controllability, Efficiency, Helpfulness, and Learnability, plus an overall usability score. Each of these scores is standardized (from comparison to their reference database), so a score of 50 is average and 100 is perfect.

## 6.6.2 American Customer Satisfaction Index

The American Customer Satisfaction Index (ACSI—*www.TheACSI.org*) was developed at the Stephen M. Ross Business School of The University of Michigan. It covers a wide range of industries, including retail, automotive, and manufacturing. ForeSee Results (*www.ForeSeeResults.com*) applies the methodology of the ACSI to measure customer satisfaction with the online experience and produce industry-specific indices. The ACSI has become particularly popular for analyzing U.S. government websites. For example, 92 websites were included in the 2nd Quarter 2006 analysis of e-government websites (ForeSee Results, 2006). Similarly, ForeSee Results' annual Top 40 Online Retail Satisfaction Index assesses such popular sites as Amazon.com, NetFlix, L.L. Bean, J.C. Penney, Dell, and CompUSA.

The ForeSee Results ACSI-based questionnaire for websites is composed of a core set of 14 to 20 questions (example shown in Figure 6.19 on page 154) customized to the function of the website (e.g., information, e-commerce, etc.). Each model question asks for a rating on a 10-point scale of different attributes of the web experience such as the quality of information, freshness of information, clarity of site organization, overall satisfaction with the site, and future behaviors (e.g., likelihood to return to the site or recommend the site). In addition, custom questions are added to the survey to profile site visitors in terms of visit intent, visit frequency, and other specific information that helps organizations profile visitors in terms meaningful to their business or mission.

As shown in Figure 6.20 (see page 155), which is an example of an informational website, the results for the website are divided into six quality-related elements that drive satisfaction—Content, Functionality, Look & Feel, Navigation, Search, and Site Performance—and overall satisfaction. The screenshot shows not only the ratings for satisfaction elements, but the relative impact of improving satisfaction for each element on increasing satisfaction overall. In addition, ratings are provided for two Future Behaviors—Likelihood to Return and Likelihood to Recommend the site to Others. All scores are on a 100-point index scale. This cause-and-effect

**152**

**wammi**

| Statement 1-10 of 20 | Strongly Agree | | | | Strongly Disagree |
|---|---|---|---|---|---|
| This web site has much that is of interest to me. | ○ | ○ | ○ | ○ | ○ |
| It is difficult to move around this web site. | ○ | ○ | ○ | ○ | ○ |
| I can quickly find what I want on this web site. | ○ | ○ | ○ | ○ | ○ |
| This web site seems logical to me. | ○ | ○ | ○ | ○ | ○ |
| This web site needs more introductory explanations. | ○ | ○ | ○ | ○ | ○ |
| The pages on this web site are very attractive. | ○ | ○ | ○ | ○ | ○ |
| I feel in control when I'm using this web site. | ○ | ○ | ○ | ○ | ○ |
| This web site is too slow. | ○ | ○ | ○ | ○ | ○ |
| This web site helps me find what I am looking for. | ○ | ○ | ○ | ○ | ○ |
| Learning to find my way around this web site is a problem. | ○ | ○ | ○ | ○ | ○ |

| Statement 11-20 of 20 | Strongly Agree | | | | Strongly Disagree |
|---|---|---|---|---|---|
| I don't like using this web site. | ○ | ○ | ○ | ○ | ○ |
| I can easily contact the people I want to on this web site. | ○ | ○ | ○ | ○ | ○ |
| I feel efficient when I'm using this web site. | ○ | ○ | ○ | ○ | ○ |
| It is difficult to tell if this web site has what I want. | ○ | ○ | ○ | ○ | ○ |
| Using this web site for the first time is easy. | ○ | ○ | ○ | ○ | ○ |
| This web site has some annoying features. | ○ | ○ | ○ | ○ | ○ |
| Remembering where I am on this web site is difficult. | ○ | ○ | ○ | ○ | ○ |
| Using this web site is a waste of time. | ○ | ○ | ○ | ○ | ○ |
| I get what I expect when I click on things on this web site. | ○ | ○ | ○ | ○ | ○ |
| Everything on this web site is easy to understand. | ○ | ○ | ○ | ○ | ○ |

**FIGURE 6.17**

The 20 rating scales used by the WAMMI online service. *Source:* Reprinted with permission from Dr. J. Kirakowski, Human Factors Research Group, University College, Cork, Ireland.

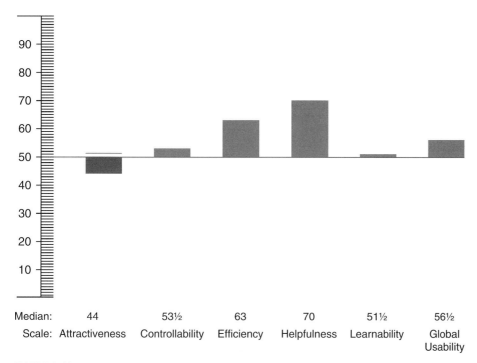

**FIGURE 6.18**

Sample data from the WAMMI online service showing average scores in each of five categories, plus an overall usability score. Reprinted with permission from Dr. J. Kirakowski, Human Factors Research Group, University College, Cork, Ireland.

modeling shows the quantitative relationships between what drives satisfaction, overall satisfaction, and behaviors resulting from satisfaction that have a financial impact on the organization.

Finally, they also make assessments of the impact that each of the quality scores has on overall satisfaction. This allows you to view the results in four quadrants, as shown in Figure 6.21, plotting the quality scores on the vertical axis and the impact on overall satisfaction on the horizontal axis. The scores in the lower right quadrant (high impact, low score) indicate the areas where you should focus your improvements to get the maximum return on satisfaction and on investment.

### 6.6.3 OpinionLab

A somewhat different approach is taken by OpinionLab (*www.OpinionLab.com*), which provides for page-level feedback from users. In some ways, this can be thought of as a page-level analog of the task-level feedback discussed earlier. As

Customer Satisfaction
Survey

Thank you for visiting our site. You have been randomly selected to take part in this survey to let us
know what we are doing well and where we need to do better. Please take a minute or two to give us
your opinions. The feedback you provide will help us enhance our site and serve you better in the
future. All responses are strictly confidential.

**1:** Please rate the **quality of information** on this site.
1=Poor                                                        10=Excellent
1    2    3    4    5    6    7    8    9    10          Don't Know

**2:** Please rate the **freshness of content** on this site.
1=Poor                                                        10=Excellent
1    2    3    4    5    6    7    8    9    10          Don't Know

**3:** Please rate the **convenience of the services** on this site.
1=Poor                                                        10=Excellent
1    2    3    4    5    6    7    8    9    10          Don't Know

**4:** Please rate the **ability to accomplish what you wanted to** on this site.
1=Poor                                                        10=Excellent
1    2    3    4    5    6    7    8    9    10          Don't Know

**5:** Please rate the **clarity of site organization**.
1=Poor                                                        10=Excellent
1    2    3    4    5    6    7    8    9    10          Don't Know

**6:** Please rate the **clean layout** of this site.
1=Poor                                                        10=Excellent
1    2    3    4    5    6    7    8    9    10          Don't Know

**7:** Please rate the **ability to find information you want** on this site.
1=Poor                                                        10=Excellent
1    2    3    4    5    6    7    8    9    10          Don't Know

**8:** Please rate the **clarity of site map/directory**.
1=Poor                                                        10=Excellent
1    2    3    4    5    6    7    8    9    10          Don't Know

**9:** Please rate the **reliability of site performance** on this site.
1=Poor                                                        10=Excellent
1    2    3    4    5    6    7    8    9    10          Don't Know

**10:** What is your **overall satisfaction** with this site?
1=Poor                                                        10=Excellent
1    2    3    4    5    6    7    8    9    10

**11:** How well does this site **meet your expectations**?
1=Poor                                                        10=Excellent
1    2    3    4    5    6    7    8    9    10

**12:** How does this site **compare to your idea of an ideal website**?
1=Poor                                                        10=Excellent
1    2    3    4    5    6    7    8    9    10

**13:** How likely are you to **return to this site**?
1=Not Very Likely                                            10=Very Likely
1    2    3    4    5    6    7    8    9    10

**14:** How likely are you to **recommend this site to someone else**?
1=Not Very Likely                                            10=Very Likely
1    2    3    4    5    6    7    8    9    10

**15:** How **frequently** do you visit this site?
Please Select

**16:** What would like to see improved on our site? *(optional)*

Thank you for taking the time to complete this survey. We value your input as we strive to continuously
improve our site to serve you better.

Submit    Cancel

**FIGURE 6.19**

Typical questions in an ACSI-based survey for a website. Used with permission.

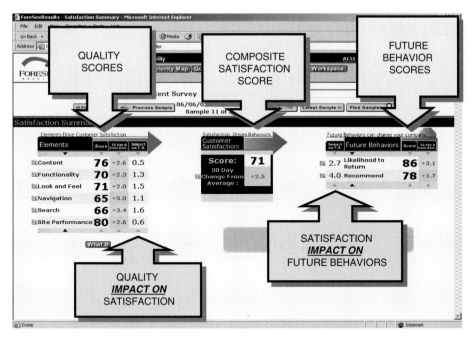

**FIGURE 6.20**

Sample results from a ForeSee Results analysis for a website: scores for six quality areas (*left*) along with values estimating the impact that each score has on overall customer satisfaction (*center*); scores for two "future behavior" areas (*right*) along with values estimating the satisfaction impact on those areas. *Source:* From ForeSee Results. Used with permission.

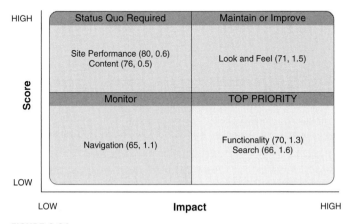

**FIGURE 6.21**

Sample results from a ForeSee Results analysis for a website. High and low scores for the six quality areas are represented on the vertical axis, and high and low impact scores are shown on the horizontal axis. The quality areas that fall in the lower right quadrant (Functionality and Search) should be top priorities for improvement. *Source:* From ForeSee Results. Used with permission.

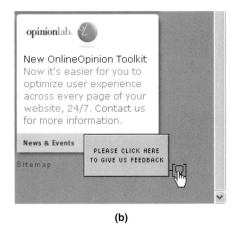

(a)        (b)

**FIGURE 6.22**

Web page (a) containing OpinionLab's feedback mechanism (*lower right*). This animated icon stays in that position while the user scrolls the page. Moving the mouse pointer over the icon reveals another version (b).

(a)        (b)

**FIGURE 6.23**

Examples of OpinionLab mechanisms for capturing feedback about a web page. The version on the left (a) allows the user to give the page a quick overall rating. The version on the right (b) allows for more detailed feedback on a few different scales.

shown in Figure 6.22, a common way for OpinionLab to allow for this page-level feedback is through a floating icon that always stays at the bottom right corner of the page regardless of the scroll position.

Clicking on that icon then leads to one of the methods shown in Figure 6.23 for capturing the feedback. The OpinionLab scales use five points that are marked simply as: $--$, $-$, $+-$, $+$, and $++$. OpinionLab provides a variety of techniques for visualizing the data for a website, including the one shown in Figure 6.24, which

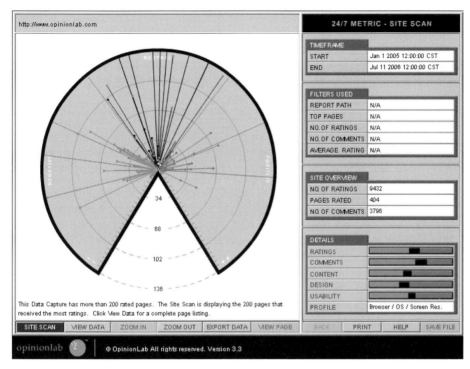

**FIGURE 6.24**

OpinionLab provides a variety of techniques for visualizing website data. On the left of the visualization shown here, the most-rated 200 pages are represented graphically. The pages receiving the most negative ratings are at the left, those with neutral ratings at the top, and those with the most positive ratings at the right.

allows you to easily spot the pages that are getting the most negative feedback and those that are getting the most positive feedback.

## 6.6.4 Issues with Live-Site Surveys

The following are some of the issues you will need to address when you use live-site surveys.

*Number of questions.* The fewer questions you have, the higher your response rate is likely to be. That's one reason that companies like OpinionLab keep the number of questions to a minimum. You need to strike a balance between getting the information you need and "scaring off" potential respondents. With every question you consider adding, ask yourself if you absolutely must have the information. Some researchers believe that 20 is about the maximum number of questions you should ask in this type of survey.

*Self-selection of respondents.* Because respondents make a decision about whether to complete the survey, they are self-selecting. You should at least ask yourself if this biases the responses in any way. Some researchers argue that people who are unhappy with the website are more likely to respond than those who are happy (or at least satisfied). If your main purpose is to uncover areas of the site to improve, that may not be a problem.

*Number of respondents.* Many of these services work on the basis of a percentage of visitors to offer the survey to. Depending on the amount of traffic your site gets, this percentage could be quite small and still generate a large number of responses. You should closely monitor responses to see if you need to increase or decrease the percentage.

*Nonduplication of respondents.* Most of these services provide a mechanism for noting (typically via a browser cookie) when the survey has already been offered to someone. As long as the user doesn't clear her cookies and is using the same computer, the survey won't be presented to her again for a specified time period. This prevents duplicate responses from an individual and also prevents annoying those users who don't want to respond.

## 6.7 OTHER TYPES OF SELF-REPORTED METRICS

Many of the self-report techniques described so far have sought to assess users reactions to products or websites as a whole or to tasks performed using them. But depending on a usability study's objectives, you might want to assess users reactions to specific product *attributes* overall or specific product *elements*.

### 6.7.1 Assessing Specific Attributes

Here are some of the attributes of a product or website that you might be interested in assessing:

- Visual appeal
- Perceived efficiency
- Usefulness
- Enjoyment
- Credibility
- Appropriateness of terminology
- Ease of navigation
- Responsiveness

Covering in detail the ways you might assess all the specific attributes you are interested in is beyond the scope of this book. Instead, we will describe a few examples of usability studies that have focused on assessing specific attributes.

Gitte Lindgaard and her associates at Carleton University in Ottawa, Ontario, were interested in learning how quickly users form an impression of the visual appeal of a web page (Lindgaard et al., 2006). They flashed images of web pages for either 50 msec or 500 msec to the participants in their study. Each web page was rated on an overall scale of visual appeal and on the following bipolar scales: Interesting/ Boring, Good Design/Bad Design, Good Color/Bad Color, Good Layout/Bad Layout, and Imaginative/Unimaginative. They found that the ratings on all five of these scales correlated very strongly with visual appeal ($r^2 = 0.86$ to 0.92). They also found that the results were consistent across the participants at both the 50-msec and 500-msec exposure levels, indicating that even at 50 msec (or 1/20th of a second), users can form a consistent impression about the visual appeal of a web page.

Several years ago, we conducted an online study of ten different websites to learn more about what makes a website *engaging*. We defined an engaging website as one that (1) stimulates your interest and curiosity, (2) makes you want to explore the site further, and (3) makes you want to revisit the site. After exploring each site, the participants responded to a single rating worded as "This website is: Not At All Engaging . . . Highly Engaging" using a 5-point scale. The two sites that received the highest ratings on this scale are shown in Figure 6.25.

One of the techniques often used in analyzing the data from subjective rating scales is to focus on the responses that fall into the extremes of the scale: the top one or two or bottom one or two values. As mentioned earlier, these are often referred to as "top-2-box" or "bottom-2-box" scores. We recently used this technique in an online study assessing participants' reactions to various load times for an intranet homepage. We artificially manipulated the load time over a range of 1 to 11 seconds. Different load times were presented in a random order, and the participants were never told what the load time was. After experiencing each load time, the participants were asked to rate that load time on a 5-point scale of "Completely Unacceptable" to "Completely Acceptable." In analyzing the data, we focused on the "Unacceptable" ratings (1 or 2) and the "Acceptable" ratings (4 or 5). These are plotted in Figure 6.26 as a function of the load time. Looking at the data this way makes it clear that a "crossover" from acceptable to unacceptable happened between three and five seconds.

B. J. Fogg and his associates at the Stanford Persuasive Technology Lab conducted a series of studies to learn more about what makes a website *credible* (Fogg et al., 2001). For example, they used a 51-item questionnaire to assess how believable a website is. Each item was a statement about some aspect of the site, such as "This site makes it hard to distinguish ads from content," and an associated 7-point scale from "Much less believable" to "Much more believable," on which the users rated the impact of that aspect on how believable the site is. They found that data from the 51 items fell into seven scales, which they labeled as Real-World Feel, Ease of Use, Expertise, Trustworthiness, Tailoring, Commercial Implications, and Amateurism. For example, one of the 51 items that weighted strongly in the "Real-World Feel" scale was "The site lists the organization's physical address."

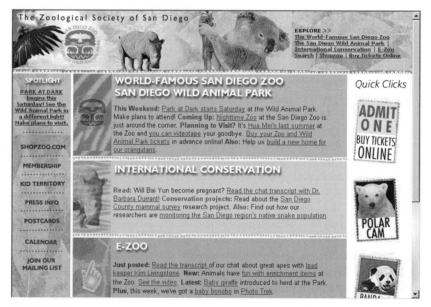

**FIGURE 6.25**

Screenshots of two websites that were rated as the most engaging of the ten sites that were examined.

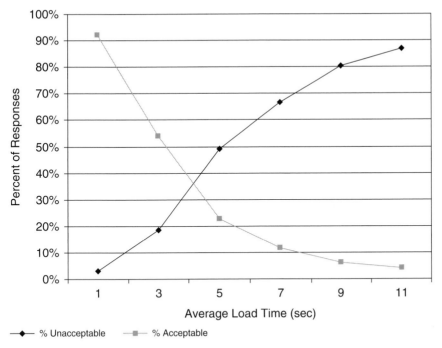

**FIGURE 6.26**

Data from participants who rated the acceptability of various load times for an intranet homepage presented in a random order. The ratings were on a 5-point scale, and the data from the online study shown here are for the bottom two (Unacceptable) and top two (Acceptable) values only.

---

**SHOULD YOU NUMBER SCALE VALUES?**

One of the issues that comes up in designing rating scales is whether to show a numeric value for each scale position. The examples we've shown in this chapter have included both numbered and unnumbered scales. Our sense is that with scales of no more than five or seven values, adding numeric values for each position is probably not necessary. But as you increase the number of scale values, numbers might become more useful in helping the user keep track of where she or he is on the scale.

---

## 6.7.2 Assessing Specific Elements

In addition to assessing specific *aspects* of a product or website, you might be interested in assessing specific *elements* of it, such as instructions, FAQs, or online help; the homepage; the search function; or the site map. The techniques for assessing subjective reactions to specific elements are basically the same as for assessing specific aspects. You simply ask the participant to focus on the specific element and then present some appropriate rating scales.

The Nielsen Norman Group (Stover, Coyne, & Nielsen, 2002) conducted a study that focused specifically on the site maps of ten different websites. After interacting with a site, the participants completed a questionnaire that included six statements related to the site map:

- The site map is easy to find.
- The information on the site map is helpful.
- The site map is easy to use.
- The site map made it easy to find the information I was looking for.
- The site map made it easy to understand the structure of the website.
- The site map made it clear what content is available on the website.

Each statement was accompanied by a 7-point Likert scale of "Strongly Disagree" to "Strongly Agree." They then averaged the ratings from the six scales to get an overall rating of the site map for each of the ten sites. This is an example of getting more reliable ratings of a feature of a website by asking for several different ratings of the feature and then averaging them together.

Tullis (1998) conducted a study that focused on candidate homepage designs for a website. (In fact, the designs were really just templates containing "placeholder" text.) One of the techniques he used for comparing the designs was to ask participants in the study to rate the designs on three rating scales: page format, attractiveness, and use of color. Each was rated on a 5-point scale ($-2$, $-1$, $0$, $1$, $2$) of "Poor" to "Excellent." The results for the five designs are shown in Figure 6.27. The design that received the best ratings was Template 1, and the design that received the worst ratings was Template 4.

This study also illustrates another common technique in studies that involve a comparison of alternatives. The participants were asked to rank-order the five templates from their most preferred to least preferred. These data can be analyzed by looking at the average rank for each alternative or at the percentages of high or low ranks. In this study, 48 percent of the participants ranked Template 1 as their first choice, while 57 percent ranked Template 4 as their last choice.

### 6.7.3 Open-Ended Questions

Most questionnaires in usability studies include some open-ended questions in addition to the various kinds of rating scales that we've discussed in this chapter. In fact, one common technique is to allow the participant to add comments related to any of the individual rating scales. Although the utility of these comments to the calculation of any metrics is probably limited, they can be very helpful in identifying ways to improve the product.

Another flavor of open-ended question commonly used in usability studies is to ask the participants to list three to five things they like the *most* about the product

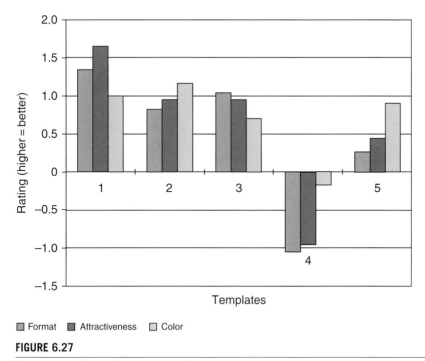

**FIGURE 6.27**

Data in which five different designs for a website's homepage were each rated on three scales: format, attractiveness, and use of color. *Source:* Adapted from Tullis (1998).

and three to five things they like the *least*. These can be translated into metrics by counting the number of instances of essentially the same thing being listed and then reporting those frequencies.

## 6.7.4 Awareness and Comprehension

A technique that somewhat blurs the distinction between self-reported data and performance data involves asking the users some questions about what they saw or remember from interacting with the application or website after they have performed some tasks with it, and not being allowed to refer back to it. One flavor of this is a check for awareness of various features of a website. For example, consider the homepage shown in Figure 6.28. First, the participant would be given a chance to explore the site a little and complete a few very general tasks like reading the latest news about the International Space Station, finding out how to get images from the Hubble Space Telescope, and learning more about the continuing impact of Hurricane Katrina. Then, with the site no longer available to the participant, a questionnaire is given that lists a variety of specific pieces of content that the site may or may not have had.

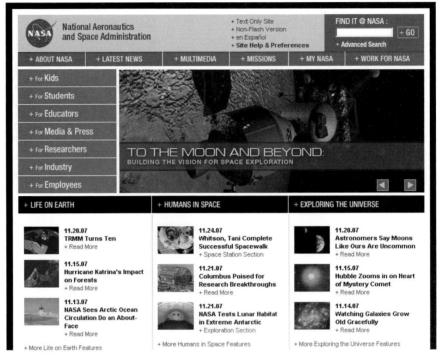

**FIGURE 6.28**

This NASA homepage illustrates one technique for assessing how "attention-grabbing" various elements of a web page are. After letting participants interact with it, you ask them to identify from a list of content items which ones were actually on the site.

These would generally be content *not* directly related to the specific tasks that the participant was asked to perform. You're interested in whether some of these other pieces of content "stood out." The participant then indicates on the questionnaire which of the pieces of content he or she remembers seeing on the site. For example, two of the items on the questionnaire might be "NASA's testing of a possible lunar habitat" and "studies of Arctic Ocean circulation," both of which are links on the homepage. One of the challenges in designing such a questionnaire is that it must include logical "distracter" items as well—items that were not on the website (or page, if you limit the study to one page) but that look like they could have been.

A closely related technique involves testing for the participants' learning and comprehension related to some of the website's content. After interacting with a site, they are given a quiz to test their comprehension of some of the information on the site. If the information is something that some of the participants might have already known prior to using the site, it would be necessary to administer a pretest to determine what they already know and then compare their results from the post-test to that. When the participants are not overtly directed to the information during their interaction with the site, this is usually called an "incidental learning" technique.

### 6.7.5  Awareness and Usefulness Gaps

One type of analysis that can be very valuable is to look at the difference between participants' *awareness* of a specific piece of information or functionality and the perceived *usefulness* of that same piece of information or functionality once they are made aware of it. For example, if a vast majority of participants are unaware of some specific functionality, but once they notice it they find it very useful, you should promote or highlight that functionality in some way.

To analyze awareness–usefulness gaps, you must have both an awareness and a usefulness metric. We typically ask participants about awareness as a yes/no question—for example, "Were you aware of this functionality prior to this study? (yes or no)." Then we ask: "On a 1 to 5 scale, how useful is this functionality to you? (1 = Not at all useful; 5 = Very useful)." This assumes that they have had a couple of minutes to explore the functionality. Next, you will need to convert the rating-scale data into a top-2-box score so that you have an apples-to-apples comparison. Simply plot the percent of participants who are aware of the functionality next to the percent of those who found the functionality useful (percent top-2-box). The difference between the two bars is called the *awareness–usefulness gap* (see Figure 6.29).

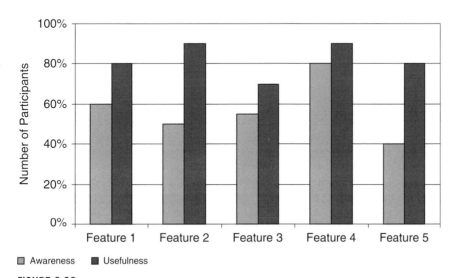

**FIGURE 6.29**

Data from a study looking at awareness–usefulness gaps. Items with the greatest difference between the awareness and usefulness ratings, such as Features 2 and 5, are those you should consider making more obvious in the interface.

## 6.8 SUMMARY

Many different techniques are available for getting usability metrics from self-reported data. The following are some of the key points to remember.

1. Consider getting self-reported data both at a task level and at the end of the usability session. Task-level data can help you identify areas that need improvement. Session-level data can help you get a sense of overall usability.

2. When testing in a lab, consider using one of the standard questionnaires for assessing subjective reactions to a system. The System Usability Scale has been shown to be robust even with relatively small numbers of participants (e.g., 8–10).

3. When testing a live website, consider using one of the online services for measuring user satisfaction. The major advantage they provide is the ability to show you how the results for your website compare to a large number of sites in their reference database.

4. Be creative in the use of other techniques in addition to simple rating scales. When possible, ask for ratings on a given topic in several different ways and average the results to get more consistent data. Carefully construct any new rating scales. Make appropriate use of open-ended questions, and consider techniques like checking for awareness or comprehension after interacting with the product.

# Behavioral and Physiological Metrics

During a typical usability test, most participants do much more than complete tasks and fill out questionnaires. They may laugh, groan, shout, grimace, smile, fidget in their chair, look aimlessly around the room, or drum their fingers on the table. These are all behaviors that are potentially measurable and offer insights into the usability of the product being tested. Most of this body language and verbalization can be observed and noted by an attentive test administrator, but some types of subtle or fleeting behavior are harder to observe. For example, facial expressions can change very rapidly, making a good-quality video recording of the participant's face very useful. And there are still other behaviors that most people aren't even conscious of, such as increased heart rate, pupil dilation, and slight increases in sweating, which require specialized equipment to monitor. All of these behaviors, those that are directly observable and those that require special instruments, are the subject of this chapter.

---

**UNPLANNED RESPONSES IN THE USABILITY LAB**

We once had a participant in our usability lab who was eight months pregnant. She was testing a prototype of a particularly challenging internal application. At one point during the session she said the interface was so bad that it was giving her labor pains! Thankfully, she admitted she was joking just before we called the paramedics.

---

## 7.1 OBSERVING AND CODING OVERT BEHAVIORS

There are probably as many different approaches to taking notes during a usability test as there are evaluators conducting usability tests. Each approach tends to be highly personalized. Some like a free-form "stream-of-consciousness" approach where they narrate the events of the session, others like to use forms where they note specific events and behaviors, and still others like to use sophisticated data-logging tools that automatically time-stamp all their entries. All of these approaches are useful, depending on the purposes of the usability study, but to be useful as a metric, some type of structure must be applied to these observations. Although it's possible to apply some structure to free-form notes *after* a test session, it's more effective to identify some degree of structure *before* the test, while also allowing for the indication of behaviors that don't fit within the structure.

A participant's overt behaviors in a usability session can be divided into two general categories: verbal and nonverbal. Verbal behaviors include anything the participant actually *says*. Nonverbal behaviors include a range of other things that the participant might *do*. Both can be helpful in identifying parts of an interface or product that cause problems for users or, conversely, that delight users.

## 7.1.1 Verbal Behaviors

Verbal behaviors provide valuable insight into a participant's emotional and mental state while they are using a product. The participant will probably make many comments, some negative ("This is hard" or "I don't like this design") and some positive ("Wow, this is much easier than I expected" or "I really like the way this looks"). Some comments are neutral or just hard to interpret, such as "This is interesting."

The most meaningful metric related to verbal behaviors is the ratio of positive to negative comments. To do this type of analysis, you first need to catalog all verbal behaviors and then categorize each one as positive, negative, or neutral. Once this is complete, simply look at the ratio of positive to negative comments, as illustrated in Figure 7.1. Only knowing that positive behaviors outnumbered negative comments by a 2:1 ratio does not say a lot by itself. However, it's much more meaningful if the ratios are compared across different design iterations or between different products. For example, if the ratio of positive to negative comments has increased significantly with each new design iteration, this would be an indicator of an improved design.

It's also possible to get more granular by differentiating among different types of verbal behaviors, such as the following:

- Strongly positive comments (e.g., "This is terrific!")
- Other positive comments (e.g., "That was pretty good.")
- Strongly negative comments (e.g., "This website is terrible!")
- Other negative comments (e.g., "I don't much like the way that worked.")
- Suggestions for improvement (e.g., "It would have been better if . . .")
- Questions (e.g., "How does this work?")
- Variation from expectation (e.g., "This isn't what I was expecting to get.")
- Stated confusion or lack of understanding (e.g., "This page doesn't make any sense.")
- Stated frustration (e.g., "At this point I'd just shut it off!")

These types of data are analyzed by examining the frequency of comments within each category. Like the previous example, comparing across design iterations or

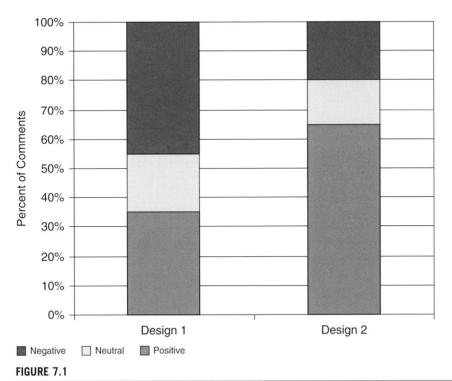

**FIGURE 7.1**

Example of coding the percentage of neutral, positive, and negative comments for two different designs.

products is the most useful. Categorizing verbal behaviors beyond just the positive, negative, or neutral can be somewhat challenging. It's helpful to work with another usability specialist to get to some level of agreement about categorizing each verbal behavior. Make good use of video recording. Even the best note takers can miss something important. Forms may be very helpful in documenting both verbal and nonverbal behaviors. Figure 7.2 shows an example of a form that could be used for coding observations and other data during a usability test.

## 7.1.2 Nonverbal Behaviors

Nonverbal behaviors can be very revealing about a participant's experience with a product. These might include facial expressions (frowning, smiling, looks of surprise, furrowing brow) or body language (fidgeting, leaning close to the screen, rubbing the head). Deriving any meaningful metrics from these nonverbal behaviors is somewhat challenging and most useful only for certain types of products. If you're evaluating websites, software, or other products that have very few physical demands, these metrics may have limited utility. But there are cases where some

**Usability Test Observation Coding Form**

Date: _____ Participant #: _____ Task #: _____

Start Time: _____ End Time: _____

**Verbal Behaviors**           Notes

☐ ☐ ☐ Strongly positive comment _____

☐ ☐ ☐ Other positive comment _____

☐ ☐ ☐ Strongly negative comment _____

☐ ☐ ☐ Other negative comment _____

☐ ☐ ☐ Suggestion for improvement _____

☐ ☐ ☐ Question _____

☐ ☐ ☐ Variation from expectation _____

☐ ☐ ☐ Stated confusion _____

☐ ☐ ☐ Stated frustration _____

Other: _____

**Nonverbal Behaviors**      Notes

☐ ☐ ☐ Frowning/Grimacing/Unhappy _____

☐ ☐ ☐ Smiling/Laughing/Happy _____

☐ ☐ ☐ Surprised/Unexpected _____

☐ ☐ ☐ Furrowed brow/Concentration _____

☐ ☐ ☐ Evidence of impatience _____

☐ ☐ ☐ Leaning in close to screen _____

☐ ☐ ☐ Variation from expectation _____

☐ ☐ ☐ Fidgeting in chair _____

☐ ☐ ☐ Random mouse movement _____

☐ ☐ ☐ Groaning/Deep sigh _____

☐ ☐ ☐ Rubbing head/eyes/neck _____

Other: _____

**Task Completion Status**           Notes:

Incomplete:           Complete:

☐ Participant gave up      ☐ Fully complete

☐ Task "called" by moderator      ☐ Complete with assistance

☐ Thought complete, but not      ☐ Partial completion

**FIGURE 7.2**

Form for coding observations during a usability test. This form is designed to be completed for each task that the participant attempts. It helps to have multiple observers complete the form independently and then reach a consensus later.

of these nonverbal behaviors may be indicative of frustration or impatience on the part of the user that may be very important. A number of years ago we were conducting a usability test of a web-based application that had unusually long response times to certain user requests. Although some participants in the test explicitly verbalized their frustration with the long delays, others did things like drum their fingers on the table, groan, or rub their head while waiting for the response.

Nonverbal behaviors may be particularly useful if the product has some physical, perceptual, or cognitive demands. For example, the setup procedure of a popular MP3 player requires the user to enter a serial number from the device when installing the software. The serial number is quite small and printed in white characters on a metallic surface, making it very difficult to read. Nonverbal behaviors such as squinting, turning the device, moving it into better light, or getting a teenager to read the number are good indicators that this task presents some difficulty for users. In this situation, it may be helpful to analyze the frequency of these nonverbal behaviors. As with verbal behaviors, it's also helpful to see how nonverbal behaviors change across different design iterations or when comparing various products.

## 7.2 BEHAVIORS REQUIRING EQUIPMENT TO CAPTURE

Whereas the previous section focused on overt behaviors that a skilled observer can reasonably detect in real time during a usability test, we're now going to turn to a finer-grained analysis that typically requires equipment to capture. These include a detailed analysis of facial expressions, eye-tracking, pupil diameter, skin conductance, and others.

### 7.2.1 Facial Expressions

Recognizing and interpreting facial expressions is a key part of human-to-human communication. The lack of that visual channel is one of the reasons that we sometimes miss subtleties in telephone conversations or e-mail. Many psychologists and others argue that facial expressions are a more accurate window into what people are actually feeling than what they say. Perhaps a more detailed analysis of the facial expressions that the participants in a usability test make could give us useful insight into their reactions to the product and how it could be improved.

One technique is for a trained observer to do a detailed analysis of the facial expressions from a good-quality video recording. This could be done using some method of classifying specific facial expressions. In the 1970s Paul Ekman and Wallace Friesen (1975) developed a taxonomy for characterizing every conceivable facial expression. They called it the Facial Action Coding System (FACS), which included 46 specific actions involving the facial muscles. More recently, they developed the FACS Affect Interpretation Dictionary (FACSAID) to specify the complex linkage between facial actions and emotional response (Ekman, Friesen, & Hager, 2002).

Of course, the main drawback of this kind of analysis of facial expressions is that it's very labor-intensive. That has prompted some researchers to investigate automated ways of measuring facial expressions. Two general approaches have been studied: video-based systems that attempt to recognize specific facial expressions and electromyogram (EMG) sensors that measure activity of specific muscles of the face.

---

### EARLY ANALYSES OF FACIAL EXPRESSIONS

The scientific analysis of facial expressions dates back at least to Charles Darwin, who published *The Expression of the Emotions in Man and Animals* in 1872. He described in great detail a variety of facial expressions for such feelings as anxiety, grief, despair, joy, anger, contempt, disgust, guilt, astonishment, and horror. Darwin argued that these expressions cut across cultures, noting that "the young and the old of widely different races, both with man and animals, express the same state of mind by the same movements." Interestingly, Darwin's book was one of the first to include photos.

---

### Video-Based Systems

Although video-based systems are far less intrusive than EMG systems, the analyses involved are computationally challenging, largely due to the varying appearances of people and their facial expressions. There have, however, been some successes, such as the work of Essa and Pentland (1997), who developed a system capable of recognizing six static facial expressions: anger, disgust, happiness, surprise, eyebrow raise, and neutral. More recently, den Uyl and van Kuilenburg (2005) tested a system called FaceReader against a reference database of 980 images of facial expressions. They found that the system accurately classified 89 percent of the expressions it was shown into one of six emotions: happy, angry, sad, surprised, scared, disgusted, and neutral.

Consider the images in Figure 7.3, which are taken from a video recording of a usability test participant. These images were captured while the participant was performing a particularly challenging and frustrating task. It's easy to see that there is information in her facial expressions. The key is figuring out how to capture and characterize the information in an efficient way.

### Electromyogram Sensors

An alternative to video analysis is the use of electromyogram (EMG) sensors to measure facial expressions, as illustrated in Figure 7.4. These sensors measure electrical activity in certain muscles of the face. They are most commonly used to measure activity of two muscle groups: the corrugator muscle of the forehead, which is associated with frowning, and the zygomatic muscle of the cheeks, which is associated with smiling (Benedek & Hazlett, 2005). But can any of this actually be of value in a usability test?

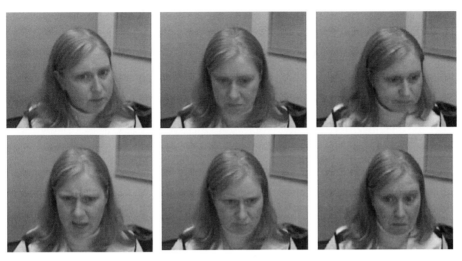

**FIGURE 7.3**

Captured images from a video recording of a test participant performing a particularly challenging and frustrating task. One of the things we discovered in capturing these images is how fleeting facial expressions can be, with many lasting less than a second.

**FIGURE 7.4**

Facial EMG sensors on a participant in a usability study. The sensors on the forehead measure electrical activity of the corrugator muscle, which is associated with frowning. The sensors on the cheek measure activity of the zygomatic muscle, which is associated with smiling. *Source:* From Benedek and Hazlett (2005). Used with permission.

Richard Hazlett of the Johns Hopkins University School of Medicine reported a study in which he used EMG sensors on the corrugator muscles of 28 participants while they performed five tasks on one of two websites: Jones of New York and Tylenol (Hazlett, 2003). He calculated a continuous Frustration Index for each participant from the corrugator EMG by comparison to a baseline established prior to the tasks. Hazlett demonstrated that this Frustration Index correlated well with more conventional measures of task and site difficulty. He found that the mean Frustration Index was significantly greater for tasks answered incorrectly than for those answered correctly. The Frustration Index, which is a continuous measure, also helped to identify specific pages in the sites that were the most problematic.

More recently, Hazlett teamed with Joey Benedek of Microsoft to assess the value of facial EMG in measuring reactions to software (Benedek & Hazlett, 2005). In one study, participants wearing facial EMG sensors were shown a demonstration of possible new features of a desktop operating system. After the demonstration, the participants were asked to list the features of the system that they particularly liked. The researchers calculated a "Desirability Rating" from the EMG data while participants viewed each of the features of the system. This Desirability Rating was based on cases where the zygomatic EMG was at least one standard deviation above the baseline (i.e., a positive response) and there was no accompanying corrugator EMG (i.e., a negative response). They found a good correlation between this Desirability Rating for each of the features and the participants' recall of the features they liked.

In a second study, Benedek and Hazlett measured EMG responses while participants performed nine tasks (e.g., burning a CD, making a playlist) using one of two versions of a media player. The researchers defined a measure of "elevated tension" as the number of seconds that the participant had a corrugator EMG value greater than one standard deviation above that participant's overall corrugator mean. They found that four of the tasks yielded very similar levels of this elevated tension measure for the two media players. But for the other five tasks, Media Player B showed significantly lower levels of elevated tension. They also looked at the correlation between time-on-task and elevated tension, and they found only a moderate correlation ($r = 0.55$). Elevated tension was associated with longer task time for six of the nine tasks, but the effect was reversed for the other three tasks. Their explanation for these three tasks was that the participants were simply enjoying themselves while taking longer to perform the tasks (which included tasks like "Play all classical music"). This shows that time-on-task by itself may not always be a good indicator of task difficulty and that another measure, such as elevated tension based on facial expressions, can add value.

### *Measuring Facial Expressions in Everyday Usability Testing*

Unfortunately, the analysis of facial expressions isn't quite ready for prime-time usability testing, unless you have access to EMG equipment and don't mind submitting your participants to it, or you're willing to devote the time and effort to detailed analyses of video recordings. Therefore, we recommend that until the technology becomes more readily available and less intrusive, you should use informal observation of facial expressions as a way to help you identify situations where you might want to probe users about their thoughts or reactions.

### 7.2.2 **Eye-Tracking**

Eye-tracking in usability testing has become significantly more common over the past few years. Thankfully, these systems have also become more reliable and easier to use. Although still not a mainstay of most usability labs, perhaps they will be in the not-too-distant future.

Although a few different technologies are used, many eye-tracking systems, such as the one shown in Figure 7.5, use a combination of an infrared video camera and infrared light sources to track where the participant is looking. The infrared light sources create reflections on the surface of the participant's eye (called the corneal reflection), and analysis routines compare the location of that reflection to the location of the participant's pupil. The location of the corneal reflection relative to the pupil changes as the participant moves his eyes. You must first calibrate the system by asking the participant to look at a series of known points; then the system can subsequently interpolate where he is looking based on the location of the corneal reflection.

Some eye-tracking systems use a head-mounted apparatus to allow for movement of the head, whereas other systems use either an optical or a magnetic system to track the participant's head and keep up with his eyes remotely. The latest eye-tracking systems are very unobtrusive, using optical tracking of the participant's eyes and allowing for accurate gaze tracking with minimal setup and calibration.

The information provided by an eye-tracking system can be remarkably useful in a usability test. Simply enabling observers of the test to see where the participant is

**FIGURE 7.5**

An eye-tracking monitor from Tobii Technology. Infrared light sources and an infrared video camera are built into the bezel of the monitor. The system tracks the participant's eyes automatically, with no need for a head-tracking apparatus.

looking in real time is extremely valuable. Even if you do no further analyses of the eye-tracking data, just this real time display provides insight that would not be possible otherwise. For example, assume a participant is performing a task on a website and there's a link on the homepage that would take him directly to the page required to complete the task. The participant keeps exploring the website, going down "dead-ends," returning to the homepage, but never reaching the required page.

In a situation like this, you would like to know whether the participant ever saw the appropriate link on the homepage or whether he saw the link but dismissed it as not what he wanted (e.g., because of its wording). Although you could subsequently ask participants that question, their memory may not be completely accurate. With an eye-tracking system you can tell whether the participant at least fixated on the link long enough to read it.

Figure 7.6(a) shows a plot of the series of fixations that an individual participant made on the USA.gov homepage. A fixation is defined by a pause in the eye's movement within a well-defined area. The fixations are numbered to indicate their sequence. The size of each circle is proportional to the length or duration of the fixation. The *saccades*, or movements between fixations, are shown by the lines. The series of fixations by multiple participants on the same page can be analyzed to create a "heat map," shown in Figure 7.6(b). In this visualization, the lightest areas represent greater density of fixations.

### Proportion of Users Looking at a Specific Element or Region

One of the simplest analyses that can be done with an eye-tracking system is determining what percentage of participants in a usability test fixated on a specific element or region of interest. For example, we compared four different treatments for the same area on a web page. It was a small rectangular region of the page (a "bricklet") that was always in the same location and had the same content, but we varied the design of the area itself. Participants in the usability session performed four different tasks using the prototype. Only one of the tasks was directly related to the contents of this area.

Our goal was to see which designs resulted in more fixations on this bricklet. The results are shown in Figure 7.7. Analyzing this data is fairly straightforward, but you should keep a couple of things in mind:

1. Define the specific element of interest in terms of $x$, $y$ coordinates on the page. Most eye-tracking analysis programs make this easy to do. These elements are usually called "areas of interest," "look-zones," or something similar.

2. Define a minimum total fixation time for the element of interest. For the data in Figure 7.7, we chose a minimum of 500 msec; we estimated that this would be the minimum time needed to get any useful information out of the element.

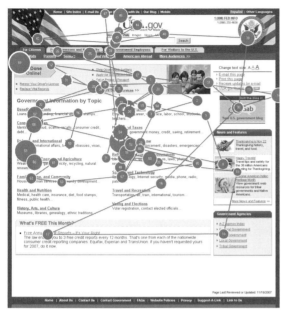

**(a)**

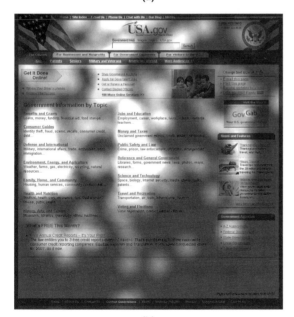

**(b)**

## FIGURE 7.6

Gaze plot (a) showing a series of fixations one participant made while viewing the USA.gov homepage. The size of each circle corresponds to fixation's time. Heat map (b) reflecting density of fixations across a number of participants on different parts of the web page. The lightest areas indicate the most fixations.

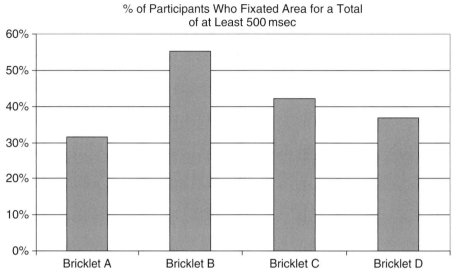

**FIGURE 7.7**

Percentage of participants who fixated for at least 500 msec total on each of the four bricklets. More of them looked at bricklet B than any of the others.

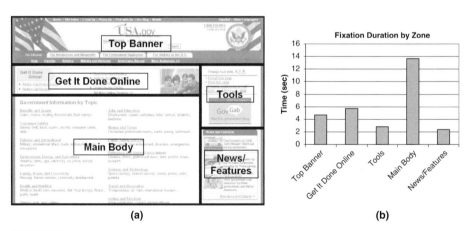

**FIGURE 7.8**

Fire regions defined on the USA.gov homepage (a), and the total fixation duration for each of those regions (b).

### *Time Spent Looking at a Specific Element or Region*

Another way to analyze eye-tracking data is shown in Figure 7.8. In this example, regions of the page are defined (a), and the visualization represents the percentage of time that the participants spent looking in each of those regions (b).

Another way to use eye-tracking in usability studies is to compare the effectiveness of different locations on a web page for the same element. For example, Albert (2002) studied two locations—above or below the top branding area—for an ad on the results page of a web search engine. He found that participants spent about seven times longer looking at ads below the branding area than above it, as shown in Figure 7.9.

When analyzing the time spent looking at different regions, keep the following in mind:

- Clearly define each region. Do not leave any space undefined. Each region should be fairly homogeneous, such as navigation, content, ads, legal information, and so forth.

- Analyze the time as a percentage of total time spent on the page, not as an absolute amount of time, since the absolute amount of time can vary widely between participants.

- Only look at time data when the participant is engaged with the task. Do not include any time data when the participant is debriefing about her experience and still being tracked.

- When presenting data by look zones, the question about where participants actually looked within the zones typically comes up. Therefore, we recommend including a heat map, as in Figure 7.6, that shows the continuous distribution of fixations.

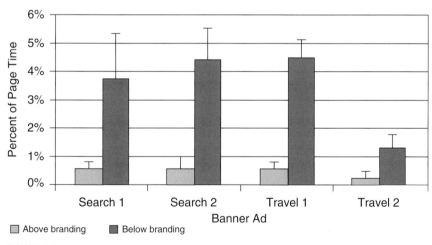

**FIGURE 7.9**

Data showing the percentage of total page viewing time that participants spent looking at ads. Four different ads (Search 1 & 2, Travel 1 & 2) and two different placements (above or below branding area) were tested. *Source:* Adapted from Albert (2002); used with permission.

### Time to Notice a Specific Element

In some situations it's helpful to know how long it takes users to notice a particular element. For example, you may know that users spend only seven seconds on average on the page, but you want to make sure that a specific element, such as a "continue" or "sign up" button, is noticed within the first five seconds. It's helpful that most eye-tracking systems time-stamp each fixation (i.e., the exact time that each fixation occurred).

One way to analyze these data is to take an average of all the times at which the particular element was first fixated. The data should be treated as elapsed time, starting from the initial exposure. The average represents the amount of time taken to first notice the element, for all of those who *did* notice it. Of course, it's possible that some of the participants may not have noticed it all, let alone within the first five seconds. Therefore, you may come up with some misleading data showing an artificially quick time by not taking all the participants into account.

Perhaps a better way to analyze these data is to consider the proportion of participants who noticed the specific element within the specified time period. To do this, simply filter for those fixations that occurred within the specified time period. Then determine whether each participant had a fixation (or set of fixations) on the element during this window of time.

### Scan Paths

Two other metrics from an eye-tracking system can be helpful in evaluating the effectiveness of an interface: length of eye movements and duration of fixations. For example, Fukuda and Bubb (2003) used these two metrics to compare the effectiveness of three different designs for web pages displaying subway timetables. They tested two groups of users: younger (17–29 years) and older (62–74 years). They found that two of the designs resulted in shorter eye movements than the other design for the first two tasks, but the opposite was true for the last two tasks. In general, a design that results in shorter eye movements can be considered a more efficient design because users have to move their eyes less to get the required information. They also found that the navigation elements in the designs that used smaller fonts (e.g., 10-point or smaller) tended to get longer fixations than those that used larger fonts. Longer fixation times generally indicate longer reading or processing times.

## 7.2.3 Pupillary Response

Closely related to the use of eye-tracking in usability studies is the use of information about the response of the pupil. Most eye-tracking systems must detect the location of the participant's pupil and calculate its diameter to determine where he or she is looking. Consequently, information about pupil diameter "comes for free" in most eye-tracking systems. The study of pupillary response, or the contractions and dilations of the pupil, is called pupillometry. Most people know that the pupil

---

**PUPILLARY RESPONSE AND POKER**

One of the most common "tells" in poker is a player's eyes, and especially his or her pupils. It's almost impossible for most players to keep their pupils from dilating when they get a hand that they're excited about. This is one reason most serious poker players wear sunglasses or a visor.

---

contracts and dilates in response to the level of ambient light, but many people don't know that it also responds to cognitive processing, arousal, and increased interest.

You can easily see this for yourself in a couple of ways. If you happen to have a cat, dangle an attractive target in front of it to encourage it to "pounce." As the cat prepares to pounce, watch how its eyes rapidly dilate. Although most of us don't pounce anymore, we have a similar pupillary response when focusing intensely on something. Another way to demonstrate this is to enlist a friend to do some mental arithmetic (e.g., 528 + 356) while you watch his pupils.

The psychological study of pupillary response began in earnest in the 1960s. One of the earliest studies to find evidence of pupil dilation in response to mental effort was by Hess and Polt (1964). It was further studied by Kahneman and Beatty (1966) and later described by Kahneman (1973) in his classic book *Attention and Effort*. But one of the challenges of using pupil dilation as a metric in usability studies is that it has been shown to correlate with a variety of different states of the user, including physical effort (Nunnally, Knott, Duchnowski, & Parker, 1967), mental effort (Hess & Polt, 1964), level of interest (Libby, Lacey, & Lacey, 1973), and emotional response (Steinhauer, Boller, Zubin, & Pearlman, 1983).

To confuse matters even more, there is also some evidence that in a memory overload condition, the pupil actually contracts (Granholm, Asarnow, Sarkin, & Dykes, 1996). In spite of these complications, some researchers have forged ahead to develop practical applications of pupillary response data. Sandra Marshall (2000) at San Diego State University developed an "Index of Cognitive Activity," or ICA, based on pupillary response. Her approach was sufficiently original that she was granted a U.S. patent for it.

Iqbal, Zheng, and Bailey (2004) studied pupillary response while participants performed easy or difficult versions of four different computer tasks: object manipulation (dragging and dropping e-mail messages), reading, mathematical reasoning, and searching for a product from a list of similar products. As shown in Figure 7.10, they found that when they focused on the cognitive components of the tasks (factoring out the motor components), the participants showed significantly larger pupil dilations in response to the difficult tasks than to the easier tasks.

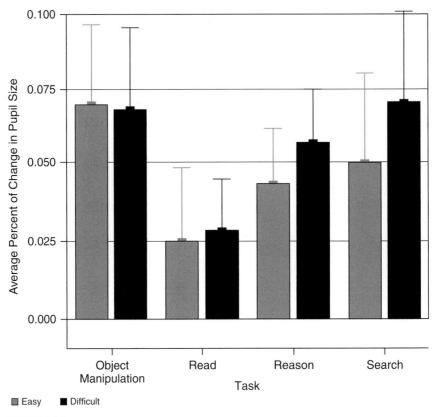

**FIGURE 7.10**

Data showing the change in pupil diameter (relative to baseline) for easy and difficult versions of four different tasks. Iqbal et al. found that when they focused on the cognitive components of the tasks (Reason and Search), the more difficult versions yielded a significantly greater change in pupil diameter. *Source:* Adapted from Iqbal, Zheng, and Bailey (2004); used with permission.

### Pupillometry in Everyday Usability Testing

Because pupil dilation is correlated with so many different mental and emotional states, it's difficult to say whether pupillary changes indicate successes or failures in everyday usability testing. However, measuring pupil diameter may be useful in certain situations where the focus is on the amount of mental concentration or emotional arousal. For example, if you are mainly interested in eliciting an emotional response to a new graphic on a website, then measuring changes in pupil diameter (from baseline) may be very useful. To do this, simply measure the percentage deviation away from a baseline for each participant and then average those deviations across the participants. Alternatively, you can measure the percentage of participants who experienced dilated pupils (of a certain amount) while attending to a particular graphic or performing a specific function.

### 7.2.4 Skin Conductance and Heart Rate

Two physiological measures that have long been known to correlate with stress are skin conductivity and heart rate. Skin conductivity is typically measured using Galvanic Skin Response, or GSR, which measures electrical resistance. As we sweat even small amounts, the additional moisture in the skin increases its conductivity. Heart rate, of course, is also associated with stress: The heart beats faster under stress. Closely related is what's called Heart Rate Variability (HRV). As stress increases, HRV—the heart's ability to beat faster or slower in response to emotional or physical demands—tends to decrease. GSR, heart rate, and HRV are all used in various forms of biofeedback, where the participant uses feedback from devices monitoring these levels to learn to relax. In fact, a computer game called *The Journey to Wild Divine* includes devices for measuring GSR, heart rate, and HRV. In the game, the user explores a virtual world that includes soothing music and beautiful imagery. As a part of the exploration, various exercises are introduced to practice relaxation.

Several studies have sought to determine whether skin conductivity and heart rate could be used as indicators of stress or other adverse reactions in a usability setting. For example, Ward and Marsden (2003) used skin conductance and heart rate to measure user reactions to two versions of a website: a well-designed version and a poorly designed version. The poorly designed version included extensive use of drop-down lists on the homepage to "hide" much of the functionality, provided impoverished navigational cues, used gratuitous animation, and had occasional pop-up windows containing ads. The heart rate and skin conductance data were plotted as changes from the participant's baseline data established during the first minute of the session.

Both measures showed a decrease in heart rate and skin conductance for the well-designed website. For the poorly designed site, the skin conductance data showed an increase over the first five minutes of the session, followed by a return to baseline over the final five minutes. The heart rate data for the poorly designed version showed some variability, but the overall trend was to stay at the same level as the baseline, unlike the well-designed version, which showed a decrease relative to the baseline. Both measures appear to reflect greater stress in interacting with the poorly designed site.

In a study of participants playing a 3D video game (*Super Mario 64*), Lin, Hu, Omata, and Imamiya (2005) looked at the relationships among task performance, subjective ratings of stress, and skin conductance. The tasks involved playing three different parts of the game as quickly and accurately as possible. Participants played each part (task) for ten minutes, during which period they could potentially complete the goal (succeed) multiple times. As shown in Figure 7.11, there was a strong correlation between participants' ratings of how stressful

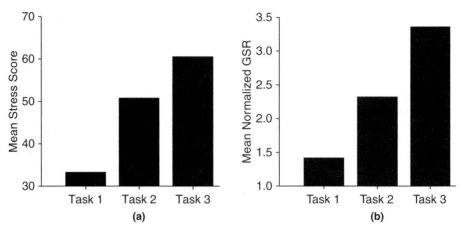

**FIGURE 7.11**

Data showing subjective ratings of stress (a) and normalized GSR (b) for three different tasks in a video game. Both show that Task 3 was the most stressful, followed by Task 2 and then Task 1. *Source:* Adapted from Lin et al. (2005): *Proceedings of OZCHI 2005,* the conference of the Computer–Human Interaction Special Interest Group (CHISIG) of the Human Factors and Ergonomics Society of Australia (HFESA), Todd Bentley and Sandrine Balbo (Eds). Canberra (Australia), 21–25 November 2005. (ACM International Conference Proceedings Series under the ACM ISBN 1–59593–222–4.)

each of the tasks was and their normalized GSR (change relative to the participant's baseline GSR) during performance of each task (a). In addition, the participants who had more successes during the performance of each task tended to have lower GSR levels, indicating that failure was associated with higher levels of stress (b).

Trimmel, Meixner-Pendleton, and Haring (2003) measured skin conductance and heart rate to assess the level of stress induced by the response times for web pages to load. They artificially manipulated page load times to be 2, 10, or 22 seconds. They found significant increases in heart rate as response time (page load time) increased, as shown in Figure 7.12. A similar pattern was found for skin conductance. This is evidence of physiological stress associated with the longer response times.

There have been some advances in the development of devices for measuring skin conductance and heart rate that are less obtrusive than traditional methods and potentially make the devices more suitable for usability testing. For example, Rosalind Picard and Jocelyn Scheirer (2001) of the MIT Media Laboratory invented a device called the Galvactivator glove (Figure 7.13) for measuring skin conductance using a glove that slips on the hand but leaves the fingers completely free. Likewise, Jukka Lekkala's research group at the Technical Research Centre of

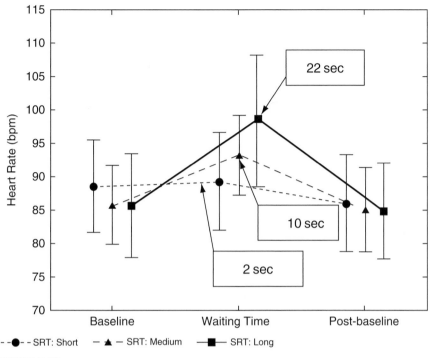

**FIGURE 7.12**

Data showing the heart rate of participants as they experienced different levels of response time waiting for web pages to load. Wait times of 10 and 22 seconds yielded progressively greater increases in heart rate relative to the baseline, indicating physiological stress. *Source:* Adapted from Trimmel et al. (2003); used with permission.

Finland invented a device called the EMFi chair (also shown in Figure 7.13) for unobtrusively measuring the heart rate of someone sitting in it (Anttonen & Surakka, 2005).

### *Measuring Stress in Everyday Usability Testing*

Measuring stress as part of a typical usability study is rarely done, not because it wouldn't be valuable but because the instruments available today are simply too obtrusive for a typical usability lab. Participants are already under considerable pressure when they come into a lab with video cameras, possibly a one-way mirror, and even an eye-tracker. If they were asked to place clips on their fingers to measure stress levels, they might head straight for the door. Perhaps in the next few years new technology will become readily available, like that shown in Figure 7.13, that can measure stress levels on a continuous basis while not impeding the user experience.

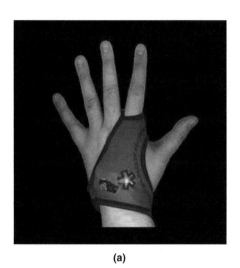

(a)                                                                    (b)

**FIGURE 7.13**

Advances in technology may allow for less obtrusive ways to measure skin conductance and heart rate. The Galvactivator glove (a) from the MIT Media Lab measures skin conductance while leaving the fingers free. The EMFi chair (b) from the Technical Research Center of Finland measures the heart rate of someone sitting in the chair. *Source:* (a) Courtesy of MIT Media Lab. (b) Courtesy of Affective Computing Research Group.

### 7.2.5 Other Measures

A few creative researchers have come up with some other techniques that might be appropriate for assessing the user's level of frustration or engagement while interacting with a computer. Most notably, Rosalind Picard and her team in the Affective Computing Research Group at the MIT Media Lab have investigated a variety of new techniques for assessing the user's emotional state during human–computer interaction. Two of these techniques that might have application to usability testing are the PressureMouse and the Posture Analysis Seat.

The PressureMouse (Reynolds, 2005), shown in Figure 7.14, is a computer mouse with six pressure sensors that detect how tightly the user is gripping the mouse. Researchers had users of the PressureMouse fill out a 5-page

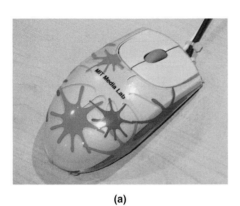 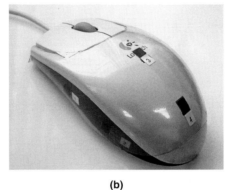

(a)                                              (b)

**FIGURE 7.14**

The PressureMouse is an experimental mouse that can detect how tightly the user is gripping it. The plastic overlay (a) transmits pressure to six sensors on the top and sides of the mouse (b). As users become frustrated with an interface, many of them subconsciously grip the mouse tighter. *Source:* The pressure-sensitive mouse was developed by Carson Reynolds and Rosalind Picard of the MIT Media Lab.

web-based survey (Dennerlein et al., 2003). After submitting one of the pages, participants were given an error message indicating that something was wrong with their entries on that page. After acknowledging the error message, the participants were then taken back to that page, but all the data they had entered had been deleted and they had to reenter it.

As illustrated in Figure 7.15, participants who had been categorized as members of a "high-response" group (based on their negative ratings in a usability questionnaire about the online survey) gripped the mouse significantly tighter for the 15 seconds *after* their loss of data than they did for the 15 seconds *before*.

The Posture Analysis Seat measures the pressure that the user is exerting on the seat and back of the chair. Kapoor, Mota, and Picard (2001) found that they could reliably detect changes in posture on the part of the participant, such as sitting upright, leaning forward, slumping backward, or leaning sideways. These may be used to infer different levels of engagement or interest on the part of the participant.

These new technologies have yet to be used in everyday usability testing, but they look promising. As these or other technologies for measuring engagement or frustration become both affordable and unobtrusive, they can be used in many situations in which they could provide valuable metrics, such as designing products for children who have limited attention spans, evaluating users' patience for download times or error messages, or measuring teenagers' level of engagement with new social networking applications.

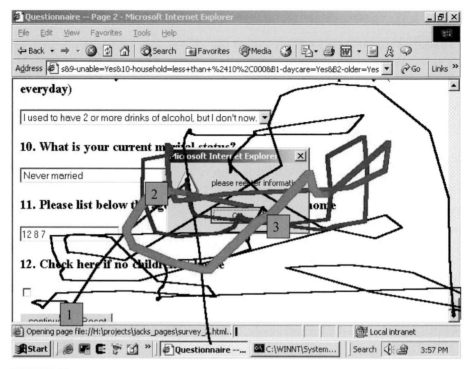

**FIGURE 7.15**

In this visualization of data from the PressureMouse, the mouse leaves a "trail" on the screen. The thickness of the trail indicates how tightly the participant is gripping the mouse. In this example, the participant is initially gripping with normal pressure while completing the online survey. When he clicked on the "Continue" button (#1), the pressure was still normal, until he started reading the error message, which caused him to grip the mouse tighter (#2). Finally, after dismissing the dialog box and seeing that the data he had entered was now gone, his grip on the mouse got even tighter (#3). *Source:* Adapted from Reynolds (2005); used with permission.

## 7.3 SUMMARY

In this chapter we covered a variety of behavioral and physiological measures that might be helpful in usability testing as additional ways of learning about the users' experiences with a product and their reactions to it. Some of these can be detected by careful observation, and some require specialized equipment. But the point about all of them is that you don't want to rely entirely on what the users say or how they perform tasks. These techniques are designed to give you additional insights that might help pinpoint parts of the interface that are working particularly well for the users or that are particularly frustrating. Here's a summary of some of the key points to remember.

1. A structured approach to collecting observational data (both verbal and nonverbal) during a usability test can be very helpful in subsequent analysis (e.g., tabulating the number of positive and negative comments made by participants during each of the tasks). A form with check boxes and other places to mark key events and behaviors on the part of the participant during each task can help facilitate this.

2. Facial expressions that participants make during a usability test may give you additional insight into what they are thinking and feeling beyond what they say. A trained observer can detect and categorize many of these expressions (e.g., frowns, smiles), but some are very fleeting and may require video analysis. Automated techniques for capturing this information using sensors on the face are more intrusive than desired for normal usability testing, but techniques using automated video analysis are being actively researched.

3. Eye-tracking can be a significant benefit in many kinds of usability tests. The technology continues to improve, becoming more accurate, easier to use, and less intrusive. Perhaps its key value can be in determining whether participants in a usability test even looked at a particular element of the interface. We've found that web designers and visual designers are keenly interested in the kinds of analyses you can get from eye-tracking data, such as the "heat maps" of where participants looked on the pages of a website.

4. If you're using eye-tracking, it might be worthwhile to also look at the pupil diameter data that the system captures. Participants' pupils tend to dilate with higher mental workload and with overall arousal.

5. Skin conductance and heart rate can be used to detect parts of an interface that participants find particularly frustrating. But the technology readily available today for measuring these is too intrusive for normal usability testing. Less intrusive technology may be available in the future.

6. Other techniques for capturing information about the participant's behavior, such as a mouse that registers how tightly it is being gripped, are on the horizon and may become useful additions to the battery of tools available for use in usability testing.

# Combined and Comparative Metrics

# 8

Usability data are building blocks. Each piece of usability data can be used to create new metrics. The raw usability data might be task completion rates, time-on-task, or self-reported ease of use. All of these usability data can be used to derive new metrics that were not previously available, such as an overall usability metric or a usability scorecard. Two ways to derive new usability metrics from existing data are (1) by combining more than one metric into a single usability measure and (2) by comparing existing usability data to expert or ideal results. We will review both methods in this chapter.

## 8.1 SINGLE USABILITY SCORES

In many usability tests, you collect more than one metric, such as task completion rate, task time, and perhaps a self-reported metric such as a System Usability Scale (SUS) score. In most cases, you don't care so much about the results for each of these metrics individually as you do about the total picture of the usability of the product as reflected by *all* of them. This section covers the various ways you can combine or represent different metrics to get an overall view of the usability of a product, or of different aspects of a product, perhaps as revealed by different tasks.

The most common question asked after a usability test is "How did it do?" The people who ask this question (often the product manager, developer, or other members of the project team) usually don't want to hear about task completion rates, task times, or questionnaire scores. They want an overall score of some type: Did it do well or not? How did it do in comparison to the last round of usability testing? Making these kinds of judgments in a meaningful way involves combining the metrics from a usability test into some type of single usability score. The challenge is figuring out how to combine scores from different scales appropriately (e.g., task completion rates in percentages and task times in minutes or seconds).

191

### 8.1.1 Combining Metrics Based on Target Goals

Perhaps the easiest way to combine different metrics is to compare each data point to a target goal and represent one single metric based on the percentage of participants who achieved a combined set of goals. For example, assume that the goal is for participants to successfully complete at least 80 percent of their tasks in no more than 70 seconds each on the average. Given that goal, consider the data in Table 8.1, which shows the task completion rate and average time per task for each of eight participants in a usability test. Also shown is an indication of whether each participant met the objective of completing at least 80 percent of the tasks in no more than 70 seconds.

Table 8.1 presents some interesting results. The average values for task completion (82 percent) and task time (67 seconds) would seem to indicate that the goals for this test were met. Even if you look at the number of participants who met the task completion goal (six participants, or 75 percent) or the task time goal (five participants, or 62 percent), you still find the results reasonably encouraging. However, the most appropriate way to look at the results is to see if each individual participant met the stated goal (i.e., the *combination* of completing at least 80 percent of the tasks in no more than 70 seconds). It turns out, as shown in the last column of the table, that only three, or 38 percent, of the participants actually met the goal. This demonstrates the importance of looking at individual participant data rather than just looking at averages.

This method of combining metrics based on target goals can be used with any set of metrics. The only real decision is what target goals to use. Target goals can be based on business goals and/or comparison to ideal performance. The math is easy (each person just gets a 1 or a 0), and the interpretation is easy to explain (the percentage of participants who had an experience that met the stated goal during the test).

**Table 8.1** Sample Task Completion and Task Time Data

| Participant Number | Task Completion | Task Time (sec) | Goal Met? |
|---|---|---|---|
| 1 | 85% | 68 | 1 |
| 2 | 70% | 59 | 0 |
| 3 | 80% | 79 | 0 |
| 4 | 75% | 62 | 0 |
| 5 | 90% | 72 | 0 |
| 6 | 80% | 60 | 1 |
| 7 | 80% | 56 | 1 |
| 8 | 95% | 78 | 0 |
| **Average** | **82%** | **67** | **38%** |

## 8.1.2 Combining Metrics Based on Percentages

Although we are well aware that we should have measurable target goals for our usability tests, in practice we often don't have them. So what can we do to combine different metrics when we don't have target goals? One simple technique for combining scores on different scales is to convert each score to a percentage and then average them. For example, consider the data in Table 8.2, which show the results of a usability test with ten participants.

One way to get an overall sense of the results from this study is to first convert each of these metrics to a percentage. In the case of the number of tasks completed and the subjective rating, it's easy because we know the maximum ("best") possible value for each of those scores: There were 15 tasks, and the maximum possible subjective rating on the scale was 4. So we just divide the score obtained for each participant by the corresponding maximum to get the percentage.

In the case of the time data, it's a little trickier since there's no predefined "best" or "worst" time—the ends of the scale are not known beforehand. One way to handle this is to treat the fastest time obtained as the "best" (25 seconds) and then express the other times in relation to it. Specifically, you divide the shortest time by each time observed to convert it to a percentage. This way, the shortest time becomes 100 percent. If a given time was twice as long as the shortest, it

**Table 8.2** Sample Data from a Usability Test

| Participant Number | Time per Task (sec) | Tasks Completed (of 15) | Rating (0–4) |
|---|---|---|---|
| 1 | 65 | 7 | 2.4 |
| 2 | 50 | 9 | 2.6 |
| 3 | 34 | 13 | 3.1 |
| 4 | 70 | 6 | 1.7 |
| 5 | 28 | 11 | 3.2 |
| 6 | 52 | 9 | 3.3 |
| 7 | 58 | 8 | 2.5 |
| 8 | 60 | 7 | 1.4 |
| 9 | 25 | 9 | 3.8 |
| 10 | 55 | 10 | 3.6 |

Note: Time per Task is the average time to complete each task, in seconds. Tasks Completed is the number of tasks (out of 15) that the participant successfully completed. Rating is the average of several 5-point subjective rating scales, where higher is better.

**Table 8.3** Data from Table 8.2 Transformed to Percentages

| Participant Number | Time | Tasks | Rating | Average |
|---|---|---|---|---|
| 1 | 38% | 47% | 60% | 48% |
| 2 | 50% | 60% | 65% | 58% |
| 3 | 74% | 87% | 78% | 79% |
| 4 | 36% | 40% | 43% | 39% |
| 5 | 89% | 73% | 80% | 81% |
| 6 | 48% | 60% | 83% | 64% |
| 7 | 43% | 53% | 63% | 53% |
| 8 | 42% | 47% | 35% | 41% |
| 9 | 100% | 60% | 95% | 85% |
| 10 | 45% | 67% | 90% | 67% |

*Note: For the Task Completion data, the score was divided by 15. For the Rating data, the score was divided by 4. For the Time data, the shortest time (25) was divided by the time obtained.*

becomes 50 percent. Using that method of transforming the data, you get the percentages shown in Table 8.3.

Table 8.3 also shows the average of these percentages for each of the participants. If any one participant had successfully completed all the tasks in the shortest average time and had given the product a perfect score on the subjective rating scales, that person's average would have been 100 percent. On the other hand, if any one participant had failed to complete any of the tasks, had taken the longest time per task, and had given the product the lowest possible score on the subjective rating scales, that person's average would have been closer to 0 percent. (The average can't actually reach 0 percent because the time data expressed as a percentage can only approach 0 percent, not actually reach it.) Of course, rarely do you see either of those extremes. Like the sample data in Table 8.3, most participants fall between those two extremes. In this case, the averages range from a low of 39 percent (Participant 4) to a high of 85 percent (Participant 9), with an overall average of 62 percent.

So, if you had to give an "overall score" to the product whose test results are shown in Tables 8.2 and 8.3, you could say it scored 62 percent overall. Most people wouldn't be too happy with 62 percent. Many years of grades from school have probably conditioned most of us to think of a percentage that low as a "failing grade." But you should also consider how accurate that percentage is. Since it's an average based on the scores from ten different participants, you can construct a confidence interval for that average, as explained in section 2.4.4. The 95 percent confidence interval in this case is 51 to 72 percent. Running more participants would probably give you a more accurate estimate of this value, whereas running fewer would probably have made it less accurate.

One thing to be aware of is that when we averaged the three percentages together (from the task completion data, task time data, and subjective ratings), we gave equal weight to each measure. In many cases, that is a perfectly reasonable thing to do, but sometimes the business goals of the product may indicate a different weighting. In this example, we're combining two performance measures (task completion and task time) with one self-reported measure (rating). By giving equal weight to each, we're actually giving twice as much weight to performance as to the self-reported measure. That can be adjusted by using weights in calculating the averages, as shown in Table 8.4. Each individual percentage is multiplied by its associated weight; these products are summed and that sum is divided by the sum of the weights (4 in this example).

In Table 8.4, the subjective rating is given a weight of 2, and each of the two performance measures is given a weight of 1. The net effect is that the subjective rating gets as much weight in the calculation of the average as the two performance measures together. The result is that these weighted averages for each participant tend to be closer to the subjective ratings than the equal-weight averages in Table 8.3. The exact weights you use for any given product should be determined by the business goals for the product. For example, if you're testing a website for use by the general public, and the users have many competitors' websites to choose from, you might want to give more weight to self-reported

**Table 8.4** Calculation of Weighted Averages

| Participant Number | Time | Weight | Tasks | Weight | Rating | Weight | Weighted Average |
|---|---|---|---|---|---|---|---|
| 1 | 38% | 1 | 47% | 1 | 60% | 2 | 51% |
| 2 | 50% | 1 | 60% | 1 | 65% | 2 | 60% |
| 3 | 74% | 1 | 87% | 1 | 78% | 2 | 79% |
| 4 | 36% | 1 | 40% | 1 | 43% | 2 | 40% |
| 5 | 89% | 1 | 73% | 1 | 80% | 2 | 81% |
| 6 | 48% | 1 | 60% | 1 | 83% | 2 | 68% |
| 7 | 43% | 1 | 53% | 1 | 63% | 2 | 55% |
| 8 | 42% | 1 | 47% | 1 | 35% | 2 | 40% |
| 9 | 100% | 1 | 60% | 1 | 95% | 2 | 88% |
| 10 | 45% | 1 | 67% | 1 | 90% | 2 | 73% |

measures because you probably care more about the users' *perception* of the product than anything else.

On the other hand, if you're dealing with a safety-critical product such as an Automated External Defibrillator (AED), you probably want to give more weight to performance measures. You can use any weights that are appropriate for your situation, but remember to divide by the sum of those weights in calculating the weighted average.

To look at transforming one more set of metrics, consider the data shown in Table 8.5. In this case, the number of errors is listed, which would include specific ones, such as data-entry errors, the 12 participants made. Obviously, it is possible (and desirable) for a participant to make no errors, so the minimum possible is 0. But there's usually no predefined maximum number of errors that a participant could make. In a case like this, the best way to transform the data is to divide the number of errors obtained by the maximum number of errors and then subtract from 1. This is how the error percentages in Table 8.5 were obtained.

If any participant had no errors (optimum), her percentage would be 100 percent. The percentage for any with the highest number of errors would be 0 percent. Notice that in calculating any of these percentages, we always want higher percentages to be better—to reflect better usability. So in the case of errors, it makes more sense to think of the resulting percentage as an "accuracy" measure.

When transforming any usability metric to a percentage, the general rule is to first determine the minimum and maximum values that the metric can possibly have. In many cases this is easy; they are predefined by the conditions of the usability test. Here are the various cases you might encounter:

- If the minimum possible score is 0 and the maximum possible score is 100 (e.g., a SUS score), then you've already got a percentage.

- In many cases, the minimum is 0 and the maximum is known, such as the total number of tasks or the highest possible rating on a rating scale. In that case, simply divide the score by the maximum to get the percentage. (This is why it's generally easier to code rating scales starting with 0 as the worst value.)

- In some cases, the minimum is 0 but the maximum is not known, such as the example of errors. In that situation, the maximum would need to be defined by the data—the highest number of errors any participant made. Specifically, the number of errors would be transformed by dividing the number of errors obtained by the maximum number of errors any participant made and subtracting that from 1.

- Finally, in some cases neither the minimum nor maximum possible scores are predefined, as with time data. Assuming higher numbers are worse, as is the case with time data, you usually want to transform the data by dividing the lowest (best) score by the score obtained.

**Table 8.5** Sample Data from a Usability Test

| Participant Number | Tasks Completed (of 10) | Number of Errors | Satisfaction Rating (0–6) | Tasks | Accuracy | Satisfaction | Average |
|---|---|---|---|---|---|---|---|
| 1 | 8 | 2 | 4.7 | 80% | 60% | 78% | 73% |
| 2 | 6 | 4 | 4.1 | 60% | 20% | 68% | 49% |
| 3 | 7 | 0 | 3.4 | 70% | 100% | 57% | 76% |
| 4 | 5 | 5 | 2.4 | 50% | 0% | 40% | 30% |
| 5 | 9 | 2 | 5.2 | 90% | 60% | 87% | 79% |
| 6 | 5 | 4 | 2.7 | 50% | 20% | 45% | 38% |
| 7 | 10 | 1 | 5.1 | 100% | 80% | 85% | 88% |
| 8 | 8 | 1 | 4.9 | 80% | 80% | 82% | 81% |
| 9 | 7 | 3 | 3.1 | 70% | 40% | 52% | 54% |
| 10 | 9 | 2 | 4.2 | 90% | 60% | 70% | 73% |
| 11 | 7 | 1 | 4.5 | 70% | 80% | 75% | 75% |
| 12 | 8 | 3 | 5.0 | 80% | 40% | 83% | 68% |

Note: Tasks Completed is the number of tasks (out of 10) that the participant successfully completed. Number of Errors is the number of specific errors that the participant made. Satisfaction Rating is on a scale of 0 to 6.

### 8.1.3 **Combining Metrics Based on *z*-Scores**

Another technique for transforming scores on different scales so that they can be combined is using *z*-scores. (See, for example, Martin & Bateson, 1993, p. 124.) These are based on the normal distribution and indicate how many units any given value is above or below the mean of the distribution. When you transform a set of scores to their corresponding *z*-scores, the resulting distribution by definition has a mean of 0 and standard deviation of 1. This is the formula for transforming any raw score into its corresponding *z*-score:

$$z = (x - \mu)/\sigma$$

where

$x =$ the score to be transformed
$\mu =$ the mean of the distribution of those scores
$\sigma =$ the standard deviation of the distribution of those scores

This transformation can also be done using the STANDARDIZE function in Excel.

The data in Table 8.2 could also be transformed using *z*-scores, as shown in Table 8.6 (on page 200). For each original score, the *z*-score was determined by subtracting the mean of the score's distribution from the original score and then dividing by the standard deviation. This *z*-score tells you how many standard deviations above or below the mean that score is.

Table 8.6 shows the mean and standard deviation for each set of *z*-scores, which should always be 0 and 1, respectively. Note that in using *z*-scores, we didn't have to make any assumptions about the maximum or minimum values that any of the scores could have. In essence, we let each set of scores define its own distribution and rescaled them so those distributions would each have a mean of 0 and a standard deviation of 1.

In this way, when they are averaged together, each of the *z*-scores makes an equal contribution to the average *z*-score. Notice that when averaging the *z*-scores together, each of the scales must be going in the same direction—in other words, higher values should always be better. In the case of the time data, the opposite is almost always true. Since *z*-scores have a mean of 0, this is easy to correct simply by multiplying the *z*-score by (−1) to reverse its scale.

If you compare the *z*-score averages in Table 8.6 to the percentage averages in Table 8.3, you will find that the ordering of the participants based on those averages is nearly the same: Both techniques yield the same top three participants (9, 5, and 3) and the same bottom three participants (4, 8, and 1).

One disadvantage of using *z*-scores is that you can't think of the overall average of the *z*-scores as some type of overall usability score, since by definition that

## STEP-BY-STEP GUIDE TO CALCULATING z-SCORES

Here are the steps for transforming any set of raw scores (times, percentages, clicks, whatever) into z-scores:

1. Enter the raw scores into a single column in Excel.

2. Calculate the average and standard deviation for this set of raw scores using "=AVERAGE(range of raw scores)" and " =STDEV(range of raw scores)."

3. In the cell to the right of the first raw score, enter the formula "=STANDARDIZE(<raw score>,<average>,<std dev>)," where <raw score> is replaced by a reference to the first raw score to be converted to a z-score, <average> is a reference to the average of the raw scores, and <std dev>is a reference to the standard deviation of the raw scores. The figure that follows shows an example. Note that the references to the cells containing the average (B11) and standard deviation (B12) include "$" in them. That's so that the references are "locked" and don't change as we copy the formula down the rows.

4. Copy this "standardize" formula down as many rows as there are raw scores.

5. As a double-check, copy the formulas for the average and standard deviation over to the z-score column. The average should be 0, and the standard deviation should be 1.

**Table 8.6** Sample Data from Table 8.2 Transformed Using z-Scores

| Participant Number | Time per Task (sec) | Tasks Completed (of 15) | Rating (0—4) | z-Time | z-Time (—1) | z-Tasks | z-Rating | Average |
|---|---|---|---|---|---|---|---|---|
| 1 | 65 | 7 | 2.4 | 0.98 | −0.98 | −0.91 | −0.46 | −0.78 |
| 2 | 50 | 9 | 2.6 | 0.02 | −0.02 | 0.05 | −0.20 | −0.06 |
| 3 | 34 | 13 | 3.1 | −1.01 | 1.01 | 1.97 | 0.43 | 1.14 |
| 4 | 70 | 6 | 1.7 | 1.30 | −1.30 | −1.39 | −1.35 | −1.35 |
| 5 | 28 | 11 | 3.2 | −1.39 | 1.39 | 1.01 | 0.56 | 0.99 |
| 6 | 52 | 9 | 3.3 | 0.15 | −0.15 | 0.05 | 0.69 | 0.20 |
| 7 | 58 | 8 | 2.5 | 0.53 | −0.53 | −0.43 | −0.33 | −0.43 |
| 8 | 60 | 7 | 1.4 | 0.66 | −0.66 | −0.91 | −1.73 | −1.10 |
| 9 | 25 | 9 | 3.8 | −1.59 | 1.59 | 0.05 | 1.32 | 0.98 |
| 10 | 55 | 10 | 3.6 | 0.34 | −0.34 | 0.53 | 1.07 | 0.42 |
| **Mean** | **49.7** | **8.9** | **2.8** | **0.0** | **0.0** | **0.0** | **0.00** | **0.00** |
| **Standard Deviation** | **5.6** | **2.1** | **0.8** | **1.0** | **1.0** | **1.0** | **1.00** | **0.90** |

overall average will be 0. So when would you want to use *z*-scores? They are useful mainly when you want to compare one set of data to another, such as data from iterative usability tests of different versions of a product, data from different groups of participants in the same usability session, or data from different conditions or designs within the same usability test.

For example, consider the data shown in Figure 8.1 from Chadwick-Dias, McNulty, and Tullis (2003), which shows *z*-scores of performance for two iterations of a prototype. This research was studying the effects of age on performance in using a website. Study 1 was a baseline study. Based on their observations of the participants in Study 1, and especially the problems encountered by the older participants, the authors of the study made changes to the prototype and then conducted Study 2 with a new group of participants. The *z*-scores were equal-weighted combinations of task time and task completion rate.

It's important to understand that the *z*-score transformations were done using the *full set* of data from Study 1 and Study 2 combined. They were then plotted appropriately to indicate from which study each *z*-score was derived. The key finding was that the performance *z*-scores for Study 2 were significantly higher than the performance *z*-scores for Study 1, and the effect was the same regardless of age (as reflected by the fact that the two lines are parallel to each other). If the

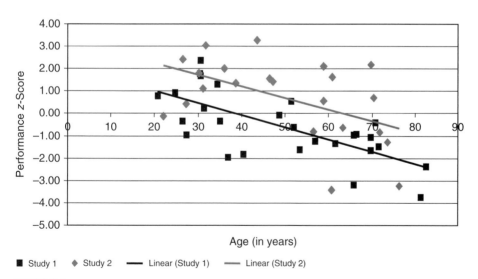

**FIGURE 8.1**

Data showing performance *z*-scores from two studies of a prototype with participants over a wide range of ages. The performance *z*-score was an equal-weighted combination of task time and task completion rate. Changes were made to the prototype between Study 1 and Study 2. The performance *z*-scores were significantly better in Study 2, regardless of the participant's age. *Source:* Adapted from Chadwick-Dias et al. (2003); used with permission.

*z*-score transformations had been done *separately* for Study 1 and Study 2, the results would have been meaningless because the means for Study 1 and Study 2 would both have been forced to 0 by the transformations.

### 8.1.4 Using SUM: Single Usability Metric

Jeff Sauro and Erika Kindlund (2005) have developed a quantitative model for combining usability metrics into a single usability score. Their focus is on task completion, task time, error counts per task, and post-task satisfaction rating (similar to ASQ described in section 6.3.2). Note that all of their analyses are at the task level, whereas the previous sections have described analyses at the "usability test" level. At the task level, task completion is typically a binary variable for each participant: that person either completed the task successfully or did not. At the usability-test level, task completion, as we have seen in the previous sections, indicates how many tasks each person completed, and it can be expressed as a percentage for each participant.

Sauro and Kindlund used techniques derived from Six Sigma methodology (e.g., Breyfogle, 1999) to standardize their four usability metrics (task completion, time, errors, and task rating) into a Single Usability Metric (SUM). Conceptually, their techniques are not that different from the *z*-score and percentage transformations described in the previous sections. In addition, they used Principal Components Analysis to determine if all four of their metrics were significantly contributing to the overall calculation of the single metric. They found that all four were significant and, in fact, that each contributed about equally. Consequently, they decided that each of the four metrics (once standardized) should contribute equally to the calculation of the SUM score.

An Excel spreadsheet for entering the data from a usability test and calculating the SUM score is available from Jeff Sauro's "Measuring Usability" website at *http://www.measuringusability.com/SUM/*. For each task and each participant in the usability test, you must enter the following:

- Whether the participant completed the task successfully (0 or 1).

- Number of errors committed on that task by that participant. (You also specify the number of error opportunities for each task.)

- Task time in seconds for that participant.

- Post-task satisfaction rating, which is an average of three post-task ratings on 5-point scales of task ease, satisfaction, and perceived time—similar to ASQ.

After entering these data for all the tasks, the spreadsheet standardizes the scores and calculates the overall SUM score and a confidence interval for each task. Standardized data for each task for ten participants and six tasks is illustrated in Table 8.7. Notice that a SUM score is calculated for each task, which allows for overall comparisons of tasks. In these sample data, the

| Task | SUM | | | Completion | Satisfaction | Time | Errors |
|------|-----|------|------|-----------|--------------|------|--------|
| | Low | Mean | High | | | | |
| Reserve a room | 62% | 75% | 97% | 81% | 74% | 68% | 76% |
| Find a hotel | 38% | 58% | 81% | 66% | 45% | 63% | 59% |
| Check room rates | 49% | 66% | 89% | 74% | 53% | 63% | 74% |
| Cancel reservation | 89% | 91% | 99% | 86% | 91% | 95% | 92% |
| Check restaurant hours | 22% | 46% | 68% | 58% | 45% | 39% | 43% |
| Get directions | 56% | 70% | 93% | 81% | 62% | 66% | 71% |
| **Overall SUM** | **53%** | **68%** | **88%** | | | | |

**Table 8.7** Sample Standardized Data from a Usability Test

participants did best on the "Cancel reservation" task and worst on the "Check restaurant hours" task. An overall SUM score, 68 percent in this example, is also calculated, as is a 90 percent confidence interval (53 to 88 percent), which is the average of the confidence intervals of the SUM score for each task.

## 8.2 USABILITY SCORECARDS

An alternative to combining different metrics to derive an overall usability score is to graphically present the results of the metrics in a summary chart. This type of chart is often called a Usability Scorecard. The goal is to present the data from the usability test in such a way that overall trends and important aspects of the data can be easily detected, such as tasks that were particularly problematic for the participants. If you have only two metrics that you're trying to represent, a simple combination graph from Excel may be appropriate. For example, Figure 8.2 shows the task completion rate and subjective rating for each of ten tasks in a usability test.

The combination chart in Figure 8.2 has some interesting features. It clarifies which tasks were the most problematic for participants (Tasks 4 and 8) because they have the lowest values on both scales. It's obvious where there were significant disparities between the task completion data and the subjective ratings, such as Tasks 9 and 10, which had only moderate task completion rates but the highest subjective ratings. Finally, it's easy to distinguish the tasks that had reasonably high values for both metrics, such as Tasks 3, 5, and 6.

This type of combination chart works well if you have only two metrics to represent, but what if you have more? One way of representing summary data for

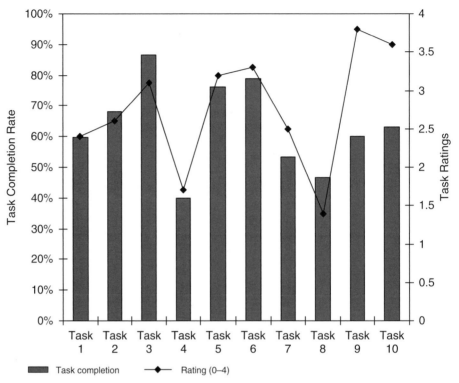

**FIGURE 8.2**

Sample combination column and line chart for ten tasks. Task completion data is shown via the columns and labeled on the *left* axis. Subjective rating is shown via the lines and labeled on the *right* axis.

three or more metrics is with radar charts (which were also illustrated in Chapter 6). Figure 8.3 shows an example of a radar chart for summarizing the results of a usability test with five factors: task completion, page visits, accuracy (lack of errors), satisfaction rating, and usefulness rating. In this example, although task completion, accuracy, and usefulness were relatively high (good), page visits and satisfaction were relatively low (poor).

Although radar charts can be useful for a high-level view, it's not really possible to represent task-level information in them. The example in Figure 8.3 averaged the data across the tasks. What if you want to represent summary data for three or more metrics but also maintain task-level information? One technique for doing that is using what are called Harvey Balls. A variation on this technique has been popularized by *Consumer Reports*. For example, consider the data shown earlier in Table 8.7, which presents the results for six tasks in a usability test, including

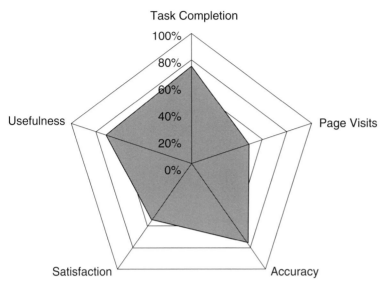

**FIGURE 8.3**

Sample radar chart summarizing task completion, page visits, accuracy (lack of errors), satisfaction rating, and usefulness rating from a usability test. Each score has been transformed to a percentage using the techniques outlined earlier in this chapter.

task completion, time, satisfaction, and errors. These data are summarized in the comparison chart shown in Figure 8.4. This type of comparison chart allows you to see at a glance how the participants did for each of the tasks (by focusing on the rows) or how the participants did for each of the metrics (by focusing on the columns).

---

**WHAT ARE HARVEY BALLS?**

Harvey Balls are small, round pictograms typically used in a comparison table to represent values for different items:

They're named for Harvey Poppel, a Booz Allen Hamilton consultant who created them in the 1970s as a way of summarizing long tables of numeric data. There are five levels, progressing from an open circle to a completely filled circle. Typically, the open circle represents the worst values, and the completely filled circle represents the best values. Links to images of Harvey Balls of different sizes can be found on our website, *www.MeasuringUserExperience.com*. Harvey Balls shouldn't be confused with Harvey Ball, who was the creator of the smiley face ☺!

| Task | SUM Score | Completion | Satisfaction | Time | Errors |
|------|-----------|------------|--------------|------|--------|
| Cancel reservation | 91% | ◕ | ● | ● | ● |
| Reserve a room | 75% | ◕ | ◑ | ◔ | ◑ |
| Get directions | 70% | ◕ | ◕ | ◔ | ◑ |
| Check room rates | 66% | ◑ | ○ | ◔ | ◑ |
| Find a hotel | 58% | ◔ | ○ | ◔ | ○ |
| Check restaurant hours | 46% | ○ | ○ | ○ | ○ |

Excellent ● 90–100%   Very good ◕ 80–89%   Good ◑ 70–79%

Fair ◔ 60–69%   Poor ○ <60%

**FIGURE 8.4**

Sample comparison chart using the data from Table 8.7. The tasks have been ordered by their SUM score, starting with the highest. For each of the four standardized scores (task completion, satisfaction, task time, and errors), the value has been represented by a coded circle (known as a Harvey Ball), as shown in the key.

## 8.3 COMPARISON TO GOALS AND EXPERT PERFORMANCE

Although the previous section focused on ways to summarize usability data without reference to an external standard, in some cases you may have one that can be used for comparison. The two main flavors of an external standard are predefined goals and expert, or optimum, performance.

### 8.3.1 Comparison to Goals

Perhaps the best way to assess the results of a usability test is to compare those results to goals that were established before the test. These goals may be set at the task level or at an overall level. Goals can be set for any of the metrics we've discussed, including task completion, task time, errors, and self-reported measures. Here are some examples of task-specific goals:

■ At least 90 percent of representative users will be able to successfully reserve a suitable hotel room.

■ At least 85 percent of representative users will be able to open a new account online within ten minutes.

■ At least 95 percent of new users will be able to purchase their chosen product online within five minutes of selecting it.

Similarly, examples of overall goals could include the following:

■ Users will be able to successfully complete at least 90 percent of their tasks.

■ Users will be able to complete their tasks in less than three minutes each, on the average.

■ Users will give the application an average SUS rating of at least 80 percent.

Typically, usability goals address task completion, time, accuracy, and/or satisfaction. The key is that the goals must be measurable. You need to be able to determine whether the data in a given situation support the attainment of the goal. For example, consider the data in Table 8.8.

The data in the table show how many of the ten participants in the usability test actually completed each of the tasks and reached the stated goal. In this case, the goal is the same for each task (nine of ten participants), but the goals could be different for each task. One way of representing the data could be by showing the comparison of the actual number who completed each task as a percentage of the goal, as shown in Figure 8.5. This makes it easier to spot the tasks where participants had the most trouble (i.e., Tasks 5 and 10). Of course, this technique could be used to represent the percentage of participants who met any particular objective (e.g., time, errors, SUS rating, etc.) at either the task level or the overall level.

**Table 8.8** Sample Task Completion Data and Goals

| Task | Actual Number of Participants Who Completed | Goal |
|------|---------------------------------------------|------|
| 1 | 9 | 9 |
| 2 | 8 | 9 |
| 3 | 9 | 9 |
| 4 | 7 | 9 |
| 5 | 5 | 9 |
| 6 | 8 | 9 |
| 7 | 9 | 9 |
| 8 | 8 | 9 |
| 9 | 7 | 9 |
| 10 | 6 | 9 |

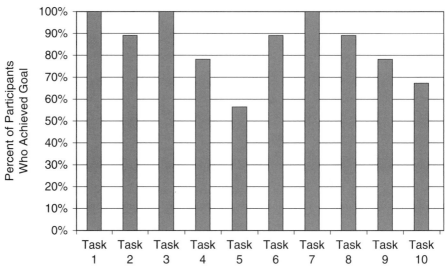

**FIGURE 8.5**

Alternative representation of the data in Table 8.8, showing the percentage of goal attainment for each task.

## 8.3.2 Comparison to Expert Performance

An alternative to comparing the results of a usability test to predefined goals is to compare the results to the performance of an "expert." The best way to determine the expert performance level is to have one or more presumed "experts" actually perform the tasks and to measure the same things that you're measuring in the usability test. Obviously your "experts" really need to be experts—people with subject-matter expertise, in-depth familiarity with the tasks, and in-depth familiarity with the product, application, or website being tested. And your data will be better if you can average the performance results from more than one expert.

Comparing the results of a usability test to the results for experts allows you to compensate for the fact that certain tasks may be inherently more difficult or take longer, even for an expert. The goal, of course, is to see how close the performance of the participants in the test actually comes to the performance of the experts.

Although you could theoretically do a comparison to expert performance for any performance metric, it's probably most common to do so for time data. With task completion data, the usual assumption is that a true expert would be able to perform all the tasks successfully. Similarly, with error data the assumption is that an expert would not make any errors. But even an expert would require some amount of time to perform the tasks. For example, consider the task time data in Table 8.9; it shows the average actual time per task, the expert time per task, and the ratio of expert to actual time.

| **Table 8.9** Sample Time Data from Ten Tasks | | | |
|---|---|---|---|
| **Task** | **Actual Time** | **Expert Time** | **Expert/Actual** |
| 1 | 124 | 85 | 69% |
| 2 | 101 | 50 | 50% |
| 3 | 89 | 70 | 79% |
| 4 | 184 | 97 | 53% |
| 5 | 64 | 40 | 63% |
| 6 | 215 | 140 | 65% |
| 7 | 70 | 47 | 67% |
| 8 | 143 | 92 | 64% |
| 9 | 108 | 98 | 91% |
| 10 | 92 | 60 | 65% |
| **Averages** | **119** | **78** | **66%** |

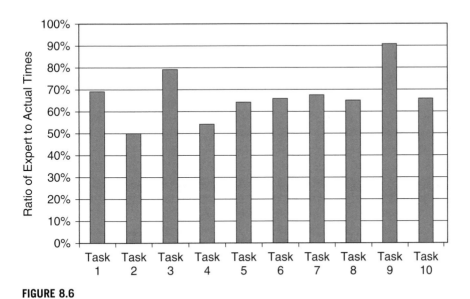

**FIGURE 8.6**

Graph of the ratio of the expert to actual times from Table 8.9.

Graphing the ratio of expert to actual times, as shown in Figure 8.6, makes it easy to spot the tasks where the test participants did well in comparison to the experts (Tasks 3 and 9) and the tasks where they did not do so well (Tasks 2 and 4). Notice that the average ratio of expert to actual performance—66 percent in this example—can also be used as an overall "usability score" for a usability test.

## 8.4 SUMMARY

Some of the key takeaways from this chapter are as follows.

1. An easy way to combine different usability metrics is to determine the percentage of participants who achieve a combination of goals. This tells you the overall percentage of participants who had a good experience with your product (based on the target goals). This method can be used with any set of metrics and is easily understood by management.

2. One way of combining different metrics into an overall usability score is to convert each of the metrics to a percentage and then average them together. This requires being able to specify, for each metric, an appropriate minimum and maximum score.

3. Another way to combine different metrics is to convert each metric to a $z$-score and then average them together. Using $z$-scores, each metric gets equal weight when they are combined. But the overall average of the $z$-scores will always be 0. The key is in comparing different subsets of the data to each other, such as data from different iterations, different groups, or different conditions.

4. The SUM technique is another method for combining different metrics, specifically task completion, task time, errors, and task-level satisfaction rating. The method requires entry of individual task and participant data for the four metrics. The calculations yield a SUM score, as a percentage, for each task and across all tasks, including confidence intervals.

5. Various types of graphs and charts can be useful for summarizing the results of a usability test in a usability scorecard. A combination line and column chart is useful for summarizing the results of two metrics for the tasks in a test. Radar charts are useful for summarizing the results of three or more metrics overall. A comparison chart using Harvey Balls to represent different levels of the metrics can effectively summarize the results for three or more metrics at the task level.

6. Perhaps the best way to determine the success of a usability test is to compare the results to a set of predefined usability goals. Typically these goals address task completion, time, accuracy, and satisfaction. The percentage of participants whose data met the stated goals can be a very effective summary.

7. A reasonable alternative to comparing results to predefined goals, especially for time data, is to compare the actual performance results to the results for experts. The closer the actual performance is to expert performance, the better.

# Special Topics

This chapter introduces a number of topics related to the measurement or analysis of usability data but not traditionally thought of as part of "mainstream" usability data. These include information you can glean from live data on a production website, data from card-sorting studies, data related to the accessibility of a website, the topic of Six Sigma and how it relates to usability, and usability Return on Investment (ROI). Our primary goal in this chapter is to make you aware of these topics, provide an overview of each of them, and then point you to additional resources for more detailed information.

## 9.1 LIVE WEBSITE DATA

If you're dealing with a live website, there's a potential treasure trove of data available to you about what the visitors to your site are actually doing—what pages they're visiting, what links they're clicking on, and what paths they're following through the site. The challenge usually isn't getting the raw data but making sense of it.

Entire books have been written only on the subject of web metrics and web analytics (e.g., Kaushik, 2007; Peterson, 2004; Sterne, 2002). There's even a *For Dummies* book on the topic (Sostre & LeClaire, 2007). So obviously we won't be able to do justice to the topic in just one section of one chapter in this book. What we'll try to do is introduce you to some of the things you can learn from live website data and specifically some of the implications they might have for the usability of your site.

### 9.1.1 Server Logs

Some websites get huge numbers of visitors every day. But regardless of how many visitors your site gets (assuming it gets some), you can learn from what they're doing on the site.

Early attempts at analyzing server log files focused on the number of requests to the server associated with each page. But each inline element of a page (e.g., each image) generates a separate request to the server, so these numbers can be misleading. Two metrics that generate more accurate numbers are *page views* and *visits* to a page. A *page view* is a request to the server for a specific page but not for its various components. A *visit* is a request for a specific page by a given user (commonly identified by IP address) within a specified time period (often 30 minutes).

Simply looking at the number of page views or visits for various pages in your site can be enlightening, especially over time or across iterations of the site. For example, assume that a page about Product A on your site was averaging 100 page views per day for a given month. Then you modified the homepage for your site, including the description of the link to Product A's page. Over the next month, the Product A page averaged 150 page views per day. It would certainly appear that the changes to the homepage significantly increased the number of visitors accessing the Product A page. But you need to be careful that other factors didn't cause the increase. For example, in the financial-services world, certain pages have seasonal differences in their number of page views. A page about contributions to an Individual Retirement Account (IRA), for example, tends to get more visits in the days leading up to April 15 because of the deadline for contributing to the prior year's IRA.

It's also possible that something caused your site as a whole to start getting more visitors, which certainly could be a good thing. But it could also be due to factors not related to the design or usability of your site, such as news events related to the subject matter of your site. This also brings up the issue of the impact that search "bots" can have on your site's statistics. Search bots, or spiders, are automated programs used by most of the major search engines to "crawl" the web by following links and indexing the pages they access. One of the challenges, once your site becomes popular and is being "found" by most of the major search engines, is filtering out the page visits due to these search bots. Most bots (e.g., Google, Yahoo!) usually identify themselves when making page requests and thus can be filtered out of the data.

What analyses can be used to determine if one set of page views is significantly different from another set? Consider the data shown in Table 9.1, which shows the number of page views per day for a given page over two different weeks. Week 1 was before a new homepage with a different link to the page in question was launched, and Week 2 was after. The new homepage contained different wording for the link to this page.

These data show a pattern that's typical in some web statistics, which is a difference in the number of page views for the weekend versus the weekdays. These data can be analyzed using a paired *t*-test to see if the average for Week 2 (519 page views per day) is significantly different from the average for Week 1 (454 page views per day). It's important to use a paired *t*-test because of the variability due to the days of the week; comparing each day to itself from the previous week takes out the variability due to days. A paired *t*-test shows that this difference is statistically significant ($p < .01$). (See section 2.5.2 for details on how to run a paired *t*-test in Excel.)

**Table 9.1** Numbers of Page Views for a Given Web Page over Two Different Weeks

|           | Week 1 | Week 2 |
|-----------|--------|--------|
| Sunday    | 237    | 282    |
| Monday    | 576    | 623    |
| Tuesday   | 490    | 598    |
| Wednesday | 523    | 612    |
| Thursday  | 562    | 630    |
| Friday    | 502    | 580    |
| Saturday  | 290    | 311    |

## 9.1.2 Click-Through Rates

Click-through rates can be used to measure the effectiveness of different ways of presenting a link. They indicate the percentage of visitors who are shown a particular link who then actually click on it. If a link is shown 100 times and it is clicked on one of those times, its click-through rate is 1 percent. Most commonly the term is used to measure the effectiveness of web ads, but the concept applies to any link. For example, Nielsen (2001b) describes several different approaches his company took to promoting their usability conference in London. Figure 9.1 shows two different versions of search engine ads (triggered when a user entered appropriate keywords) that they tried.

The click-through rate for the ad that was more specific ("Jakob Nielsen in Europe," dates included) was 55 percent greater than the more general one. Given the number of visitors many search engines get, this could be a huge difference in the actual number of users who clicked on the ad.

What analyses can be used to determine if the click-through rate for one link is significantly different from that for another link? One such analysis is the chi-square

**FIGURE 9.1**

Two different search engine ads tested for promoting the Nielsen Norman Group's London usability conference. The percentages indicate the click-through rates for the European users. *Source:* From Nielsen (2001b); used with permission.

**Table 9.2** Click-Through Rates for Two Different Links

|  | Click | No Click |
|---|---|---|
| Link 1 | 145 | 10,289 |
| Link 2 | 198 | 11,170 |

**Table 9.3** Same Data as in Table 9.2 with Row and Column Sums Added

| Observed | Click | No Click | Sum |
|---|---|---|---|
| Link 1 | 145 | 10,289 | 10,434 |
| Link 2 | 198 | 11,170 | 11,368 |
| Sum | 343 | 21,459 | 21,802 |

test. A chi-square test lets you determine whether an observed set of frequencies is significantly different from an expected set of frequencies (see section 2.7.1 for more details). For example, consider the data shown in Table 9.2 that represent click rates for two different links: the number of times each link was clicked and the number of times each was presented but not clicked. The click-through rate for Link 1 is 1.4 percent [145 / (145 + 10,289)]. The click-through rate for Link 2 is 1.7 percent [198 / (198 + 11,170)]. But are these two significantly different from each other? Link 2 got more clicks, but it was also presented more times.

To do a chi-square test, you must first construct a table of expected frequencies as if there were no difference in the click-through rates of Link 1 and Link 2. This is done using the sums of the rows and columns of the original table, as shown in Table 9.3. The data are used to calculate the expected frequencies if there was no difference in the click-through rates.

By taking the product of each pair of row and column sums and dividing that by the grand total, you get the expected values as shown in Table 9.4. For example, the expected frequency for a "Click" on "Link 1" (164.2) is the product of the respective row and column sums divided by the grand total: $(343 \times 10,434)/21,802$. The "CHITEST" function in Excel can then be used to compare the actual frequencies in Table 9.2 to the expected frequencies in Table 9.4. The resulting value is $p = 0.037$, indicating that there is a significant difference between the click-through rates for Link 1 and Link 2.

You should keep two important points about the chi-square test in mind. First, the chi-square test must be done using raw frequencies or counts, *not* percentages. You commonly think of click-through rates in terms of percentages, but that's not how you test for significant differences between them. Also, the categories used must be mutually exclusive and exhaustive. That's why the preceding example

**Table 9.4** Expected Frequencies with No Difference in Click-Through Rates for Link 1 and Link 2

| Expected | Click | No Click |
|----------|-------|----------|
| Link 1 | 164.2 | 10,269.8 |
| Link 2 | 178.8 | 11,189.2 |

Note: Data shown are derived from the sums shown in Table 9.3.

used "Click" and "No Click" as the two categories of observations for each link. Those two categories are mutually exclusive, and they account for all possible actions that could be taken on the link: either the user clicked on it or didn't.

### 9.1.3 Drop-Off Rates

Drop-off rates can be a particularly useful way of detecting where there might be some usability problems on your site. The most common use of drop-off rates is to identify where in a sequence of pages users are dropping out of or abandoning a process, such as opening an account or completing a purchase. For example, assume that the user must fill out the information on a sequence of five pages to open some type of account. Table 9.5 reflects the percentage of users who started the process who actually completed each of the five pages.

In this example, all of the percentages are relative to the number of users who started the entire process—that is, who got to Page 1. So 89 percent of the users who got to Page 1 successfully completed it, 80 percent of that original number completed Page 2, and so on. Given the data in Table 9.5, which of the five pages do the users seem to be having the most trouble with? The key is to look at how many users dropped off from each page—in other words, the difference between how many got to the page and how many completed it. Those "drop-off percentages" for each of the pages are shown in Table 9.6.

**Table 9.5** Percentage of Users Who Started and Completed Each Step in a Multipage Process

| Page 1 | 89% |
|--------|-----|
| Page 2 | 80% |
| Page 3 | 73% |
| Page 4 | 52% |
| Page 5 | 49% |

| **Table 9.6** Drop-Off Percentages for Each Page Shown in Table 9.5 ||
|---|---|
| Page 1 | 11% |
| Page 2 | 9% |
| Page 3 | 7% |
| Page 4 | 21% |
| Page 5 | 3% |

This makes it clear that the largest drop-off rate, 21 percent, is associated with Page 4. If you're going to redesign this multipage process, you would be well advised to learn what's causing the drop-off at Page 4 and then try to address that in the redesign.

### 9.1.4 A/B Studies

A/B studies are a special type of live-site study in which you manipulate the pages that users see. The traditional approach to A/B testing on a website involves posting two alternative designs for a given page. Some visitors to the site see the "A" version and others see the "B" version. In many cases, this assignment is random, so about the same number of visitors sees each version. In some cases, the majority of visitors see the existing page, and a smaller percentage see an experimental version that's being tested. Although these studies are typically called A/B tests, the same concept applies to any number of alternative designs for a page.

Technically, visitors to a page can be directed to one of the alternative pages in a variety of ways, including on random number generation, the exact time (e.g., an even or odd number of seconds since midnight), or several other techniques. Typically, a cookie is set to indicate which version the visitor was shown so that if he or she returns to the site within a specified time period, the same version will be shown again. Keep in mind that it's important to test the alternative versions at the same time because of the external factors mentioned before that could affect the results if you tested at different times.

Usborne (2005) described an A/B/C test of three different versions of a page explaining a report and including a form to complete for purchasing the report. Page A was the existing page. Page B used the same basic page layout and design but modified the text or "copy." Page C was a redesign that involved changing from a single-column layout to a two-column layout; the goal was to bring more of the key content "above the fold." These three versions of the same basic page were then tested simultaneously. The key metric for comparing the three versions was the number of sales of the report each generated. The results are shown in Table 9.7

**Table 9.7** Data from an A/B/C Test

|  | Page A | Page B | Page C |
|---|---|---|---|
| Percent of traffic | 34% | 33% | 33% |
| New sales | 244 | 282 | 114 |
| Change relative to A | N/A | 15.6% | 53.3% |

*Source: Adapted from Usborne (2005); used with permission.*

The "Percent of traffic" reflects the fact that each of the three versions of the page was shown the same number of times. The key is the number of "New sales," which is the number of visitors who actually purchased the report. Since Page A was the existing page, the others were compared to it: Page B resulted in a 15.6 percent increase in sales, whereas Page C resulted in a 53.3 percent *decrease* in sales! The lesson to learn from this is that the actual text on a page really makes a difference (as shown by the improvement with Page B) and that sometimes the design and layout decisions you make may not always have the effect you intend (as in Page C).

Carefully designed A/B tests can give you significant insight into what works and what doesn't work on your website. Many companies are constantly doing A/B tests on their live sites, although most users don't notice it. In fact, as Kohavi and Round (2004) explained, A/B testing is constant at Amazon, and experimentation through A/B testing is one of the ways they make changes to their site.

## 9.2 CARD-SORTING DATA

Card-sorting as a technique for organizing the elements of an information system in a way that makes sense to the users has been around at least since the early 1980s. For example, Tullis (1985) used the technique to organize the menus of a mainframe operating system. More recently, the technique has become popular as a way of informing decisions about the information architecture of a website (e.g., Maurer & Warfel, 2004). Over the years the technique has evolved from being a true card-sorting exercise using index cards to an online exercise using virtual cards. Although many usability professionals are familiar with the basic card-sorting techniques, fewer seem to be aware that various metrics can be used in the analyses of card-sorting data.

The two major types of card-sorting exercises are (1) open card-sorts, where you give participants the cards that are to be sorted but let them define their own groups that the cards will be sorted into, and (2) closed card-sorts, where you give participants the cards to be sorted as well as the names of the groups to sort them into. Although some metrics apply to both, others are unique to each.

---

**CARD-SORTING TOOLS**

A number of tools are available for conducting card-sorting exercises. Some are desktop applications and others are web-based. Here are some of the ones we're familiar with:

- CardSort (*http://www.cardsort.net/*)—a Windows application
- CardZort (*http://www.cardzort.com/cardzort/*)—a Windows application
- Classified (*http://www.infodesign.com.au/usabilityresources/classified/*)—a Windows application
- OptimalSort (*http://www.optimalsort.com/*)—a web-based service
- UzCardSort (*http://uzilla.mozdev.org/cardsort.html*)—a Mozilla extension
- WebCAT (*http://zing.ncsl.nist.gov/WebTools/WebCAT/overview.html*)—a free web-based tool you can install on your server if you're a techno-geek!
- Websort (*http://www.websort.net/*)—a web-based service
- XSort (*http://www.ipragma.com/xsort*)—a Mac OS X application

Although not a card-sorting tool, you can also use PowerPoint or similar programs to do card-sorting exercises. Simply create a slide that has the cards to be sorted along with empty boxes and then e-mail that to participants, asking them to put the cards into the boxes and to name the boxes. Then they simply e-mail the file back.

---

### 9.2.1 Analyses of Open Card-Sort Data

One way to analyze the data from an open card-sort is to create a matrix of the "perceived distances" among all pairs of cards in the study. For example, assume you conducted a card-sorting study using ten fruits: apples, oranges, strawberries, bananas, peaches, plums, tomatoes, pears, grapes, and cherries. Assume one participant in the study created the following groups:

- "Large, round fruits": apples, oranges, peaches, tomatoes
- "Small fruits": strawberries, grapes, cherries, plums
- "Funny-shaped fruits": bananas, pears

You can then create a matrix of "perceived distances" among all pairs of the fruits for each participant by using the following rules:

- If this person put a pair of cards in the same group, it gets a distance of 0.
- If this person put a pair of cards into different groups, it gets a distance of 1.

Using these rules, the distance matrix for the preceding participant would look like what's shown in Table 9.8.

We're only showing the top half of the matrix for simplicity, but the bottom half would be exactly the same. The diagonal entries are not meaningful because the distance of a card from itself is undefined. (Or it can be assumed to be zero if needed in the analyses.) So for any one participant in the study, the entries in this matrix will only be 0's or 1's. The key is to then combine these matrices for all the

**Table 9.8** Distance Matrix for a Participant's Card-Sorting Results

| | Apples | Oranges | Strawberries | Bananas | Peaches | Plums | Tomatoes | Pears | Grapes | Cherries |
|---|---|---|---|---|---|---|---|---|---|---|
| Apples | — | 0 | 1 | 1 | 0 | 1 | 0 | 1 | 1 | 1 |
| Oranges | | — | 1 | 1 | 0 | 1 | 0 | 1 | 1 | 1 |
| Strawberries | | | — | 1 | 1 | 0 | 1 | 1 | 0 | 0 |
| Bananas | | | | — | 1 | 1 | 1 | 0 | 1 | 1 |
| Peaches | | | | | — | 1 | 0 | 1 | 1 | 1 |
| Plums | | | | | | — | 1 | 1 | 0 | 0 |
| Tomatoes | | | | | | | — | 1 | 1 | 1 |
| Pears | | | | | | | | — | 1 | 1 |
| Grapes | | | | | | | | | — | 0 |
| Cherries | | | | | | | | | | — |

participants in the study. Let's assume you had 20 participants do the card-sorting exercise with the fruits. You can then sum the matrices for the 20 participants. This will create an overall distance matrix whose values can, in theory, range from 0 (if all participants put that pair into the same group) to 20 (if all participants put that pair into different groups).

Table 9.9 shows an example of what that might look like. In this example, only 2 of the participants put the oranges and peaches in different groups, whereas all 20 of the participants put the bananas and tomatoes into different groups.

---

### A CARD-SORT ANALYSIS SPREADSHEET

Donna Maurer has developed an Excel spreadsheet for the analysis of card-sorting data. She uses some very different techniques for exploring the results of a card-sorting exercise than the more statistical techniques we're describing here, including support for the person doing the analysis to standardize the categories by grouping the ones that are similar. The spreadsheet and instructions can be downloaded from *http://www.rosenfeldmedia.com/books/cardsorting/blog/card_sort_analysis_spreadsheet/*.

---

This overall matrix can then be analyzed using any of several standard statistical methods for studying distance (or similarity) matrices. Two that we find useful are hierarchical cluster analysis (e.g., Aldenderfer & Blashfield, 1984) and multidimensional scaling, or MDS (e.g., Kruskal & Wish, 2006). Both are available in a variety of commercial statistical analysis packages. One that we use is NCSS (NCSS, 2007), which was used for both of the following analyses.

### Hierarchical Cluster Analysis

The goal of hierarchical cluster analysis is to build a tree diagram where the cards that were viewed as most similar by the participants in the study are placed on branches that are close together. For example, Figure 9.2 shows the result of a hierarchical cluster analysis of the data in Table 9.9. The key to interpreting a hierarchical cluster analysis is to look at the point at which any given pair of cards "join together" in the tree diagram. Cards that join together sooner are more similar to each other than those that join together later. For example, the pair of fruits with the lowest distance in Table 9.9 (peaches and oranges; distance = 2) join together first in the tree diagram.

Something to be aware of is that several different algorithms can be used in hierarchical cluster analysis to determine how the "linkages" are created. Most of the commercial packages that support hierarchical cluster analysis let you choose which method to use. The linkage method we think works best is one called the Group Average method. But you might want to experiment with some of the other linkage methods to see what the results look like; there's no absolute rule saying one is better than another.

One thing that makes hierarchical cluster analysis so appealing for use in the analysis of card-sorting data is that you can use it to directly inform how you might

**Table 9.9** Overall Distance Matrix for 20 Fruit Card-Sorting Study Participants

| | Apples | Oranges | Strawberries | Bananas | Peaches | Plums | Tomatoes | Pears | Grapes | Cherries |
|---|---|---|---|---|---|---|---|---|---|---|
| Apples | — | 5 | 11 | 16 | 4 | 10 | 12 | 8 | 11 | 10 |
| Oranges | | — | 17 | 14 | 2 | 12 | 15 | 11 | 12 | 14 |
| Strawberries | | | — | 17 | 16 | 8 | 18 | 15 | 4 | 8 |
| Bananas | | | | — | 17 | 15 | 20 | 11 | 14 | 16 |
| Peaches | | | | | — | 9 | 11 | 6 | 15 | 13 |
| Plums | | | | | | — | 12 | 10 | 9 | 7 |
| Tomatoes | | | | | | | — | 16 | 18 | 14 |
| Pears | | | | | | | | — | 12 | 14 |
| Grapes | | | | | | | | | — | 3 |
| Cherries | | | | | | | | | | — |

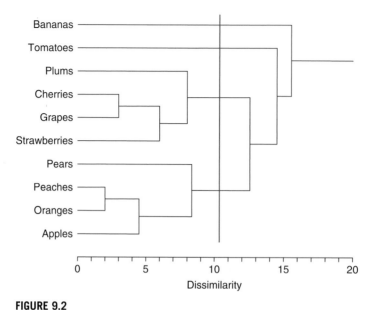

**FIGURE 9.2**

Result of a hierarchical cluster analysis of the data shown in Table 9.9.

organize the cards (pages) in a website. One way to do this is to take a vertical "slice" through the tree diagram and see what groupings that creates. For example, Figure 9.2 shows a 4-cluster "slice": The vertical line intersects four horizontal lines, forming the four groups—(1) bananas; (2) tomatoes; (3) plums, cherries, grapes, and strawberries; and (4) pears, peaches, oranges, and apples. How do you decide how many clusters to create when taking a "slice" like this? Again, there's no fixed rule, but one method we like is to calculate the average number of groups of cards created by the participants in the card-sorting study and then try to approximate that.

After taking a "slice" through the tree diagram and identifying the groups created by that, the next thing you might want to do is determine how those groups compare to the original card-sorting data—in essence, to come up with a "goodness of fit" metric for your derived groups. One way of doing that is to compare the pairings of cards in your derived groups with the pairings created by each participant in the card-sorting study and to identify what percentage of the pairs match. For example, for the data in Table 9.8, only 7 of the 45 pairs do *not* match those identified in Figure 9.2. The 7 nonmatching pairings are apples–tomatoes, apples–pears, oranges–tomatoes, oranges–pears, bananas–pears, peaches–tomatoes, and peaches–pears. That means 38 pairings do match, or 84 percent (38/45). Averaging these matching percentages across all the participants will give you a measure of the goodness of fit for your derived groups relative to the original data.

### Multidimensional Scaling

Another way of analyzing and visualizing the data from a card-sorting exercise is using multidimensional scaling, or MDS. Perhaps the best way to understand MDS

### HOW MANY PARTICIPANTS ARE ENOUGH FOR A CARD-SORTING STUDY?

Tullis and Wood (2004) conducted a card-sorting study in which they addressed the question of how many people you need for a card-sorting study if you want to get reliable results from your analyses. They did an open sort with 46 cards and 168 participants. They then analyzed the results for the full dataset (168 participants) as well as many random subsamples of the data from 2 to 70 participants. The correlations of the results for those subsamples to the full dataset looked like the chart here.

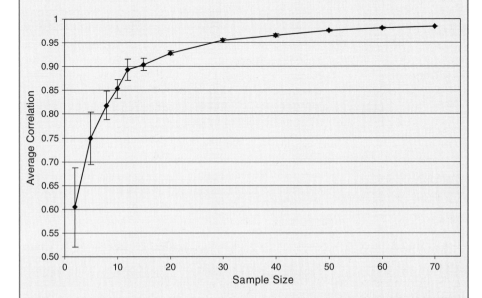

The "elbow" of that curve appears to be somewhere between 10 and 20, with a sample size of 15 yielding a correlation of 0.90 with the full dataset. Although it's hard to know how well these results would generalize to other card-sorting studies with different subject matter or different numbers of cards, they at least suggest that about 15 may be a good target number of participants.

is through an analogy. Imagine that you had a table of the mileages between all pairs of major U.S. cities but not a map of where those cities are located. An MDS analysis could take that table of mileages and derive an approximation of the map showing where those cities are relative to each other. In essence, MDS tries to create a map in which the distances between all pairs of items match the distances in the original distance matrix as closely as possible.

The input to an MDS analysis is the same as the input to a hierarchical cluster analysis—a distance matrix, like the example shown in Table 9.9. The result of an MDS analysis of the data in Table 9.9 is shown in Figure 9.3. The first thing that's apparent from this MDS analysis is how the tomatoes and bananas are isolated from

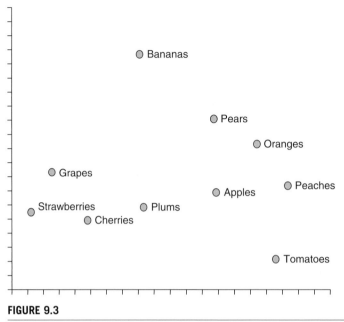

**FIGURE 9.3**

MDS analysis of the distance matrix in Table 9.9.

all the other fruit. That's consistent with the hierarchical cluster analysis, where those two fruits were the last two to join all the others. In fact, our 4-cluster "slice" of the hierarchical cluster analysis (Figure 9.2) had these two fruits as groups unto themselves. Another thing apparent from the MDS analysis is how the strawberries, grapes, cherries, and plums cluster together on the left, and the apples, peaches, pears, and oranges cluster together on the right. That's also consistent with the hierarchical cluster analysis.

Notice that it's also possible to use more than two dimensions in an MDS analysis, but we've rarely seen a case where adding even just one more dimension yields particularly useful insights into card-sorting data. Another point to keep in mind is that the orientation of the axes in an MDS plot is arbitrary. You could rotate or flip the map any way you want, and the results would still be the same. The only thing that's actually important is the relative distances between all pairs of the items.

The most common metric that's used to represent how well an MDS plot reflects the original data is a measure of "stress" that's sometimes referred to as *Phi*. Most of the commercial packages that do MDS analysis can also report the stress value associated with a solution. Basically, it's calculated by looking at all pairs of items, finding the difference between each pair's distance in the MDS map and its distance in the original matrix, squaring that difference, and summing those squares. That measure of stress for the MDS map shown in Figure 9.3 is 0.04. The smaller the value, the better. But how small does it really need to be? A good rule of thumb is that stress values under 0.10 are excellent, whereas stress values above 0.20 are poor.

We find that it's useful to do both a hierarchical cluster analysis and an MDS analysis. Sometimes you see interesting things in one that aren't apparent in the other. And they are different statistical analysis techniques, so you shouldn't expect them to give exactly the same answers. For example, one thing that's sometimes easier to see in an MDS map is which cards are "outliers"—those that don't obviously belong with a single group. There are at least two reasons why a card could be an outlier: (1) It could truly be an outlier—a function that really is different from all the others, or (2) it could have been "pulled" toward two or more groups. When designing a website, you would probably want to make these functions available from *each* of those areas.

### 9.2.2 Analyses of Closed Card-Sort Data

Closed card-sorts, where you give participants not only the cards but also the names of the groups in which to sort them, are probably done less often than open card-sorts. Typically, you would start with an open sort to get an idea of the kinds of groups that users would naturally create and the names they might use for them. Sometimes it's helpful to follow up an open sort with one or more closed sorts, mainly as a way of testing your ideas about organizing the functions. With a closed card-sort you have an idea about how you want to organize the functions, and you want to see how close users come to matching the organization you have in mind.

We recently used closed card-sorting to compare different ways of organizing the functions for a website (Tullis, 2007). We first conducted an open sort with 54 functions. We then used those results to generate six different ways of organizing the functions that we then tested in six parallel closed card-sorting exercises. Each closed card-sort used the same 54 functions but presented different groups to sort the functions into. The number of groups in each "framework" (set of group names) ranged from three to nine. Each participant only saw and used one of the six frameworks.

In looking at the data from a closed card-sort, the main thing you're interested in is how well the groups "pulled" the cards to them that you intend to belong to those groups. For example, consider the data in Table 9.10, which shows the percentage of the participants in a closed card-sorting exercise who put each of the ten cards into each of the three groups provided.

The other percentage, shown on the right in Table 9.10, is the highest percentage for each card. This is an indicator of how well the "winning" group pulled the appropriate cards to it. What you hope to see are cases like Card 10 in this table, which was very strongly pulled to Group C, with 92 percent of the participants putting it in that group. The ones that are more troubling are cases like Card 7, where 46 percent of the participants put it in Group A, but 37 percent put it in Group C—so participants were very "split" in deciding where that card belonged in this set of groups.

**Table 9.10** Percentage of Closed Card-Sort Participants Who Put Each Card in Each of the Three Groups Provided

| Card | Group A | Group B | Group C | Max |
|------|---------|---------|---------|-----|
| 1 | 17% | 78% | 5% | **78%** |
| 2 | 15% | 77% | 8% | **77%** |
| 3 | 20% | 79% | 1% | **79%** |
| 4 | 48% | 40% | 12% | **48%** |
| 5 | 11% | 8% | 81% | **81%** |
| 6 | 1% | 3% | 96% | **96%** |
| 7 | 46% | 16% | 37% | **46%** |
| 8 | 57% | 38% | 5% | **57%** |
| 9 | 20% | 75% | 5% | **75%** |
| 10 | 4% | 5% | 92% | **92%** |
| | | | **Average** | **73%** |

One metric you could use for characterizing how well a particular set of group names fared in a closed card-sort is the average of these maximum values for all the cards. For the data in Table 9.10, that would be 73 percent. But what if you want to compare the results from closed card-sorts with the same cards but different sets of groups? That average maximum percentage will work well for comparisons as long as each set contained the same number of groups. But if one set had only three groups and another had nine groups, as in the Tullis (2007) study, it's not a fair metric for comparison. If participants were simply acting randomly in doing the sorting with only three groups, by chance they would get a maximum percentage of 33 percent. But if they were acting randomly in doing a sort with nine groups, they would get a maximum percentage of only 11 percent. So using this metric, a framework with more groups is at a disadvantage in comparison to one with fewer groups.

We experimented with a variety of methods to correct for the number of groups in a closed card-sort. The one that seems to work best is illustrated in Table 9.11. These are the same data as shown earlier in Table 9.10 but with two additional columns. The "2nd Place" column gives the percentage associated with the group that had the next-highest percentage. The "Difference" column is simply the difference between the maximum percentage and the 2nd-place percentage. A card that was pulled strongly to one group, such as Card 10, gets a relatively small penalty in this scheme. But a card that was more evenly split, such as Card 7, takes quite a hit.

**Table 9.11** Same Data as in Table 9.10 with an Additional Two Columns

| Card | Category A | Category B | Category C | Max | 2nd Place | Difference |
|------|-----------|-----------|-----------|-----|-----------|-----------|
| 1 | 17% | 78% | 5% | **78%** | **17%** | **61%** |
| 2 | 15% | 77% | 8% | **77%** | **15%** | **62%** |
| 3 | 20% | 79% | 1% | **79%** | **20%** | **60%** |
| 4 | 48% | 40% | 12% | **48%** | **40%** | **8%** |
| 5 | 11% | 8% | 81% | **81%** | **11%** | **70%** |
| 6 | 1% | 3% | 96% | **96%** | **3%** | **93%** |
| 7 | 46% | 16% | 37% | **46%** | **37%** | **8%** |
| 8 | 57% | 38% | 5% | **57%** | **38%** | **18%** |
| 9 | 20% | 75% | 5% | **75%** | **20%** | **55%** |
| 10 | 4% | 5% | 92% | **92%** | **5%** | **87%** |
| | | | **Average** | **73%** | | **52%** |

Note: The 2nd Place column refers to the next-highest percentage after the maximum percentage, and the Difference column indicates the difference between the maximum percentage and the 2nd-Place percentage.

The average of these differences can then be used to make comparisons between frameworks that have different numbers of groups. For example, Figure 9.4 shows the data from Tullis (2007) plotted using this method. We call this a measure of the percent agreement among the participants about which group each card belongs to. Obviously, higher values are better.

Notice that the data from a closed card-sort can also be analyzed using hierarchical cluster analysis and MDS analysis, just like the data from an open card-sort. These give you visual representations of how well the framework you presented to the participants in the closed card-sort actually worked for them.

## 9.3 ACCESSIBILITY DATA

*Accessibility* usually refers to how effectively someone with disabilities can use a particular system, application, or website (e.g., Henry, 2007; Kirkpatrick et al., 2006). We believe that accessibility is really just usability for a particular set of users. When viewed that way, it becomes obvious that most of the other metrics discussed in this book (e.g., task completion rates and times, self-reported metrics) can be applied to measure the usability of any system for users with different types

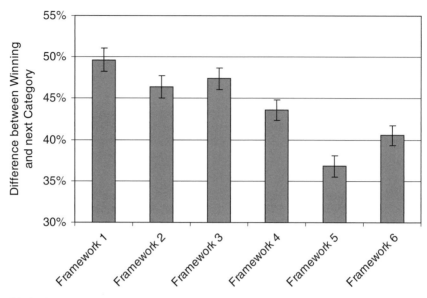

**FIGURE 9.4**

Comparison of six frameworks in six parallel closed card-sorts. Since the frameworks had different numbers of groups, a correction was used in which the percentage associated with the 2nd-place group was subtracted from the winning group. *Source:* Adapted from Tullis (2007); used with permission.

**Table 9.12** Website Usability Test Results for Normal, Blind, and Low-Vision Users

|  | Screen Reader Users | Screen Magnifier Users | Control |
|---|---|---|---|
| Task Success | 12.5% | 21.4% | 78.2% |
| Task Time | 16:46 | 15:26 | 7:14 |
| Errors | 2 | 4.5 | 0.6 |
| Subjective Rating | 2.5 | 2.9 | 4.6 |

*Source: Adapted from Nielsen (2001c); used with permission.*

of disabilities. For example, Nielsen (2001c) reported four usability metrics from a study of 19 websites with three groups of users: blind users, who accessed the sites using screen-reading software; low-vision users, who accessed the sites using screen-magnifying software; and a control group who did not use assistive technology. Table 9.12 shows the results for the four metrics.

These results point out that the usability of these sites is far worse for the screen-reader and screen-magnifier users than it is for the control users. But the other important message is that the best way to measure the usability of a system or website for users with disabilities is to actually test with representative users. Although that's a very desirable objective, most designers and developers don't have the resources to test with representative users from all the disability groups that might want to use their product. That's where accessibility guidelines can be helpful.

Perhaps the most widely recognized web accessibility guidelines are the Web Content Accessibility Guidelines (WCAG) from the World-Wide Web Consortium (W3C) (World-Wide Web Consortium, 1999). These guidelines are divided into three categories:

*Priority 1:* Sixteen guidelines that *must* be met
*Priority 2:* Thirty guidelines that *should* be met
*Priority 3:* Nineteen guidelines that *may* be met

One way of quantifying how well a website meets these criteria is to assess how many of the pages in the site fail one of more of each of these guidelines.

Some automated tools can check for certain obvious violations of these guidelines (e.g., missing "Alt" text on image). Although the errors they detect are generally true errors, they also commonly miss many errors. Many of the items that the automated tools flag as *warnings* may in fact be true errors, but it takes a human to find out. For example, if an image on a web page has null Alt text defined (ALT=""), that may be an error if the image is informational, or it may be correct if the image is purely decorative. The bottom line is that the only really accurate way to determine whether accessibility guidelines have been met is by manual inspection of the code or by evaluation using a screen reader or other appropriate assistive technology. Often both techniques are needed.

---

**AUTOMATED ACCESSIBILITY-CHECKING TOOLS**

Some of the tools available for checking web pages for accessibility errors include the following:

- Bobby (*http://www.watchfire.com/products/webxm/bobby.aspx*); there's also a free 1-page checking version available at *http://webxact.watchfire.com/*
- Cynthia Says (*http://www.contentquality.com/*)
- HiSoftware's AccMonitor (*http://www.hisoftware.com/products/access_101.htm*)
- Accessibility Valet Demonstrator (*http://valet.webthing.com/access/url.html*)
- WebAIM's WAVE tool (*http://www.wave.webaim.org/wave35/index.jsp*)
- University of Toronto Web Accessibility Checker (*http://checker.atrc.utoronto.ca/index.html*)
- TAW Web Accessibility Test (*http://www.tawdis.net/taw3/cms/en*)

Once you've analyzed the pages against the accessibility criteria, one way of summarizing the results is to count the number of pages with the different types of errors. In most cases, the number of pages containing errors is a more meaningful metric than the actual number of errors. For example, Figure 9.5 shows the results of an analysis of a website against all three priorities of the WCAG guidelines. This shows that only 21 percent of the pages have no errors, whereas 30 percent have the most severe (Priority 1) errors. Notice that any given page may contain multiple errors of different priority levels. Each page containing errors is categorized according to the most severe errors on the page. So, for example, a page containing any Priority 1 errors is categorized as Priority 1 regardless of any other errors on the page. A page categorized as Priority 3 cannot have any Priority 1 or 2 errors.

Another useful way of analyzing and reporting accessibility errors is by counting the total number of errors (of whatever type you are checking for) per page and then looking at the number of pages containing various numbers of errors, as shown in Figure 9.6. The logic behind this analysis is that pages with significantly more errors tend to represent more of a barrier to access than those with fewer errors.

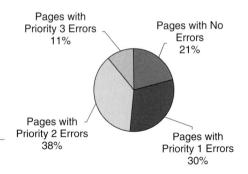

**FIGURE 9.5**

Results of analysis of a website against all three priority levels of the WCAG guidelines.

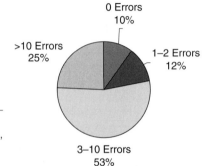

**FIGURE 9.6**

Data from an accessibility analysis showing the percentage of pages containing no errors, one to two errors, three to ten errors, and more than ten errors.

In the United States, another important set of accessibility guidelines is the so-called Section 508 guidelines, or, technically, the 1998 Amendment to Section 508 of the 1973 Rehabilitation Act (Section 508, 1998; also see Mueller, 2003). This law requires federal agencies to make their information accessible to people with disabilities, including what's on their websites. The law applies to all federal agencies when they develop, procure, maintain, or use electronic and information technology. Section 508 specifies 16 standards that websites must meet. Although there is significant overlap with the Priority 1 WCAG guidelines, Section 508 also includes some standards not listed in WCAG. As with the WCAG guidelines, we believe the most useful metric is a page-level metric, indicating whether the page passes all 16 standards or not. You can then chart the percentage of pages that pass versus those that fail.

## 9.4 RETURN-ON-INVESTMENT DATA

A book about usability metrics wouldn't be complete without at least some discussion of Return on Investment (ROI), since the usability metrics discussed in this book often play a key role in calculating ROI. But because entire books have been written on this topic (Bias & Mayhew, 2005; Mayhew & Bias, 1994), our purpose is to just introduce some of the concepts.

The basic idea behind usability ROI, of course, is to calculate the financial benefit attributable to usability enhancements for a product, system, or website. These benefits are usually derived from such measures as increased sales, increased productivity, or decreased support costs that can be attributed to the usability improvements. The key is to identify the cost associated with the usability improvements and then compare those to the financial benefits.

To illustrate some of the issues and techniques in calculating usability ROI, we'll look at an example from Diamond Bullet Design (Withrow, Brinck, & Speredelozzi, 2000). This case study involved the redesign of a state government web portal. The researchers conducted usability tests of the original website and a new version that had been created using a user-centered design process. The same ten tasks were used to test both versions. A few of them were as follows:

- You are interested in renewing a [*State*] driver's license online.
- How do nurses get licensed in [*State*]?
- To assist in traveling, you want to find a map of [*State*] highways.
- What four-year colleges are located in [*State*]?
- What is the state bird of [*State*]?

Twenty residents of the state participated in the study, which was a between-subjects design (with half using the original site and half using the new). The data collected included task times, task completion rates, and various self-reported metrics. The researchers found that the task times were significantly shorter for

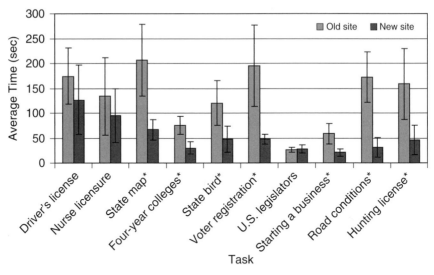

**FIGURE 9.7**

Task times for the original and the redesigned sites (* = Significant difference).
*Source:* Adapted from Withrow et al. (2000); used with permission.

**Table 9.13** Summary of the Task Performance Data

|  | **Original Site** | **Redesigned Site** |
|---|---|---|
| Average Task Completion Rate | 72% | 95% |
| Average Task Time (mins) | 2.2 | 0.84 |
| Average Efficiency | 33% | 113% |

the redesigned site and the task completion rates were significantly higher. Figure 9.7 shows the task times for the original and redesigned sites. Table 9.13 shows a summary of the task completion rates and task times for both versions of the site, as well as an overall measure of efficiency for both (task completion rate per unit time).

So far, everything is very straightforward and simply illustrates some of the usability metrics we've discussed in this book. But here's where it gets interesting. To begin calculating ROI from the changes made to the site, Withrow et al. (2000) made the following assumptions and calculations related to the *time savings*:

- Of the 2.7 million residents of the state, we might "conservatively estimate" a quarter of them use the website at least once per month.

- If each of them save 79 seconds (as was the average task savings in this study), then about 53 million seconds (14,800 hours) are saved per year.

- Converting this to labor costs, we find 370 person-weeks (at 40 hours per week) or 7 person-years are saved per month. 84 person-years are saved each year.

- On average, a citizen in the target state has an annual salary of $14,700.

- This leads to a yearly benefit of *$1.2 million* based only on the time savings.

Notice that this chain of reasoning had to start with a pretty big assumption: that a quarter of the residents of the state use the site at least once per month. So that assumption, which all the rest of the calculations hinge on, is certainly up for debate. A better way of generating an appropriate value with which to start these calculations would have been from actual usage data for the current site.

Then they went on to calculate an increase in revenue due to the increased task completion rate for the new site:

1. The task failure rate of the old portal was found to be 28 percent, whereas the new site was 5 percent.

2. We might assume that 100,000 users would pay a service fee on the order of $2 per transaction at least once a month.

3. Then the 23 percent of them who are succeeding on the new site, whereas formerly they were failing, are generating an additional $552,000 in revenue per year.

Again, a critical assumption had to be made early in the chain of reasoning: that 100,000 users would pay a service fee to the state on the order of $2 per transaction at least once a month.

A better way of doing this calculation would have been to use data from the live site specifically about the frequency of fee-generating transactions (and the amounts of the fees). These could then have been adjusted to reflect the higher task completion rate for the redesigned site. If you agree with their assumptions, these two sets of calculations yield a total of about $1.75 million annually, either in time savings to the residents or in increased fees to the state.

This example points out some of the challenges associated with calculating usability ROI. In general, there are two major classes of situations where you might try to calculate a usability ROI: when the users of the product are employees of your company and when the users of the product are your customers. It tends to be much more straightforward to calculate ROI when the users are employees of your company. You generally know how much the employees are paid, so time savings in completing certain tasks (especially highly repetitive ones) can be directly translated to dollar savings. In addition, you may know the costs involved in correcting certain types of errors, so reductions in the rates of those errors could also be translated to dollar savings.

Calculating usability ROI tends to be much more challenging when the users are your customers (or really anyone not an employee of your company). Your benefits are much more indirect. For example, it might not make any real difference to your bottom line that your customers can complete a key income-generating transaction in 30 percent less time than before. It probably does *not* mean that they will then be performing significantly more of those transactions. But what it *might* mean is that over time those customers will remain your customers and others will become your customers who might not have otherwise (assuming the transaction times are significantly shorter than they are for your competitors), thus increasing revenue. A similar argument can be made for increased task completion rates.

## 9.5 SIX SIGMA

Six Sigma is a business methodology focused on measuring quality improvement. *Sigma* refers to the standard deviation, so *Six Sigma* refers to six standard deviations. In a manufacturing process, Six Sigma is equivalent to 3.4 defects per 1 million parts manufactured. Six Sigma, as a process improvement methodology, was originated by Bill Smith at Motorola (Motorola, 2007). Since then, the methodology has been adopted by a number of companies, and many books have been written on the topic (e.g., Gygi et al., 2005; Pande & Holpp, 2001; Pyzdek, 2003).

The basic concept underlying Six Sigma is illustrated in Figure 9.8. By going 3 standard deviations ($\sigma$, or sigma) above and below the mean, you account for about 99.7 percent of the cases. That leaves only 0.3 percent of the cases outside of that range. The basic goal of Six Sigma is to achieve that level of quality—that the frequency of defects in whatever you're dealing with is at the level of only 0.3 percent or lower. But in many cases, it's not really possible to exactly measure the

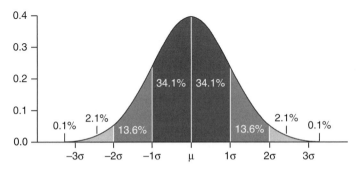

**FIGURE 9.8**

The normal distribution, illustrating the fact that $\pm 3$ standard deviations (i.e., Six Sigma) account for about 99.7 percent of the cases. *Source:* From Wikimedia Commons, based on an original graph by Jeremy Kemp.

frequency of defects. Instead, the goal is often to achieve a Six-Sigma improvement in whatever you are measuring.

So how does any of this apply to usability data? Sigma can certainly be calculated for most of the metrics we've discussed (e.g., task completion, time, errors, satisfaction). At least one interpretation of how Six Sigma could be applied to usability metrics is that you want to try to achieve improvement in a usability metric, across iterations, that's at least three standard deviations higher (better) than where you started. But is that possible with usability data?

Let's look at the data from LeDoux, Mangan, and Tullis (2005), who reported the results of two usability tests of an intranet site: one before a redesign of the site and the other after. Figure 9.9 shows the distribution of SUS scores for the two versions of the site. For the original site, the mean SUS score was 49.1, with a standard deviation of 6.25. Three times the standard deviation would be 18.8, meaning that the "critical mean SUS score" to beat would be 49.1 + 18.8, or 67.9. For the redesigned site, the mean SUS score was 81.8, with a standard deviation of 13.54. The standard error of the mean was 3.50, which means that the lower limit of the 99.7 percent confidence interval for the mean would be 71.4. Since that

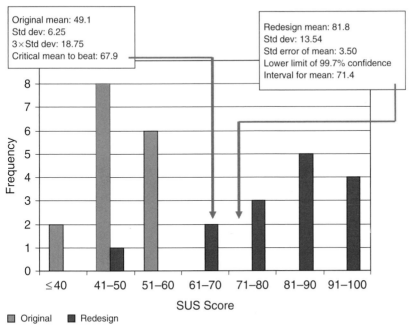

**FIGURE 9.9**

Data with annotations to illustrate the Six-Sigma improvement in the SUS score from the original version to the redesigned version. *Source:* Adapted from LeDoux, Connor, and Tullis (2005); used with permission.

lower limit is higher than the critical mean to beat from the original version (67.9), you can say that the redesign achieved a Six-Sigma improvement in the SUS rating.

So this is at least one illustration that a Six-Sigma improvement in a usability metric is possible. Is it common to achieve this much improvement in a usability metric in just one design iteration? Probably not. But nobody ever said Six Sigma was easy. Achieving it over multiple iterations may be much more realistic.

## 9.6 SUMMARY

Here are some of the key takeaways from this chapter:

1. If you're dealing with a live website, you should be studying what your users are doing on the site as much as you can. Don't just look at page hit counts. Look at click-through rates and drop-off rates. Whenever possible, conduct live A/B tests to compare alternative designs (typically with small differences). Use appropriate statistics (e.g., chi-square) to make sure any differences you're seeing are statistically significant.

2. Card-sorting can be immensely helpful in learning how to organize some information or an entire website. Consider starting with an open sort and then following up with one or more closed sorts. Hierarchical cluster analysis and multidimensional scaling (MDS) are useful techniques for summarizing and presenting the results. Closed card-sorts can be used to compare how well different information architectures work for the users.

3. Accessibility is just usability for a particular group of users. Whenever possible, try to include older users and users with various kinds of disabilities in your usability tests. In addition, you should evaluate your product against published accessibility guidelines or standards, such as WCAG or Section 508.

4. Calculating ROI data for usability work is sometimes challenging, but it usually can be done. If the users are employees of your company, it's generally easy to convert usability metrics like reductions in task times into dollar savings. If the users are external customers, you generally have to extrapolate usability metrics, like improved task completion rates or improved overall satisfaction, to decreases in support calls, increases in sales, or increases in customer loyalty.

5. One way of applying Six Sigma concepts to usability data is to see if you can achieve a Six-Sigma improvement in a given usability metric (e.g., task completion rates, task times, satisfaction ratings) from one design iteration or release of a product to another. If so, you can claim that you're moving toward the goals of Six Sigma.

# Case Studies

In this chapter we present six case studies showing how other usability research-ers and practitioners have used metrics in their work. We would like to thank the authors of these case studies: Hoa Loranger; Jim Lewis; Bob Bailey, Cari Wolfson, and Janice Nall; Scott Weiss and Chris Whitby; Agnieszka (Aga) Bojko; and Todd Zazelenchuk.

## 10.1 REDESIGNING A WEBSITE CHEAPLY AND QUICKLY—By Hoa Loranger

A well-known company in the entertainment news and content industry asked me to help with their website redesign project. The main goal of the redesign was to increase the number of site visitors and motivate them to spend more time exploring the site's content and offerings. Since much of the revenue generated on the site was from paid advertising, the number of page views and ad impres-sions was vital to the success of the website.

The challenge was to create a new site that was appealing to visitors while supporting business needs. If ads needed to stay, then the team needed to develop advertising strategies that were acceptable and, even better, appealing to users.

Similar to other redesign projects I have worked on in the past, this one needed to be completed quickly and cheaply. We had four months for multiple iterations of design and usability testing. The best way to tackle this challenge was to do it incrementally. Instead of trying to design the perfect solution at once, which is virtually impossible, we took a multiphase approach.

### 10.1.1 Phase 1: Testing Competitor Websites

Before delving too deeply into redesign, we first learned from the successes and failures of other similar websites by conducting a competitive study. The first phase was designed to discover people's reaction to concepts of the new site and to find out what worked and what did not work on a few other competitor **237** sites. In a one-on-one lab environment, I gave participants tasks to do on three different websites and observed their behavior as they attempted to accomplish the tasks. Fifteen people participated in this study. All participants were interested in movies and entertainment and had a least a year of web experience, although most had significantly more.

### Sample Tasks

Your friend just told you about a movie that is called [*Movie name*]. Check out *www.companyname.com* to see whether you might be interested in seeing this movie.

- Find the most convenient place and time to see [*Movie name*].
- Find out what TV shows and movies [*Actor name*] has been in.

It was important that I stressed to the team that although this part of the study was termed "Competitive," it was not meant to be truly competitive. I reiterated (and reiterated) that we were not interested in seeing what websites people picked as the "winner." The purpose of this test was to identify the elements of each design that worked well and elements that did not work so well, so that we could eventually produce the best single design with the best aspects of all of them.

### Questionnaire

After each site evaluation, participants were asked to rate the site on different characteristics. (Ratings were not used on the Company X design because it was still in its infancy and not comparable to the competitive sites.) The questionnaire is shown in Figure 10.1.

### Results

The scores from the questionnaire were combined, resulting in the Website Appeal score. The average Website Appeal results are shown in Figure 10.2. This

---

*Please pick a number from the scale to show how well each word or phrase below describes the website.*

*Strongly Disagree*   1   2   3   4   5   6   7   *Strongly Agree*

\_\_\_\_\_ Credible      \_\_\_\_\_ Easy to use    \_\_\_\_\_ Annoying

\_\_\_\_\_ Fun to use    \_\_\_\_\_ Frustrating    \_\_\_\_\_ Boring

\_\_\_\_\_ Engaging      \_\_\_\_\_ Helpful

**FIGURE 10.1**

Questions used in Phase 1 to measure website appeal.

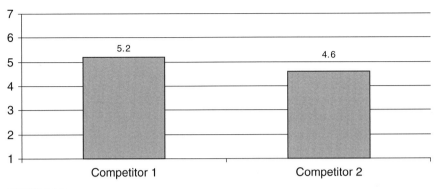

**FIGURE 10.2**

Average score for website appeal. Competitor 1 scored higher in desirable attributes than Competitor 2.

study helped the team identify major usability issues with the conceptual design, as well as provided insight into the advantages and disadvantages between other competitive sites.

## 10.1.2 Phase 2: Testing Three Different Design Concepts

Seven people participated in this part of the study. Based on the qualitative and quantitative information learned from Phase 1, the designers created alternative visual designs for the new website.

We did not have the time or budget to have different studies to measure graphical design and advertising conditions separately. We made the most of what we had by combining the various conditions. Again, we were relying on both quantitative data (people's comments and reactions) and the survey data to point us in the right direction.

### The Designs Tested

Each participant evaluated two out of the following three designs.

- *Version 1*: Medium graphical treatment with high level of unrelated ads
- *Version 2*: Minimal graphical treatment with low level of related and unrelated ads
- *Version 3*: High graphical treatment with moderate level of related ads

I first asked them to provide their first impressions of the homepage and then gave them tasks to do on the websites. I noted user interactions, comments, and success scores for each task. After attempting tasks on each design, participants filled out a questionnaire to measure their preference.

### Questionnaire

After each site evaluation, participants were asked to rate the site. The questionnaire is shown in Figure 10.3.

### Results: Satisfaction

In general, respondents were relatively satisfied with all three designs. When comparing the overall satisfaction scores of the three designs, there was only a moderate difference between people's satisfaction ratings for each design (see Figure 10.4). For example, between Design 2 and Design 3, there is only approximately a half-point incremental difference.

From a usability standpoint, the prototypes performed virtually the same. Most people were able to accomplish the tasks without much difficulty. This was not surprising because the interaction design for each version was virtually identical.

| *Please circle the number from the scale to indicate your opinion of the website.* | | | | | | | | |
|---|---|---|---|---|---|---|---|---|
| | | | **Scale** | | | | | |
| *Very Dissatisfying to Use* | 1 | 2 | 3 | 4 | 5 | 6 | 7 | *Very Satisfying to Use* |
| *Very Unattractive* | 1 | 2 | 3 | 4 | 5 | 6 | 7 | *Very Attractive* |
| *Not Very Credible* | 1 | 2 | 3 | 4 | 5 | 6 | 7 | *Very Credible* |

**FIGURE 10.3**

Questions used to measure design preference.

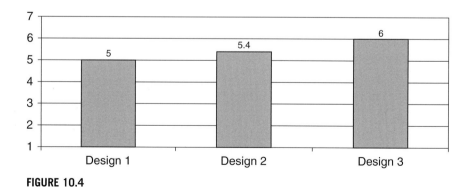

**FIGURE 10.4**

Phase 2: Satisfaction scores of three different website designs.

Therefore, differences in satisfaction ratings could mainly be attributed to the visual design differences and/or advertising conditions.

### Results: Attractiveness and Credibility

When people scored the different sites strictly on attractiveness and visual appeal, Design 3 scored much higher than the other two designs, and they consistently chose Design 3 as their preferred choice (six out of seven users). In contrast to the results of the satisfaction ratings, there was a much greater difference in attractiveness scores (see Figure 10.5). Design 3 was rated much higher in attractiveness than the other two designs. The results from the attractiveness rating are consistent with what people said they would pick as their favorite design when given the option to choose one of the three visual designs.

Design 3 had the most attractive design, which also scored highest in credibility, even though it contained a moderate level of related ads (see Figure 10.6). People

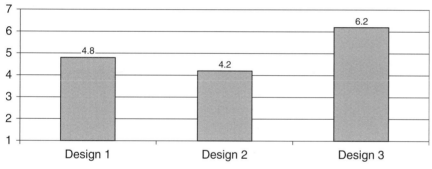

**FIGURE 10.5**

Phase 2: Attractiveness scores of three different website designs. Six out of seven participants chose Design 3.

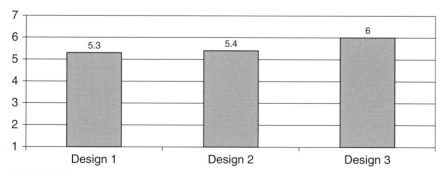

**FIGURE 10.6**

Phase 2: Credibility scores of three different website designs.

didn't seem to mind advertising as long as it was related to the site's content. The conditions that scored lower in attractiveness and had the highest levels of unrelated ads scored lowest in credibility.

### Negative Reactions

I measured the number of unprompted negative comments made by users during the study. Results showed that Design 1 (many unrelated ads) prompted the most negative reactions (see Figures 10.7 and 10.8). These findings suggested that although the number of ads could affect participant experience, the relevancy of the ads had a stronger effect on people's perception of the site. Ads that were

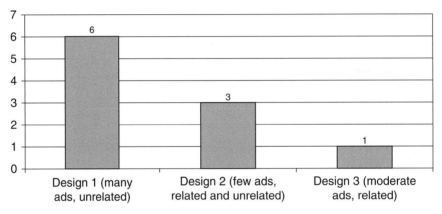

**FIGURE 10.7**

Number of negative comments. Design 1 received the most negative comments. Having many unrelated ads on a website generated the most negative reactions.

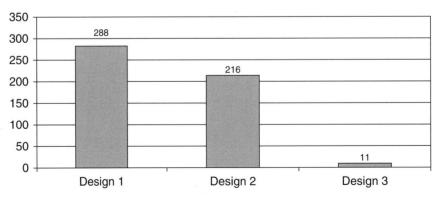

**FIGURE 10.8**

Seconds spent on negative comments. Respondents spent the least amount of time making negative comments when using Design 3, whereas Designs 1 and 2 evoked longer negative reactions.

unrelated to the site's content evoked stronger and more negative reactions than designs that had related advertising content.

### Outcome: Phase 2

We were not particularly interested in statistical significance; we were interested in trends and design insight. Even with feedback from only seven participants, the findings from this study strongly influenced the team's decision on which visual design to keep and which ones to scrap. This study also helped influence advertising guidelines, such as the placement, design, and types of advertisement allowed on the site.

### 10.1.3 **Phase 3: Testing a Single Design**

By Phase 3, the team felt relatively confident that they had a solid design. The designers made minor modifications to the design that respondents preferred and put it through another round of usability testing. This phase had even fewer participants—only five—but this was fine because the process allowed for several validation points. Similar tasks were given to the new set of respondents. Again, success scores and user interactions were noted. At the end of each session, participants were asked to rate their satisfaction level with using the website.

### Results: Phase 3

This design resulted in an average satisfaction rating of 5.8 out of 7. Overall, people were relatively successful in accomplishing the tasks. The average success score across all tasks was 92 percent (see Figure 10.9).

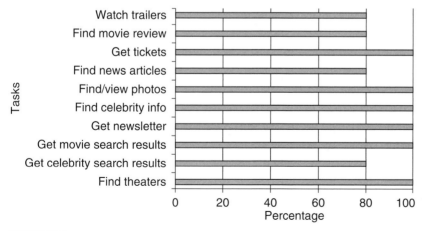

**FIGURE 10.9**

Average success rate. The high rate of success gave us a boost in confidence—we were heading in the right direction.

### *Outcome: Phase 3*

The positive results from this study were an indication that we were on the right path. The data suggested that people can easily accomplish tasks on the site. Our diligence paid off. The satisfaction score was slightly lower than I originally expected, but this could be due to the lack of functionality available on the prototype. For example, people were disappointed when the search engine was not available, and this might have affected their rating.

## 10.1.4 Conclusion

In a few short months, the team was able to completely redesign an entertainment content site to meet both user and business goals. Augmenting quantitative techniques with simple quantitative methodologies provided sufficient data to help the design team make decisions quickly. Only seven days total were spent user testing, and only 27 people participated in the study. However, even with such seemingly small numbers, the data were sufficient to guide us in making the right decisions. After Phase 3, the design went through another round of iterations. I conducted a design review, and the new website was launched shortly after with great success.

## 10.1.5 Biography

*Hoa Loranger* is a User Experience Specialist at Nielsen Norman Group, where she consults with many large, well-known companies in various industries, including finance, entertainment, technology, e-commerce, and mobile devices. She co-authored the book *Prioritizing Web Usability* (New Riders Press). Her extensive research has spanned the globe, including Asia, Australia, and Europe. She is a frequent speaker and has published reports on a variety of web usability topics.

# 10.2 USABILITY EVALUATION OF A SPEECH RECOGNITION IVR—By James R. Lewis

The purpose of this study was to investigate the immediate usability of a speech recognition interactive voice response (IVR) system. The application supports self-service and call-routing activities, such as finding nearby stores, finding nearby service centers, and purchasing products and accessories.

## 10.2.1 Method

Six participants completed the following four tasks.

- *Task 1*: Find the nearest service location
- *Task 2*: Find an accessory and a nearby store
- *Task 3*: Buy an accessory
- *Task 4*: Order a new product

After each task, participants completed an After Scenario Questionnaire (ASQ; Lewis, 1995). After finishing all tasks, participants completed a Post-Study System Usability Questionnaire (PSSUQ; Lewis, 1995, 2002).

The ASQ contains three questions, each scored from 1 to 7, with lower scores indicating greater satisfaction and ease of use. The overall score is the arithmetic mean of the three item scores. The PSSUQ contains 16 items for which participants indicate their level of agreement on a 7-point scale, with lower ratings indicating greater subjective usability. The PSSUQ has three subscales: System Usefulness (SysUse), Information Quality (InfoQual), and Interface Quality (IntQual).

Each participant read through each of the tasks, asked for any necessary clarifications, and indicated to the experimenter when he or she was ready to begin the tasks. Participants received instruction to complete an ASQ following each task.

## 10.2.2 Results: Task-Level Measurements

For each task, the mean call-completion time was less than three minutes and the upper limits of the confidence intervals (CIs) were all under three and a half minutes (see Table 10.1). It's difficult to interpret time-on-task without a comparative context, but the observed times-on-task can provide a baseline for future studies of similar systems.

Participants completed Tasks 2, 3, and 4 with 100 percent success. The failures for Task 1 occurred when two participants incorrectly selected "Find a store" instead of "Find service" from the main menu.

The satisfaction scores (7-point scales in which 1 is the best rating) for Tasks 1, 2, and 3 were very good. The rating for Task 4 was slightly poorer, primarily due to confusion over the wording of a main menu option. Five of the six participants indicated some feeling of confusion about the option, even though they all eventually chose the correct option. In addition to this, two participants spoke subsets of the prompted phrase that were out of grammar and not recognized by the application.

**Table 10.1** Task-Level Usability Measurements

| Task | Completion Time | | Success Rate | | Satisfaction | |
|---|---|---|---|---|---|---|
| | Mean | 90% CI | Rate | 90% CI | Mean | 90% CI |
| 1 | 2.1 | 1.8–2.3 | 0.67 | 0.27–0.94 | 1.5 | 1.0–2.0 |
| 2 | 2.9 | 2.3–3.4 | 1.00 | 0.61–1.00 | 1.9 | 1.2–2.6 |
| 3 | 2.6 | 2.0–3.2 | 1.00 | 0.61–1.00 | 2.1 | 1.0–3.1 |
| 4 | 1.3 | 0.9–1.6 | 1.00 | 0.61–1.00 | 2.4 | 0.9–3.9 |

**Table 10.2** PSSUQ Data by Scale

| Satisfaction | Mean | 90% CI |
|---|---|---|
| Overall | 2.0 | 1.0–3.1 |
| SysUse | 2.0 | 1.0–3.1 |
| InfoQual | 2.2 | 1.0–3.3 |
| IntQual | 1.8 | 1.0–2.8 |

### 10.2.3 PSSUQ

The overall mean PSSUQ score (with 90 percent CI) was 2.0 ±1.1. Table 10.2 gives the means and 90 percent confidence intervals for the PSSUQ scales. The observed means were well below the scale midpoint (in the direction of favorable perceived usability), and the upper limits of their 90 percent confidence intervals were also below the scale midpoint, indicating that for this design, these tasks, and these types of users, the perception of usability was favorable.

### 10.2.4 Participant Comments

Each participant provided comments for the three most-liked and least-liked system attributes, as shown in Table 10.3. The most frequently mentioned application characteristics that participants liked were that the application was easy to understand, easy to use, had good recognition accuracy, and had a useful repeat function. The most frequently mentioned dislikes were that one of the main menu options was confusing, some information (especially telephone numbers) was spoken too quickly, and some of the information presented was too wordy.

**Table 10.3** Participant Comments

| Participant Comments: Favorable | Count |
|---|---|
| Easy to understand (1, 2, 5, 6) | 4 |
| Easy to use (3, 4, 6) | 3 |
| Good recognition (1, 3) | 2 |
| Able to have system repeat (2, 4) | 2 |
| Able to barge in (4) | 1 |
| Quick (1) | 1 |
| Prerecorded audio (2) | 1 |

**Table 10.3** *cont...*

| Participant Comments: Unfavorable | Count |
|---|---|
| One main menu prompt terminology confusing (1, 2, 4) | 3 |
| Some information was spoken too quickly (1, 5) | 2 |
| Too wordy (1, 5) | 2 |
| Found barge-in didn't always work (6) | 1 |
| Lack of DTMF input (6) | 1 |
| Voice recognition unforgiving (5) | 1 |
| *Note: Participants' numbers are in parentheses.* | |

## 10.2.5 Usability Problems

Table 10.4 lists the usability problems discovered during this study, organized by task. The numbers in the cells of the participant columns indicate the impact level of the problem on that participant, using the following scale:

1. Caused participant to fail to complete the task successfully
2. Required more than one minute to recover from the problem
3. Required less than one minute to recover from the problem
4. Minor inefficiency

Table 10.5 shows the usability problems, organized in order of descending severity. The severity score is calculated by multiplying the frequency of occurrence of the problem in the study (the percentage of participants who experienced the problem) by an impact weight. Greater impact levels receive greater weight, with Level 1 having a weight of 10, Level 2 having a weight of 5, Level 3 having a weight of 2, and Level 4 having a weight of 1. Thus, the highest possible severity score is 1,000 (frequency of 100 times an impact weight of 10).

## 10.2.6 Adequacy of Sample Size

This assessment of the adequacy of the sample size of a problem-discovery (formative) usability study uses the relatively new techniques described in Lewis (2006). An analysis of the participant by problem matrix in Table 10.4 indicated that the observed rate of problem discovery was 0.278 and, adjusting for the sample size and pattern of problem discovery, produced an adjusted estimate of 0.134. Given $p = 0.134$, the best estimate of the percentage of discovered problems is 0.578

**Table 10.4** Usability Problems by Participant

| Problem Number | Description | Task | P1 | P2 | P3 | P4 | P5 | P6 |
|---|---|---|---|---|---|---|---|---|
| 1 | System did not recognize zip code. | 1 | | 2 | | | | |
| 2 | Asked for store rather than service location. | 1 | | | | 1 | 1 | |
| 3 | Phone numbers play a little fast. | 1 | 4 | 4 | | | 4 | |
| 4 | Had to repeat phone number. | 2 | | 3 | | | | |
| 5 | Picked store from list, didn't wait for prompt to request zip code. | 2 | | | 4 | | | |
| 6 | Experienced "Was that <silence>?" | 2 | | | | 3 | | |
| 7 | System did not recognize an ungrammatical utterance. | 2 | | | | | | 3 |
| 8 | Tried to enter zip with keypad. | 2 | | | | | | 3 |
| 9 | Went back to main menu to order accessory. | 3 | | 3 | | | | |
| 10 | Participant said entire model number, then rejected 4-digit "Was that" response. | 3 | | | | | 3 | |
| 11 | A main menu option was confusing. | 4 | 3 | 3 | 3 | 3 | | 3 |
| 12 | Participant said ungrammatical variant of prompted option, had to listen to help and retry. | 4 | | | | | 3 | 3 |

$[1 - (1 - 0.134)^6]$. At this rate of discovery, the best estimate of the total number of problems available for discovery given this application and the tasks is about 21 (12 / 0.578). Table 10.6 shows the expected rate of continuing problem discovery.

This projection shows that the 12 problems discovered in this study by these six participants represent about 57.8 percent of the problems available for discovery. At this relatively slow rate of discovery, it is likely that running additional participants will only turn up one additional problem per participant for the next two or three participants and will then continue declining until it becomes necessary to run multiple participants to discover each new problem. This low rate of problem discovery and generally low problem severities are indicative of a well-designed user interface in which there are few high-frequency problems to find.

**Table 10.5** Usability Problems by Severity

| Problem Number | Description | Task | Impact Level | Frequency | Impact Weight | Severity |
|---|---|---|---|---|---|---|
| 2 | Asked for store rather than service location. | 1 | 1 | 33 | 10 | 333 |
| 11 | A main menu option was confusing. | 4 | 3 | 83 | 2 | 167 |
| 1 | System did not recognize zip code. | 1 | 2 | 17 | 5 | 83 |
| 12 | Participant said ungrammatical variant of prompted option, had to listen to help and retry. | 4 | 3 | 33 | 2 | 67 |
| 3 | Phone numbers play a little fast. | 1 | 4 | | 1 | 50 |
| 4 | Had to repeat phone number. | 2 | 3 | 17 | 2 | 33 |
| 6 | Experienced "Was that <silence>?" | 2 | 3 | | 2 | 33 |
| 7 | System did not recognize an ungrammatical utterance. | 2 | 3 | 17 | 2 | 33 |
| 8 | Tried to enter zip with keypad. | 2 | 3 | 17 | 2 | 33 |
| 9 | Went back to main menu to order accessory. | 3 | 3 | 17 | 2 | 33 |
| 10 | Participant said entire model number, then rejected 4-digit "Was that" response. | 3 | 3 | 17 | 2 | 33 |
| 5 | Picked store from list, didn't wait for prompt to request zip code. | 2 | 4 | 17 | 1 | 17 |

| Table 10.6 Expected Rate of Continuing Problem Discovery | | | |
|---|---|---|---|
| **N** | **p** | **Problems** | **Delta** |
| 7 | 0.635 | 13.3 | 1.2 |
| 8 | 0.684 | 14.4 | 1.0 |
| 9 | 0.726 | 15.2 | 0.9 |
| 10 | 0.763 | 16.0 | 0.8 |
| 11 | 0.795 | 16.7 | 0.7 |
| 12 | 0.822 | 17.3 | 0.6 |
| 13 | 0.846 | 17.8 | 0.5 |
| 14 | 0.867 | 18.2 | 0.4 |
| 15 | 0.884 | 18.6 | 0.4 |
| 16 | 0.900 | 18.9 | 0.3 |
| 17 | 0.913 | 19.2 | 0.3 |
| 18 | 0.925 | 19.4 | 0.2 |
| 19 | 0.935 | 19.6 | 0.2 |
| 20 | 0.944 | 19.8 | 0.2 |
| 21 | 0.951 | 20.0 | 0.2 |

## 10.2.7 Recommendations Based on Participant Behaviors and Comments

*Recommendation 1:* Investigate reordering the main menu options to reduce the likelihood that a user seeking service will select "Find a store" when the desired function is "Find service." The basis for this recommendation is that two of the six participants made this high-impact error when completing Task 1. Placing "Find service" immediately after "Find a store" will increase the likelihood that callers will hear both options before saying, "Find a store." (We have observed that when callers barge in, they often do so after hearing one option past the option that they ultimately select.)

*Recommendation 2:* Replace the confusing main menu option with alternative wording. Five of six participants indicated that they found one of the main menu options somewhat confusing.

*Recommendation 3:* Slightly slow the text-to-speech (TTS) speech rate, especially for telephone numbers. Two participants commented that some of the speech was too fast, and three participants specifically commented on the speed of playback of telephone numbers, which is done via TTS. One participant had the application repeat a phone number, presumably due to the speed of the speech.

*Recommendation 4:* Consider allowing zip code entry with the keypad. One participant tried to enter a zip code using the keypad rather than speech. If the impact to code is slight, then enable the keypad for zip code entry. If the impact to code is high, then leave the application as is because the participant recovered rapidly and completed the task successfully.

## 10.2.8 Discussion

This case study of a formative usability study illustrates a number of different usability metrics. Even though the focus was on problem discovery, it didn't require much additional investment to provide the standard task-level measurements of completion time, success rate, and satisfaction rating (and the study-level satisfaction ratings of the PSSUQ). To document the limits of measurement accuracy with a sample size of six participants, the report included 90 percent confidence intervals for completion time and satisfaction ratings and 90 percent binomial confidence intervals for success rates. From a usability perspective, the task- and study-level measurements are of limited immediate usefulness but could be useful as benchmarks for tests of later versions of the application or tests of similar tasks in other similar applications.

The primary focus of the study was on discovering and prioritizing usability problems and developing recommendations to eliminate the problems or reduce their impact. At the usability problem level of analysis, the key measurements were frequency of occurrence and impact on the user, with those measurements combined to derive a severity score used to prioritize the usability problems.

Finally, I assessed the adequacy of the sample size for the purpose of problem discovery. The techniques used for this assessment are fairly new, but I now routinely apply them at the end of these types of studies to get an idea of whether it is reasonable to run additional participants in the study. For the development group with whom I currently work, the presentation of results in tabular form is very effective, so I only rarely present results in graphic form.

## 10.2.9 Biography

*James R. (Jim) Lewis* has worked as a Human Factors Engineer for IBM since 1981. He has published research on sample sizes for formative usability studies and the measurement of user satisfaction. He served in 2005 as the chair for the NIST working group on formative usability metrics, and wrote the chapter on usability testing for the 3rd edition (2006) of the *Handbook of Human Factors and Ergonomics*.

## 10.2.10 References

Lewis, J. R. (1995). IBM computer usability satisfaction questionnaires: Psychometric evaluation and instructions for use. *International Journal of Human-Computer Interaction*, 7, 57–78.

Lewis, J. R. (2002). Psychometric evaluation of the PSSUQ using data from five years of usability studies. *International Journal of Human-Computer Interaction*, 14, 463–488.

Lewis, J. R. (2006). Usability testing. In G. Salvendy (Ed.), *Handbook of human factors and ergonomics* (pp. 1275–1316). New York: John Wiley.

## 10.3 REDESIGN OF THE CDC.gov WEBSITE—By Robert Bailey, Cari Wolfson, and Janice Nall

In 2006, the Centers for Disease Control and Prevention (CDC) elected to revise and update its website, CDC.gov. One of the primary goals during this redesign process was to optimize the usability of the homepage and a few new second-level pages.

A 6-person User Experience team—Janice Nall, Robert Bailey, Catherine Jamal, Colleen Jones, Nick Sabadosh, and Cari Wolfson—was organized and headed by Janice Nall. The team created a plan to ensure that major, meaningful usability-related activities would be appropriately applied. Over a 6-month period, the major usability activities included the following:

- Conducting a review of past usability studies at CDC
- Interviewing users, stakeholders, partners, and web staff
- Conducting a detailed analysis of web and search and call logs
- Analyzing the user survey data from the American Customer Satisfaction Index
- Surveying the ideas and attitudes of CDC leadership, employees, and web staff
- Conducting a card-sort activity
- Conducting parallel design sessions
- Producing a series of wireframes
- Creating graphically oriented prototypes

This case study focuses only on the major usability activity of usability testing, particularly as it was related to revising the CDC.gov homepage. The usability testing included a baseline test, first-click tests, and final prototype tests. Overall, 170 participants were tested using more than 100 task scenarios in three major usability tests. These usability tests eventually showed a success rate improvement of 26 percent and a satisfaction score improvement of 70 percent.

### 10.3.1  Usability Testing Levels

We used the model of usability testing levels Bailey developed in 2006 to help guide our decisions about the types of usability tests to perform. This model proposes five usability testing levels:

*Level 1:* Traditional inspection evaluations, such as heuristic evaluations, expert reviews, and so forth

*Level 2:* Algorithmic reviews with scenarios

*Level 3:* Usability tests that are moderately controlled and use a relatively small number of test participants (about eight)

*Level 4:* Usability tests that are tightly controlled but use only enough participants to make weak inferences to the population

*Level 5:* Usability tests that are very tightly controlled and use a sufficient number of participants to make strong inferences to the population

Because of the well-documented weaknesses of inspection evaluations (Bailey, 2004), the User Experience team elected not to use any Level 1 testing and to do Level 2 testing only on the final, revised homepage. The final algorithmic evaluation was based on the usability guidelines book (Koyani, Bailey, & Nall, 2006).

The existing CDC.gov homepage had been around with very few changes since February 2003 (almost four years). During this time, there had been many surveys, studies, and tests, recommending small changes to the homepage. We were interested in collecting data where we could make fairly strong inferences to the user population, and consequently we did few Level 3 tests. Most of our usability tests were either Level 4 or Level 5.

### 10.3.2  Baseline Test

The original baseline test was used to establish the human performance and user satisfaction levels for the existing site. We also used the baseline test to help us understand some of the major usability issues that may help to guide future changes to the new homepage. The baseline tests took place in August 2006 at three different locations in the United States. The in-person usability tests were conducted in government usability labs, conference rooms, and offices.

The participants were both federal employees and people who had no affiliation with the government. We tested a total of 68 participants that included public health professionals; healthcare workers (physicians, nurses, etc.); general consumers; researchers and scientists; and journalists, legislators, and students. The participants had a mix of gender, age, education, race, and Internet experience that matched typical users of CDC.gov. The usability testing sessions were about one hour long and were conducted using Keynote's *WebEffective* and Techsmith's *Morae*.

The User Experience team created 36 scenarios that reflected the tasks performed most frequently on CDC.gov. Considerable time and effort went into identifying the most frequently performed tasks on the website. Information was used from interviews, surveys, reports from the call center, evaluations of web logs (Omniture), ACSI results, and so on.

Each participant dealt with ten scenarios. All participants were told to browse to the correct answer, and not to use the website's search capability. Later, a "search-only" test was conducted to determine the impact (if any) of not allowing users to search. As can be seen in Table 10.7, there was little difference in success rates, average time, average page views, or satisfaction scores.

Participants were instructed to work as quickly and accurately as possible. They answered prescenario questions, responded to several task scenarios, and then answered postscenario questions (including a satisfaction metric: the System Usability Scale—SUS). If they did not find the answer to a scenario question within three minutes, they were automatically moved to the next scenario and were considered "unsuccessful" on that scenario.

The overall success rate across all 36 scenarios was 54 percent. In other words, users were able to successfully complete only about half of the scenarios in the allowed 3-minute time limit. Figure 10.10 shows success rates for 11 of the scenarios.

### 10.3.3 Task Scenarios

Using information gained during the baseline test, we focused on making changes to those scenarios that elicited the poorest performance. For those

**Table 10.7** Overall Performance Comparisons between "Browse" and "Search" Activities

|  | Browse | Search |
|---|---|---|
| Success rate | 54% | 49% |
| Average time | 2.4 min | 2.8 min |
| Average page views | 7.1 pages | 7.7 pages |
| Satisfaction (out of 100) | 46 | 49 |

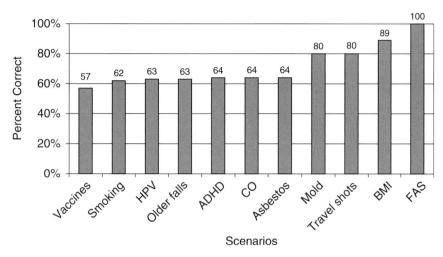

**FIGURE 10.10**

Success rates of eleven scenarios from the baseline test.

scenarios shown in Figure 10.10, this would be those that had success rates of 64 percent or less. As can be seen from Figure 10.10, there were some scenarios that elicited very good performance. We tried to encourage designers *not* to make changes that would lower the success rates of these scenarios. We found it necessary to continuously remind designers to stay focused on those scenarios where the success rate was lowest, and to look for general reasons why they were low. This was one of the major uses of the usability testing sessions: It kept designers focused on those homepage issues that most needed their attention.

## 10.3.4 Qualitative Findings

It should be noted that the qualitative findings from the usability testing were used to inform the proposed changes to the homepage. We had participants type their overall impressions, specify what they liked best and least, and indicate what changes they would make if given the chance. During many of the tests, evaluators took notes about problems that participants were having and asked questions in a debriefing at the end of each test. Here are some of the observations after the baseline test:

- Many felt that the homepage had too much information (overwhelming).
- Participants struggled to find information because of busy, cluttered pages.
- Participants who found the A–Z index liked it and used it quite frequently (it was hard to find).

- Participants thought that the website was inconsistent in layout, navigation, and look and feel.
- Participants did not feel that the categories of information were clear.
- Participants thought that they had to go through too many layers to find information.
- Participants *did* find that the features and the page descriptions were useful.

We found these observations to be invaluable after deciding which scenarios were leading to the most usability problems. These insights from both testers and users assisted us in deciding what changes had the best chance of improving the website.

## 10.3.5 Wireframing and FirstClick Testing

Once the problems were better understood and several solutions had been proposed, we created several competing wireframes to see which would best elicit the success levels we were seeking. All of these eventually were combined into three homepage wireframes (A, B, and C). After only one quick test, B was eliminated and the final two wireframes (A and C) were tested "head-to-head" (see Figure 10.11).

We had 65 participants attempt to complete 136 scenarios (68 using Wireframe A and 68 using Wireframe C). Each participant spent about one hour completing the scenarios using Wireframe A and then Wireframe C (or Wireframe C and then Wireframe A).

We used a FirstClick testing methodology, where we collected and analyzed only the first click they made after reading the scenario. In previous testing, we had observed that the first click was a very critical action. If they had difficulty with that original decision, they frequently had problems finding the correct answer, and when the first click was wrong, it took much longer to complete a scenario than it should have.

This type of testing enabled us to considerably expand the number of scenarios (each scenario took participants less than 30 seconds) and to see which of the two wireframes elicited the best *initial* performance. The test was conducted using Bailey's *Usability Testing Environment* and Techsmith's *Morae*.

The test results showed no reliable difference between the two wireframes in terms of success, but Wireframe C did elicit reliably *faster* performance. Figures 10.12 and 10.13 show the percent of participants that clicked first on each of the links for two different scenarios. Those with a light background were correct, and those with a dark background were incorrect.

We were particularly interested in two different response patterns. Figure 10.12 shows a scenario where a fairly large number of participants tended to agree on the *wrong* response—in other words, the wrong link.

This means that there is something about that link that erroneously elicits clicks, whereas the correct response does not elicit the clicks. This usually can be fixed by

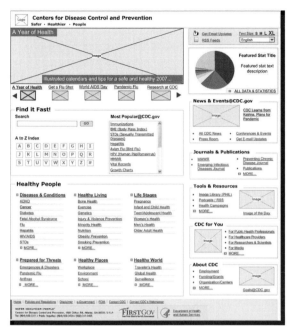

**(a)**

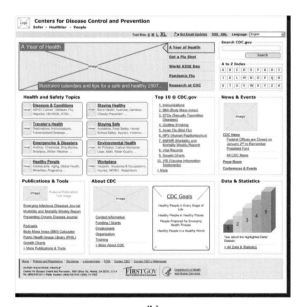

**(b)**

**FIGURE 10.11**

The two wireframes used for conducting the FirstClick tests.

**FIGURE 10.12**

Sixty-seven percent of the participants had an incorrect FirstClick response (call-out percent with dark background).

changing the link names. Figure 10.13 shows a different pattern of responses. In this case, few people could agree on the correct response, and even fewer on the incorrect response. Those making wrong responses showed little consistency in their responses. It is much more difficult to find a workable solution for a problem like this.

Some of the scenarios that elicited poor success rates in the baseline test continued to show poor performance in the FirstClick test. This was after making many changes to the homepage that were expected to improve user performance on these scenarios. For example, in the baseline test "Budget" had an overall success rate of only 17 percent, and in the FirstClick test "Budget" still had only 59 percent making the first click successfully. We noted that two scenarios that elicited good success rates in the baseline test continued to show very good performance in the FirstClick test. The FAS scenario, for example, had perfect performance in both tests. For some scenarios there were big differences between the performance levels on the two different prototypes. These were evaluated further.

## 10.3.6 Final Prototype Testing (Prelaunch Test)

Some design decisions on both wireframes led to better performance, and we used the best from both wireframes to produce a final wireframe. The final wireframe

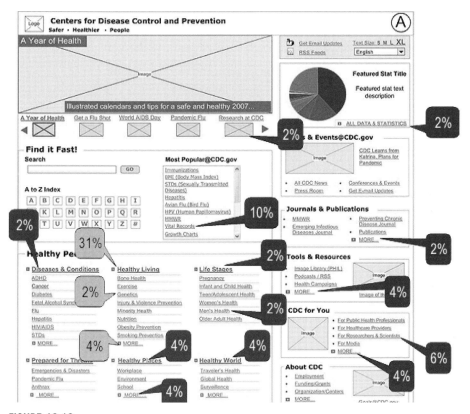

**FIGURE 10.13**

Most participants were incorrect in their FirstClick response. (Call outs with a light background were correct; call outs with a dark background were incorrect.)

was then used as the basis for developing a graphic prototype. The graphic prototype, with images, colors, and a variety of type fonts for headers, was used for the final prelaunch usability test.

The participants were a mixture of federal and nonfederal employees. The majority of participants included the primary audience for this site, which were healthcare providers, public health professionals, and consumers. Again, these tests were conducted using Bailey's *Usability Testing Environment*.

The prelaunch usability tests were divided into two parts: a pilot test and the final test. The pilot test was conducted on Monday using 18 participants and 56 task scenarios that were divided into three categories: 24 FirstClick from the homepage, 24 FirstClick from one of the new second-level pages, and 9 "homepage to content page." All participants saw all scenarios in one-hour in-person testing sessions. After the testing was complete, the data were summarized and analyzed, and a set of observations and recommendations were prepared. On

Tuesday morning, the usability team met with the primary designers and conveyed the recommendations. On Tuesday afternoon and evening, many changes were made to the homepage, and a few changes were made to the test itself. The final in-person tests were conducted all day on Wednesday, using 56 slightly revised scenarios and 19 different participants.

For purposes of this case study, we will only discuss the findings related to the nine "homepage to content page" scenarios in the final in-person (pre-launch) tests. In the "homepage to content page" scenarios, users were allowed to navigate through the website to find information, exactly as they had done in the original baseline test. This provided us with an estimate of the percent improvement from the baseline to the final prelaunch test. The results showed a success rate of 78 percent that could be compared back to the original success rate of 62 percent for these same scenarios (an improvement of 26 percent). In addition, the satisfaction score was measured as 78, which could be compared with the original satisfaction score of 46 (an improvement of 70 percent). A summary of improvements is shown in Table 10.8. Notice that all human performance and user satisfaction scores were substantially improved.

As can be seen in Figure 10.14, the changes made to the homepage for some of these nine scenarios led to substantial increases in performance (Budget, ADHD, and BMI). Four others had moderate increases in performance. Eight of the nine scenarios (89 percent) showed improved performance. Looking back at the FirstClick data, two of these scenarios were shown to elicit good performance (BMI and FAS), whereas one of them still showed that it was a problem (Budget). Obviously, useful changes were made to the website to bring the success rate for "Budget" from 17 percent in the baseline test to 59 percent in the FirstClick test to 91 percent in the prelaunch test.

Only one of these scenarios had a decrease in performance: "NewsRelease." The "NewsRelease" scenario shows how certain changes can result in no substantial changes to the success rate, whereas others actually can cause difficulties. The success rate for "NewsRelease" went from a low 67 percent in the baseline to an

**Table 10.8** Comparison of Performance and Preference Results between Baseline and Prelaunch Tests

| | Baseline Test | Prelaunch Test | Percent Improvement |
|---|---|---|---|
| Success rate | 62 | 78 | 26% |
| Average time | 96 | 81 | 19% |
| Average page views | 8.3 | 4.9 | 69% |
| Satisfaction score (out of 100) | 46 | 78 | 70% |

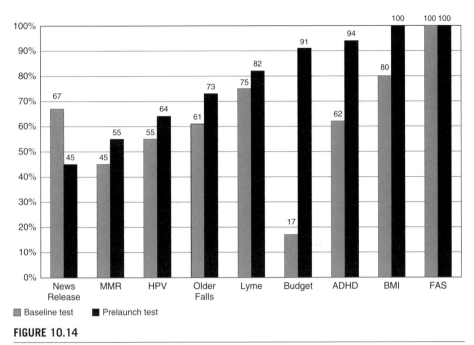

**FIGURE 10.14**

Change in performance between the baseline test and the prelaunch test.

even lower 48 percent in the FirstClick to a 45 percent in the prelaunch test. None of these success rates were acceptable, and this task continues to pose a problem for users who are looking for news information on the homepage.

## 10.3.7 Conclusions

There are three main uses of usability testing metrics in the revision of existing web pages and websites. The first is to establish an overall baseline success rate for comparison against other sites, usability objectives, a revised website, and so on.

The second major use is to identify the individual scenarios where users have the most problems. This helps in finding the weakest areas of the site and enables designers to focus the majority of their efforts on strengthening those areas. In other words, a good usability test can help guide designers to the most problematic areas of the site. We continuously stayed focused on those scenarios that had the lowest success rates. This also enabled us to look for patterns across several scenarios. For example, making the A–Z Index more apparent had a positive impact on several scenarios. In another situation, we noted that virtually all of the CDC statistics-related scenarios performed poorly.

With each change to the website and the resulting test results, we watched to see if success increased. Once the success rate reached the goal for each scenario, we stopped trying to improve performance on that scenario. We tried to use our limited resources and to stay focused on those scenarios that were causing the most usability problems.

A third use of the usability test metrics was to identify those scenarios that consistently elicited high levels of human performance. These areas do *not* require attention, and focusing on them would only waste time and detract from more useful activities.

After each test, changes were made to the homepage. With each set of usability tests and resulting changes made to the homepage (i.e., each "iteration"), we watched closely to see if the success level of the targeted scenarios increased, decreased, or remained about the same. We knew from past testing that some changes to the website would lead to improved performance, others would have no effect, and others could actually make things worse. This is the major reason why it is so important *always* to test after making changes to the site.

In the CDC.gov revision of the homepage, and certain second-level pages, we found the usability testing program to be very valuable. The new homepage was substantially improved over the original page. Based on our experiences, we find it hard to imagine how valid, useful, and important changes could be made to improve a website without conducting high-level usability testing to assist the change process.

## 10.3.8 Biographies

*Robert W. Bailey* is the president of Computer Psychology, Inc. He holds a Ph.D. degree from Rice University, worked for years in the Human Performance Technology Center at Bell Laboratories, and has served on the faculties of numerous schools, including Columbia University. Dr. Bailey has an international reputation as an author, researcher, and lecturer.

*Cari A. Wolfson* is president of Focus on U!, a usability and user-centered design firm that has led the redesign of several high-profile websites, including Usability.gov. Prior to founding Focus on U!, Wolfson was a Usability Engineer at the National Cancer Institute and a Senior Information Architect with a large Internet consulting firm. Wolfson holds a B.A. in communications from Drake University.

*Janice R. Nall* is the director of eHealth Marketing at the National Center for Health Marketing at the Centers for Disease Control and Prevention (CDC). She is responsible for CDC's websites and leading e-health and new media initiatives. Previously, she managed user experience activities at the General Services Administration (GSA), and National Cancer Institute (NCI).

## 10.3.9 References

Bailey, R. W. (2006). Applying usability metrics. *Web Managers University,* May 16.

Bailey, R. W. (2004). Comparing heuristic evaluation and performance testing. *User Interface Update.*

Koyani, S. J., Bailey, R. W., and Nall, J. R. (2006). *Research-based web design & usability guidelines*. Washington, DC: U.S. Government Printing Office.

## 10.4  USABILITY BENCHMARKING: MOBILE MUSIC AND VIDEO— By Scott Weiss and Chris Whitby

Usable Products Company studied U.S. mobile phone-based download and play-back of video and music by way of a comparative, quantitative user experience benchmark. The studied mobile phone user interfaces for music and video play-back were poor, despite the availability of high-quality dedicated media players in the marketplace. Despite polished visual design, usability participants had a diffi-cult time purchasing and playing video and music on mobile phones.

### 10.4.1  Project Goals and Methods

This research focused on understanding the strengths and weaknesses of today's implemented means for shopping, purchase, and playback of video and music on mobile handsets. In the first and second quarters of 2006 in New York City, we compared the three media download and playback services available for mobile handsets by way of usability interviews with target users of these services. At the same time, we utilized improvements in our benchmarking process and learned from new mistakes made in information presentation. For the first time, we included video clips in the presentation files, but the sheer density and quantity of information prevented our participants from finding what they needed quickly.

### 10.4.2  Qualitative and Quantitative Data

This study combined quantitative and qualitative methods to compare three mobile handsets from different carriers and manufacturers. The quantitative data provided the core of the evidence for usability findings (Ebling & John, 2000). The quantitative data and statistical analysis provided support for and scope of the qualitative issues (Sauer & Kindlund, 2005). The quantitative metrics provided points of comparison for each of the three handsets tested and uncovered issues not discovered through qualitative means.

### 10.4.3  Research Domain

A limited number of handsets were available that supported both music and video downloads at the time of this study. Only three operators, one of which was an MVNO (Mobile Virtual Network Operator), supported the technology. All were CDMA, as high-speed GSM networks were not yet launched in the United States. Verizon and Sprint featured multiple handsets, and we chose the most comparable handsets from two major manufacturers, Samsung and LG. Amp'd Mobile had only one handset at the time, from Kyocera, which was available in two colors. We chose the Angel, a pearlescent white slider phone.

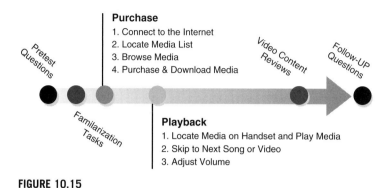

**FIGURE 10.15**

Purchase and playback tasks used in the study.

## 10.4.4 Comparative Analysis

Respondent tasks were categorized as either "purchase" or "playback" (see Figure 10.15). By collecting time, success rate, and satisfaction data for each task, not only were we able to get a more granular level of quantitative data that pertained to particular task flows, but we were also able to compare tasks flows between handsets and between different tasks on the same handset.

*Connect to the Internet* was presented to respondents as "Find a place where you can start to browse for clips that you can purchase." The *Media List* was "a list of media, or media categories." These two segments were distinct in the Amp'd Kyocera Angel but were combined on the Sprint and Verizon handsets, which immediately brought up Media Lists.

Respondents were first asked to find and play back the song, clip, or channel they had purchased. Then they were asked to play the *next* piece of content of the same type (song, video) and adjust the playback volume. The playback task was repeated on the two clamshell handsets that featured external media controls to determine the usability differential between internal and external user interfaces (UIs). Each respondent performed two sets of tasks, once with music and once with video. The music and video tasks were alternated between respondents.

## 10.4.5 Study Operations: Number of Respondents

Research published on sample sizes and user testing focuses on using online methods to extend lab-based research. Spool and Schroeder (2001) discussed how the size and complexity of websites require additional research participants to "ferret out problems." Schulman (2001) argued that quantitative research provides the answers to this problem through online usability testing methods. Online testing is valid for desktop PC software and websites, but it cannot help in the case of testing multiple mobile telephone handsets. In order to acquire the data for mobile telephones, which cannot be instrumented like websites or PC software, in-person one-on-one usability interviews are required. For this project, an "interview" was a user testing session during which performance and preference measurements were taken. Participants were asked to complete tasks under observation in a one-on-one laboratory setting.

Our study was comparative in nature, so it was important to prevent "single-user effects" from coloring these averages. Based on past experience and successful case studies similar in nature, we arrived at 20 as an acceptable compromise for the number of user interviews per handset.

### 10.4.6 Respondent Recruiting

Sixty respondent interviews were required to complete the research (three handsets at 20 interviews per handset). To meet this recruiting goal, we developed an online panel early in the pilot phase and our panel development was continuous throughout the research.

We targeted mobile phone users representing a mix of gender, age, ethnicity, household income, educational level, and mobile phone data use, skewed slightly toward younger people, who more actively purchase handset-based media. Each panelist completed an extensive online survey designed to facilitate the recruiting process. A combination of database applications, e-mail, and telephone was used in the recruiting effort.

We developed customized recruiting software for this project (see Figure 10.21), which interfaced the respondent database with the project's data warehouse. This custom UI was used by an administrative assistant to filter, schedule, and track respondents for the study. The software generated a web calendar of respondents for moderators who were in separate buildings in New York City.

### 10.4.7 Data Collection

We used the freely available logging tool from Ovo Studios (*http://www.ovo.com*) during interviews. This tool enabled systematic data capture, covering performance and perception measures, summarized in Table 10.9. Free-form moderator observations that formed the basis for qualitative analysis were also captured with this logging tool, which also provided task times and observation categories. Synching the software's timer with that of the DVD recorders capturing the interview allowed the moderator to set checkpoints in the logs after a potentially presentable video clip (a segment during which a respondent properly articulates the perceived general sentiment about an aspect of a handset's usability) so they could be harvested afterwards. Any ambiguities or missing data in the logs could be retrieved by reviewing the DVD recordings of interviews.

**Table 10.9** Performance and Perception Metrics Collected

| Performance Metrics | Perception Metrics |
| --- | --- |
| ■ Time to complete tasks<br>■ Success rates<br>■ Number of attempts | ■ Feelings about handsets before and after one hour's use (affinity)<br>■ Perceived cost<br>■ Perceived weight of handset<br>■ Ease of use<br>■ Perceived time to complete tasks<br>■ Satisfaction |

### 10.4.8 Time to Complete

Successful tasks were timed from a predefined start point to a predefined stop point. For example, the Download Place segment started from when a respondent started to use the handset after receiving instructions and lasted until the respondent successfully connected to the media service. At two minutes, respondents were offered help. If they accepted help, the task was failed. Without help, tasks were failed at three minutes.

### 10.4.9 Success or Failure

Success was determined when a respondent achieved the requested goal within the time limit.

### 10.4.10 Number of Attempts

In our previous studies, a respondent's attempt count was incremented by one each time he or she returned to the handset's idle screen while trying to complete a task. However, after a case study conducted by Usable Products Company between 2004 and 2005, we stopped recording attempt counts because successful respondents were almost always completing a task on their first or second attempt. Respondents who exceeded two attempts either gave up on the task or ran out of allotted time (Martin & Weiss, 2006). For the purpose of this study, the moderator did not maintain an attempt count, but rather he carefully monitored and recorded the actions of respondents as they tried to complete tasks.

### 10.4.11 Perception Metrics

As shown in Table 10.9, preferences were also measured, all on a 5-point scale, with 1 being the worst measure and 5 being the best measure. We found the "Before and After Affinity" to be most interesting, since the change in the measure from before the interview to after was affected only by participant experience of the handset. We asked respondents to state how they felt about the handset, from "1 = Hate It" to "5 = Love It."

### 10.4.12 Qualitative Findings

Qualitative analysis followed the typical usability reporting format, with issues and illustrations arranged by task. With this arrangement, useful comparisons could be made between the particular media paths on a handset, and comparisons for the same task stage could be made across handsets.

To provide extra value, the report included Information Architecture diagrams with photographs of the display mapping the task flows for all handsets. These diagrams were actual screenshots from the handsets arranged with linking arrows to walk readers through typical usage patterns for task completion.

### 10.4.13 Quantitative Findings

Presentation of the qualitative data included charts for every category of quantitative data collected. In all, we produced 73 charts, perhaps too many for our readership. Our readers informed us that they would prefer a more condensed analysis of our findings. We utilized the Summative Usability Metric (SUM) method for single-scoring and ranking usability (see Figure 10.16). In future studies we will produce fewer charts and rely more heavily on SUM scores.

### 10.4.14 Summary Findings and SUM Metrics

In studying usability publications, we came upon the Summative Usability Metric, based on the work of Sauro and Kindlund (2005). In this method, time, success, and ease of use perception data are normalized with respect to benchmark goals and averaged, giving a value on a Six Sigma scale. Based on the assumption of a normal distribution, SUM charts show how likely the task performance is to exceed the ideal measures we set for these tasks.

In Figure 10.16, the Sprint LG Fusic clearly had the best usability with regard to adjusting the volume. The worst usability came from the Amp'd Kyocera Angel, with regard to locating and playing downloaded songs. Analysis of the data in the benchmark required that we look to the information architecture diagrams and individual handset qualitative analyses. In each outlier case, there were specific design flaws in the user experience that explained the handset's poor performance in the SUM chart, validating the measure from a logical standpoint.

### 10.4.15 Data Manipulation and Visualization

Data was stored using the Microsoft Access database and analyzed with SPSS, often considered the industry standard in statistical software. Microsoft Access

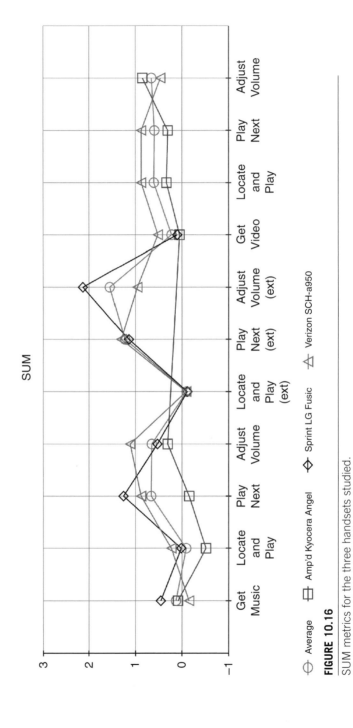

SUM

**FIGURE 10.16**

SUM metrics for the three handsets studied.

compartmentalized the data storage and processes stages in the analysis and sped up the data integrity checks and quality assurance work done before report delivery. Using SPSS rather than Microsoft Excel allows one to increase the number of statistical procedures available without adding to development time, outside basic scripting.

Charts were designed and coded with Visual Basic for Applications (VBA) in the Microsoft Access environment, relying on the Scalable Vector Graphics (SVG) format for output. The SVG markup language provides precise control of vector graphics via an easily scripted markup language. Since SVG is a full graphic platform and not a charting plug-in for Microsoft Access, crafting the visualizations and charting conventions became a much simpler process, and we were able to incorporate the visualizations into our reports in a high-quality fashion.

Video clips of respondents making significant remarks were harvested from the DVD recordings of interviews before being edited for quality using Adobe Premier.

## 10.4.16 Discussion

The end result of the study was a set of best practices that explained common problems respondents encountered while attempting music and video download and playback tasks. The documentation included embedded respondent video clips and flowchart diagrams using screenshots to help visualize the usability challenges of the handsets.

The main usability challenge was the vague link between the devices' hard buttons and their corresponding functions. For example, the functionality of the Amp'd Kyocera Angel's "Back" button was inconsistent between user interfaces. When the Amp'd Media Player was accessed on the device, the "Back" button's functionality became "broken." During playback of a media file, the "Back" button only served to move playback to the start of the file, not to return to the previous screen, which confused respondents, who spent more time navigating than would otherwise have been necessary.

It was unclear to respondents that the download place might not be accessible through the web browser, as was the case with the Verizon and Sprint handsets. Respondents, who associated downloading media with the interim step of "connecting," were confused when the Verizon and Sprint web browsers did not provide access to media services.

While browsing, differentiating between types of media was difficult for respondents when using the Amp'd Live service. Music was easily identified, but the "TV" category included TV-show themed wallpaper in addition to video clips.

Respondents also had difficulty locating downloaded media on all three handsets. The option to immediately view or listen to the media immediately after download at the purchase confirmation screen was unavailable, forcing respondents to then search for the media before playback. It was nonobvious to respondents that downloaded songs and video could be found through the purchasing service; instead, they checked local media folders (e.g., "My Content") and media players before checking the purchase place as a last resort. The Amp'd Kyocera Angel employed cryptic filenames (e.g., "UMG_0034561"), further confusing respondents.

During playback, respondents were unable to switch between local media files without exiting the media player. Although all tested players had the ability to switch songs within the player, the barrier we discovered was the default playlists that were used when the players were opened. Players that opened songs without including other downloaded songs on the playlist had, in effect, disabled their navigation buttons, and their single-song playlists were useless for switching between songs.

### 10.4.17  Benchmark Changes and Future Work

Our clients indicated their preference for more concise findings. We erred on the side of providing comprehensive analysis to prove the points made in our best practices. In future work, we will use summaries and best practices for the early matter and provide more detailed evidence for findings later in the documentation. Some charts will simply be left out if they are of minimal value. We will also use larger type throughout the document, requiring fewer words and more illustrations. Larger type benefits everyone—print and screen readers alike.

We found that the data collected in this project would have been nice to compare to our earlier syndicated study of ring tone, wallpaper, and game downloads and installation. However, the data from that project was siloed, preventing easy cross-project analysis. We will embark on a data warehousing project to consolidate usability projects from multiple projects so that we can expand our analysis capabilities. For our next research, we plan to study either mobile search or mobile community user interfaces.

### 10.4.18  Biographies

*Scott Weiss* is the president of Usable Products Company, a usability design and research agency specializing in usability benchmarking and UI design for mobile phones and consumer electronics. Usable Products worked with Samsung on the design of the YP-K5 MP3 player UI, and with Vodafone on the Simply handset UI. Scott's prior employers were Apple, Microsoft, Sybase, and Autodesk.

*Chris Whitby* is a Usability Analyst with Usable Products Company. His responsibilities include discussion guide development, respondent recruitment, moderating, data analysis, and presenting findings. Chris graduated from New York University with a bachelor of arts degree in sociology.

### 10.4.19  References

Ebling, M. R., and John, B.E. (2000). On the contributions of different empirical data in usability testing. *Proceedings of the Conference on Designing Interactive Systems: Processes, Practices, Methods, and Techniques, 289–296.*

Martin, R., and Weiss, S. (2006). Usability benchmarking case study: Media downloads via mobile phones in the U.S. *Proceedings of the 8th Conference on Human-Computer Interaction with Mobile Devices and Services,* 195–198.

Sauro, J. (2004). Premium usability: Getting the discount without paying the price. *Interactions, 11*(4), 30–37.

Sauro, J., and Kindlund, E. (2005). A method to standardize usability metrics into a single score. *Proceedings of the SIGCHI Conference on Human Factors in Computing Systems,* 401–409.

Schulman, D. (2001). *Quantitative usability: Extending lab research for larger sample sizes.* Retrieved January 14, 2005, from *http://www.3.ibm.com/ibm/easy/eou_ext.nsf/Publish/1854/$File/1854.pdf* .

Spool, J., and Schroeder, W. (2001). Testing web sites: Five users is nowhere near enough. *CHI 2001 Proceedings,* 286–286.

## 10.5 MEASURING THE EFFECTS OF DRUG LABEL DESIGN AND SIMILARITY ON PHARMACISTS' PERFORMANCE—By Agnieszka (Aga) Bojko

In an effort to make drug packaging production more cost effective, Abbott created a standard template for its prescription drug labels. Although replacing the myriad labels for Abbott's drugs appeared daunting, the initiative also provided the opportunity to add new anticounterfeiting features to the label. The standardization would also help reduce regulatory review time of new drugs.

Throughout the redesign process, Abbott focused on safety because any label change could easily add to the estimated 1.7 percent of dispensing errors that occur in pharmacies (Flynn, Barker, & Carnahan, 2003). To ensure that the template did not have a negative impact on pharmacists' performance relative to the existing labels, User Centric was asked to conduct a series of studies that investigated various applications and elements of the new label.

Initial studies showed that the new label, when applied to drug bottles, improved performance in terms of both search efficiency and information-processing efficiency. These improvements led to shorter times required to locate and identify critical drug information with the new labels as compared to the existing labels (Bojko, Gaddy, Lew, Quinn, & Israelski, 2005). So what exactly caused the improvement? Applying a template to all Abbott drug labels meant two things: change in label design (the visual design of the template was different from all existing label designs) and increase in consistency across labels (all labels were created according to the template). Although we knew that the template had a positive effect, we did not know exactly why. Was the observed improvement due to the new design or the interlabel similarity?

The main objective of the present study was to investigate whether the proposed standardized label template had an impact on user performance when the template was applied to drug cartons (containing tablets or capsules individually sealed in blister packs) rather than drug bottles (containing loose tablets or capsules). If there was an impact, we also wanted to determine whether it was due to the different label design, the increased similarity across all Abbott labels, or some combination of these two factors.

Since bottles are much more common than cartons in U.S. pharmacies, we decided to conduct the study in Europe, where cartons are the primary form of prescription drug packaging. Pharmacists were invited to our user research lab in Rome and asked to perform typical drug selection tasks using the new and existing label designs in a situation that approximated their work environment.

Considering Abbott's concern for safety, the ideal metric to assess user performance would be error rate. However, drug-dispensing errors attributed to label design are quite rare and presumably would be even less frequent in a lab setting. Thus, although we needed to collect error data, we also decided to measure factors that can *contribute* to error, such as difficulties in finding information or increased cognitive processing demands. The effect of these factors can be accentuated and lead to errors in stressful situations and under high mental workload.

Therefore, in addition to error rate, we measured the number of eye fixations prior to target selection as an indicator of search efficiency (Kotval & Goldberg, 1998), average fixation duration as a measure of information processing difficulty (Fitts, Jones, & Milton, 1950), and pupil diameter of the participants as a global measure of cognitive workload (Kahneman, 1973). As a gross measure of overall task efficiency, we also analyzed participant response times needed to locate and select the correct drug.

## 10.5.1 Participants

Twenty pharmacists (14 women and 6 men) between the ages of 26 and 45 ($M = 34$) participated in individual 60-minute sessions. Their pharmaceutical experience ranged from 2 to 17 years ($M = 6.5$), and they worked in pharmacies of varying sizes (3–13 employees) and script volumes (150–1,500 scripts per day). The participants were compensated for their time with a one-year subscription to a professional journal.

## 10.5.2 Apparatus

The stimuli were presented on a 17-inch monitor interfaced with a PC with a 1.79 GHz AMD Athlon XP 2100+ processor. The screen resolution was set to $1024 \times 768$ pixels. Each participant used a keyboard to indicate responses. Eye movements were recorded with a Tobii 1750 binocular remote eye-tracker with 50 Hz temporal resolution and a .5-degree spatial resolution.

## 10.5.3 Stimuli

In countries where cartons are more prevalent than bottles, prescription drugs tend to be stored in drawers, as shown in Figure 10.17. In an effort to simulate the

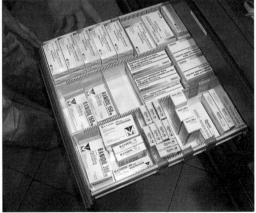

**FIGURE 10.17**

Drawers with cartons in an Italian pharmacy.

experience of standing over a drawer and selecting a drug to fill a prescription, we created 16 digital drawings of carton labels arranged in a $4 \times 4$ grid representing a top-down view of a drawer, examples of which are shown in Figure 10.18. Each drawer stimulus contained 16 cartons with 8 unique drugs, some including multiple dosage strengths. The arrangement of the labels corresponded to a common drug organization—alphabetically by trade name, followed by dosage strength within the name.

Four different Abbott label designs were tested: the new template and three existing designs (E1, E2, and E3), with two label similarity levels (low and high), resulting in the eight experimental conditions illustrated in Figure 10.19. Each condition consisted of a set of two drawers. The high-similarity condition shown in Figure 10.18(a) was achieved by using the same label design as a template for all labels in the drawer. In the low-similarity condition shown in Figure 10.18(b), the Abbott label design of interest was used for only five cartons per drawer (for two different drugs). The other 11 cartons (six different drugs) used various non-Abbott labels, presented as products of a fictitious manufacturer "Biomed."

The eight sets of drawers (one set per condition) were equivalent in terms of color and all label elements. All elements except for the drugs' trade names were mapped exactly (e.g., in one of the drawers in each set, the top left label was always yellow with 125 mg, as shown in Figure 10.19). The trade names were different in each drawer, but they all consisted of exactly three syllables with a name length of seven to ten letters. All trade and generic drug names were fictitious to control for familiarity effects and ensure content equivalency across drawers by allowing us to systematically manipulate the different label elements without confusing the participants.

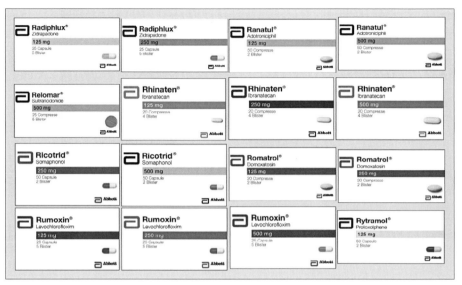

(a)

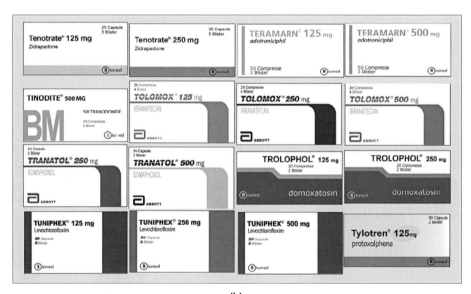

(b)

**FIGURE 10.18**

Two of the 16 stimuli used in the study: (a) high-similarity drawer with the new labels; (b) low-similarity drawer with one of the existing label designs—E1.

| | | Design | | | |
|---|---|---|---|---|---|
| | | Existing 1 (E1) | Existing 2 (E2) | Existing 3 (E3) | New |
| | | 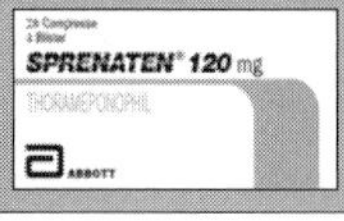  | 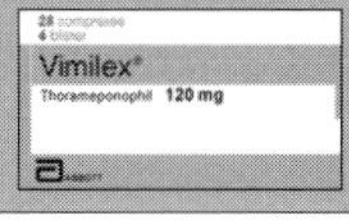  | 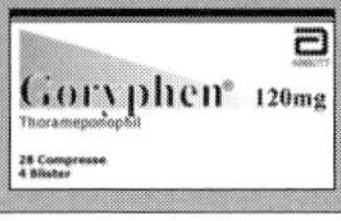  | 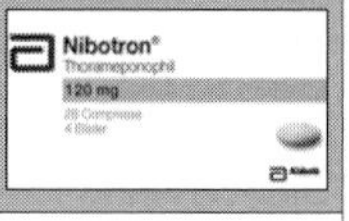  |
| Similarity | High | Example not shown | Example not shown | Example not shown | **Example in Figure 10.18(a)** |
| | Low | **Example in Figure 10.18(b)** | Example not shown | Example not shown | Example not shown |

**FIGURE 10.19**

The eight experimental conditions.

Only three different dosage strengths were presented in a single drawer (either 125, 250, and 500 mg, or 120, 240, and 480 mg). This forced users to examine both the drug name and dosage strength because the target could not be identified by looking at one of these elements alone.

### 10.5.4 Procedure

For each task, participants saw a picture of a "drawer" and were asked to locate a drug according to task instructions (e.g., "Find Medotil 500 mg"). The instructions were always displayed at the bottom of the screen. After reading the instructions, participants had to press the space bar for the drawer stimulus to appear above the instructions. As soon as the participants identified the target label, they responded by pressing one of four keys on the keyboard (*d*, *f*, *k*, and *l*) to indicate the column (I, II, III, or IV) in which the target drug was located. The key press began the next trial by displaying a new set of instructions.

Participants used their index and middle fingers from each hand to press the keys, which were marked with stickers to make them easy to locate. We used key press responses instead of mouse clicks to ensure that our visual search data were uncontaminated by the selection behavior associated with aiming the mouse pointer.

Each condition was presented in a separate block, which consisted of 16 trials (tasks), with 8 trials per drawer. Each trial had a unique target. In each low-similarity drawer, 4 trials had an Abbott label as a target and 4 trials had a non-Abbott label as a target. In each high-similarity drawer, all 8 trials had an Abbott label as a target because all labels used the same Abbott template.

To compensate for order effects, the order of the trials within each block was randomized, and the order of the blocks was counterbalanced across participants. Organization of the drugs in each drawer remained constant, as is usually the case in pharmacies. Participants were instructed to find the target drug as quickly as possible but without sacrificing accuracy. To familiarize them with the procedure and response mappings, a practice block of 16 trials was administered at the beginning of the session.

### 10.5.5 **Analysis**

The data we collected included error rate, time-on-task, and three eye-related measures: pupil diameter, fixation count, and average fixation duration. We precisely defined the metrics to ensure valid results:

*Error rate* was defined as the percentage of responses (key presses) that did not match the location of the target in question.

*Time-on-task* was the time it took participants to read task instructions, locate the correct label, and respond. It was measured from the onset of the instructions to the participant's key press indicating the location of the drug in question, and it was computed for successful tasks only.

*Pupil diameter* was the average size of the participant's pupil throughout the entire block (condition). Pupils dilate slowly, so collecting this measure on a per-trial basis (or excluding data from unsuccessful trials) would not be useful because of the difficulty in matching the data to the particular stimulus caused by the delay.

*Fixation count* was the average number of fixations per Abbott label. Fixations were determined using the dispersion-threshold method (Salvucci & Goldberg, 2000), where the dispersion threshold radius was 0.5° and duration threshold was 100 ms. This measure was computed for successful tasks only.

*Fixation duration* was the average length of a fixation on Abbott labels. This measure was computed for all tasks (both successful and not).

An initial analysis of the fixation data revealed that each Abbott label in the low-similarity condition received, on average, more fixations than each of the Abbott labels in the high-similarity condition. However, on closer examination of the data, we realized that this was an artifact caused by the much higher target-to-Abbott-label ratio in the low-similarity condition (4 targets/5 Abbott labels) than in the high-similarity condition (8 targets/16 Abbott labels).

Targets tended to attract more attention because participants had to examine both the name and dosage strength of the drug to make sure that the label matched the drug in the instructions (while elimination of nontargets was possible by looking at one of these elements only). Also, participants often employed strategies where once they found the correct drug, they would look at the instructions again, and then go back to the label to verify. These two factors significantly increased the number of fixations on the labels that served as targets, thus increasing the average for the Abbott labels in the low-similarity condition as compared to the high-similarity condition.

To avoid this artifact in the fixation analysis, we decided to analyze only those labels in the high-similarity drawers that matched the locations of the five Abbott labels in the low-similarity drawers. The chosen locations, in addition to being equivalent along multiple dimensions (as described in Section 10.5.3), also had the same probability of being a target (i.e., four of five of these labels were always targets on the eight trials with each drawer).

Once all measures were defined, to determine the impact of the new label template on pharmacists' performance, we computed a 4 (design: E1, E2, E3, and New) $\times$ 2 (similarity level: low and high) repeated measures analysis of variance (ANOVA) for all five metrics collected during the study.

### 10.5.6 Results and Discussion

On average, participants needed 9 seconds to read the task instructions and correctly identify the target drug among 15 others. Each participant responded erroneously on 5.9 percent of the tasks, which translates into almost one error per condition. However, at least some of the errors resulted from an incorrect response rather than an incorrect intention because participants would often comment that they pressed the wrong key unintentionally. The error and time analyses revealed no main effects for design or label similarity and no significant interaction between the two factors ($p > 0.05$), which suggests that the new template had no negative impact at least on the overt aspects of participant performance.

Participant pupil diameter was recorded throughout the session to assess the perceptual, cognitive, and response-related processing demands of the different labels and label sets. Similar to findings on error rate and time, the size of the pupil was not affected by label design or level of label similarity, nor was any interaction found between the two factors ($p > 0.05$). This indicates that the new template design or the between-drug similarity that the template introduced did not increase the workload of the pharmacists, keeping it consistent (3.53 mm on average) across the different drawers.

The fixation data, however, revealed some interesting findings. Although there was no main effect of similarity and no interaction between design and similarity for either fixation count or fixation duration ($p > 0.05$), a main effect of label design was found for fixation count ($p < 0.05$). The new template required *fewer* fixations (0.88 fixation per Abbott label per trial) than one of the existing designs, E3 (1.1 fixations). This suggests that the new design improved participants' search efficiency, which could be attributed to the key label elements (i.e., drug name and dosage strength) being closer together than in the existing designs. The closer proximity of the label elements created a smaller area that needed to be scanned to obtain the key information. In the new design, both elements were often pro-cessed with a single fixation, whereas the existing design sometimes required multiple fixations (Figure 10.20).

The fixation duration analysis also revealed a main effect for label design ($p < 0.0001$). However, this effect was counter to the number of fixations result; the new template required *longer* fixations ($M = 279$ ms) than existing design E3 ($M = 220$ ms). Increased fixation duration can be caused by unclear or ambiguous information, but because the drawers were equivalent in terms of content, this explanation was ruled out. A more plausible cause was the smaller font and higher

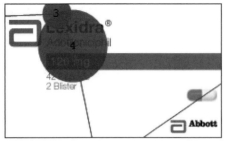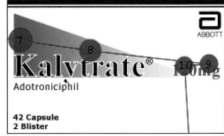

**FIGURE 10.20**

New label design (*left*) and one of the existing label designs, E3 (*right*), with superimposed sample fixation data. The circles indicate fixations, with the circle size being proportional to duration of fixation.

information density in the new template, which demanded more processing time per fixation. However, this result cannot be considered negative because it was accompanied by a decrease in the number of fixations, and time-on-task was not ultimately affected. It should also be noted that the font sizes in the new template were chosen to ensure both consistency across labels and readability of critical information at an estimated worst case distance of 24 inches (arm's length).

The purpose of this study was to determine the impact of the new template on pharmacists. Overall, we concluded that the new labels did no worse than the existing labels we tested. However, our previous study found significant performance improvements associated with the new template when it was applied to bottles. So why did the template not show much improvement when it was applied to cartons? One explanation that comes to mind involves the existing label designs to which we compared the new template. Some of the existing labels used in the previous study had very poor contrast and extremely high information density, and they were thus not nearly as readable as the labels used in the present study. The results of both studies indicate that although the new design is not superior to every Abbott label design that exists, it is better than some and, in the worst case, equal to others.

We realize that just like any study, this one has its limitations. Although our participants were domain experts, they were novices with regard to the particular (fictitious) drugs we showed them. Therefore, our findings only generalize to novice participants in early stages of learning. It is however possible that the across-drug label similarity that will accompany the introduction of the template will affect expert performance, preventing experts from relying on their top-down processes when searching for drugs. Instead of being able to conduct an efficient search by discriminating labels parafoveally, they might have to examine them one by one if they are not distinctive enough. Label similarity may also affect learnability because it is difficult to memorize what each drug looks like if they all look similar.

Although the smaller font used in the new template did not have a detrimental impact on the pharmacists in this study, it might cause issues when the distance between the eye and the drawer increases and possibly exceeds 24 inches. This impact could be exacerbated in high-similarity conditions where it is difficult to see the name and dosage strength of the drug and there are no other cues to identify it from the distance.

One recommendation is to conduct research with longer sessions or multiple sessions over a period of time to assess learning and expert performance. Another is to extend the study to physical (rather than digital) drawers and cartons experienced under a variety of conditions (e.g., various viewing distances or different cognitive workload levels), which would improve the ecological validity of this research.

In this study, a great deal of attention was given to the selection, definition, and collection of measures. When selecting measures, we had to account for the fact that error rate might be insufficient. Understanding the relationship between easily observable performance measures and other less overt physiological metrics allowed us to investigate underlying cognitive processes to assess performance.

Next, we defined the measures and determined how they would be analyzed. For example, deciding to collect the number of fixations was not enough. We had to define a fixation and choose whether to analyze this measure for the entire drawer, for all Abbott labels, or just for some of them. Recognizing factors that may impact these measures (e.g., targets attract more fixations, pupillary response has a delay, or mouse clicks create additional fixations) helped us refine these measures and adjust procedures and analyses to ensure that we were not collecting just data but valid data.

## 10.5.7  Biography

*Agnieszka (Aga) Bojko* is a chief scientist and associate director at User Centric, Inc. She directs global user research studies and publishes methodology papers that focus on integrating behavioral measures with eye movement metrics. Aga holds graduate degrees in Human Factors and Human–Computer Interaction from University of Illinois and DePaul University, respectively.

## 10.5.8  References

Bojko, A., Gaddy, C. Lew, G. S., Quinn, A., and E. Israelski. (2005). Evaluation of drug label designs using eye tracking. *Proceedings of the 49th Annual Meeting of the Human Factors and Ergonomics Society,* Orlando, FL.

Fitts, P. M., Jones, R. E., and Milton, J. L. (1950). Eye movements of aircraft pilots during instrument landing approaches. *Aeronautical Engineering Review*, 9(2), 24–29.

Flynn, E. A., Barker, K. N, and Carnahan, B. J. (2003). National observational study of prescription dispensing accuracy and safety in 50 pharmacies. *Journal of the American Pharmaceutical Association*, 43(2), 191–200.

Kahneman, D. (1973). *Attention and effort.* Englewood Cliffs, NJ: Prentice-Hall.

Kotval, X. P., and Goldberg, J. H. (1998). Eye movements and interface components grouping: An evaluation method. *Proceedings of the 42nd Annual Meeting of the Human Factors and Ergonomics Society,* Chicago.

Salvucci, D. D., and Goldberg, J. H. (2000). Identifying fixations and saccades in eye-tracking protocol. *Proceedings of the Eye Tracking Research and Applications Symposium,* Palm Beach Gardens, FL.

## 10.6  MAKING METRICS MATTER—By Todd Zazelenchuk

Collecting usability and other design-related metrics has become a hot topic in recent years, as usability has become more of a mainstream concept for many organizations. The consumer software industry, the world of home appliance design, and institutions of higher education are just a few examples of where organizational leaders have found themselves enamored with the collection of metrics as a way of helping their organizations "move the needle" in their product design efforts. Collecting quantitative measures of a product's performance, however, is only part of the equation. In order for usability metrics to stand a chance of influencing the future direction of a product, several criteria must be met. Without them, the effort may resemble a successful academic exercise, but it will most likely fail to have the desired impact on the product's direction. The following case study illustrates one such example where usability metrics were successfully collected, but their ultimate impact was limited.

### 10.6.1  OneStart: Indiana University's Enterprise Portal Project

Indiana University (IU) embarked on its enterprise portal project in the year 2000 with design research and iterative prototype development leading the way. Technically, the project had begun two years earlier with the publication of an information technology strategic plan for the university (McRobbie, 1998). This plan identified a broadening base of information consumers who were becoming increasingly tech-savvy and whose expectations for convenient, quick access to information and services were rapidly expanding. Although the plan never actually mentioned the word *portal*, it effectively described the need for what would become *OneStart*, a "next-generation" enterprise portal responsible for providing a full range of university services to over 500,000 students, staff, faculty, and alumni (Thomas, 2003).

Integral to the IU Strategic Plan was *Action 44*, the requirement for a user-centered design approach to all information technology projects. From 1995 to 2003, Usability Consulting Services, an internal consulting group based within IU's University Information Technology Services (UITS), supported project teams in the design and evaluation of their numerous software development initiatives. Known as the User Experience Group today, this team has since contributed significantly to the successful technologies delivered by UITS and Indiana University. In the case of the OneStart project alone, more than a dozen research studies have been conducted on various aspects of the portal over the past seven years, including usability testing, user surveys, and focus groups.

In 2000, not yet able to test any designs of its own, the OneStart team began with a comparative evaluation of some existing web-based portals. Three portals (MyExcite, MyFidelity, and MyYahoo) were evaluated with a sample of student and faculty users. The emphasis was largely on navigation and personalization tasks (selecting content for display, arranging a custom layout, changing background themes and colors). From this study, the team gained insights into many of the design elements that made portals of that era either easy or difficult for users to interact with and comprehend.

By early 2001, the team had a working prototype of OneStart in place, and the next phase of testing began. There were several motivations for the next round of research. At the most basic level, the team wished to understand how users would react to their university information and services being consolidated into the new portal environment. We anticipated that users may be confused about the relationship between the new portal and the traditional homepage of the IU website. Further motivation involved a desire to learn whether the content organization and personalization features of the portal were both usable and useful for the target population of users. Finally, the author was selfishly motivated to complete his dissertation related to the topic of measuring satisfaction as an attribute of usability. The combination of these motivating factors led to an empirical study with the following goals:

- Identify the major usability problems associated with the portal's navigation and personalization features in order to help direct the next iteration of OneStart.

- Establish usability benchmark data (comprising effectiveness, efficiency, and satisfaction metrics) for the core tasks currently supported by the portal in order to allow comparison with future design iterations of OneStart.

- Investigate the theoretical questions of whether certain methods of administering user satisfaction surveys have an impact on the ratings themselves and whether correlations between efficiency, effectiveness, and satisfaction exist for portal users.

- Identify why users rate their satisfaction with the portal the way they do (i.e., what are the contributing factors of a portal experience to users' satisfaction or frustration with the product?).

## 10.6.2 Designing and Conducting the Study

To achieve the goals outlined for the research, a usability lab study was designed and conducted with a sample of 45 participants representing the student portion of the overall OneStart target population. This was a much larger sample than the lab normally recruited for formative evaluation studies, but the desire to collect certain metrics and apply inferential statistical methods made it necessary. Had it not been for the dissertation-related questions, a smaller sample and descriptive statistics would have sufficed.

The study applied a between-subjects, one-variable, multiple-conditions design (Gall, Borg, & Gall, 1996), in which the 45 participants were distributed across three groups of 15, each of which encountered the same portal design and core tasks to be performed but experienced different conditions for rating their satisfaction levels with the product.

The tasks for each participant included a combination of information retrieval and personalization tasks. Information retrieval tasks consisted of locating "channels," or groups of content to be added to the participants' portal page. Personalization tasks required the participant to change the look and organization of their interface (e.g., screen color, layout, add content, etc.).

A traditional two-room, mirrored glass lab facility was utilized with the researcher moderating the study from the test room, while the participant worked through assigned tasks in the participant room. The ISO definition of usability (ISO 9241-11, 1998), comprising the three attributes—*effectiveness*, *efficiency*, and *satisfaction*—was used as the basis for the metrics collected. For *effectiveness*, a rubric was established to judge whether task performances were scored as a pass or fail. A stopwatch was used to measure the attribute of *efficiency*, the time spent per task in minutes and seconds.

The third attribute, *satisfaction*, was collected using two different instruments: the After-Scenario Questionnaire (ASQ) and the Post-Satisfaction Survey of Usability Questionnaire (PSSUQ; Lewis, 1995). The ASQ consisted of three questions asked after the completion of each task. The PSSUQ consisted of 19 questions asked after the completion of the entire study. Both questionnaires utilized a 7-point scale (1 = Strongly Agree, 7 = Strongly Disagree) that was reversed prior to data analysis.

## 10.6.3 Analyzing and Interpreting the Results

We analyzed our qualitative data looking for high-frequency patterns of behavior that might suggest inherent problems with the design. We found several, along with problems that were lower frequency yet potentially severe in their impact on the user experience. Once this analysis was completed, we prioritized the problems based on frequency and our subjective ratings of severity to help prioritize the order of presentation in our final report.

The most frequently demonstrated problems involved personalization activities, with key problem areas including tasks such as creating a custom page for personal content, changing the color of a page, and viewing the completed page. These were all considered to be rather serious problems at the time, given the importance that the team believed personalization features would have on user adoption of the portal.

For the quantitative data collected, we calculated descriptive statistics for effectiveness, efficiency, and satisfaction to share with the project team. We evaluated effectiveness by calculating the mean values of task completion for each task, as well as the mean and standard deviation for all tasks combined ($M = 0.731$, $SD = 0.238$). Efficiency (mean time per task) was presented for

| Table **10.10** Correlations between Usability Metrics | |
|---|---|
| **ISO Attributes of Usability** | **Correlations Found** |
| Satisfaction effectiveness | $(-0.593, p < 0.01)$ |
| Satisfaction and efficiency | $(-0.452, p < 0.01)$ |
| Effectiveness and efficiency | $(-0.394, p < 0.01)$ |

individual tasks as well as for the full set of tasks ($M = 467.4$s, $SD = 145.0$s). Satisfaction was evaluated by reversing the scale values and computing the mean post-test PSSUQ scores for each group and for all participants ($M = 5.1$, $SD = 1.1$).

The theoretical questions for the study were analyzed further using SPSS to discover moderate to high correlations existing between effectiveness, efficiency, and satisfaction (see Table 10.10). The different satisfaction collection methods revealed no significant difference between methods (Zazelenchuk, 2002).

## 10.6.4  Sharing the Findings and Recommendations

The findings from the study were compiled and reported to the OneStart design team in both a written report and a presentation supplemented with video highlights of the most frequently occurring, highest-severity issues. Although this author has rarely compiled test session video highlights for presentation, this study represented an exception due to the large sample size. The impact of viewing tightly edited sequences of multiple participants (often ten or more) demonstrating the same unanticipated behaviors certainly drove the message home to the design team for many of the findings.

The quantitative data representing effectiveness and efficiency were shared with the design team on a per-task basis (see Figures 10.21 and 10.22). Given that there was no significant difference discovered between the three conditions applied in the study, users' satisfaction measures were presented as an average post-task score for all 45 participants.

From a practical perspective, the most actionable data collected from the study were the qualitative findings revealed in the prioritized problem lists and supported by the video excerpts in the summary presentation. A total of seven qualitative themes were identified representing participants' rationales for their ratings of satisfaction with the portal (Zazelenchuk & Boling, 2003) and in 2005 were part of Educause's recommended reading list for the Top Ten Issues in Information Technology (Educause, 2005).

The quantitative metrics were also shared with the design team, but a reliable frame of reference for their interpretation was lacking. Had the initial competitive evaluation of existing portals been conducted with the goal of establishing benchmarks for certain tasks, those results could potentially have represented a

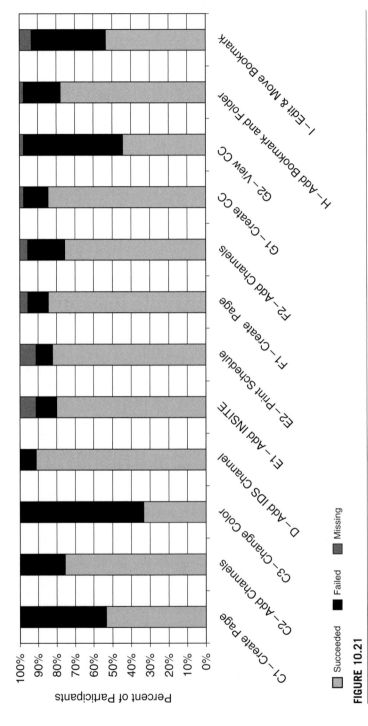

**FIGURE 10.21**

Task success and failure rates.

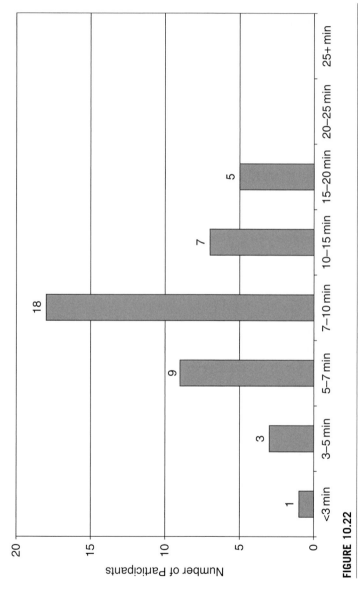

**FIGURE 10.22**

Mean time per task.

meaningful frame of reference for the analysis. Without those baseline scores, however, the metrics collected in this study were limited to answering the academic questions associated with the author's dissertation and providing an initial benchmark for future evaluations of the portal.

### 10.6.5 **Reflecting on the Impact**

Six years after the original study, and four years after the author's last direct experience with OneStart, an update from the design team provided additional insights into the challenges associated with making usability metrics matter. The metrics collected in the 2001 study had provided negligible long-term value. Although they successfully addressed the academic questions associated with the original study, their practical impact on the actual product was low. There were two primary reasons for this: Both represent important considerations for today's organizations as they race to institute a metrics-driven usability process.

Usability metrics only provide value when there is a frame of reference. Without it, teams are left to wonder whether 80 percent task completion is a good score, if 85 percent may be necessary, or just how much of a problem it is when someone "takes 30 seconds to locate the popcorn command the first time they use a microwave oven." When there is a clear plan in place for reliable, repeated measures to be collected in the future, an effective frame of reference can be established, and valuable comparisons and learning may begin.

In the case of OneStart, the metrics collected in the 2001 study represented the first attempt at measuring the usability of the portal. As a result, the numbers lacked a meaningful reference point and were much less actionable than the qualitative findings from the study.

Usability metrics are most reliable and informative when the tasks being measured represent core tasks that will likely persist throughout the life of the product. Spending time collecting metrics on anything but a product's core tasks contributes to the "frame of reference" problem by constantly measuring new tasks for the first time.

In the case of the original OneStart study, the tasks measured were largely feature-driven. In other words, they represented the tasks that the portal supported at that time, rather than those that were truly core tasks for the product over the long term. Moreover, those feature tasks have since been found to be less important than once imagined. Web server log data (another valuable usability metric), representing the actual usage of OneStart's personalization features over the past four years, have revealed that only 1 percent of users have ever visited the portal's personalization features. This has helped lead the team to rethink their emphasis on personalization options in the latest 2007 release by scaling back personalization to focus on simplicity, clarity of organization, and navigation. Given this change in direction, it suggests that collecting repeated measures of the original personalization tasks would not have been the best use of their time.

### 10.6.6 Conclusion

The OneStart case study represents a common example of where the efforts expended to carefully measure a product exceeded the returns. It reminds us that collecting usability metrics should be kept in perspective; they are a means to an end, where the "end" is the improvement of your product or process. By ensuring that you have in place a frame of reference to help you interpret your metrics, and that you restrict your focus to core tasks that can be revisited in future evaluations, you are more likely to produce metrics that matter.

### 10.6.7 Acknowledgment

Thanks to Dr. Philip Hodgson, Dr. Helen Wight, James Thomas, and Nate Johnson for their critical feedback on earlier drafts of this section.

### 10.6.8 Biography

*Todd Zazelenchuk* is a user experience researcher at Intuit in Mountain View, CA. He earned his Ph.D. in Instructional Technology from Indiana University in 2002. Prior to the consumer software industry, Todd worked in academia (Indiana University) and consumer goods (Whirlpool Corporation), gaining insights in to both the value and the challenges of applying usability metrics to the product design process.

### 10.6.9 References

Educause. (2005). Recommended readings on the top-ten IT issues—*www.educause.edu/ir/library/pdf/ERM0566.pdf.*

Gall, M. D., Borg, W. R, and Gall, J. P. (1996). *Educational research: An introduction* (6th ed.). White Plains, NY: Longman.

International Standards Organization (ISO). (1998). ISO 9241-11: Ergonomic requirements for office work with visual display terminals (VDTs). Part 11—Guidance on usability, 22.

Lewis, J. R. (1995). IBM computer usability satisfaction questionnaires: Psychometric evaluation and instructions for use. *International Journal of Human-Computer Interaction*, 7(1), 57–78.

McRobbie, M. (1998). *Architecture for the 21st century: An information technology strategic plan for Indiana University*. Bloomington: Indiana University.

Thomas, J. (2003). Indiana University's enterprise portal as a service delivery framework, in *Designing portals. Opportunities and challenges*. A. Jafari and M. Sheehan, Eds. Hershey, PA: Information Science Publishing.

Zazelenchuk, T. W. (2002). Measuring satisfaction in usability tests: A comparison of questionnaire administration methods and an investigation into users' rationales for satisfaction. Dissertation Abstracts International.

Zazelenchuk, T. W., and Boling, E. (2003). Considering user satisfaction in designing web-based portals. *Educause Quarterly*, 26(1), 35–40.

# Moving Forward

Some of the concepts and approaches we've described may be new to some readers, and maybe even a bit overwhelming at first, so we wanted to distill the key elements of this book into ten steps to help you move forward. These steps will help you establish a culture of usability metrics within your organization. These are lessons we've learned—sometimes the hard way—over the years.

## 11.1 SELL USABILITY AND THE POWER OF METRICS

One of the most important factors contributing to the success of a usability program is the degree to which management buys into the whole concept of usability. Several techniques can be very helpful in making this happen. First, we recommend that you bring key decision makers into the lab to observe as many sessions as possible. If you don't have a lab, arrange to use a conference room for the day. A screen-sharing application and a conference call can make for a very effective makeshift observation gallery. Nothing speaks louder than observing the user experience firsthand.

Once key decision makers start to see a consistent pattern of results, you won't need to spend much effort convincing them of the need for a design change. But be careful when someone only observes a single usability session. Watching one participant struggle can easily be dismissed as an edge case (e.g., "Our participants will be much smarter than that person!"). Conversely, seeing someone easily fly through the tasks can lead to a false sense of security that there are no usability issues with the design. The power of observation is in consistent patterns of results.

Another excellent way to sell usability is with short video clips. Embedding short video clips into a presentation can make all the difference in selling usability. The most effective way to illustrate a usability issue is by showing short clips of two or three different participants encountering the same problem. Showing reliable patterns is essential. In our experience, participants who are more animated usually make for better clips. Make sure each clip is short—ideally less than 30 seconds. The last thing you want is to lose the power of a clip by dragging it **289**

---

**TIPS FOR GETTING PEOPLE TO OBSERVE USER SESSIONS**

- *Provide a place for observing.* Even if it's a remote session, provide a room with projection or a large screen for observers to watch the session as a group. An important part of observing a usability session is the interaction among the observers.

- *Provide food.* For some odd reason, more observers show up when test sessions are scheduled during the lunch hour and food is provided for everyone!

- *Get the sessions on their calendars.* Many people live by their online calendars. If it's not on the calendar, it doesn't happen (for them). Send meeting invitations using your company's scheduling system.

- *Provide information.* Observers need to understand what's going on. Make sure that a session schedule, moderator's guide, and any other relevant information are readily available to the observers, both before and during the sessions.

- *Engage the observers.* Give the observers something to do besides just watching. Provide whiteboards or sticky notes for them to record issues. If there are breaks between sessions, have them do a quick review of the key takeaways from the last session.

---

out too long. Before showing a clip, provide appropriate context about the participant (without revealing any private information) and what he or she is trying to do.

If bringing observers into the lab or putting video clips in front of them doesn't work, try presenting a few key usability metrics. Basic metrics around task success, efficiency, and satisfaction generally work well. Ideally, you'll be able to tie these metrics to return on investment (ROI). For example, if you can show how a redesign will increase ROI or how abandonment rates are higher on your product compared to your competition, you'll get the attention of senior management.

Finding a champion for user experience in upper management is also very important. This person should help you fight for the user experience, get the budget you need for staff and other resources, and convince other senior managers about the importance of the user experience. The more champions you have, the more impact you will have, and ultimately the better the user experience for your products.

## 11.2 START SMALL AND WORK YOUR WAY UP

Don't try to boil the entire ocean. When deciding which metrics to use for a usability study, start off with something small and manageable. It's critical that you be successful in your first uses of metrics. If you're trying to incorporate metrics in routine formative testing, start with categorizing types of issues and issue severity. By logging all the issues, you'll have plenty of data to work with. Also, it's easy to collect System Usability Scale (SUS) data at the conclusion of each usability session. It only takes a few minutes to administer the survey, and it can provide valuable data in the long run. As you get comfortable with some of the more basic metrics, you can work your way up the metrics ladder.

A second phase might include some efficiency metrics such as completion times and lostness. Consider some other types of self-reported metrics such as usefulness–awareness gaps or expectations. Also, explore different ways to represent task success, such as through levels of completion. Finally, start to combine multiple metrics into an overall usability metric, or even build your own usability scorecard.

Over time you'll build up a repertoire of different metrics. By starting off small, you'll learn which metrics work for your situation and which don't. You'll learn the advantages and disadvantages of each metric and start to reduce the noise in the data collection process. In our work, it has taken us many years to expand our metrics toolkit to where it is today. So don't worry if you're not collecting all the metrics you want at first; you'll get there eventually. Also, be aware that your audience will have an adjustment period. If your audience is only used to seeing qualitative findings, it may take them a while to get adjusted to seeing metrics. If you throw too much at them too quickly, they may become resistant or think you just got back from math camp.

## 11.3 MAKE SURE YOU HAVE THE TIME AND MONEY

One of the most frustrating experiences is having the desire to do the job right but no money or time to do it. It's critical to make sure you have the right amount of time and budget before starting any usability study. Be very careful in planning out how much time and money every usability study is going to take. Ultimately, it comes down to a balancing act. On one hand, you don't want to underestimate and have to go back to your business sponsors for more money and be perceived as inefficient (not keeping to the budget) or as poor planners. On the other hand, if you overestimate, you may be perceived as being too expensive. A good way to accurately estimate time and costs is by first considering two general types of usability studies that use metrics.

1. Some usability studies involve adding a few simple metrics to a more qualitative study. The time and budget for these studies should not excessively surpass those if you didn't collect any metrics at all—perhaps up to 10 percent more. For these studies, it helps to build a track record of how much time and money was actually spent on similar types of studies. Then you can adjust up or down,

depending on how easy or difficult the recruiting is going to be, how many days you're testing, any demands to attend meetings as part of the project, and any special requirements in the analysis or presentation. For the most part, such studies are within 25 percent above or below the average estimate.

2. Other studies are more focused on collecting a wide range of metrics. It's harder to estimate time and budget for these kinds of studies. This might be a site-wide benchmark study, competitive benchmark, or online study. These kinds of studies are done less frequently, so it's more difficult to develop historical data to rely on. In addition, the variance is much greater. For these studies, you can break down your time and cost estimates into three distinct phases of any project: test preparation, data collection, and data analysis/presentation. Additional costs might include participant recruiting/compensation and licensing the technology to run online surveys. In our experience, these studies can run anywhere from half the cost of a traditional qualitative lab test up to twice the cost.

One problem you might encounter is running out of time during the analysis stage. Often you're on a very tight timeline and simply don't have the luxury of exploring the data as much as you'd like. In such cases, you can release the results of the study in two phases. In the first phase, give the top-line actionable results. In the second phase, provide a more detailed analysis of the data with follow-up from the first phase.

## 11.4 PLAN EARLY AND OFTEN

One of the key messages of this book has been the importance of planning ahead when collecting any metrics. The reason we stress this is because it is so tempting to skip, and skipping it usually has a negative outcome. If you go into a usability study not sure which metrics you want to collect and why, you're almost certainly going to be less effective.

Try to think through as many details as you can before the study. The more specific you can be, the better the outcome. For example, if you're collecting task success metrics and completion times, make sure that you define your success criteria and when exactly you'll turn off the clock. Also, think about how you're going to record and analyze the data. Unfortunately, we can't provide a single, comprehensive checklist to plan out every detail well in advance. Every metric and evaluation method requires its own unique set of plans. The best way to build your checklist is through experience.

One technique that has worked well for us has been "reverse engineering" the data. This means sketching out what the data will look like before conducting the study. We usually think of it as the key slides in a presentation. Then we work back from there to figure out what format the data must be in to create the charts. Next, we start designing the study to yield data in the desired format. This isn't faking the results but rather visualizing what the data might look like. Another simple strategy is to take a fake dataset and analyze it to make sure that you can perform the desired analysis. This might take a little extra time, but it could help save more time when you actually have the real dataset in front of you.

Of course, running pilot studies is also very useful. By running one or two pilot participants through the study, you'll be able to identify some of the outstanding issues that you have yet to address in the larger study. It's important to keep the pilot as realistic as possible and to allow enough time to address any issues that arise. Keep in mind that a pilot study is not a substitute for planning ahead. A pilot study is best used to identify the smaller issues that can be addressed fairly quickly before the actual study begins.

## 11.5 BENCHMARK YOUR PRODUCTS

Usability metrics are relative. There's no absolute standard for what is considered "good usability" and "bad usability." Because of this, it's essential to benchmark the usability of your product. This is constantly done in market research. Marketers are always talking about "moving the needle." Unfortunately, the same is not always true in usability. But we would argue that usability benchmarking is just as important as market-research benchmarking.

Establishing a set of benchmarks isn't as difficult as it may sound. First, you need to determine which metrics you'll be collecting over time. It's a good practice to collect data around three aspects of usability: effectiveness (i.e., task success), efficiency (i.e., time), and satisfaction (i.e., ease of use ratings). Next, you need to determine your strategy for collecting these metrics. This would include how often the data are going to be collected and how the metrics are going to be analyzed and presented. Finally, you need to identify the type of participants to include in your benchmarks (broken up into distinct groups, how many you need, and how they're going to be recruited). Perhaps the most important thing to remember is to be consistent from one benchmark to another. This makes it all the more important to get things right the first time you lay out your benchmarking plans.

Benchmarking doesn't always have to be a special event. You can collect benchmark data (anything that will allow you to compare across more than one study) on a much smaller scale. For example, you could routinely collect SUS data after each usability session, allowing you to easily compare SUS scores across projects and designs. It isn't directly actionable, but at least it gives an indication of whether improvements are being made from one design iteration to the next and how different projects stack up against each other.

Running a competitive usability study will put your data into perspective. What might seem like a high satisfaction score for your product might not be quite as impressive when compared to the competition. Competitive metrics around key business goals always speak volumes. For example, if your abandonment rates are much higher than your competition, this can be leveraged to acquire budget for future design and usability work.

## 11.6 EXPLORE YOUR DATA

One of the most valuable things you can do is to explore your data. Roll up your shirt sleeves and dive into the raw data. Run exploratory statistics on your dataset. Look for patterns or trends that are not so obvious. Try slicing and dicing your data in different ways. The keys to exploring your data are to give yourself enough time and not to be afraid to try something new.

When we explore data, especially large datasets, the first thing we do is to make sure we're working with a clean dataset. We check for inconsistent responses and remove outliers. We make sure all the variables are well labeled and organized. After cleaning up the data, the fun begins. We start to create some new variables based on the original data. For example, we might calculate top-2-box and bottom-2-box scores for each self-reported question. We often calculate averages across multiple tasks, such as total number of task successes. We might calculate a ratio to expert performance or categorize time data according to different levels of acceptable completion times. Many new variables could be created. In fact, many of our most valuable metrics have come through data exploration.

You don't always have to be creative. One thing we often do is to run basic descriptive and exploratory statistics (explained in Chapter 2). This is easy to do in statistical packages such as SPSS and even in Excel. By running some of the basic statistics, you'll see the big patterns pretty quickly.

Also, try to visualize your data in different ways. For example, create different types of scatterplots and plot regression lines, and even play with different types of bar charts. Even though you might never be presenting these figures, it helps give you a sense of what's going on.

Go beyond your data. Try to pull in data from other sources that confirm or even conflict with your assertions. More data from several other sources lend credibility to the data you put on the table. It's much easier to commit a multimillion-dollar redesign effort when more than one dataset tell the same story. Think of usability data as just one piece of the puzzle—and the more pieces of the puzzle, the easier it is to fit it all together and get the big picture.

We can't stress enough the value in going through your data firsthand. If you're working with a vendor or business sponsor who "owns the data," ask for the raw data. Canned charts and statistics rarely tell the whole story. They're often fraught with issues. We don't take any summary data at face value; we need to see for ourselves what's going on.

## 11.7 SPEAK THE LANGUAGE OF BUSINESS

Usability professionals must speak the language of business to have maximum impact. This means not only using the terms and jargon that management understands and identifies with but, more important, adopting their perspective. In the business world, this usually centers on how to decrease costs and/or increase revenue. So if you're asked to present your usability findings to upper management, you should tailor your presentation to focus on how the design effort will result in lower costs or increased revenue. You need to approach usability as an effective means to an end. Convey the perspective that usability is a highly effective way to reach business goals. If you keep your dialogue too academic or overly detailed, what you say probably won't have the impact you're hoping for.

Do whatever you can to tie your metrics to decreased costs or increased sales. This might not apply to every organization but certainly to the vast majority. Take the metrics you collect and calculate how costs and/or revenue are going to change as a result of your design efforts. Sometimes it takes a few assumptions to calculate an ROI, but it's still an important exercise to go through. If you're worried about your assumptions, calculate both a conservative and an aggressive set of assumptions to cover a wider range of possibilities.

Also, make sure the metrics relate to the larger business goals within your organization. If the goal of your project is to reduce phone calls to a call center, then measure task completion rates and task abandonment likelihood. If your product is all about e-commerce sales, then measure abandonment rates during checkout or likelihood to return. By carefully choosing your metrics, you'll have greater impact.

## 11.8 SHOW YOUR CONFIDENCE

Showing the amount of confidence you have in your results will lead to smarter decisions and help enhance your credibility. Ideally, your confidence in the data should be very high, allowing you to make the right decisions. Unfortunately, this is not always the case. Sometimes you may not have a lot of confidence in your results because of a low sample size or a relatively large amount of variance in the data. By calculating and presenting the confidence intervals, you'll have a much better idea of how much faith or confidence to place in the data. Without confidence intervals, deciding whether some differences are real is pretty much a wild guess, even what may appear to be big differences.

No matter what your data show, show confidence intervals whenever possible. This is especially important for relatively small samples (e.g., less than 20). The mechanics of calculating and presenting confidence intervals is pretty simple. The only thing you need to pay attention to is the type of data you are presenting. Calculating a confidence interval is different if the data are continuous (such as completion time) or binary (such as binary task success). By showing the confidence intervals, you can (hopefully) explain how the results generalize to a larger population.

Showing your confidence goes beyond calculating confidence intervals. We recommend that you calculate *p*-values to help you decide whether to accept or reject your hypotheses. For example, when comparing average task completion times between two different designs, it's important to determine whether there's a significant difference using a *t*-test or ANOVA. Without running the appropriate statistics, you just can't really know.

Of course, you shouldn't misrepresent your data or present it in a misleading way. For example, if you're showing task success rates based on a small sample size, it might be better to show the numbers as a frequency (e.g., six out of eight) as compared to a percentage. Also, use the appropriate level of precision for your data. For example, if you're presenting task completion times, and the tasks are taking several minutes, there's no need to present the data to the third decimal position. Even though you can, you shouldn't.

---

**RELATIONSHIP BETWEEN CONFIDENCE INTERVALS AND SIGNIFICANT DIFFERENCES**

If the confidence intervals for two means do not overlap, you can assume the two means are significantly different from each other. But if they do overlap, it's still possible that the difference could be significant. A *t*-test or ANOVA would be needed to check.

---

## 11.9 DON'T MISUSE METRICS

Usability metrics have a time and a place. Misusing metrics has the potential of undermining your entire usability program. Misuse might take the form of using metrics where none are needed, presenting too much data at once, measuring too much at once, or over-relying on a single metric.

In some situations it's probably better not to include metrics. If you're just looking for some qualitative feedback at the start of a project, metrics might not be appropriate. Or perhaps the project is going through a series of rapid design iterations. Metrics in these situations might only be a distraction and not add any value. It's important to be clear about when and where metrics serve a purpose. If metrics aren't adding value, don't include them.

It's also possible to present too much usability data at once. Just like packing for a vacation, it's probably wise to include all the data you want to present and then chop it in half. Not all data are equal. Some metrics are much more compelling than others. Resist the urge to show everything. That's why appendices were invented. We try to focus on a few key metrics in any presentation or report. By showing too much data, the most important message is lost.

Don't try to measure everything at once. There are only so many aspects of the user experience that you can quantify at any one time. If a product or business sponsor wants you to capture 100 different metrics, make them justify why each and every metric is essential. It's important to choose a few key metrics for any one study. The additional time to run the study and perform the analyses may make you think twice about including too many metrics at once.

Don't overrely on a single metric. If you try to get a single metric to represent the entire experience, you're likely to miss something big. For example, if you only collect data on satisfaction, you'll miss everything about the actual interaction. Sometimes satisfaction data might take aspects of the interaction into account, but it often misses a lot as well. We recommend that you try to capture a few different metrics, each tapping into a different aspect of the user experience.

## 11.10  SIMPLIFY YOUR PRESENTATION

All your hard work comes down to the point where you have to present results. How you choose to communicate your results can make or break a study. There are a few key things you should pay special attention to. First and foremost, you need to understand your audience and their goals.

Often you need to present usability findings to several different types of audiences. For example, you may need to present findings to the project team, consisting of an information architect, design lead, project manager, editor, developer, business sponsor, and prototyper. The project team is most concerned with detailed usability issues and specific design recommendations. Bottom line, they want to know the issues with the design and how to fix them.

---

**TIPS FOR AN EFFECTIVE PRESENTATION OF USABILITY RESULTS**

■ *Set the stage appropriately.* Depending on your audience, you might need to explain or demo the product, describe the usability testing process, or provide other background information. It all comes down to knowing your audience.

■ *Don't belabor procedural details of the test, but make them available.* At a minimum, your audience will usually want to know something about the participants in the test and the tasks they were asked to perform.

■ *Lead with positive findings.* Some positive results come out of almost every usability test. Most people like to hear about features of the design that worked well.

■ *Use screenshots.* Pictures really do work better than words in most cases. A screenshot that you've annotated with notes about usability issues can be very compelling.

■ *Use short video clips.* The days of an elaborate production process to create a highlights videotape are, thankfully, mostly gone. With computer-based video, it's much easier and more compelling to embed short clips directly in the appropriate context of your presentation.

■ *Present summary metrics.* Try to come up with one slide that clearly shows the key usability data at a glance. This might be a high-level view of the task completion data, comparisons to objectives, a derived metric representing overall usability, or a usability scorecard.

You also may need to present to the business sponsors or product team. They're concerned about meeting their business goals, participants' reactions to the new design, and how the recommended design changes are going to impact the project timeline and budget. You may present to senior management too. They want to ensure that the design changes will have the desired impact in terms of overall business goals and user experience. When presenting to senior managers, generally limit the metrics and focus instead on the big picture of the user experience by using stories and video clips. Too much detail usually doesn't work.

When presenting results, it's important to keep the message as simple as possible. Avoid jargon, focus on the key message, and keep the data simple and straightforward. Whatever you do, don't just describe the data. It's a surefire way to put your audience to sleep. Develop a story for each main point. Every chart or figure you show in a presentation has a story to it. Sometimes the story is that the task was difficult. Explain why it was difficult, and use metrics, verbatims, and video clips to show why it was difficult, and possibly even highlight design solutions. Paint a high-level picture for your audience. They will want perhaps two or three findings to latch onto. By putting all the pieces of the puzzle together, you can help them move forward in the decision making.

# References

Agresti, A., & Coull, B. (1998). Approximate is better than 'exact' for interval estimation of binomial proportions. *The American Statistician, 52,* 119-126.

Albert, W. (2002). Do Web users actually look at ads? A case study of banner ads and eye-tracking technology. *Proceedings of the Usability Professionals Association Conference 2002,* Orlando.

Albert, W., & Dixon, E. (2003). Is this what you expected? The use of expectation measures in usability testing. *Proceedings of the Usability Professionals Association 2003 Conference,* Scottsdale, AZ.

Aldenderfer, M., & Blashfield, R. (1984). *Cluster analysis (quantitative applications in the social sciences).* Beverly Hills, CA: Sage Publications, Inc.

American Institutes for Research. (2001). Windows XP Home Edition vs. Windows Millennium Edition (ME) public report. Concord, MA: New England Research Center. Available at *http://download.microsoft.com/download/d/8/1/d810ce49-d481-4a55-ae63-3fe2800cbabd/ME_Public.doc.*

Anttonen, J., & Surakka, V. (2005). Emotions and heart rate while sitting on a chair. *Proceedings of the SIGCHI Conference on Human Factors in Computing Systems,* Portland, OR, 491-499.

Apple Computer Inc. (1982). *Apple IIe design guidelines.* Cupertino, CA: Apple Computer, Inc.

Bailey, B. (2005). Judging the severity of usability issues on web sites: This doesn't work. *Usability Updates Newsletters.* Available at *http://www.usability.gov/pubs/102005news.html.*

Barnum, C., Bevan, N., Cockton, G., Nielsen, J., Spool, J., & Wixon, D. (2003). The "magic number 5": Is it enough for web testing? *CHI 2003,* April 5-10, Ft. Lauderdale, FL.

Benedek, J., & Hazlett, R. (2005). Incorporating facial EMG emotion measures as feedback in the software design process. *Human Computer Interaction Consortium,* February, Colorado.

Benedek, J., & Miner, T. (2002). Measuring desirability: New methods for evaluating desirability in a usability lab setting. *Usability Professionals Association Conference,* July 8-12, Orlando. Also available at *http://www.microsoft.com/usability/UEPostings/Desirability Toolkit.doc.* Also see the appendix listing the Product Reaction Cards at *http://www. microsoft.com/usability/UEPostings/ProductReactionCards.doc.*

Bias, R., & Mayhew, D. (2005). *Cost-justifying usability: An update for the Internet age,* 2nd ed. San Francisco: Morgan Kaufmann.

Birns, J. H., Joffre, J. A., Leclerc, J. F., & Paulsen, C. A. (2002). Getting the whole picture—The importance of collecting usability data using both concurrent think aloud and retrospective probing procedures. *Usability Professionals Association Conference,* July 8-12, Orlando. Also available at *http://www.usabilityair.org/publications/christinepaulsen/upa_thinkaloud_paper.pdf.*

Breyfogle, F. (1999). *Implementing Six Sigma: Smarter solutions using statistical methods.* New York: John Wiley.

Brooke, J. (1996). SUS: A quick and dirty usability scale. In P. W. Jordan, B. Thomas, B. A. Weerdmeester, & I. L. McClelland (Eds.), *Usability evaluation in industry.* London: Taylor & Francis. Also see *http://www.usability.serco.com/trump/documents/Suschapt.doc.*

Brush, A. J. B., Ames, M., & Davis, J. (2004). A comparison of synchronous remote and local usability studies for an expert interface. *Proceedings of CHI 2004 Conference.* Available at *http://www.stanford.edu/~morganya/research/chi2004-remote.pdf.*

Castillo, J. C., Hartson, H. R., & Hix, D. (1998). Remote usability evaluation: Can users report their own critical incidents? *Proceedings of CHI '98 Conference*.

Catani, M., & Biers, D. (1998). Usability evaluation and prototype fidelity. *Proceedings of the Human Factors and Ergonomic Society*.

Chadwick-Dias, A., Bergel, M., LeDoux, L., & Tullis, T. (2005). How to improve Web usability for older users. *Proceedings of HCI International 2005 Conference*, July, Las Vegas.

Chadwick-Dias, A., McNulty, M., & Tullis, T. (2003). Web usability and age: How design changes can improve performance. *Proceedings of the 2003 ACM Conference on Universal Usability*, Vancouver, BC.

Chin, J. P., Diehl, V. A., & Norman, K. L. (1988). Development of an instrument measuring user satisfaction of the human-computer interface. *ACM CHI '88 proceedings*, 213–218.

Cockton, G., & Woolrych, A. (2001). Understanding inspection methods: Lessons from an assessment of heuristic evaluation. *Joint Proceedings of HCI and IHM: People and Computers, XV*.

Darwin, C. (1872). *The expression of the emotions in man and animals*. London: John Murray, Albemarle Street. Available at *http://pages.britishlibrary.net/charles.darwin3/expression/expression_intro.htm*.

den Uyl, M. J., & van Kuilenburg, H. (2005). The FaceReader: Online facial expression recognition. *Proceedings of Measuring Behavior 2005*. Available at *http://www.noldus.com/site/content/files/other_downloads/fc_denuyl_and_vankuilenburg_2005.pdf*.

Dennerlein, J., Becker, T., Johnson, P., Reynolds, C. J., & Picard, R. W. (2003). Frustrating computer users increases exposure to physical factors. *Proceedings of the International Ergonomics Association*, August 24-29, Seoul.

Dillman, D. A., Phelps, G., Tottora, R, Swift, K, Kohrell, J., & Berck, J. (2001). Response rate and measurement differences in mixed mode surveys using mail, telephone, interactive voice response, and the Internet. Available at *http://survey.sesrc.wsu.edu/dillman/papers.htm*.

Dumas, J., Molich, R., & Jeffries, R. (2004). Describing usability problems: Are we sending the right message? *Interactions*, July–August.

Educause. (2005). Recommended readings of the top-ten IT issues. Available at *www.educause.edu/ir/library/pdf/ERM0566.pdf*.

Ekman, P., & Friesen, W. V. (1975). *Unmasking the face: A guide to recognizing emotions from facial clues*. Englewood Cliffs, NJ: Prentice Hall.

Ekman, P., Friesen, W. V., & Hager, J. C. (2002). *The facial action coding system*, 2nd ed. Salt Lake City: Research Nexus eBook.

Ekman, P., Sorenson, E. R., & Friesen, W. V. (1969). Pan-cultural elements in facial displays of emotions. *Science, 164*(3875), 86–88.

Essa, I. A., & Pentland, A. P. (1997). Coding, analysis, interpretation, and recognition of facial expressions. *IEEE Transactions on Pattern Analysis and Machine Intelligence, 19*(7), 757–763.

Everett, S. P., Byrne, M. D., & Greene, K. K. (2006). Measuring the usability of paper ballots: Efficiency, effectiveness, and satisfaction. *Proceedings of the Human Factors and Ergonomics Society 50th Annual Meeting*. Santa Monica, CA.

Few, S. (2004). *Show me the numbers: Designing tables and graphs to enlighten*. Oakland, CA: Analytics Press.

————. (2006). *Information dashboard design: The effective visual communication of data*. Sebastopol, CA: O'Reilly.

Fogg, B. J., Marshall, J., Laraki, O., Osipovich, A., Varma, C., Fang, N., Paul, J., Rangnekar, A., Shon, J., Swani, P., & Treinen, M. (2001). What makes a Web site credible? A report on a large quantitative study. *Proceedings of ACM CHI 2001 Conference on Human Factors in Computing Systems, 1,* 61-68. New York: ACM Press.

ForeSee Results (2006). *E-Government Satisfaction Index,* June 20, Ann Arbor, MI. Available at *http://www.ForeSeeResults.com.*

Fukuda, R., & Bubb, H. (2003). Eye tracking study on Web-use: Comparison between younger and elderly users in case of search task with electronic timetable service. *PsychNology Journal, 1*(3), 202-228.

Gall, M. D., Borg, W. R., & Gall, J. P. (1996). *Educational research: An introduction*, 6th ed. White Plains, NY: Longman.

Granholm, E., Asarnow, R. F., Sarkin, A. J., & Dykes, K. L. (1996). Pupillary responses index cognitive resource limitations. *Psychophysiology, 33,* 457-461.

Gygi, C., DeCarlo, N., Williams, B., & Covey, S. (2005). *Six Sigma for dummies*. Hoboken, NJ: John Wiley.

Hammontree, M., Weiler, P., & Nayak, N. (1994). Remote usability testing. *Interactions,* July 21-25.

Harris, R. L. (1999). *Information graphics: A comprehensive illustrated reference*. New York: Oxford University Press.

Hart, T. (2004). Designing "senior friendly" Websites: Do guidelines help? *Usability News, 6.1. http://psychology.wichita.edu/surl/usabilitynews/61/older_adults-withexp.htm.*

Hartson, H. R., Castillo, J. C., Kelso, J., & Neale, W. C. (1996). Remote evaluation: The network as an extension of the laboratory. *Proceedings of CHI '96 Conference*. Vancouver, BC.

Hazlett, R. L. (2003). Measurement of user frustration: A biologic approach. *Proceedings of CHI Conference on Human Factors in Computing Systems, v2*. New York: ACM Press.

Hazlett, R. L., & Benedek, J. (2005). Measuring the emotional reaction to passive first impression of software. *Proceedings of Designing Pleasurable Products and Interfaces*. Eindhoven, Netherlands: Springer-Verlag.

Henry, S. (2007). *Just ask: Integrating accessibility throughout design*. Available at *Lulu.com.*

Hertzum, M., Jacobsen, N., & Molich, R. (2002). Usability inspections by groups of specialists: Perceived agreement in spite of disparate observations. *CHI 2002,* Minneapolis.

Hess, E. H., & Polt, J. M. (1964). Pupil size in relation to mental activity during simple problem-solving. *Science, 143,* 1190-1192.

International Standards Organization—ISO 9241-11. (1998). *Ergonomic requirements for office* work *with visual display terminals (VDTs); Part 11—Guidance on usability, 22.*

Iqbal, S. T., Zheng, X. S., & Bailey, B. P. (2004). Task-evoked pupillary response to mental workload in human-computer interaction. *Extended Abstracts of the ACM Conference on Human Factors in Computing Systems,* Vienna.

Jacobsen, N., Hertzum, M., & John, B. (1998). The evaluator effect in usability studies: Problem detection and severity judgments. *Proceedings of the Human Factors and Ergonomics Society.*

Kahneman, D. (1973). *Attention and effort*. Englewood Cliffs, NJ: Prentice-Hall.

Kahneman, D., & Beatty, J. (1966). Pupil diameter and load on memory. *Science, 154,* 1583-1585.

Kapoor, A., Mota, S., & Picard, R. (2001). Towards a learning companion that recognizes affect. *AAAI Fall Symposium,* November, North Falmouth, MA.

Kaushik, A. (2007). Web analytics: An hour a day. Sybex; Pap/Cdr edition (June).

Kessner, M., Wood, J., Dillon, R., & West, R. (2001). On the reliability of usability testing. *Proceedings of CHI 2001*, Seattle.

Kirkpatrick, A., Rutter, R., Heilmann, C., Thatcher, J., & Waddell, C. (2006). *Web accessibility: Web standards and regulatory compliance.* Available online from Friends of ED at *http://www.friendsofed.com/book/html?isbn=1590596382.*

Kohavi, R., & Round, M. (2004). Front line Internet analytics at Amazon.com. *Presentation at Emetrics Summit 2004.* Retrieved on May 22, 2007, from *http://ai.stanford.edu/~ronnyk/emetricsAmazon.pdf.*

Krug, S. (2000). *Don't make me think! A common sense approach to Web usability.* Indianapolis: New Riders Press.

Kruskal, J., & Wish, M. (2006). *Multidimensional scaling (quantitative applications in the social sciences).* Beverly Hills, CA: Sage Publications, Inc.

Kuniavsky, M. (2003). *Observing the user experience: A practitioner's guide to user research.* San Francisco: Morgan Kaufmann.

LeDoux, L., Connor Mangan, E., & Tullis, T. (2005). Extreme makeover: UI edition. *Proceedings of the Usability Professionals Association Conference,* Montreal. Available at *http://www.upassoc.org/usability_resources/conference/2005/ledoux-UPA2005-Extreme.pdf.*

Lewis, J. R. (1991). Psychometric evaluation of an after-scenario questionnaire for computer usability studies: The ASQ. *SIGCHI Bulletin, 23*(1), 78–81. Also see *http://www.acm.org/~perlman/question.cgi?form=ASQ.*

———. (1992). Psychometric evaluation of the post-study system usability questionnaire: The PSSUQ. *Proceedings of the Human Factors Society 36th Annual Meeting,* 1259–1263, Santa Monica, CA.

———. (1994). Sample sizes for usability studies: Additional considerations. *Human Factors, 36,* 368–378.

———. (1995). IBM computer usability satisfaction questionnaires: Psychometric evaluation and instructions for use. *International Journal of Human-Computer Interaction,* 7(1), 57–78. Also see *http://www.acm.org/~perlman/question.cgi?form=CSUQ.*

Lewis, J., & Sauro, J. (2006). When 100% really isn't 100%: Improving the accuracy of small-sample estimates of completion rates. *Journal of Usability Studies, 1*(3), 136–150. Also see *http://www.upassoc.org/upa_publications/jus/2006_may/lewis_small_sample_estimates.pdf.*

Libby, W. L., Jr., Lacey, B. C., & Lacey, J. I. (1973). Pupillary and cardiac activity during visual attention. *Psychophysiology, 10,* 270–294.

Likert, R. (1932). A technique for the measurement of attitudes. *Archives of Psychology, 140,* 55.

Lin, T., Hu, W., Omata, M., & Imamiya, A. (2005). Do physiological data relate to traditional usability indexes? *Proceedings of OZCHI 2005,* November 23–25, Canberra, Australia.

Lindgaard, G., & Chattratichart, J. (2007). Usability testing: What have we overlooked? *Proceedings of ACM CHI Conference on Human Factors in Computing Systems.*

Lindgaard, G., Fernandes, G., Dudek, C., & Brown, J. (2006). Attention web designers: You have 50 milliseconds to make a good first impression! *Behaviour & Information Technology, 25,* 115–126.

Lund, A. (2001). Measuring usability with the USE questionnaire. *Usability and User Experience Newsletter* of the STC Usability SIG. See *http://www.stcsig.org/usability/newsletter/0110_measuring_with_use.html.*

Marshall, S. (2000). Method and apparatus for eye tracking and monitoring pupil dilation to evaluate cognitive activity. U.S. Patent approved, February.

Martin, P., & Bateson, P. (1993). *Measuring behaviour*, 2nd ed. Cambridge: Cambridge University Press.

Maurer, D., & Warfel, T. (2004). Card sorting: A definitive guide. *Boxes and Arrows*, April. Retrieved on May 26, 2007, from *http://www.boxesandarrows.com/archives/card_sorting_a_definitive_guide.php.*

Mayhew, D., & Bias, R. (1994). *Cost-justifying usability*. San Francisco: Morgan Kaufmann.

McGee, M. (2003). Usability magnitude estimation. *Proceedings of the Human Factors and Ergonomics Society Annual Meeting,* Denver.

———. (2004). Master usability scaling: Magnitude estimation and master scaling applied to usability measurement. *Proceedings of CHI Conference on Human Factors in Computer Systems,* Vienna. New York: ACM Press.

McRobbie, M. (1998). Architecture for the 21st century: An information technology strategic plan for Indiana University. Bloomington: Indiana University.

Molich, R., Bevan, N., Butler, S., Curson, I., Kindlund, E., Kirakowski, J., & Miller, D. (1998). Comparative evaluation of usability tests. *Usability Professionals Association Conference,* Washington, DC.

Molich, R., & Dumas, J. (2006). Comparative usability evaluation (CUE-4). *Behaviour & Information Technology,* 99999(1), 0144-929X. Retrieved on August 27, 2007, from *http://www.informaworld.com/10.1080/01449290600959062.*

Molich, R., Jeffries, R., & Dumas, J. (2007). Making usability recommendations useful and usable. *Journal of Usability Studies, 2*(4), 162–179. Available at *http://www.upassoc.org/upa_publications/jus/2007august/useful-usable.pdf.*

Motorola. (2007). *About Motorola University: The inventors of Six Sigma.* Retrieved on May 28, 2007, from *http://www.motorola.com/content.jsp?globalObjectId=3079.*

Mueller, J. (2003). *Accessibility for everybody: Understanding the Section 508 accessibility requirements.* Berkeley, CA: Apress.

Nancarrow, C., & Brace, I. (2000). Saying the "right thing": Coping with social desirability bias in marketing research. *Bristol Business School Teaching and Research Review, 3*(Summer).

National Institute of Standards and Technology (NIST). (1999). Common industry format for usability test reports. See *http://zing.ncsl.nist.gov/iusr/documents/cifv1.1b.htm.*

———. (2001). ANSI/INCITS 354-2001: Common Industry Format (CIF) for usability test reports. See *http://webstore.ansi.org/ansidocstore/product.asp?sku=ANSI+INCITS+354–2001.*

NCSS. (2007). NCSS: Statistical and power analysis software. Retrieved on May 26, 2007, from *http://www.ncss.com/.*

Nielsen, J. (Undated). Severity ratings for usability problems. Available at *http://www.useit.com/papers/heuristic/severityrating.html.*

———. (1993). *Usability engineering*. San Francisco: Morgan Kaufmann.

———. (1998). *Sun Microsystems 1997 Web Design*, January 13. Retrieved on May 28, 2007, from *http://www.useit.com/papers/sun/1997/*.

———. (2000). Why you only need to test with 5 users. *AlertBox*, March 19. Available at *http://www.useit.com/alertbox/20000319.html*.

———. (2001a). Jakob Nielsen's AlertBox, February 18. Success rate: The simplest usability metric. Available at *http://www.useit.com/alertbox/20010218.html*.

———. (2001b). Designing web ads using click-through data. *AlertBox*, September 2. Retrieved on May 22, 2007, from *http://www.useit.com/alertbox/20010902.html*.

———. (2001c). Beyond accessibility: Treating users with disabilities as people. *AlertBox*, November 11. Retrieved on May 27, 2007, from *http://www.useit.com/alertbox/20011111.html*.

———. (2005). Medical usability: How to kill patients through bad design. Available at *http://www.useit.com/alertbox/20050411.html*.

Nielsen, J., & Landauer, T. (1993). A mathematical model of the finding of usability problems. *ACM Proceedings, Interchi* 93, Amsterdam.

Nunnally, J. C., Knott, P. D., Duchnowski, A., & Parker, R. (1967). Pupillary response as a general measure of activation. *Perception & Psychophysics, 2,* 149–150.

Osgood, C. E., Suci, G., & Tannenbaum, P. (1957). *The measurement of meaning*. Urbana: University of Illinois Press.

Pande, P., & Holpp, L. (2001). *What is Six Sigma?* New York: McGraw-Hill.

Peterson, E. (2004). *Web analytics demystified: A marketer's guide to understanding how your Web site affects your business*. Portland, OR: Celilo Group Media.

Picard, R., & Scheirer, J. (2001). The Galvactivator: A glove that senses and communicates skin conductivity. *Proceedings of the 9th International Conference on Human–Computer Interaction,* New Orleans.

Pyzdek, T. (2003). *The Six Sigma handbook: The complete guide for greenbelts, blackbelts, and managers at all levels, revised and expanded edition*. New York: McGraw-Hill.

Rehabilitation Act as Amended, Section 508 of the 1973. (1998). Workforce Investment Act of 1998, Pub. L. No. 105-220, 112 Stat. 936 (August 7). Codified at 29 U.S.C. §794d.

RelevantView. (2006). Ratings, reviews and the customer decision process: Amazon v. Best Buy v. CircuitCity v. WalMart. March/April. Available at *http://www.relevantview.com/retailreport.htm*.

Reynolds, C. (2005). *Adversarial uses of affective computing and ethical implications*. Ph.D. Thesis, Massachusetts Institute of Technology, Cambridge. Available at *http://affect.media.mit.edu/pdfs/05.reynolds-phd.pdf*.

Rubin, J. (1994). *Handbook of usability testing. How to plan, design, and conduct effective tests*. New York: John Wiley.

Sauro, J., & Kindlund, E. (2005). A method to standardize usability metrics into a single score. *Proceedings of the Conference on Human Factors in Computing Systems (CHI 2005),* Portland, OR.

Sauro, J., & Lewis, J. (2005). Estimating completion rates from small samples using binomial confidence intervals: Comparisons and recommendations. *Proceedings of the Human Factors and Ergonomics Society Annual Meeting,* Orlando.

Shaikh, A., Baker, J., & Russell, M. (2004). What's the skinny on weight loss websites? *Usability News*, 6(1), Available at *http://psychology.wichita.edu/surl/usabilitynews/61/diet_domain.htm*.

Smith, P. A. (1996). Towards a practical measure of hypertext usability. *Interacting with Computers*, 8,(4), 365–381.

Snyder, C. (2006). Bias in usability testing. *Boston Mini-UPA Conference,* March 3, Natick, MA.

Sostre, P., & LeClaire, J. (2007). *Web analytics for dummies*. New York: John Wiley.

Spool, J., & Schroeder, W. (2001). Testing web sites: Five users is nowhere near enough. *CHI 2001,* Seattle.

Steinhauer, S. R., Boller, F., Zubin, J., & Pearlman, S. (1983). Pupillary dilation to emotional visual stimuli revisited. *Psychophysiology, 20,* 472.

Sterne, J. (2002). *Web metrics: Proven methods for measuring Web site success*. New York: John Wiley.

Stevens, S. S. (1957). On the psychophysical law. *Psychological Review, 64*(3), 153–181.

Stover, A., Coyne, K., & Nielsen, J. (2002). *Designing usable site maps for Websites*. Available at *http://www.nngroup.com/reports/sitemaps/*.

Tedesco, D., & Tullis, T. (2006). A comparison of methods for eliciting post-task subjective ratings in usability testing. *Usability Professionals Association Conference*, June 12–16, Broomfield, CO.

Thomas, J. (2003). Indiana University's Enterprise portal as a service delivery framework in designing portals: Opportunities and challenges. In A. Jafari & M. Sheehan, Eds., *Designing portals: Opportunities and challenges*. Hershey, PA: Information Science Publishing.

Trimmel, M., Meixner-Pendleton, M., & Haring, S. (2003). Stress response caused by system response time when searching for information on the Internet: Psychophysiology in ergonomics. *Human Factors, 45*(4), 615–621.

Tufte, E. R. (1990). *Envisioning information*. Chesire, CT: Graphics Press.

———. (1997). *Visual explanations: Images and quantities, evidence and narrative*. Chesire, CT: Graphics Press.

———. (2001). *The visual display of quantitative information,* 2nd ed. Chesire, CT: Graphics Press.

———. (2006). *Beautiful evidence*. Chesire, CT: Graphics Press.

Tullis, T. S. (1985). Designing a menu-based interface to an operating system. *Proceedings of CHI '85 Conference on Human Factors in Computing Systems*, San Francisco.

———. (1998). A method for evaluating web page design concepts. *Proceedings of CHI '98 Conference on Computer–Human Interaction,* Los Angeles.

———. (2005). How reliable are the results of a usability test? *Boston Mini-UPA Conference,* March 3, Natick, MA.

———. (2007). Using closed card-sorting to evaluate information architectures. *Usability Professionals Association Conference,* Austin, TX.

Tullis, T. S., Fleischman, S., McNulty, M., Cianchette, C., & Bergel, M. (2002). An empirical comparison of lab and remote usability testing of Web sites. *Usability Professionals Association Conference*, Orlando. Available at *http://home.comcast.net/~tomtullis/publications/RemoteVsLab.pdf*.

Tullis, T. S., Mangan, E. C., & Rosenbaum, R. (2007). An empirical comparison of on-screen keyboards. *Human Factors and Ergonomics Society 51st Annual Meeting,* October 1–5, Baltimore.

Tullis, T. S., & Stetson, J. (2004). A comparison of questionnaires for assessing Website usability. *Usability Professionals Association Conference*, June 7–11, Minneapolis. Available at *http://home.comcast.net/%7Etomtullis/publications/UPA2004TullisStetson. pdf.* Slides *http://www.upassoc.org/usability_resources/conference/2004/UPA-2004-TullisStetson.pdf.*

Tullis, T. S., & Tullis, C. (2007). Statistical analyses of e-commerce Websites: Can a site be usable and beautiful? *Proceedings of HCI International Conference,* Beijing.

Tullis, T. S., & Wood, L. (2004). How many users are enough for a card-sorting study? *Proceedings of the Usability Professionals Association Conference,* June 7–11, Minneapolis. Available at *http://websort.net/articles/Tullis&Wood.pdf.*

———. (2005). How can you do a card-sorting study with lots of cards? *Usability Professionals Association Conference,* Montreal.

Turner, C., Nielsen, J., & Lewis, J. (2002). Current issues in the determination of usability test sample size: How many users is enough? *Usability Professionals Association Conference,* Orlando.

Usability Professionals Association. See *http://upassoc.org/usability_resources/about_usability/definitions_of_usability.html.*

Usborne, N. (2005). Design choices can cripple a Website. *A List Apart*, November 8. Retrieved on May 22, 2007, from *http://alistapart.com/articles/designcancripple.*

Virzi, R. (1992). Refining the test phase of the usability evaluation: How many subjects is enough? *Human Factors, 34*(4), 457–468.

Ward, R., & Marsden, P. (2003). Physiological responses to different WEB page designs. *International Journal of Human–Computer Studies, 59*, 199–212.

Wilson, C. (1999). Readers' questions: Severity scales. *Usability Interface, 5*(4). Available at *http://www.stcsig.org/usability/newsletter/9904-severity-scale.html.*

Wilson, C., & Coyne, K. P. (2001). Tracking usability issues: To bug or not to bug? *Interactions*, May–June.

Withrow, J., Brinck, T., & Speredelozzi, A. (2000). *Comparative usability evaluation for an e-government portal.* Diamond Bullet Design Report, #U1-00-2, December, Ann Arbor, MI. Available at *http://www.diamondbullet.com/egovportal.pdf.*

Woolrych, A., & Cockton, G. (2001). Why and when five test users aren't enough. *Proceedings of IHM-HCI 2001, 2*, 105–108. Toulouse, France: Cépaduès-Éditions.

World-Wide Web Consortium. (1999). *Web content accessibility guidelines 1.0.* Retrieved on May 27, 2007, from *http://www.w3.org/TR/WAI-WEBCONTENT/.*

Zazelenchuk, T. W. (2002). Measuring satisfaction in usability tests: A comparison of questionnaire administration methods and an investigation into users' rationales for satisfaction. *Dissertation Abstracts International, 63*(05A): UMI No. 3054425.

Zazelenchuk, T. W., & Boling, E. (2003). Considering user satisfaction in designing web-based portals. *Educause Quarterly, 26*(1), 35–40.

# Index

## A

A/B studies, 35, 54, 216–217
Abbott prescription drug labels, 271–279
Accessibility checking tools, 229
Accessibility data, 227–231
Accessibility Valet Demonstrator, 229
AccMonitor (HiSoftware), 229
Accuracy, in reporting decimal places, 26
ACSI. *See* American Customer Satisfaction Index
Add Trend Line option (Excel), 32
Adjusted Wald Method, 69
Affective Computing Research Group, 186–188
After-Scenario Questionnaire (ASQ), 129–130
　in IVR case study, 245
　in OneStart case study, 282
Aggregating task ratings, 137–138
Albert, W., 129, 131, 179
Alternative design comparisons, 55
American Customer Satisfaction Index (ACSI),
　151, 153–155
American Institutes for Research, 147
Analysis of variance (ANOVA)
　binary successes, 67
　pharmacist performance case study, 277
　types, 30–31
Analyzing and reporting metrics
　binary success, 67–68
　card-sorting data, 218–228
　efficiency, 88–90
　errors, 84–86
　frequency of unique issues, 109–111
　frequency of participants per issue, 111–112
　issues by category, 112–113
　issues by task, 113
　learnability data, 94–96
　levels of success, 72–73
　positive issues, 114
　precision in, 26
　self-reported data, 127–128
　time-on-task data, 77–79
Anchor terms, in Likert scales, 124
Anonymity, in self-reported data collection, 127
ANOVA. *See* Analysis of variance
ANOVA: Single-Factor option, 30–31
*Apple IIe Design Guidelines*, 102
Artifact bias, 116
ASQ. *See* After-Scenario Questionnaire
Assistance factors, in levels of success, 71

## B

Attractiveness area, in WAMMI, 151, 153
Attribute assessment, in self-reported metrics,
　158–161
Automated studies, 103
Automated tools
　accessibility-checking, 229
　measuring time-on-task, 75
Awareness
　and comprehension, 163–165
　increasing, 52
Awareness–usefulness gaps, 165
Axes
　bar graphs, 36–37
　labeling, 35
　line graphs, 39–40
　MDS plots, 224
　scatterplots, 32, 40–41
　stacked bar graphs, 43

Bailey, B. P., 181–182
Bailey, Robert W., 108, 252, 262
Baker, J., 88
Ball, Harvey, 205
Ballots
　comparisons, 148–150
　errors in, 6, 82–83
Bar graphs, 36–38
　vs. line graphs, 38
　stacked, 42–44
Baseline tests, 253–254
Beginning and ending of issues, 103–104
Behavioral and physiological metrics, 52, 54, 167
　Affective Computing Research Group
　　and, 186–188
　eye-tracking, 175–180
　facial expression capture, 171–174
　overt behaviors, 167–171
　pupillary response, 180–182
　skin conductance and heart rate, 183–186
Benchmarking, 293
Benchmarking case study (mobile music
　and video), 263
　attempts, number of, 266
　changes and future work, 270
　comparative analysis, 264
　data collection, 265–266
　data manipulation and visualization, 267, 269

**307**

Benchmarking case study (mobile music and video) (*Continued*)
  discussion, 269-270
  perception metrics, 266-267
  project goals and methods, 263
  qualitative and quantitative data, 263
  qualitative and quantitative findings, 267
  research domain, 263
  respondent recruiting, 265
  respondents, number of, 264-265
  successes and failures, 266
  summary findings and SUM metrics, 267-268
  time to complete, 266
Benedek, Joey, 142, 172-174
Between-subjects studies, 18-19
Biases
  in issue identification, 116-117
  in self-reported data collection, 126-127
"Big Opportunities" quadrant (expectation vs. experience), 131
Binary successes, 66
  analyzing and presenting, 67-68
  collecting and measuring, 66-67
  confidence intervals, 69
Bobby accessibility checking tool, 229
Bojko, Agnieszka, 271, 279
Bots (search), 212
Brooke, John, 138
Bubb, H., 180
Budgets, 55-56, 291-292
Business goals, 295
Business language, 295
Butterfly ballots, 6, 82-83
Byrne, Michael, 148

**C**

Calendars, for sessions, 290
Card-sorting data, 51, 217
  analysis, 218-225
  closed sorts, 217, 225-228
  number of participants, 223
  tools, 218
CardSort tool, 218
CardZort tool, 218
Case studies, 237
  metrics impact, in enterprise portal study, 280-287
  mobile music and video, 263-271
  pharmacist performance, 271-280
  speech recognition IVR, 244-252
  website redesign, 237-244, 252-253
Category, issues by, 112-113

CDC.GOV website redesign case study, 252-253
  baseline test, 253-254
  conclusions, 261-262
  final prototype testing, 258-261
  qualitative findings, 255-256
  task scenarios, 255
  usability testing levels, 253
  wireframing and FirstClick testing, 256-258
Central tendency, measures of, 25
Chadwick-Dias, A., 201
Champions for user experience, 290
Chattratichart, J., 116-117, 119
Chi-square tests
  click-through rates, 213-214
  overview, 33-35
CHITEST function, 34, 214
CIF. *See* Common Industry Format
Click-through rates, 213-215
Clock operation, for time-on-task, 75
Closed card sorts, 51, 217, 225-228
Cockton, G., 119
Coding overt behaviors, 167-171
Cognitive effort, 87
Collecting data, 59-60
  binary successes, 66-67
  efficiency, 87-88
  errors, 83-84
  learnability, 93-94
  levels of success, 70-72
  for mobile music and video case study, 265-266
  myths about, 10
  self-reported data, 124-128
  task success metrics, 65
  time-on-task, 74-77
Color, in graphs, 35
Column graphs, 36-38
Combined metrics, 191
  based on percentages, 193-198
  based on target goals, 192
  based on z-scores, 199-202
  product comparisons, 50
  severity ratings based on, 106-107
  SUM, 202-203
  usability scorecards, 203-206
Common Industry Format (CIF), 90
Comparative Usability Evaluation (CUE), 114
Comparisons
  alternative designs, 55
  to expert performance, 208-209
  to goals, 206-208
  of independent sample means, 28-29

in mobile music and video case study, 264
of more than two samples means, 30-31
of paired samples means, 29-30
products, 50
Competitor websites, 237-239
Completed transaction metrics, 48, 50
Comprehension, in self-reported metrics, 163-164
Computer System Usability Questionnaire (CSUQ), 139-140, 144-146
CONFIDENCE function, 27
Confidence intervals, 8
   binary successes, 69
   in culture of usability, 295-296
   on graphs, 35
   overview, 27-28
   and sample size, 17-18, 27-28
Consistency
   in data cleanup, 60-61
   in identifying and prioritizing issues, 114-115
Content category, in ACSI, 151, 155
Continuous data, 22-23
Controllability area, in WAMMI, 151, 153
Converting Excel time, 75
Core measure, of efficiency, 90
Correlation function (Excel), 32
Correlations, 32-33
Costs
   in culture of usability, 291-292
   myths about, 10-11
COUNT function (Excel), 27
Counterbalancing, 19-20
Coyne, K. P., 108
Credible websites, 159
Criteria, for participants, 58-59
Critical product studies, 53
CSUQ. See Computer System Usability Questionnaire
CUE. See Comparative Usability Evaluation
Culture of usability metrics, 289
   benchmarking for, 293-294
   business language, 295
   confidence intervals, 295-296
   exploring data, 294
   planning for, 292-293
   proper use of metrics, 296-297
   selling usability and metrics, 289-290
   simplifying presentations, 297-298
   starting small, 291
   time and money, 291-292
Cynthia Says tool, 229

**D**

Darwin, Charles, 172
Data Analysis option (Excel), 24
Data cleanup, 60-61
Data collection. See Collecting data
Data Logger, 75
Data points, on line graphs, 40
Data types, 20
   interval, 22-23
   for metrics, 23-24
   nominal, 20-21
   ordinal, 21-22
   ratio, 23
Decimal places, in reporting, 26
Degrees of intervalness, in self-reported data, 128
den Uyl, M. J., 172
Dependent variables, 20
Descriptive statistics, 24-25
   confidence intervals, 27-28
   measures of central tendency, 25
   measures of variability, 26-27
Designing usability studies, 15
   counterbalancing, 19-20
   independent and dependent variables, 20
   participant selection, 16-17
   sample size, 17-18
   within-subjects and between-subjects, 18-19
Desirability Rating, 174
Diamond Bullet Design case study, 231
Disabilities guidelines, 231
Display $R$-squared value on chart option (Excel), 32
Distributions, of time-on-task data, 78-79
Dixon, E., 129, 131
"Don't Touch It" quadrant (expectation vs. experience), 131
Double-counting errors, 86
Drop-off rates, 215-216
Drug label design. See Pharmacist performance case study
Dumas, J., 101, 114

**E**

Ease of use, in post-task ratings, 128-129
Effectiveness metrics, 8, 282-283
Efficiency metrics, 8, 50, 87
   analyzing and presenting, 88-90
   collecting and measuring, 87-88
   as combination of task success and time, 90-92
   frequent use of products, 51
   in OneStart project case study, 282-283
   in product comparisons, 50
   in WAMMI, 151, 153

Effort, cognitive and physical, 87
Ekman, Paul, 171
Election ballots
    comparisons, 148-150
    errors in, 6, 82-83
Electromyogram (EMG) sensors, 172-174
Element assessment, in self-reported metrics,
        161-163
EMFi chair, 185-186
Engaging websites, 159-160
Environmental bias, 116
ErgoBrowser, 75
Errors, 81
    analyzing and presenting, 84-86
    collecting, 83-84
    determining, 82-83
    issues, 86-87
    measuring, 81-84
    metric, 53
    in pharmacist performance case study, 276
    and sample size, 17-18, 27-28
Essa, I. A., 172
Evaluation methods, in studies, 57-58
Everett, Sarah, 148
Exact Method for binary success, 69
Expectation measure, in self-reported data, 129
Expectation rating, in self-reported data, 131
Experience rating, in self-reported data, 129, 131
Expert performance, comparison to, 208-209
Eye-tracking technology, 52, 175-176
    in pharmacist performance case study, 276
    scan paths, 180
    specific elements, 179-180
    specific regions, 176-179

**F**

F-value, in comparing means, 31
FaceReader system, 172
Facial Action Coding System (FACS), 171
Facial expression capture, 171-172
    electromyogram sensors, 172-174
    in everyday testing, 174
    video-based systems, 172-173
FACS Affect Interpretation Dictionary
        (FACSAID), 172
Failure scores, in binary success, 66-67
Fake issues vs. real, 101-102
Few, Stephen, 36
Filtering data, 60
FirstClick testing, 256-258
"Fix It Fast" quadrant (expectation vs.
        experience), 131

Fixation count and duration, in eye-tracking, 276
Florida election ballots, 82-83
Focus groups, 58
Fogg, B. J., 159
Food, at usability sessions, 290
Foresee Results, 151
Formative studies, 45-46
Formats for time data, 75
Forms, for self-reported data, 126
Frequency of issues
    unique, 109-110
    users, 111
Frequent use, of product studies, 50-51
Friesen, Wallace, 171
Frustration Index, 173-174
Fukuda, R., 180
Functionality category, in ACSI, 151, 155

**G**

Galvactivator glove, 185-186
Galvanic Skin Response (GSR), 183-184
Gaze plots, 176-177
GEOMEAN function (Excel), 78
Geometric mean, 78
Goals
    business, 295
    combining metrics based on, 192
    comparison to, 206-208
    in mobile music and video case study, 263
    study, 45-47
    user, 47-48
Granularity of issues, 104
Graphs
    column and bar, 36-38
    guidelines, 35
    line, 38-40
    overview, 35-36
    pie charts, 42
    scatterplots, 40-41
    stacked bar, 42-44
Greene, Kristen, 148
GSR. *See* Galvanic Skin Response
Gut level decisions, myths about, 12
Gutenberg, Johann, 7

**H**

Haring, S., 184
Harris, Robert, 36
Hart, Traci, 147
Harvey Balls, 204-205
Hazlett, Richard L., 172-174
Heart rate, 183-186

Heart rate variability (HRV), 183
Heat maps, of eye-tracking data, 176–177
Helpfulness area, in WAMMI, 151, 153
Hertzum, M., 108
Hierarchical cluster analysis, 220, 222
Horizontal labels, on graphs, 35
Hu, W., 183
Human Factors Research Group (HFRG), 150

**I**

ICA. *See* Index of Cognitive Activity
Identifying usability issues
    bias in, 117–118
    consistency in, 114–115
Imamiya, A., 183
Impact of subtle changes, evaluating, 54–55
In-person studies, 103
Independent samples, for comparing means, 28–29
Independent variables, 20
Index of Cognitive Activity (ICA), 181
Indiana University enterprise portal project case
        study, 280–281
    analyzing and interpreting results, 282–283
    conclusion, 287
    designing and conducting, 281–282
    findings and recommendations, 283–286
    impact, 286
Information architecture studies, 51
Information, at sessions, 290
Information Quality (InfoQual) scale
        (in PSSUQ), 245
Interactive Voice Response (IVR) systems
    case study. *See* Speech recognition IVR
        case study
    evaluations of, 149
Interface Quality (IntQual) scale (in PSSUQ), 245
International Standards Organization (ISO), 4
Interval data, 22–23
iPod, 54
Iqbal, S. T., 181–182
Issue severity, 50
Issues-based metrics, 53, 55, 99
    analyzing and reporting metrics, 108–114
    automated studies, 103
    beginning and ending of issues, 103–104
    determining issues, 100–102
    identifying issues, 99–100, 114–117
    in-person studies, 103
    multiple observers, 104–105
    number of participants, 117–121
    severity ratings, 105–108
IVR. *See* Interactive Voice Response systems

**J**

Jargon, 295
Jeffries, R., 101
Jenny Craig site, 88–89
Jones, Colleen, 252
Jones of New York site, 173

**K**

Kahneman, D., 181
Kapoor, A., 187
Kindlund, Erika, 202, 267
Krug, Steve, 4
Kuniavsky, M., 108

**L**

Lab tests, 57
Labeling
    axes and units, 35
    drugs. *See* Pharmacist performance case study
Landauer, T., 118
Language, of business, 295
Learnability metrics, 51, 92–93
    analyzing and presenting, 94–96
    collecting and measuring, 93–94
    issues, 96–97
    in WAMMI, 151, 153
LeDoux, L., 235
Legends, on line graphs, 40
Lekkala, Jukka, 184
Levels of success, 69–70
    analyzing and presenting, 72–73
    collecting and measuring, 70–72
Lewis, James R., 69, 129, 139, 244,
        249–250, 252
Likelihood to return metric, 50
Likert scales, 124–125
Lin, T, 183
Lindgaard, Gitte, 116–117, 119, 159
Line graphs
    vs. bar graphs, 38
    guidelines, 38–40
Linkages, for card-sorting data, 220
Live-set metrics, 54
Live website data, 211
    A/B studies, 216–217
    click-through rates, 213–215
    drop-off rates, 215–216
    server logs, 211–213
    survey issues, 156–158
Look & Feel category, in ACSI, 151, 155
Loranger, Hoa, 237, 244

Lostness
  in efficiency, 89–90
  in information architecture, 51
Lund, Arnie, 142

# M

Magic number 5, 118–120
Magnitude estimation, in self-reported data, 132–133
Management appreciation, myths about, 13
Mangan, E., 95, 235
Marsden, P., 183
Marshall, Sandra, 181
Maurer, Donna, 220
McGee, Mick, 132
McNulty, M., 201
MDS. *See* Multidimensional scaling
Means, comparing, 25, 28
  independent samples, 28–29
  more than two samples, 30–31
  paired samples, 29–30
Means, in time-on-task, 78
Measures
  of central tendency, 25
  of variability, 26–27
Measuring the Usability of Multi-Media Systems (MUMMS), 151
Median
  overview, 25
  time-on-task, 78
MEDIAN function, 78
Meixner-Pendleton, M., 184
Memory, as metric, 52
Method selection, bias from, 116
Metrics impact case study. *See* OneStart project case study
Metrics overview, 48. *See also* Studies overview
  data types for, 23–24
  definition, 7–8
  myths, 10–13
  table, 49
  value, 8–10
Miner, Trish, 142
Mobile music and video case study, 263
  changes and future work, 270
  comparative analysis, 264
  data collection, 265–266
  data manipulation and visualization, 267, 269
  discussion, 269–270
  number of attempts, 266
  number of respondents, 264–265
  perception metrics, 266–267

project goals and methods, 263
  qualitative and quantitative data, 263
  qualitative and quantitative findings, 267
  research domain, 263
  respondent recruiting, 265
  successes and failures, 266
  summary findings and SUM metrics, 267–268
  time to complete, 266
Mode, 25
Moderator bias, 116
Molich, Rolf, 101, 114
Mota, S., 187
Mouse, pressure-sensitive, 186–188
Multidimensional scaling (MDS), 222–225
Multiple observers, benefits of, 104–105
MUMMS. *See* Measuring the Usability of Multi-Media Systems
Music. *See* Mobile music and video case study
Myths about metrics, 10–13

# N

Nall, Janice R., 252, 262
NASA web site, 168
Navigation category, in ACSI, 151, 155
Navigation studies, 51
Negative relationships, 32
New products, myths about, 12
Nielsen, Jakob, 5, 106–107, 118, 213, 228
Nielsen Norman Group, 162
Noisy data, myths about, 11–12
Nominal data
  nonparametric tests for, 33
  overview, 20–21
Nonduplication of respondents, 158
Nonparametric tests
  chi-square, 33–35
  overview, 33
Nonverbal behaviors, 169, 171
Noticeability studies, 52
Null hypotheses, 29
Number
  of participants, 117–121
  of survey questions, 156–158
  of survey respondents, 157–158
Numbered and unnumbered scales, 159

# O

Objective self-reported metrics, 123
Observability, of metrics, 7–8
Observation locations, 290
Observing overt behaviors, 167–171
Omata, M., 183

OneStart project case study, 280-281
    analyzing and interpreting
        results, 282-283
    conclusion, 287
    designing and conducting, 281-282
    findings and recommendations, 283-286
    impact, 286
Online forms, 126
Online questionnaires, 142
Online services, 150
    ACSI, 151, 153-155
    live-site survey issues, 156
    OpinionLab, 153
    WAMMI, 150-153
Online studies, 57-58
Online surveys, 58, 126
Open card sorts, 217
Open-ended questions, 128, 163
OpinionLab, 153, 156-157
OptimalSort tool, 218
Ordering, counterbalancing for, 19-20
Ordinal data
    nonparametric tests for, 33
    overview, 21-22
Osgood, Charles E., 125
Outliers
    defined, 26
    time-on-task data, 78-79
Overloading graphs, 35
Ovo Studios, 265

**P**

*p*-values
    calculating, 120-121
    in comparing means, 29-31
Page views, 212-213
Paired samples *t*-tests, 29-30
Paired values, on scatterplots, 40
Palm Beach County, Florida, election ballots,
        82-83
Paper ballots, comparisons of, 148-150
Paper forms, for self-reported data, 126
Participant knowledge, in time-on-task
        measurements, 80-81
Participants
    bias in identifying issues, 116
    card-sorting data, 223
    frequency of, 111-112
    number of, 117-121
    selecting, 16-17, 116
    studies, 58-59
Pentland, A. P., 172

Perceived distances, card-sorting data for, 218
Percentages
    combining metrics based on, 193-197
    in pie charts, 42
Perception metrics
    mobile music and video case study, 266-267
    self-reported data for, 123
Performance
    comparison to, 208-209
    vs. satisfaction, 48
    as user goal, 47
Performance metrics, 63-64
    efficiency, 87-92
    errors. *See* Errors
    learnability, 92-96
    pharmacists. *See* Pharmacist performance
        case study
    task success. *See* Successes
    time-on-task. *See* Time-on-task metrics
Perlman, Gary, 142
Pharmacist performance case study, 271-279
    analysis, 276-277
    apparatus, 272
    participants, 272
    procedure, 275
    results and discussion, 277-279
    stimuli, 272-275
Physical effort, 87
Physiological metrics. *See* Behavioral and
        physiological metrics
Picard, Rosalind, 184-187
Pie charts, 42
Planning studies, 45
    importance of, 293-294
    metric choices. *See* Studies overview
    study goals in, 45-47
    user goals in, 47-48
Poker, 181
Poppel, Harvey, 205
Positive findings, 114, 297
Positive user experiences, 54
Post-session ratings, 135, 137
    aggregating, 137-138
    comparison, 144-146
    CSUQ, 139-140
    product reaction cards, 142, 145
    QUIS, 139, 141
    SUS, 138-139
    Usefulness, Satisfaction, and Ease of Use
        Questionnaire, 142-144
Post-Study System Usability Questionnaire
        (PSSUQ), 139, 245-246

Post-task ratings
  after-scenario questionnaire, 129-130
  ease of use, 128-129
  expectation measure, 129, 131
  task comparisons, 133-137
  usability magnitude estimation, 132-133
Posture Analysis Seat, 187
Precision
  in graphs, 35
  in reporting, 26
Prelaunch tests, 258-261
Presentation
  binary successes, 67-68
  efficiency, 88-90
  errors, 84-86
  learnability, 94-96
  levels of success, 72-73
  simplifying, 297-298
  time-on-task data, 77-79
Presidential election of 2000, 6, 82-83
PressureMouse, 186-188
Printing press, 7
Prioritizing issues, 114-115
Problem discovery, 52-53, 247-248
Procedural details, 297
Product comparison studies, 50
Product reaction cards, 142, 144-145
Product use frequency studies, 50-51
Proficiency, in learnability, 93
"Promote It" quadrant (expectation vs.
  experience), 131
Prototype testing, 258-261
PSSUQ. *See* Post-Study System Usability
  Questionnaire
Pupillary response, 180-182, 276

**Q**

Qualitative findings
  benchmarking case study, 267
  CDC.GOV website redesign case study,
    255-256
  in mobile music and video
    case study, 263, 267
Quantifiability of metrics, 8
Questionnaire for User Interface Satisfaction
  (QUIS), 139, 141, 144-146
Questionnaires, online, 142

**R**

*R*-squared value, 32
Radar charts, 143, 204-205
Random sampling, 16

Ranges
  overview, 26
  time-on-task data, 78
Ranked data, 21-22
Ratings
  post-session. *See* Post-session ratings
  post-task. *See* Post-task ratings
  for self-reported data, 127
  severity, 21, 105-108
Ratios
  in magnitude estimation, 132
  overview, 23
Real issues vs. false, 101-102
Redesigning website case study. *See* Website
    redesign case study
Rehabilitation Act, 231
Relationships, between variables, 31-33
Repeated-measures studies, 18-19
Reporting. *See* Analyzing and reporting metrics
Retrospective probing technique, 80
Return on investment (ROI), 9, 231-234
Reynolds, C., 186-188
Rosenbaum, R., 95
Rubin, J., 106-107
Russell, M., 88

**S**

Sabadosh, Nick, 252
Safety, drug label design for. *See* Pharmacist
    performance case study
Safety-critical products, 196
Samples, 17-18
  in comparing means, 28
  myths about, 13
  participants, 59
  in speech recognition IVR case study, 249-250
  techniques, 16
Samples of convenience, 17
Satisfaction
  metrics, 8, 50
  vs. performance, 48
  as user goal, 47-48
Sauro, Jeff, 69, 202, 267
Scalable Vector Graphics (SVG) formats, 269
Scales
  Likert, 124-125
  scatterplots, 40
Scan paths, in eye-tracking, 180
Scatterplots, 32, 40-41
Scheirer, Jocelyn, 184
Schroeder, W., 119, 264
Schulman, D., 264

Scorecards, usability, 203-206
Scoring methods, in levels of success, 71
Screenshots, 297
Search and Site Performance category, in ACSI, 151, 155
Search bots, 212
Section 508 guidelines, 231
Segments, in pie charts, 42
Selecting, of participants, 16-17, 116
Self-reported metrics, 57-58, 123
    analyzing, 127-128
    attribute assessment, 158-161
    awareness, 163-165
    collecting, 124-128
    element assessment, 161-163
    online services. *See* Online services
    open-ended questions, 163
    post-session ratings. *See* Post-session ratings
    post-task ratings. *See* Post-task ratings
    rating scales for, 127
    SUS, 147-150
Self-selection, of respondents, 158
Selling usability and metrics, 289-290
Semantic differential scales, 125
Senior-friendly website comparisons, 147
Server logs, 211-213
Severity ratings, 21, 105
    caveats, 107
    combination of factors, 106-107
    user experience, 105-106
    working with, 107-108
Shaikh, A., 88
Signage disaster, 5-6
Significance level, in confidence intervals, 27-28
Simplifying presentations, 297-298
Single error opportunity, tasks with, 84-85
Single-factor ANOVA, 30-31
Single Usability Metric (SUM), 202-203
Single usability scores, 191
    based on percentages, 193-197
    based on target goals, 192
    based on *z*-scores, 199-202
    SUM, 202-203
Site map study, 161-162
Six Sigma methodology, 202, 234-236
Skin conductance, 183-186
Small improvements, myths about, 11
Small sample size, myths about, 13
Smith, Bill, 234
Smith, P. A., 89-90
Snyder, Carolyn, 116

Social desirability bias, 126-127
Software Usability Measurement Inventory (SUMI) tool, 150-151
Software Usability Research Laboratory, 147
Spearman rank correlation, 134
Speech recognition IVR case study, 244
    discussion, 251-252
    method, 244-245
    participant comments, 246-247
    PSSUQ score, 246, 282
    recommendations, 250-251
    results, 245
    sample size, 249-250
    usability problems, 247-249
Spiders (search), 212
Spool, J., 119, 264
Spreadsheet for card-sorting data, 220
Stacked bar graphs, 42-44
Standard deviation, 26-27
STANDARDIZE function (Excel), 198
Starting small, 291
Statistics, descriptive, 24-25
    confidence intervals, 27-28
    measures of central tendency, 25
    measures of variability, 26-27
STDEV function (Excel), 27, 198
Stetson, J., 144
Steven M. Ross Business School, 151
Stopping rules, for unsuccessful tasks, 73-74
Stratified sampling, 16
Stress measures, 183-186
Studies, types of, overview, 48
    alternative design comparisons, 55
    awareness, 52
    budgets and timelines, 55-56
    completing transactions, 48, 50
    critical products, 53
    data cleanup, 60-61
    data collection, 59
    evaluation methods, 57-58
    frequent use of products, 50-51
    goals, 45-47
    impact of subtle changes, 54-55
    navigation and information architecture, 51
    participants, 58-59
    positive user experience, 54
    problem discovery, 52-53
    product comparisons, 50
    table, 49
Subjective self-reported metrics, 123
Subtle changes impact, 54-55

Successes, 53, 64-65
  binary, 66-69
  data collection, 65
  in efficiency, 90-92
  issues in, 73-74
  levels, 69-73
  in time-on-task data, 80
SUM. *See* Summative Usability Metric method
SUMI. *See* Software Usability Measurement Inventory tool
Summarizing self-reported data, 128
Summary metrics, 297
Summative testing, 46-47
Summative Usability Metric (SUM) method, 202-203, 267-268
Surveys
  live-site, 156-158
  online, 58, 126
SUS. *See* System Usability Scale
SVG. *See* Scalable Vector Graphics formats
System Usability Scale (SUS), 22, 144-146
  good and bad scores, 149
  overview, 138-139
  for paper ballots comparisons, 148-150
  for senior-friendly website comparisons, 147
  for Windows ME and Windows XP comparisons, 147-148
System Usefulness (SysUse) scale (in PSSUQ), 245
Systematic sampling, 16

**T**

*t*-tests
  binary successes, 67
  mean comparisons, 28-30
Tabulating time data, 76-77
Target audience, in participant selection, 16
Target goals, combining metrics based on, 192
Task completion
  studies, 48, 50
  time. *See* Time-on-task metrics
Task-level measurements, in IVR case study, 245
Tasks
  aggregating ratings, 137-138
  issues by, 113
  with multiple error opportunities, 85-86
  selection bias, 116
  success metrics. *See* Successes
TAW Web Accessibility Test tool, 229
Technical Research Centre, 185
Tedesco, D., 133-135
Terms and jargon, 295
Text-to-speech (TTS), 250

Think-aloud protocol, 80
3D graphs, 35
Thresholds, in time-on-task data, 78
Time and time data
  collection myths, 10
  in efficiency, 90-92
  in Excel, 75
  requirements, 291-292
  savings, 233
  tabulating, 76-77
Time-on-task metrics, 74
  analyzing and presenting data, 77-79
  collecting and measuring, 74-77
  in frequent use of product studies, 51
  importance, 74
  issues, 79-81
  in pharmacist performance case study, 276
Timelines, for studies, 55-56
TiVo, 54
Top-2-box scores, 128
Top 40 Online Retail Satisfaction Index, 151
Transaction completion studies, 48, 50
Transferring data, 61
Trend lines, 32, 40
Trials, in learnability, 96-97
Trimmel, M., 184
Tufte, Edward, 36
Tullis, C., 40-41
Tullis, T.
  card-sorting data, 217, 223, 225-227
  identifying issues, 115
  learnability, 95
  self-reported metrics, 133-135, 144, 162
  Six Sigma, 235
  visual appeal ratings, 40-41
  *z*-scores, 201
Tylenol site, 173

**U**

Unique issues, frequency of, 109-110
Units, labeling, 35
Usability Information Technology Services (UITS), 280
Usability magnitude estimation, 132-133
Usability overview
  definition, 4
  importance, 5-7
  metrics, 7-8
  myths, 10-13
  value, 8-10
Usability Professionals Association (UPA), 4, 6
Usability scorecards, 203-206

Usability Testing Environment (UTE), 75, 259
Usborne, N., 216
Usefulness, Satisfaction, and Ease of Use (USE)
        questionnaire, 142-144
Usefulness, in self-reported metrics, 164-165
User errors metric, 53
User expectations studies, 50
User experience, severity ratings based on,
        105-106
User goals, 47-48
User issues, frequency of, 111
UzCardSort tool, 218

**V**

Value of usability metrics, 8-10
van Kuilenburg, H., 172
Variability measures, 26-27
Variables
    creating, 60
    independent and dependent, 20
    relationship between, 31-33
Variance, 26-27
Verbal behaviors, 168-170
Verifying responses, 60
Video-based systems, for facial expression
        capture, 172-173
Video clips
    in presentations, 297
    for selling usability, 290
Video playback case study. *See* Mobile music
        and video case study
Visits, to pages, 212-213
Voice of the Customer (VoC) studies, 150

**W**

Wald Method, 69
Ward, R., 183
WAVE tool, 229

Web Content Accessibility Guidelines (WCAG),
        229-231
WebCAT tool, 218
Website Analysis and Measurement Inventory
        (WAMMI), 150-153
Website redesign case study, 237
    conclusion, 244
    testing competitor websites, 237-239
    testing design concepts, 239-243
    testing single design, 243-244
Websort tool, 218
Weight-loss sites, 88-89
Weight, of graph lines, 40
Weight Watchers site, 88-89
Weighted averages, 195
Weiss, Scott, 263, 270
Whitby, Chris, 263, 270
Wilson, C., 106, 108
Windows ME and Windows XP comparison,
        147-148
Wireframing, in website redesign case study,
        256-258
Within-subjects studies, 18-19
Withrow, J., 232
Wolfson, Cari A., 252, 262
Wood, L., 223
Woolrych, A., 119

**X**

X/Y plots, 40-41

**Z**

z-scores
    calculating, 198
    combining metrics based on, 198-202
Zazelenchuk, Todd, 280, 287
Zheng, X. S., 181-182